CW00796967

PERFORMANCE

A BIOGRAPHY OF THE CLASSIC SIXTIES FILM

PERFORMANCE

A BIOGRAPHY OF THE CLASSIC SIXTIES FILM

PAUL BUCK

London / New York / Paris / Sydney / Copenhagen / Berlin / Madrid / Tokyo

Cover designed by Fresh Lemon
Picture research by Jacqui Black

ISBN: 978.0.85712.791.4
Order No: OP53878

Exclusive Distributors
Music Sales Limited,
14/15 Berners Street,
London, W1T 3LJ.

Music Sales Corporation,
257 Park Avenue South,
New York, NY 10010, USA.

Macmillan Distribution Services,
56 Parkwest Drive
Derrimut, Vic 3030,
Australia.

Printed in the EU

A catalogue record for this book is available from the British Library.

Visit Omnibus Press on the web at www.omnibuspress.com

Contents

1) trailer

A JET shoots across the sky, the fastest of its time, a high-performance plane. A Rolls pulls up, more than once, the cream of status and money. A tough guy goes through his paces in the sexual act. A blinding left. Flash of performers swing through a mirror. The gangster goes about his daily job, enforcement with bravado, intimidation. His boss stands before a Magritte, a thoroughbred at his shoulder. A rock icon jumps into frame, in a flash. Jack the lad. Mick Jagger. Everyone knows him, everyone needs somebody. Drugs take us into a world where they perform, we perform. Jagger sings. Chas too is a performer. A juggler. A jongleur. I bet you do. I know a thing or two about performing.

That is a touch or two, two or three things we know about performing, to paraphrase Godard. And we all perform, as we all prostitute ourselves on a daily basis. The Times. Sign of the times.

What a turn-up for the books. Talk about the tragedy of revenge. Sixty-nine. Eighty-one.

Paint it black. Red. Dyed. Dead.

Welcome to *Performance*, a mosaic in the making, the film that Donald Cammell conceived, drawing in others as associates: Mick Jagger, James Fox, Anita Pallenberg and more . . . enlisting Nic Roeg as his cohort and co-conspirator. And that is just to scratch the surface. To run the razor's edge across the image, to perform a Buñuelian act on the viewer, or the gangster's predilection (later excised), to unravel, cultivate and explore.

2) the beginning is also the end

THE seeds of *Performance* can be found in an earlier draft for a film to be called *The Liars*. Reduced to its essentials, *The Liars* tells the story of Corelli, an American hitman, in Paris on business. Pursued by the police when things go wrong, and discovering that he has misplaced his flight ticket, he makes for the nearest city where he believes he will be able to slip quietly to ground: London. Unable to find a suitable hotel at night, he heads for the area around Earls Court on the recommendation of the taxi driver, his intention being to rent a room. Corelli finds himself in the flat of Haskin, a reclusive pop star, who has quit his band, Spinal Kord, which was also the name for Turner's band in the first drafts towards the *Performance* script, his resignation based on disagreements over the commercialisation of the band's music.

Also living in the flat is Simon, a runaway teenager. She strikes up a relationship with the American, which becomes more amorous as the day proceeds. Haskin meanwhile ventures out into the Swinging London of Chelsea and Soho, taking in the sights and picking up Pherber, a groupie, who winds up in his bed and his bath.

This script, written in 1967, runs to 69 pages, but it is not finished. It does appear, though, to have aspects of *Performance* in the making, a "plot that was essentially the same plot as *Performance*", as Donald Cammell said in an interview recorded in 1992 that was included in the documentary *The Ultimate Performance*, produced after his death in 1996 by his brother David Cammell. It also has an affinity with two earlier films: *The Touchables* (1968), directed by Robert Freeman, even if that film has less obvious traces of the initial scriptwriting, and *Avec Avec*, which materialised as *Duffy* (1968), directed by Robert Parrish and starring James Coburn, James Mason, James Fox and Susannah York. This trio of scripts, in which Donald Cammell had varying degrees of involvement, are attempts, like many others of that period, to tap into the era's youth culture, a way to push the buttons on what was required to sell a script and gain admittance to the film world. The Beatles had starred in *A Hard Day's Night* (1964) and *Help!* (1965), The Dave Clark Five had had a lesser hit with *Catch Us If You Can* (1965), and there were other endeavours with other pop stars that barely survive in our memories. Some could now be termed Britpop exploitation movies; films like *Just for Fun* (1963), or similar vehicles such as *Band of Thieves* (1963) and *Every Day's a Holiday* (1965). They satisfied the desire to see more music stars, since television was such a weak provider of pop culture, its two main programmes, *Top of the Pops* and *Ready Steady Go!*, being the only ones to have an important lifespan and impact. As the decade progressed, the tag of Swinging London would be attached to more substantial films, such as *Darling* (1965), *The Knack . . . and How to Get It* (1965), *Alfie* (1966), *Morgan: A Suitable Case for Treatment* (1966), *Blowup* (1966) . . .

There are a couple of threads to pull out briefly at this point. Haskin, the pop star in *The Liars*, bears traits of Brian Jones, with whom Donald Cammell had become friends in Paris through one of his girlfriends, Anita Pallenberg. Indeed, this friendship with Jones was to become Donald's door into the world of The Rolling Stones. Haskin's resignation from the band could easily relate to Jones' own dissatisfaction with the commercial direction of *his* own band (I use *his* advisedly). And further, Jones was gaining an interest in Moroccan music that Cammell was very aware of, for he had introduced Jones to Morocco in the first place. There is also other overlapping common ground, as will unravel.

That said, the character of Haskin, like the character of Corelli, is not properly formed in this draft, whereas the character of Pherber displays a remarkable likeness to Anita Pallenberg, whom Donald was involved with. She was to feature later not only as one of the stars before the camera in *Performance*, but also acknowledged as playing a considerable part in shaping the whole nature of what was to become *Performance*. Her name changes in this script from Pilar to Phoebe to Pherber.

It is also worth noting in passing that at this stage the other young woman is called Simon, not Simone, the character who would develop into Lucy. Thus the androgynous aspect is hinted at right from the beginning, an angle that fascinated Donald and would be allowed to bear fruit in *Performance*.

One might also conceive that Haskin derives from Sam Haskins, an international photographer, whose book *Cowboy Kate* (1965) sold more than a million copies at the time. Though Haskins didn't return to live in London, just off the King's Road, until 1968, for someone with Donald's interests Sam Haskins' work at the cutting edge of commercial nude photography would not have passed unnoticed.

This treatment, *The Liars,* had come about because Donald was signed to Sandy Lieberson, who worked for Creative Management Associates, an agency whose books had a number of writers, directors, actors and others, including The Rolling Stones (for film and television work). It was in their interests to combine these talents to maximise and create 'deals' that they could then offer to film companies.

Sandy Lieberson had taken on Donald after being impressed by the script for *Duffy*. "He was an original in terms of his personality, character, outlook on life. We formed a really close friendship very quickly and talked about movies and what we both wanted to do. At that time, everybody was leaving the agency business to become film producers and I thought, why don't I do that? So Donald and I decided to try and do something together."

And thus, with the sketchy treatment, "we decided to approach Mick (Jagger) and Marlon Brando," said Lieberson. "Donald and I thought Mick had something rather particular about him that would work in movies."

Donald thought that Marlon Brando could be the American hitman. They had met some years earlier, in the late Fifties, in Paris, through the French actor Christian Marquand, a close friend of Brando. This 'closeness' gave rise to Brando naming his son Christian, after Marquand, the following year, though it appears the mother of the child, Anna Kashfi, always refused to refer to her son by that name because, she said, "Marlon and Marquand displayed an affection toward each other that far over-reached the usual expressions of friendship." Not that Brando denied his homosexuality, telling Gary Carey, one biographer: "Homosexuality is so much in fashion it no longer makes news. Like a large number of men, I, too, have had homosexual experiences and I am not ashamed. I have never paid much attention to what people think about me." I have determined to note some of the sexual terrain that underlies *Performance* and the world in which the main practitioners resided in order to reflect the normality of this aspect of their relationships, which in turn will help us to understand the film and why the sexual angle was taken in its stride by those involved. To date, nobody has subdued, or exerted pressure to subdue, the sexual undertones of Donald Cammell's sexual preferences, at least none of those involved in the production of *Performance.*

Marlon Brando had an attachment to Paris, dating back to 1949, when he was first drawn to the Left Bank and the world of the existentialists. It was there that he met Christian Marquand, who was lunching on the terrace of La Coupole with Roger Vadim, his flatmate. A relationship sprung up between the three men. Finding that Brando was staying in a fleabag of a hotel, the Hôtel d'Alsace, they invited him to join them at their flat. Though all three men were known as healthy heterosexuals, they enjoyed an intimate relationship, indeed a *ménage à trois* from the off. Vadim remarked later that "Brando and Marquand had an unconventional love affair that would span the decades, and fidelity to each other had nothing to do with it. I don't think I ever saw a more compatible couple." Later, when Brando moved with them into another, larger apartment, which they shared with Daniel Gélin, Brando also took that actor as a lover. The story comes full circle in 1972, when Brando went to Paris to face more scandals to film Bertolucci's *Last Tango in Paris*, starring opposite the young actress Maria Schneider, who was the daughter of Daniel Gélin.

Donald's meeting with Brando occurred in less than salubrious surroundings. Brando, in Paris to film *The Young Lions* with Montgomery Clift in 1957, had accidentally scalded his testicles and been taken to hospital. Cammell recalled to Chris Rodley in a *20/20* interview: "A certain French girl had jumped onto (Brando's) lap, while he was waiting for a set-up on the shoot of *The Young Lions*. He had a hot cup of French coffee in his hand and it spilt and scalded his balls quite severely. Second degree burns, so he told me, on his private parts!" Christian Marquand insisted Cammell accompany him on a visit to the actor in hospital. "He took a magnificent gift – a book of drawings by Leonardo da Vinci. A French coffee-table deluxe item."

Though Brando's relationship with Donald Cammell was to span the rest of his life, their plans to work together led to years of wasted energy and one disappointment after another. When presented with that initial idea of *The Liars* in 1967, Brando was not interested. Lieberson said: "We submitted *The Liars* to Brando, but he was caught up in doing other things, and it would have meant a lot of courting and a lot of waiting, and we decided that would be unrealistic. So instead we decided to develop it for James Fox, who had become quite friendly with Donald."

The Liars was set to be transformed into *The Performers*.

Who was Donald Cammell, the writer of these film scripts, one of which was on its way to becoming a cult classic? From a world of painting into a world of films, Cammell had lived in London, New York and Paris, had inhabited a society that included Mick Jagger and others from that rich, bohemian group known as the 'Chelsea Set'. This book strives to be the biography of the film, not a biography of any of its participants, at least not in any great detail. Where one draws the line is another matter. In fact, where one draws the line with anything regarding this film is questionable. Its blurredness and its instability are fundamental to its success on all levels, and that is what I'm seeking to catch.

Donald Cammell was born on January 17, 1934, the elder son of Charles Richard Cammell and Iona Macdonald, his second wife. As an heir to the Cammell Laird shipbuilding company, Charles Cammell had used his not inconsiderable wealth to explore his interests as a writer and 'aesthete', though these pursuits were foreshortened by the global financial crash of the Thirties, and his writing skills by necessity turned towards earning a living.

Donald was born in Edinburgh, in the Outlook Tower, beneath the camera obscura that offered a panoramic view of the city. As a number of people have pointed out, when Donald took his life 62 years later, it was on Lookout Mountain in Hollywood. This observation fits in with the pattern of his approach towards his work. "Any film, like any story, forms an elaborate pattern," Cammell said in one of his few interviews. "It is not a statement of truth, it's a design, a mandala, it's a construct whose virtue lies in its harmonies and its paradoxes and its evocations."

Donald had two brothers. One, David, was born three years later in 1937 in Richmond, on the outskirts of London, the family having moved south. David was destined also to become part of the *Performance* family.

In Richmond, the Cammells became friends with Aleister Crowley, the infamous occultist, magician and poet, who lived nearby, across the Green. Their friendship developed to the degree that Charles Cammell became Crowley's biographer, writing a slim volume called *Aleister Crowley: The Man, the Mage, the Poet* (1951). Crowley enters the story, and indeed the myths that surround *Performance*, with the notion that he was Donald's godfather, though how old Donald was when Crowley took on that mantle is not known. It all sounds as if it started as a joke (the 'Devil's Disciple' taking on the distinction of 'godfather'), partly entertained by Donald for some years, until finally he found he was unable to jettison it entirely as others thought it was a 'hip' or 'cool' connection to have. His brother David says that he too sometimes played with the notion of Crowley as godfather, but ultimately it was a sort of fantasy for both of them that Donald took too far and was unable to shake off. The American beat poet Harold Norse, who met Donald in Florence, reported that Donald's father "was convinced that poetry ended with Tennyson; to him Yeats, whom he knew personally, was an abomination. He believed another friend, Aleister Crowley, was a greater poet who wasted himself on the black arts." We should also note that the word 'biographer' is not exactly correct. Though Crowley had wanted Charles Cammell to write a one-volume book for the general reader based on the six volumes of his *Confessions*, "perhaps Memoir is the best word; for I have done no more (…) than stroll along the lanes of Memory, with this or that book of Crowley's for companion."

With the onset of the Second World War the Cammells moved from London to Devon to escape the bombings. Though the family came back to the capital when things seemed quieter, the boys were sent up to the Scottish Highlands. Donald was boarded at a prep school in Fort Augustus, until his mother brought him back in 1942 and placed him closer to their home at Shrewsbury House School in Surbiton.

Donald had shown an interest in drawing and painting from the age of three. Indeed, he was judged an art prodigy. His father promoted his drawing skills, having his work exhibited at the Royal Drawing School. Donald's development as an artist was pursued through schooling at Westminster, and then the Byam Shaw Art School, which led to a scholarship to the Royal Academy School of Art. In the early Fifties he went to Florence as an apprentice to Pietro Annigoni, one of the leading portrait painters in Europe, who became internationally renowned for his painting of Queen Elizabeth II in 1956. Annigoni was also an acquaintance of Charles Cammell, Donald's father, who had written his biography.

Donald's connection with the London of the Chelsea Set began on his return to set up his own studio in Flood Street. His portrait of Sheridan, the Marquis of Dufferin and Ava, who was a pageboy for the Queen's Coronation, was the 1953 'society portrait of the year' according to *The Times*.

Donald married a Greek actress, Maria Andipa, in 1954. He was far from pleased when a son was born some years later, causing the marriage to fall apart and instigating his departure for New York in late 1959 to seek another life.

Even though London is regarded as one of the stars of *Performance*, Donald's feel for the place being part of the fabric, he never exactly lived in the capital again. "I went to live in America when I was in my early twenties and then I was living in France after that. I was living in France when I made *Performance*. Just came here. I wrote the story in France." That was how he explained it to Jon Savage in an interview in *Vague*, leading to the suggestion that perhaps being away from the city enabled him to perceive it more sharply.

Donald was, as he said, "bored with painting and with myself". Nevertheless, he occasionally undertook portraits to earn money right into the Seventies. In New York he explored other painting fields, what he called his "abstract expressionist period". He had a show at the Bertha Schaefer Gallery, though it was not as well received as he had hoped, and there is a review that indicates an influence of the Spanish artist, Antoni Tàpies, in his style.

It was during this New York period that he met Deborah Dixon, who had arrived from Texas to become a model. She had been sent to see the photographer Louis Faurer, who lived on 58W 57th Street, where Donald also had a studio. They were to live together for eight years, through most of the Sixties, and Deborah was a technical advisor (not costume consultant as credited) on *Performance*, even though they had separated some months before filming commenced.

Though the New York stay only lasted around 18 months, until the summer of 1961, Deborah feels this period has been somewhat neglected.

"His life in New York was a strong influence on him, but nobody ever mentions it," Deborah said recently. "A mix of people from jazz musicians and actors to painters and very interesting people who helped to form his ideas, so that when he came to Paris the New York aura, more than the English one, made him a magnet to a lot of people."

They formed a strong friendship with Roscoe Lee Browne, and James Earl Jones and Cicely Tyson, all of whom they saw in the first Off-Broadway production of Genet's *The Blacks*. The jazz connection is re-enforced by their friendship with Peggy Hitchcock, "a very bohemian heiress" whose family estate was in Millbrook, where Deborah and Donald would go and stay. Another close friendship came from Ludwig Bemelmans, the author of the *Madeline* series, who obtained illustration work for Donald. This snapshot gives a glimpse of the new world that Donald was experiencing. The ability to draw and the skill of the draughtsman can be seen in the works of two artists who also became friends: Mati Klarwein and Domenico Gnoli.

When Donald and Deborah moved to Europe, they established their home and studio in a flat on the rue Delambre in the Montparnasse district of Paris. Donald was quite keen to remain in New York, but it was Deborah who initially wished to live in Paris. She had a lucrative income from modelling, enough to sustain a fairly high living standard for both of them.

Life in Paris revolved around café culture and entwined various strands of art activities: literature, visual arts and film. The art community that Donald became involved with also had connections with the vibrant film world that was evolving in the early Sixties around the *nouvelle vague* movement, though Donald also had other film acquaintances such as Christian Marquand, Roger Vadim and Roman Polanski.

Of particular interest in relation to the *nouvelle vague* was Jean-Luc Godard, and, more by accident than design, Eric Rohmer. Eric Rohmer's *La Collectionneuse* was filmed in the late summer of 1966 and released the following year. Donald had a small role, seen briefly with the young woman of the film, Haydée, on the terrace of a café in St Tropez. This appearance was probably due to Donald and Deborah's habit of going to St Tropez regularly during the summer, whether for weekends or longer stays. They often rented an apartment overlooking the bay of St Tropez in Grimaud. Rohmer's *La Collectionneuse* reflects the crossover of the art and film world, with Alain Jouffroy, the writer and art critic, opening the second section of the prologue in discussion with artist Daniel Pommereulle.

"We used to take a flat in Grimaud every spring and early autumn and Patrick (Bauchau) was a friend, and also Daniel Pommereulle." Deborah recalls that "Patrick brought all the cast up to the flat and I think they rehearsed there," suggesting they hadn't gained admittance to the house where they were to film at that point.

The film's premise is interesting in that the main character, Adrien (Patrick Bauchau), wants to stay for the summer at a friend's house, just outside St Tropez, and do nothing, nothing at all. His friend Daniel (Daniel Pommereulle, the artist) is there too. Unfortunately, there is a young woman, Haydée (Haydée Politoff), a 17-year-old, also in residence, who is spending her holiday engaged in relationships with the area's young men. Adrien is determined that he will not have sex with her, as he doesn't want to be drawn into that game. The two men regard her as a 'collector' of men, initially bringing the string of different lovers to the house, later staying the night elsewhere after Adrien and Daniel object to their peace being disturbed. Haydée is not that many years younger than these two men, but enough to see herself as a youngster exploring sexuality rather than looking for love or a partner. There is an overriding misogyny to the film, in that, in accordance with the times, the men see it as their duty to seduce the woman. Whatever the circumstance, Rohmer tends towards supporting the female. The film's title is the female form of the word 'collector'. For both men, just by 'being' she is a threat. She is young, inexperienced, a 'proto-hippie' as one critic observed, her future far from shaped, unlike theirs. We are also in the terrain of pre-feminism here. While Haydée is the main focus, she is not overly articulate. The men and their problems buzz around her. One can't help but laugh at flappings such as:

"Adrien: And you're chasing me.

Haydée: I'm not.

Adrien: You are. I can tell when a girl's interested. Another time, you could have had me. I'm weak-willed, and too nice."

Rohmer pointed out in an interview: "You should never think of me as an apologist for my male character, even (or especially) when he is being his own apologist. On the contrary, the men in my films are not meant to be particularly sympathetic characters."

The idea that books are either left around a set, 'dressed', as they say, or incorporated into the film's texture is very much part of Godard, as we will see later, but it also occurs in *La Collectionneuse*. Whether Cammell was just accepting a part, or whether he agreed to take it because he knew that the film was a more philosophical work (the book being picked up for holiday reading is one of the collected writings of Rousseau), which he would have gathered from Pommereulle, his friend, is unknown. In fact, he could also have learnt it from his friendship with (another with an uncredited bit part) Pierre-Richard Bré, who wrote earlier for *Cahiers du Cinéma*, or from Eric Rohmer, who had been *Cahiers*' editor at that time before turning to directing. Cammell did know that films had the potential for serious discussion, and were not just entertainment. And besides, his role was not exactly unappealing. His 18 seconds of screen time were spent with his arms around the young Haydée, keeping her warm, having suggested they go for a walk together.

It's interesting, too, that Daniel and Haydée, both non-actors, used their own names in the film. It should also be noted that this film was shot in a large house in which the cast and crew lived together during its five-week shoot, the social commitment and interplay being used in the film. Deborah Dixon recalls "going to the first day of shooting and finding the cameraman was Néstor Almendros, who had been my Spanish teacher at university". Almendros had indeed taught for a short period at Vassar College, employed, he thought, "because they needed someone who could run the audio-visual equipment in the newly opened language laboratory".

Donald and Deborah knew both Bauchau and Pommereulle from Paris, the latter in particular. Pommereulle was an artist, with dangerous edges to his work – in *La Collectionneuse*, a paint tin with razor blades fixed perpendicularly around it was presented as a vicious sculpture, *Objet hors saisie*. (Another time, this author saw an exhibition in Paris that included a larger work with bayonets protruding from a similar round core, the gallery placing no barrier to stop anyone from approaching and seriously injuring themselves.)

Daniel Pommereulle would form part of a group who came together under the banner Zanzibar Films (a name taken from the Maoist island nation in East Africa), a decidedly informal collective of about a dozen artists, writers and students making their first films. Their financier for the couple of years of its existence was Sylvina Boissonnas, a young French heiress and patroness of the arts. While the *nouvelle vague* filmmakers had started out in their late twenties and early thirties, the Zanzibar group were younger (Philippe Garrel, one of the key figures, was just 20) and inspired by the heady spirit and times of May 1968. Despite their diversity, the Zanzibar films (which appear to number 15 in total) were distinguished by minimal scripts, improvisation and the use of non-actors, many with strong ties to the worlds of both art and fashion. (Several of the Zanzibar participants spent time in Warhol's Factory in the mid-Sixties.) Their films represented the French equivalent of the American underground, standing for an anti-*auteur* attitude, despite some having connections to the *Cahiers du Cinéma* directors and their *auteur* label.

Donald's interest in film was not centred around the director as *auteur*. He says in his *Cinema Rising* interview, also confirmed by Patrick Bauchau, that he was self-taught, "totally uninterested in the *auteur* theory – or any other". Donald thought "reverence for the director of a film as sole creator has been vastly exaggerated, through critical efforts. I'm thinking particularly of the *Cahiers du Cinéma* 'author' concept – I've been living in Paris, and have been quite aware of it for a long time. The kind of theory of creativity that's arisen there (and in related worlds in New York) is, succinctly, crap."

Some of the artists who formed part of Zanzibar films had a different perspective towards art than Donald, who had a more traditional grounding (which was probably why they were rather scathing of his abilities as an artist). Olivier Mosset, Daniel Pommereulle, Didier Léon and Frédéric Pardo are the four artists usually named. The men were also typified by calling themselves dandies. Pommereulle often quoted Oscar Wilde: "An idea which is not dangerous does not merit being called an idea." They believed in physical attractiveness. The women who appeared in or were involved in their films were often models: Caroline de Bendern, Zouzou, Nico . . . and indeed Deborah Dixon, who was the subject of Pommereulle's short *One More Time*. Hence the query in the third prologue of *La*

Collectionneuse of how anyone can fall in love with someone who is ugly: "Ugliness is an insult to others. One is responsible for one's appearance."

Though Donald and Deborah were only involved on the periphery and the group's impetus didn't start until after May 68, by which time Donald was in London and focussed on *Performance*, the social milieu of many of its participants was nevertheless part of their world. However, on many levels there was little connection to the type of films Donald had in mind. He could subscribe to the improvisational aspect, but was also interested in the more complex nature of film, akin to a form of home movie cut into a grand style of Hollywood filmmaking.

There were, of course, other painters in Paris who were venturing into film, or whose work derived from film imagery. They were often grouped together as 'Figuration narrative' and included Jacques Monory, Gérard Fromanger, Bernard Rancillac, Antonio Recalcati and Eduardo Arroyo. These artists frequently used stills, or made work that looked as if it related to cinema. In the case of Monory, he had extended his work into films by the end of the decade. And although there was a social and political tone to their works, there was also a strong erotic aspect, particularly with Monory.

If none of these worlds seem totally central to Donald's interests, the world of the painter Balthus certainly was. Donald was friends with Prince Stanislas Klossowski de Rola, known as 'Stash', who later also became a friend of Brian Jones and others in London's bohemian circle. Donald offered Stash a roof over his head at one point when he was suddenly penniless and homeless. Stash was the youngest son of Balthus, and there are suggestions that he took some of his father's abandoned drawings from the studio, which were then 'finished' by Donald, later turning up for sale in the window of an antiques shop in the rue Bonaparte.

Balthus' work is distinguished by paintings that show pre-pubescent girls in erotic positions, always offered up for the voyeuristic gaze of the viewer. "I really don't understand why people see the paintings of girls as Lolitas," Balthus said in 1996. "My little model is absolutely untouchable to me. Some American journalist said he found my work pornographic. What does he mean? Everything now is pornographic. Advertising is pornographic. You see a young woman putting on some beauty product who looks like she's having an orgasm. I've never made anything pornographic. Except perhaps *The Guitar Lesson*."

Donald's painting in Paris returned to figurative work and was influenced by Balthus, with young girls as his subjects. These erotic paintings were not destroyed by Donald, but left behind in Paris, later to be put in storage when Deborah moved, and finally damaged when the storage space was flooded.

Balthus' brother was Pierre Klossowski, the writer and (later) painter, whose focal interest was sexual works with a deep theological base. It is partly through Klossowski's writings on de Sade that the Marquis was drawn back into contemporary thinking. A key concept for Klossowski revolves around his 'laws of hospitality', originally exemplified in *Roberte Ce Soir* in 1953 and in subsequent writings, which Donald might have known about, if not actually read. The English translation did not appear until 1969. Notions of hospitality rest on the host offering his wife to his guests, with him watching, in order to know himself better; in the process eroticism "becomes a category of the human being, not a means of pleasure, but a door opening on to knowledge". Klossowski, of course, was one of those radical theorists who had affiliations with another key erotic thinker, Georges Bataille.

Whilst Deborah and Donald went to the cinema regularly, for Paris at that time, more than London, was peppered with cinemas, Donald always stated that his interest was more in books than films. Paris in the Fifties and Sixties famously pushed at the boundaries of what was sexually permissible in print. Not to go into too much detail about the history of Olympia Press and its predecessors, it's enough to say that Olympia Press became synonymous with a new freedom in literature. Klossowski and Bataille were not widely translated into English until later, though the Olympia Press did publish *Story of the Eye* as *A Tale of Satisfied Desire* (1953), and *Madame Edwarda* as *The Naked Beast at Heaven's Gate* (1956). Grove Press in New York added a reprint (from the impeccable Yale French Studies) of the Klossowski essay on Sade to the translations they issued, starting in 1965, to give the books some weight and stave off censorship issues, reprinting the earlier Olympia versions: *The Bedroom Philosophers* (1953), *The 120 Days of Sodom* (1954), *Justine* (1953) and *Juliette* (1958–64).

The visitor to Paris seeking a 'traveller's companion' for his baggage home was provided for by the bold exploits of Maurice Girodias, Olympia

Press' boss. Whether one read them or not, the olive-green books enlarged the allure of the French capital's sexual climate. These volumes were targeted by the sharp-eyed customs officers at British and American borders, presenting a challenge to defy the law. Those that were destined for fame included *Candy* by Terry Southern and Mason Hoffenberg, plus Henry Miller's philosophy of life with *Plexus* and *Sexus*, *Quiet Days in Clichy*, and *Tropic of Cancer* and *Tropic of Capricorn*. Those with an underground reputation included Alexander Trocchi's (with female pseudonyms) *White Thighs*, *Helen and Desire*, *Thongs, The Carnal Days of Helen Seferis* and *School for Sin* as well as Harriet Daimler's (pseudonym of Iris Owens) *Darling*, *Innocence*, *The Organisation* and *The Woman Thing* . . . because there were a few female writers who contributed. Indeed, Pauline Réage's *The Story of O* first saw the light of day with Olympia.

In Mason Hoffenberg's *Sin for Breakfast*, his character Margot (who is undoubtedly Daimler/Owens) says: "Let's face it – the thing that's unique about these particular books is that, for once, the writers have the liberty to deal with sex as frankly as they wish. If they do it well, they accomplish something that's really significant: they throw a light on a very, very important subject that's always been a forbidden one for authors. If they don't do it well, then their books may be what a lot of people claim them to be – pornography. That's why, if you're writing one, I say you're justified in going to any lengths to acquire the material . . ."

Entwined with these 'dbs' (dirty books), as they were termed, were the literary works that were banned or ignored elsewhere, at least for the moment, like Vladimir Nabokov's *Lolita*, J.P. Donleavy's *The Ginger Man*, and William Burroughs' *Naked Lunch*, *The Soft Machine* and *The Ticket that Exploded*, not to mention novels by Samuel Beckett (*Watt* and *Molloy*) and the translations of Jean Genet's *The Thief's Journal* and *Our Lady of the Flowers*.

Burroughs, Genet and Nabokov (with his novel *Despair*, published elsewhere in 1965) were to become instrumental in the mosaic of references relevant to *Performance*. Deborah Dixon confirms that whilst they could read French, they were basically reading English-language books, which would include Olympia Press publications. She also notes that she knew some of the young women who wrote pornographic novels, mentioning Marilyn Meeske by name. Meeske had written, under the pseudonym

Henry Crannach, a book entitled *Flesh and Bone*, and another, *The Pleasure Thieves*, with Iris Owens. Iris Owens was the star among Olympia Press' female writers and her four books as Harriet Daimler remain classics. However, by the time Donald and Deborah had arrived in Paris, Owens found herself with writer's block and had slipped quietly back to anonymity in New York, stepping aside from her Daimler persona.

Much of this activity would not have happened if it hadn't been for the presence of writers like Alexander Trocchi, who was also editing *Merlin*, or translators like Richard Seaver and the unflagging Austryn Wainhouse. Their magic talents were a vital part of the success of the publishing ventures of both Trocchi and Girodias.

Among the French books that Donald owned, and that were left behind in Paris, were books on Hans Bellmer, another favoured artist, and many editions from the publisher Pauvert, particularly erotic illustrative works, including Georges Bataille's *Les Larmes d'Eros* and Benayoun's *Erotique et surréalisme*. A copy of Bataille's *L'Erotisme* in the 10/18 edition exists, though Deborah suspects it has not been read, as those books' spines soon reflect wear and tear.

Donald and Deborah were both charmed by Paris and the French way of life proved more than a passing fancy. In fact, Deborah still lives there today. It's also reported that Donald took up French citizenship and remained a French citizen for the rest of his life. Though we might read something deep into this, a rejection of his British roots perhaps, or an alignment with a French cultural heritage, today both his brother David and Donald's partner of the time, Deborah Dixon, think there was little behind it other than tax reasons. That said, Donald always claimed, even after years spent living in America, that Paris was his home.

As mentioned above, it was more the aura of America, and perhaps the people they met in New York, that led to the company Deborah and Donald found in Paris. Perhaps that is why one regularly notices Donald being referred to as a former American painter.

Another writer whom Deborah remembers with pleasure is Harry Mathews, who lived in Paris at the time, cutting a fine figure, exploring a world where playfulness was given full rein in his writings, meaning he was never going to be a commercial author. Indeed, Mathews would say: "I've always had the audience I wanted, and that was the audience that reads poetry. What I want is enthusiasm among friends and their friends, people who I know are serious readers."

By unravelling all these connections it gives the impression that Paris was little more than a hotbed of sexual activity, a life well suited to the debauchery that is generally associated with Donald's story. No one denies any of the stories surrounding Donald, and no one has dug too deep to unearth further tales. There seems to be no need. But by bringing Harry Mathews into the picture it does reveal that not every literary connection's writings were steeped in sexual content. Likewise, not everyone was as liberal in their thinking as they appeared. This writer remembers only too well going to Georges Bataille's office, a room in Diane Bataille's flat in rue Saint-Sulpice, in the early Seventies to meet Stash's brother Thadée Klossowski, who was editing Bataille's *Oeuvres Complètes* for Gallimard at the time. Under my arm I was carrying a copy of *La Monnaie Vivante* by Pierre Klossowski which I had just bought, a work lavishly illustrated with photos by Pierre Zucca of Klossowski's wife Denise in various erotic states to illustrate his theoretical positions. She was hardly naked, but it was explicit enough for Thadée to express his utter shame and displeasure at the manner in which his auntie had displayed herself.

This then gives the flavour of the world that Donald and Deborah inhabited. A few years earlier, in the late Forties, just after the war, it would have been the world of the Café de Flore and Le Tabou, Juliette Gréco and Boris Vian, Jean-Paul Sartre and the existentialists around St-Germain-des-Prés. Or the era before, when Henry Miller was in residence, perhaps coming up against Anaïs Nin and friends. Or another period with Gertrude Stein, Sylvie Beach, Ernest Hemingway, Djuna Barnes, Natalie Barney . . . The lists could go on, each with intriguing stories, each intertwining, a labyrinth, another mosaic. Donald and Deborah must have ventured there in the early Sixties to seek the ambience of that period. Paris was romantic. Fresh air. Paris was the centre of the cultured world. One set off for it with wild intent, even if one didn't know where it would lead. One sensed, though, that it was the right decision.

Our story reaches a further turning point when Anita Pallenberg walked into the lives of Donald Cammell and Deborah Dixon in the early Sixties. She met Deborah either on a modelling job or at a nightclub: "I'd just come from New York (...) and I was modelling in Paris and I think I met his girlfriend first, Deborah, on the job, or something like that. Or in a club; we used to go to Castel's a lot, and dance." She didn't recall it that way in Rebecca and Sam Umland's biography of Donald Cammell: "I was hanging out in Paris with a bunch of Americans at the time and that's how I came to meet Deborah. It wasn't through modelling. I think I met Donald through Deborah."

There's some intriguing research to be done tracing the way the world of models slides into the world of the arts, particularly music. The credentials one needed in the Fifties and Sixties to join this world have probably, to some degree, changed today. One wonders if there is still a high percentage of society girls who have little to do and drift into it, or whether it is nowadays seen as simply another way to bag oneself a partner who is a rock star, footballer, rich heir or City banker, whether for fun or for a husband. Or whether it is seen as another route into the film business. Anita was once tagged as a model, but she was undoubtedly destined for other things in life.

Whether Anita became a girlfriend or joined the household for a *ménage à trois* is not exactly clear. Donald was always regarded as a charmer and seducer. Patrick Bauchau, the Belgian actor and friend of Donald and Deborah at the time in Paris, remembers that Deborah used to attract other women. "Donald and Deborah, of course to me, were a team. It wasn't just Donald. It was Donald and Deborah. They both together made quite a powerful impact on quite a number of people in Paris. Because Deborah was making pots of money in those days. She was a top model."

To summarise Anita Pallenberg's early life is to outline a family history that has a firm footing in art. Though an early relative was painted by Holbein, it is usual to delineate Anita as the great-great-granddaughter of Arnold Böcklin, the nineteenth-century German-Swiss symbolist painter, and to stress that enough family members were involved in the arts for her to be accustomed to an environment of writers, painters and musicians. She was born in Rome, and called herself Italian-born, if not Italian. She was fluent in Italian, French and German, and studied art restoration and graphic design. She summarised herself in one interview: "I was in Rome in 1960 just as La Dolce Vita was happening and met Fellini, Alberto Moravia, Visconti and Pasolini. Then I went to model in New York in 1963 and hung out with Andy Warhol and all the Pop artists, and met the beat poets. And then I went to Paris." She omits that she knew The Living Theatre in New York, a fact that is relevant to our story.

Anita was 21 when she set sail for New York with her then boyfriend Mario Schifano. Though referred to at the time as a photographer, he was to become a leading Italian postmodernist painter. Anita worked as an assistant in Jasper Johns' studio and had intentions to study art further, but also often found herself 'standing in' for models who hadn't shown up for Schifano and other photographers. Given her 'ravishing' looks (one adjective that regularly describes her), it was inevitable that before long she would find herself accepting fashion assignments all over Europe.

"I'd been around a lot before I met any of The Rolling Stones," says Pallenberg. And so the next injection into our mosaic comes with the arrival of Brian Jones.

There is some confusion over where Anita and Brian first met. Most accounts say it occurred in Munich after a gig by The Rolling Stones. Anita at various times has confirmed this. But on other occasions she says that it was earlier, in Paris, and from there she took Jones to Donald and Deborah's place.

Perhaps we should take our lead from Bill Wyman, the Stones' bassist, who appears to have been a veritable Samuel Pepys, chronicling the daily routines and finances of the band. "Between our two concerts on 14 September (1965) in Munich, Brian met Anita Pallenberg for the first time. This was a romance which would dramatically affect his, and our, future. Anita, a model in town on a fashion job, went to the first show and saw us perform. After the show she persuaded a Swedish photographer to smuggle her backstage. She returned to the hotel for the night with a tearful Brian, who was reeling from a verbal hammering we'd all given him about his Pat Andrews problem." Wyman is referring to the child support lawsuits that had been slapped on Brian Jones by both Pat Andrews and Linda Lawrence.

Anita was in town on a modelling assignment, and had indeed ventured backstage at the Oktoberfest Circus, where the Stones had just performed. "When I got backstage, I went straight to Brian because he was the one I fancied. I tapped him on the shoulder and had a big smile ready for him when he turned around. I could hardly believe it, he was on the verge of tears. For a weird moment I thought it was somehow my fault. He was the only one of the Stones who really bothered to talk to me. He could even speak a little German."

He asked her to go back to the hotel with him. "I don't want to be alone," he said. So she went with him. "Almost the whole night he spent crying." Another time she expressed her attraction another way: "Brian seemed sexually the most flexible. Guys or girls? It didn't matter. The others all seemed to have a chick on their side with a toupee, false eyelashes and all that. You know what I mean? And foam for the fanny and stuff for not getting pregnant and all that shit. Brian – I knew I could just talk to him. As a matter of fact, when I met him I was his groupie, really."

However, in the Umlands' exhaustive and detailed biography, their evidence leads to April 1965 in Paris as the meeting point for Brian and Anita, because Donald met the Stones in Paris at that time, and "because he (Brian) fell in love with a girlfriend of mine called Anita Pallenberg". David Cammell helps to confirm that date, saying that later that summer he called in on Donald in Paris on his way back from Tangier and was asked by Anita, whom he was meeting for the first time, to give her a lift to London in his red Lotus Elan. He recalls taking her to the Scotch of St James club, where she met up with Brian, as they had planned.

According to Stanley Booth, another Stones biographer, they met a girl backstage at the Olympia in Paris, "a north Italian fashion model named Anita Pallenberg". Booth adds the Munich meeting later, when Anita and Brian spent the night together. (At least he didn't suggest, as has another, that Anita first met Brian in Donald's flat in Paris.)

The confusion is perhaps resolved (or given another twist) by bringing Nico into the frame. Nico was another young model/actress, who became a singer once Brian Jones had introduced her to Andy Warhol. Nico suggests that she had met Brian at a party in London, and he had indicated that she "catch us somewhere" as the Stones were starting a tour the next day. Brian added: "We can talk after the show." That date turned out to be on the second of the three nights at the Olympia, on April 17, 1965. Discovering that a friend of hers, the actress Zouzou, had spent time with Brian facilitated admittance to the backstage area after the concert. There she hooked up with Brian, and for a few months they had a relationship. It seems that a number of documented sources have confused Anita with

Nico because they had fairly similar looks. As Dick Witts, Nico's biographer and friend, wrote: "To those men of the press and the aides of the group who later wrote their memoirs, one 'German chick' was the same as the next."

I don't apologise for injecting these confusions, because, as we will see, the confusion of Mick Jagger for Brian Jones will help greatly in this web, or mosaic as I'm terming it, that was under way round this film. And the idea of identities being exchanged fascinated Donald Cammell and was at the core of *Performance*.

That said, Anita's beauty set her apart from others according to all accounts. One of the Stones' hired hands at the time, Tony Sanchez, offers this description: "She had only to walk along the street to cause a string of traffic accidents. She had tumbling, shining blonde hair, a long lithe body and wickedly beautiful cat's eyes. She was no dumb blonde, either, and the combination of witty conversation and devastating looks rapidly turned her into the darling of aristocratic London." Marianne Faithfull was equally taken: "Dazzling, beautiful, hypnotic and unsettling. Her smile – those carnivorous teeth! – obliterated everything. Other women evaporated next to her."

In those early days, Anita remembers being very aware that the other band members regarded her with suspicion. "You could see them exchanging looks like, 'Who is this weird bird?'" It's not unusual to hear that they treated her with hostility. Or that Keith was terrified of her at the beginning. "Mick really tried to put me down, thereby putting Brian down in the process, but there was no way that this sort of crude, lippy guy was going to do a number on me. I was always able to squelch him – I found out, you stand up to Mick, he crumbles. He tried to get Brian to stop seeing me, called me poison. He ordered his girlfriend, Chrissie, not to go near me. I figured he was jealous because I was the one close to Brian."

The way she summed up the others' partners didn't make for easy times. Later she said: "Except for Brian, all the Stones at that time were really suburban squares. Mick's girlfriend, Chrissie Shrimpton, was a secretary type, nine to five, Miss Proper, hairdresser's on Thursday, and so was the girl Keith had – very normal, very plain, no challenge. Charlie Watts had a kind of drab wife he kept in the background, and Bill Wyman, too – you know, background women, with personalities like elevator music."

One could believe that when Pallenberg went on the road with the band, perhaps helping Jones wrest power back from the others, or Jagger and Richards in particular, she was not going to make life smooth. "Anita was an exotic, ambitious, sexy, decadent, *dangerous* woman," noted their photographer of the time, Gered Mankowitz. "In a word, she was trouble."

"This was a romance which would dramatically affect his, and our, future," as Bill Wyman succinctly put it. This is not the place to examine the Brian Jones story in detail, but some documentation of his relationship with Anita is necessary, for Brian's life within the Stones was deteriorating and would collide with the events around *Performance*. Anita said that when she first met Brian, she thought he was the 'leader of the group', as that is the impression he gave.

What should be documented is the way in which the relationship was destructive, as it provides a useful frisson to the film. Their relationship was one of such violence that rock critic Nick Kent summed it up as: "He couldn't stand to be without her for a minute but when he was with her he couldn't stand not to hit her." After his assaults he would be overcome with remorse and pour forth tears as he begged for forgiveness. Yet during his violent outbursts his strength and savageness were uncontrollable, as he hurled pots of hot coffee or small tables at her, covering her with welts and bruises. Eventually, Anita had to admit that "Brian was a terrible person, really. And I put up with a lot. He was a tortured personality, insecure as hell. He was ill very early on – totally paranoiac."

The antiques dealer and designer Christopher Gibbs, who knew the couple well, said: "They fought about everything – cars, prices, restaurant meals. Brian could never win an argument with Anita, although he always made the mistake of trying. There would be a terrific scene with both of them screaming at each other. The difference was that Brian didn't know what he was doing. Anita did know what she was doing."

Keith Richards notes in *Life*, his autobiography, that when Jones and Pallenberg were accompanying Christopher Gibbs in Tangier in 1966, Gibbs had to take Brian to hospital "with a broken wrist after a punch he'd thrown at Anita had hit the metal window frame in the El Minzah Hotel in Tangier. He was never good at connecting with Anita. I learned later just how violent Brian had already become with her, as the downward slide began, throwing knives, glass, punches at her, forcing her to barricade herself behind sofas."

But before everything started going downhill, there was a real bond between them. "Brian was very moody," she said, "which I like, and he was physically attractive as well – he looked kind of like a girl in a funny kind of way; sexually I like girls as well as men and Brian seemed to combine both sexes for me."

There was also an intellectual compatibility: "He had a wonderful curiosity – curious about new things, new places, wanted to know everything that was going on, wanted to meet new people, new ideas . . ." And also to get into mischief, something that seems to recur in different ways over the years where Anita is concerned. "And we got introduced to a lot of mischief by Robert Fraser, who was a London art dealer, Eton type, connected with high society and royalty."

Anita had first met Robert Fraser in 1961, through Mario Schifano. He opened his own gallery at 69 Duke Street, coming to represent or show some of the most important artists of the day, including Peter Blake, Richard Hamilton, Jim Dine, Andy Warhol, Ed Ruscha, Claes Oldenburg . . . even René Magritte gets into the picture. "Robert was way ahead of everything that was going on," Anita recalled. "I'd spent six months in New York and was very informed about that art scene. So I found it comforting to be around Robert."

It was Fraser who introduced Anita to Christopher Gibbs. He was something of a bibliophile, and was quick to pick up on Anita. "When I talked to her, I discovered she was highly intelligent and extremely well read. She'd read obscure German Romantic novelists like Hoffmann as well as all the usual Hermann Hessery."

Anita is credited with introducing The Rolling Stones and others in their music circles to the high-class bohemian field. Marianne Faithfull writes that Anita "almost single-handedly engineered a cultural revolution in London by bringing together the Stones and the *jeunesse dorée*". When she introduced Brian as 'the leader of The Rolling Stones', they were excited. "They were all infatuated with pop stars," as Marianne writes. Besides Christopher Gibbs and Robert Fraser, and indeed Donald Cammell, this circle included Sir Mark Palmer, Tara Browne and Lord Harlech's children (Jane, Julian and Victoria Ormsby-Gore), Paul Getty . . . the "King's Road dandies".

Fraser and Gibbs were both gay, and acted up in true Oscar Wilde fashion. Marianne describes Gibbs in terms of the opening lines of *The Picture of Dorian Gray*: "From the corner of the divan of Persian saddle-bags on which he was lying, Lord Henry elevated his eyebrows, and looked at him in amazement through the thin blue wreaths of smoke that curled up in such fanciful whorls from his heavy opium-tainted cigarette."

Donald's take on Anita's position was: "At the time she first started to hang out with those guys she opened up a whole world to them. She was the most attractive girl any of them had ever been around and she had a genuine feeling for books and poetry, and the guts to get involved with things."

Robert Fraser's place in Mount Street was an environment that appealed to Anita and Brian. It was "a fascinating group of people who were on the cutting edge of what was happening in high society, great cultural evenings, wonderful intellectual talk, plenty of hash and marijuana and speed and LSD. Brian and I were having a ball." Or as Marianne described it: "desultory intellectual chitchat, drugs, hip aristocrats, languid dilettantes and high naughtiness."

Jones' motto was "Let's try anything." That was one of the draws for Anita. Jones and Keith Richards took LSD together for the first time after a concert in Los Angeles, attending the second Acid Test party given by the writer Ken Kesey on December 5, 1965. Both had good experiences, and from then on Jones made it his drug of choice.

Anita joined Brian on these trips once he returned to London. Their first time together "he saw creatures coming out of the ground, the walls, the floors. He was looking in the cupboards for people, 'where are they?' That's when he said to me, 'Dress me up like singer Françoise Hardy.'"

Not only is it acknowledged that Anita brought together the Stones and the rich bohemians, but she is also regularly given credit for developing the Stones' dress sense, summed up by Victor Bockris: "Her fashion sense – mixing ace miniskirts, black tights, and knee-high boots with satin and velvet blouses and coats (often designed by Ossie Clark) – influenced generations."

By encouraging Brian to wear her clothes, jewellery and make-up, she took him out of the cupboard, out of the flat and onto the streets. While many might think that Biba was a natural home for their shopping outings, Anita said, "Biba was too big. I wasn't into that very English look. In Italy we'd always had salsa, the mamba, all those Latin dances which gave me a different feel for things, so my style was fedoras, belts, little Twenties jackets, lace that I'd collected. If I wore mini-skirts I'd have them made by Granny's. We'd try on clothes and have a joint in the back. Granny's was very small, just two rooms, so everyone knew each other." In fact, the shops of choice were Emmerton & Lambert in the Chelsea Antiques Market, Hung On You and Granny Takes a Trip.

Brian would be seen wearing a stunning amalgam of men's and women's clothes, "a broad-brimmed plumed hat that could have been worn by one of the three Musketeers, a tunic with pearl buttons, striped silk pants, a woman's satin blouse, gaily coloured silk scarves tied to his wrists and knees, several beaded necklaces, and high-heeled boots," as one observer noted. Bill Wyman recalls that in New York, "Brian had indulged himself in expeditions to the ladies jewellery departments of such stores as Saks Fifth Avenue and Bergdorf Goodman. A New York journalist friend (Al Aronowitz) commented: 'If he gave nothing else to the world, Brian was the first heterosexual male to start wearing costume jewellery from Saks Fifth Avenue.'"

Brian and Anita forged an androgynous look in public, to the extent that they started to look identical. "They had grown to look like each other; their hair and clothes were becoming identical. They'd merged their personas, stylistically at least," as Keith Richards notes. Looking good and exciting was very important to both of them. Brian relished blurring the boundaries between male and female, yet at the same time remaining masculine. "I had expected him to be girlish," one friend remarked, "which was how he looked. What really took me back a step was the fact that he was the very opposite. He had this very deep posh voice and was surprisingly manly. It wasn't how I'd imagined him at all."

Brian wasn't the only one dressing in his partner's clothes. Mick Jagger was too. "It was this strong masculine-feminine force, which manifested itself when they were performing, that caused some people to regard them as bisexual," as Ossie Clark observed.

And later, when Anita was living with Keith, he too adopted that style. "I was beginning to wear her clothes most of the time," he writes in *Life*.

"I would wake up and put on what was lying around. Sometimes it was mine, and sometimes it was the old lady's, but we were the same size so it didn't matter."

A huge space just off the Gloucester Road, at 1 Courtfield Road, was the aptly named place where Brian and Anita held court. Whether it was musicians like Hendrix, Lennon and George Harrison, or others such as Donald Cammell, Paul Getty and the rich bohemians, people just passed through.

Such a place needed décor and Christopher Gibbs relished the chance, giving it a Moroccan theme, since Brian had taken a liking to the country following his first trip there with Cammell in summer 1965. The rooms were vaulted and 30-feet high, the walls covered with embroidered Arabic rugs, the floors piled with cushions. A carved wood minstrels' gallery, that led to their panelled bedroom, ran round the top of the main room.

Settled cosily in such an environment Brian felt less need to venture out. Drugs became a way of life. "Inner demons had started eating away at the Renaissance angel's head," Marianne Faithfull commented. LSD fed Brian's paranoia. The couple's mischief allowed them to indulge in the latest trend of spiking an unsuspecting guest's glass with acid and watching the reaction.

"1966 was incredibly psychedelic," said Stash. "Mick said to me one morning it was very difficult to carry on doing the job you were doing when you've lost your ego. Psychedelics made everything seem multi-dimensional, and revealed consensus reality as threadbare. After it, the game of life had changed."

Brian and Anita indulged their sexual fantasies as a result, whether it was bisexual scenes or sado-masochistic games. One of their guests, an old friend, Dave Thomson, said: "I actually saw her one night going into their room with a bloody great whip. I could hear her whipping Brian."

Nico recounts tales about Brian's use of candles either as dildos or for dripping hot wax. He was out to experience all he could, and in that way Anita was great. She excited him, seemed to know the risks, and could take it further than most.

Perhaps Nico was right in her suggestion: "It's really very simple. He was sexy. He seduced girls. He was charming, until he locked the door."

Tony Sanchez had observed that Brian was extremely violent towards women, as if gaining pleasure from beating them. One often saw them bruised, though many came back for more, pulled by the allure of being with a Rolling Stone. He thought that while Brian had plenty of sex, it was definitely sex and not love. Brian used to denigrate and humiliate the girls, often discussing their performance loudly enough for them to overhear his attacking tongue from the next room.

Though most of the Stones' circle denied that Brian and Mick ever had a sexual liaison, Anita claims that Brian told her differently. "I only know that Brian did break up a lot of things by actually going to bed with Mick. And I think Mick always resented him for having fallen for it. In later years there have been rumours about Mick being gay, but then it was as if Brian violated Mick's privacy by revealing his weak side. So that was probably why he resented him."

It is hard when a strong woman injects herself into a band and interferes with the tensions at play. Jagger was already irritated that Anita had been given credit for the male/female look, something he thought he had a hand in, and also that she had opened doors to society circles, which had been one of his aims. With the Jagger and Richards songwriting team developing, Jones was sidelined, and felt he was being pushed out. But at the same time Richards was aware that he needed a relationship with Brian, as they were the guitarists and a style of music was evolving requiring their rhythm/lead interchanges. Thus, it was not strange when Keith and Brian started to become tight. "Brian and I were at odds for years. Sixty-five through sixty-six. He'd been playing Mick and me against each other. He was a manipulator, something you don't need when you're working that many days a year. (...) Then he turns up with Anita and – I still have to check myself today on whether I decided to become friends with Brian again so's to ingratiate myself with her. (...) As fascinating as Anita was, she scared the pants off me. She knew everything and she could say it in five languages."

Magic is another underlying motif that finds its way into the life of many of those involved. To what degree anyone was really interested, or whether it was more down to the times, is still not clear. Alexis Korner suggested that Brian Jones was "more interested in the paraphernalia than the philosophy". And Nico remembered: "he was like a little boy with a magic set. It was really an excuse for him to be nasty and sexy." Jones read

Aleister Crowley and his Silver Cloud Rolls-Royce bore the registration plate DD 666 (DD for Devil's Disciple, the Great Beast 666, as Crowley was known by his followers), although whether this was by chance or specifically acquired is not known. As the car had been purchased from George Harrison, it was probably the latter.

Kenneth Anger, the filmmaker and occultist, who became a friend to the Stones during his stay in London, thought that for the others "it was just the climate of the times", but he saw that Brian was the most psychic. He also noted that Brian had a witch's tit. "He had a supernumerary tit in a very sexy place in his inner thigh." A smiling Jones had told Anger that "in another time they would have burned me".

Marianne thought Anita was "a sort of black queen, a dark person, despite her blonde looks". She was "certainly into black magic". "It's very hard to define wickedness, but when Anita looked at you sometimes with that incredible smile on her face, it was not a smile you had ever seen before, it was a smile that seemed to be a camouflage for some great dark secret that she was hoarding. (…) The best way I can describe Anita is that she was like a snake to a bird and that she could transfix you and hold you in place until she wanted to make her move."

There's a well-documented time when Brian threw Anita out onto the street, literally, bruised and bleeding, after a fight. She took refuge in a friend's house: "I was sitting there, in tears, angry, getting my wounds treated, feeling terrible, and I decided to make a wax figure of Brian and poke him with a needle. I moulded some candle wax into an effigy and said whatever words I said and closed my eyes and jabbed the needle into the wax figure. It pierced the stomach. Next morning when I went back to where I was living with Brian, I found him suffering from severe stomach pains. He'd been up all night, and he was in agony, bottles of Milk of Magnesia and other medications all around him. (…) The world of the occult fascinated me, but after what happened to Brian, I never cast another spell."

It was when Mick's relationship with Marianne became closer that Keith felt cast afloat, and drifted back towards Brian, who was only too pleased to regain a bond within the band. He invited Keith to move in to Courtfield Road, though by all accounts he was already staying there, or 'passing by', for extended periods, sometimes days at a time.

As suggested, Keith's need to regain a musical contact with Brian probably mingled with his fascination for Anita. He might have said she terrified him, but he was undoubtedly attracted to her, drawn by that fear. Nevertheless Keith moved into Courtfield Road.

Another interesting ingredient is the arrival of heavies and bodyguards into the Stones' world. Right from the early days, as for most pop stars, their fans mobbed them. This was encouraged by management, and indeed enjoyed by many of the musicians . . . up to a point. Eventually, though, almost everyone tires of having their clothes ripped from them, despite the moments of pleasure it might provide. Nobody likes having a scarf or necklace tugged at by two opposing fans, your neck being choked between. Nobody wants their hair pulled at, ripped right out of their scalp. Jones was paranoiac about his hair being touched, let alone tugged at. No barber was even allowed to cut it. The only person who could was the trusted intimate: the girlfriend.

Tom Keylock was an early chauffeur, who also became in effect a minder. An ex-paratrooper, he meant business, not only in protecting the Stones against any fans or would-be aggressors, but also against any other employee who might try to take advantage. One chauffeur hired for Brian is alleged to have stolen two expensive cameras from his employer. Keylock knocked his teeth out and slung him out the door with the words: "You're sacked."

The 'hard men' in the entourage helped to endorse the image of the Stones. The Stones' Mafia, as the 'chauffeurs' were known, were not necessarily difficult to control for Keith Richards or Mick Jagger, but Brian Jones lacked the mental strength. They were there as minders, but to what degree they took control is one of the questions that has been continually asked. It's one that goes right through to the end with Brian, right through to the tragedy of his death in his swimming pool at Cotchford Farm, in the garden of Winnie the Pooh's creator, A.A. Milne.

After the Redlands drugs bust, a part of the story yet to come, all those involved wanted to escape Britain for a change of scenery, albeit briefly. As is well known, Anita and Keith started their relationship in the back of Keith's Bentley Continental, called Blue Lena (after Lena Horne), whilst driving through France and Spain to Morocco. As the plan was for everyone to rendezvous at the El Minzah Hotel in Tangier, Mick, Marianne, Robert Fraser and Christopher Gibbs travelled there directly by plane, while Anita, Brian and Keith flew first to Paris and waited for Tom Keylock to bring the empty Blue Lena across by ferry and collect them from their hotel. Adding Donald Cammell's partner, Deborah Dixon, the party set off for the drive south through France. Somewhere along the way Brian became ill and they stopped at Toulon, eventually checking him into the hospital with suspected pneumonia. It was arranged that he would join them by plane once he had recovered. Back on the road, there was a further delay in Barcelona, when the Bentley was vandalised whilst they were in a 'flamenco guitar joint', as Keith puts it, resulting in them all being dragged for a night into a police station, and a kangaroo court . . . enough for Deborah to abandon the journey next day and return to Paris. Left alone amongst the furs in the back of the car, Keith and Anita started their relationship. "By the time we reached Valencia," Anita recalled, "we could no longer resist each other and Keith spent the night in my room. In the morning I realised, as did Keith, that we were creating an unmanageable situation so we pulled back as best we could during the rest of the journey."

It was probably only a matter of time, once Brian joined the entourage at the hotel, with its simmering tension, that an argument would result. Brian went out into the night and returned with a Berber whore, or two – accounts vary. When Anita walked into the bedroom scene, Brian invited her to join them. Perhaps she might have done another time, but this occasion was not the one. With her mind fixed on another relationship, a dispute was triggered. When Brian hit her, she had had enough. Anita knew there was a way out, even though Keith said, "I'm feeling guilty."

To cool the situation Keith asked Keylock to find Brion Gysin and see if he would take Brian to hear some local musicians. At this point the others were leaving and Anita and Keith decided to load up the Bentley and leave too, with Keylock at the wheel. No word was left for Brian about their departure. Jones had to take a plane, flying directly to Paris. "He called me from the airport," Cammell said. "I had absolutely no idea what was going on. Brian was always so fastidious about his clothes, but when he came up to my place he was filthy; he hadn't changed his shirt and was wearing bedraggled lace and tattered velvet. He was alone, a figure of great pathos, totally distraught and out of it." Others run the story along the lines of

Brian arriving unannounced at Cammell's door, an abandoned soul, banging in the night, shouting: "They just fucked off and left me!"

Courtfield Road had lost its glamour. The place was strewn with debris; not only half-eaten takeaway meals, wardrobe doors hanging off their hinges and mirrors broken, but clothes, books and magazines were thrown across the floors and sleeveless albums piled high in a corner. Christopher Gibbs, who had helped to give Jones' home some elegance, said: "He was living in complete chaos. He had hundreds of beautiful clothes, but these were left lying about all over the floor, either burnt or covered in food. All ruined and filthy, and there'd be thousands and thousands of pounds' worth of the stuff. There were dozens of instruments that were smashed and hadn't been repaired; they were scattered everywhere. It was a terrible mess."

Gibbs recalls when Jones turned up at his home, asking to stay. "He wasn't really house-trained and would leave cigarettes burning on all the furniture, on an antique book that you valued, and I would complain, but the next minute he'd have burned a hole in the mattress or the floor, or anything. God it was so difficult not to hit him. I had to eventually tell him to make another plan. I may make him sound impossible, and he was, but actually he was very charming too. I was very fond of him, but he was pretty incoherent, rambling on and on about things. It was like someone thinking out loud."

Jones' demise followed. Sacked from the Stones with a settlement pay agreed, accounts of what happened after that become a palette of many colours. Those last few weeks – the death by drowning in the pool, the role the minders played – is another story.

When Donald met Brian in Paris, whether introduced by Anita or not, they immediately hit it off. "Brian and I became friends instantly. I had a great admiration for him and his work, his whole strange thing. He was someone who really saw his whole life in a poetic way." That was said on camera in 1996, but 12 years before in the *Vague* interview he had room to expound. "I was living a very sort of marginal existence to society at the time, because I was living in Paris and I was not involved with the pop society at all. I was involved with some artists and people, and I was also pursuing a girl a lot at the time, going through a very romantic period in 64 and 65, I remember. And I met the Stones, not in a pop society, I met them by accident. Brian through . . . because he fell in love with a girlfriend of mine called Anita Pallenberg . . . A marvellous girl. He showed up in Paris and spent a lot of time at my . . . I had a little studio over there (. . .) But then we went to Morocco – Brian and me. And Brion Gysin was there and Bill Burroughs, people whom I'd met. And as you know Brian became completely lost in that world for a while. (. . .) He was a very instinctive musician you know . . . An Artist . . . And he was always romantic. Even when he was just, you know, a sort of very pale, perpetually fatigued kid, always seemed to be living on the edge of his own adventure, which he created . . . created that strange impression of magic and it was consistent with him all the time."

Brian was introduced to Morocco by Donald, and was to travel there periodically, either with Donald or with Anita and Christopher Gibbs. It was like a spiritual home to him. Though he was paranoiac about being recognised, admonished by Christopher Gibbs, who told him no one would know him, Brian learnt to go round the marketplaces and bazaars haggling and buying up enormous amounts of clothes, from kaftans to djellabahs, cushions, tapestries, all manner of trinkets and jewellery, copperware, beaten metal lamps . . . trunk loads of goods, all to be shipped back to London.

Morocco also had a more relaxed atmosphere for drugs, particularly hashish. He also discovered another delight in the Berber prostitutes and their tattooed breasts and genitalia. It should be noted that both Donald and Brian shared a liking for *ménage à trois*, though the term 'threesome' is actually the right terminology in some cases, as *ménage à trois* usually means three people living together.

And there was the music to bind this North African experience together. It was Brion Gysin who introduced Brian Jones to the music of the Master Musicians of Jajouka, leading him to the foothills of the Rif mountains with engineer George Chkiantz to record them in summer 1968, at the time Jagger was in London filming *Performance*. When Jones returned with the tapes, he was filled with excitement. "Their music is going to cause a sensation. (. . .) The music has got this incredible, pulsing excitement, and I've got it all down on tape. It's going to make the most amazing album." The album did not appear until after his death.

The first public sign of Donald as a scriptwriter came with the developing of the draft of a script his brother David had written that was to become *The Touchables*. But it was only one stage, possibly requiring only slight touches on his part, for the director passed it to Ian La Frenais to complete.

The resultant film is more than dated, veering towards Swinging London at its worst. One wonders what aspects bore Donald's hand. It would seem that most of the plot came from either David or the director who initiated the project, the well-known photographer Robert Freeman. Relevant points in connection with *Performance* would include: the pop star focus, the protection racket of the London gangsters, the hip pad of the four girls, the wrestling (instead of boxing), the reading of a story from a book . . . The whole work is treated in a light and frothy manner, reminiscent of the period when programmes such as *The Avengers* or *The Prisoner* held sway, except this film misfires on virtually all fronts. Given that Ian La Frenais had co-written *The Likely Lads* (1964–1966) for TV just prior to this, and was later to co-write *Villain* (1971), a more substantial film with Richard Burton, and later still the classic series *Porridge* (1974–1977) for the BBC, it is surprising to find it so lacking.

The next film came from an earlier script called *Avec Avec*, written with Harry Joe Brown Jr. It drew on the exploits of the retired jewel thief, Albie Baker, whom Donald and Deborah knew in New York, and who published his story a little later as *Stolen Sweets* (1973). "When I wrote it, it was called *Avec Avec* and when it finally emerged, it was re-written, and called *Duffy*." Donald said in interviews: "It's not a serious movie, more of a bonbon, very carefree. Not worth discussing." (I suspect few saw Donald's joke – undoubtedly Albie referred to his bounty as sweets. With Donald you have to keep up with the humour of his wordplay.) It was indeed slight. David Cammell sums up the effort: "Basically it was a caper movie, and it was bought by Hollywood, and they subsequently transformed it into an absolute parody of the Swinging Sixties."

What dates it dramatically is the 'groovy' dialogue. It does reveal, though, how films are composite works. The actors – James Coburn, James Fox, James Mason and Susannah York – are of the finest order, but they all relax into their roles; nothing offers them any challenge. Robert Parrish, its director, was probably not the right person for the job. Perhaps they thought his involvement with *Casino Royale* the previous year would help.

Susannah York thought it "was a disaster as far as I was concerned, I simply couldn't get hold of the character at all. She was supposed to be 'cool' and I hadn't a notion what 'cool' meant. It was an unstructured performance and it frightened me like anything. It was a film of its period but it was also one of the worst of its period."

Donald had written the original script, but "I was fired as the writer and then I was rehired just as the movie was about to begin, to do a final draft script by a new director. Typical Hollywood stuff." Donald went on location to Almeira, in southern Spain, in early August 1967, taking Deborah along to enjoy the sun. He must have caused trouble amongst the ranks for he was dismissed by the producers 'for independent thought' after two weeks.

James Fox colours the situation somewhat further: "He was very passionate about the shooting. (...) He and I were tremendous friends by that time and we used to bemoan the terrible way the film was going. And some of the things that were being done to the film, that were being ruined, and Donald was tearing his hair out. But we forged a friendship at that time because he perhaps felt I was a kindred spirit."

Duffy, however, does contain many biographical signs; pointers that seem to be part of the Cammell vocabulary, destined to be found in *Performance* and subsequent films.

Perhaps the most pertinent one is the construct of the *ménage à trois*, which is used not once, but twice. It seems fairly common in films to see the two main characters share a woman, either at her instigation, or as an aid to one of the protagonists. In this case the three are Duffy (James Coburn), Stefane (James Fox) and Segolene (Susannah York). But unbeknown to us until the final minutes, there has been another triangle since the start, this one between Stefane, Segolene and J.C. Calvert (James Mason), Stefane's father. The deeper significance of this state of affairs is not explored. All we have in *Duffy* is a system of shifting permutations. Segolene is a classy hooker in one respect, or perhaps groupie is an equally appropriate term. Duffy accuses her of being a slut. She is outraged: "I may be a hooker. I am absolutely *not* a slut!" In her view, there is a fine distinction, since a hooker chooses her clients and is in control of her own destiny.

Hooker also plays nicely with hookah, as they step into a Tangier nightclub, The Garden of Allah, where they puff away, get stoned and dance, and where Segolene seduces Duffy to bring him on board for the heist they are planning, all with Stefane watching from the wings, complicit. There is no point going into any psychology at play, as there is no depth to the characters. The nightclub scene is also shot with lens distortion, a simple and prolonged attempt at indicating the hazy and druggy state of the participants. This is not a patch on the effective way *Performance* handles the drug moment with Nic Roeg at the helm. Short and effective, rather than prolonged, which sounds ironic given that everyone tends to think of *Performance*'s second part as long and drawn out.

There is also the use of art in *Duffy*, which must have been indicated to some degree in the script. Duffy's apartment in Tangier is filled with sculptural works made from found objects, including many based on discarded mannequin limbs which have overtones of Ed Kienholz's pieces or Richard Lindner paintings made into three dimensions, or even turning around Hans Bellmer's dolls. These objects are discussed in terms of eroticism, though Duffy likes to think they are in the "pop porno vein". The theatrical is also referenced, as Duffy remarks that Stefane is not a psychopath but "an unborn psychedelic Cecil B. DeMille . . . a showman, baby". Indeed, a performer. Whilst there is also an attempt to inject sexuality into the film, it is not blended in a natural way, in the way that's found in *Performance*. Here, it is just a smutty tastelessness.

What is relevant, though, is that Cammell spent time with James Fox on location and struck up a deeper friendship. Fox says in his autobiography that though he had met Donald before, it was during a party at Christopher Gibbs' place that Donald first approached him about appearing in *Duffy*. "He wanted me to play a hippy amateur heister who hires an American pro to help him rob some gold from a ship belonging to his father. Bob Parrish directed it and James Coburn played the American master thief with a penchant for modern art. I agreed to do it mostly out of friendship and admiration for Donald." Their friendship was strong; Fox says that whilst it wasn't a particularly happy experience making *Duffy*, "I upset the director and producer by being too much in character and somewhat critical of Hollywood's interpretation of the hippy scene in Europe (...) One thing [illegible] Donald had a tremendous talent, but he needed control of the production if his ideas were to be properly interpreted."

The die was cast. When Donald came to Fox with another project, "It became altogether more promising, because with *Duffy* he had no control over it, this time he said he was going to direct. And this time we're going to do it the way it should be done."

This was to be *Performance*.

3) straightening the script

LIKE a prospector, Donald sought to strike gold with Brando, though not necessarily in a material sense, more by hoping that the great actor would rise to the challenge of his ideas. However, Marlon Brando was not interested, or perhaps he was too busy. Given Donald's subsequent history with Brando, a succession of on/off projects that stretched right through the rest of his life, it was probably fortunate that Brando was unavailable for the birth of his directorial career, which was turbulent enough without further burdens.

In any event, Donald's friendship with James Fox had developed to the extent that Cammell saw another option for the meeting of a gangster and a rock star. The first step of the transformation of *The Liars* was given the new title, *The Performers*, and bears more relationship to what ultimately was to be called *Performance*. The American hitman would turn into a British gangster, working for a boss, who bore a similarity to Ronnie Kray of the Kray twins. The home of the pop star moved from Trebovir Road in Earls Court to Melbury Terrace, though not yet to the ambience of Powis Square, and the musician is given a deeper-seated problem than whether his music is becoming too commercial or not.

The script, though, was not quite what one normally expects of a script. Indeed, it has more of a resemblance to a novel, with descriptions of character and other elaborations. In one respect, this is quite usual for someone trying to capture their ideas on paper, adding digressions through details that will later be assimilated when the whole is rewritten into something akin to a script. After all, a script is only a document whose prime purpose is to provide the financiers with something to put their finger on when keeping track of their investment.

One has only to refer to Antonioni's published scripts in English at the time, *Screenplays* (1963; the film titles were presented in Italian: *l'avventura, il grido, la notte, l'eclisse*), to see that there was a precedent for this, although few scripts were actually published in those days for any aspiring film-maker. Antonioni's style is more that of a novelist, fighting his words onto the page, words that will conjure up the ideas he wants to be made visual. As he explained: "You have to describe images with provisional words which later will no longer have any use, and this in itself is unnatural. What is more, the description can only be general or even false because the images are in the mind without any concrete point of reference."

There are scenes that never appear in Cammell's final script, and other portions that never made it to the final film, because not everything that was shot was retained, the cutting-room floor viewing the remainder. The biggest changes though are in the final sections in Turner's house, which are simply written as possibilities, allowing the artists to adapt during filming, bringing forward ideas that happen before one's eyes which in turn generate further ideas. And this is indeed what happened, *Performance* setting its course in the process of filming (and, as we will see, in editing), eventually finding its ending, almost with a cry of 'Eureka!'. The one difference between a filmmaker and an artist in his studio, or a writer at his desk, is that the filmmaker, surrounded by a crew and actors, does not act as the sole creator, as the financial and time constraints force the pre-ordained script to be filmed. Whilst Donald did not subscribe to the *auteur* theory, at the same time he wanted to enjoy some of the benefits and freedoms that underground filmmakers embraced, working at a kind of white canvas on a daily basis.

There seem to be other characters written into this new version of the story who could have been taken from Donald's personal relationship with Robert Fraser, or with his recent partner, Deborah Dixon, perhaps drawing on those evenings and nights at the homes of Fraser, Gibbs, Jones and Jagger, to name a few, or at the Cammell/Dixon flat in Paris. Towards the end, the narrative includes a drugs bust, as if to provide the plot with some action, searching for a direction to resolve the story. "When in doubt, have a man come through a door with a gun in his hand," used to be the key for Raymond Chandler. This adaptation makes the knock at the door a drugs bust, courtesy of Jagger's experience at Redlands. The moment of tension surrounding whether the police will recognise Chas beneath his unwitting disguise, or whether a thorough search will reveal the gun, is resolved when Turner offers up his drugs, "vintage Atlas

Mountains hashish . . . three ounces of the Acapulco Gold that he bought cheap off Donovan". (This is a witticism, which relates to the attention directed at Donovan after he had made a television documentary which clearly showed his friends smoking dope. His songs also had drug references flashing colourfully.) The scripted ending has gained a twist, for it is now common knowledge that Jagger claimed the amphetamines found in his jacket at the Redlands bust were his, when in fact they belonged to Marianne, but he was prepared to take the rap, thinking there would be fewer consequences for him. As well as being a gallant act, Jagger displayed the manners of a well-brought-up middle-class lad.

The notion that some of this story development draws from personal experiences also extends to Lucy's suggestion to Chas that, instead of going to Persia, he should consider Marrakech, a place he'd like, for many of their friends "went there last summer".

And so the story is not resolved; the script is not resolved. Donald showed that he didn't know at that point how to explain the things Chas and Turner say, or might say to each other. All Cammell can say is that in the 13 hours that have occurred since the two men became involved, they have had "a considerable effect on each other". As he suggests, "it is unlikely, for example, that Chas would ask, 'Why have you helped me, Turner?' . . . in words that is. For in a certain way, he does ask. And in another way, equally clear, Turner will answer him." These things can only happen during filming, perhaps through a look, or some nuance in the dialogue, probably something visual, not something pinned down in words.

This was how the film was shaping up with Donald as he worked with two friends, James Fox and Mick Jagger, as his two protagonists. And it was this idea that Donald took to Sandy Lieberson, who believed he could convince his connections to Hollywood that it was a viable proposition. "The first objective was to get Warners in, then reveal slowly the fact that we were all people with little or no experience. Donald came up with the idea of Nic Roeg." Nic Roeg was a cameraman in the process of taking the next step – directing his own films. "At that point there were no teams of people co-directing. In the end it was a very real way for Donald to achieve telling his story." By setting up his own production company, Goodtimes Enterprises, and dealing with the agency, CMA, that he had been working for, Lieberson was able to sell the idea. Two of CMA's agents, Freddie Fields and David Begelman, handled the project and approached Ken Hyman, head of production at Warner Bros in London, to broker a deal. "The deal was sold here in London, but finalised in California." When Warners saw the name Mick Jagger, the cash register must have started to ring. "The Hollywood majors were setting their sights on the youth market. They saw him as a powerful contemporary personality." It is generally said that they imagined a vehicle not unlike The Beatles' *A Hard Day's Night*. Thus the money was forthcoming. It wasn't a large budget, but enough to work with. "£1.1m, including contingency," said Lieberson.

"They were excited about a film with Mick Jagger," Nic Roeg recalled, "a soundtrack, songs, and whatever, which they didn't get finally, but . . . it was the deal that started it. They didn't realise they didn't have a script."

Lieberson told Mick Brown for his book on the film that there was a production supervisor, Raymond Anzarat, who thought it was "absolutely ludicrous that Warners had approved the film" with all the unknown factors of two directors who had never directed, a producer who had never produced a film, all out of some office in Chelsea. It was completely against the grain. Anzarat "loathed" it and "he wrote me endless memos berating us about how unprofessional we were, the script was terrible, the budget was unrealistic".

When the film appeared, a few years later, a Warner Bros press release played on this lack of experience. Under the title '"Performance" Racks Up Score of Film Firsts', the one-page release notes: "For rock-performer Mick Jagger, it's his first dramatic role. Moreover, he wrote his first special material for a film score (...) It is versatile James Fox's first real 'heavy' role, as a vicious Cockney gangster on the run for murder. '*Performance*' also marks the first English-speaking role for actress Michele Breton, age 19, who learned English in four months for the part, and the first British film for both Miss Breton and, in the other female lead, German-Italian actress Anita Pallenberg. In addition, Donald Cammell, who wrote the original screenplay, and Nicolas Roeg, the cinematographer, make their directorial debuts, as co-directors of the motion picture."

In one of his few interviews, this one in 1988, though it wasn't published until after his death, Donald pointed out to David Del Valle that he had sought to combine the gangster and rock star world because in Britain "the underworld was typified by the Krays. The Krays were very macho, very dangerous and rather glamorous. This I saw as sort of a parallel with the rock world and, particularly, The Rolling Stones. Originally, my script was called *The Performers* because each of the characters is a performer, in one sense or another."

When he points out the glamour that was attached to the Krays, he was picking up on a rare phenomenon. In the Sixties there were three fashionable photographers in London: Terence Donovan, Brian Duffy and David Bailey, the latter an East End lad who had made it to the top and formed the basis for David Hemming's part in Antonioni's *Blowup*. In 1965 Bailey published a portfolio box of his photos, *David Bailey's Box of Pin-Ups*, reflecting that period as he saw it. It comprised his 36 glamorous people of the time, each an icon and representative of the new world of the young, a world filled with money, drugs and sexual freedom, a snapshot of Swinging London. These photos included Lennon and McCartney, Mick Jagger, Brian Jones, The Rolling Stones, P.J. Proby, Gordon Waller, Brian Epstein, Michael Caine, Andrew Loog Oldham, Rudolf Nureyev, Terence Stamp, Jean Shrimpton (one of only four women, all models), Vidal Sassoon, Terence Donovan, Cecil Beaton, Michael Cooper, David Hockney and the Kray twins. The photo of Reggie and Ronnie Kray not only became infamous in itself, but also indicates a romantic tie to the criminal fraternity. The presence of the twins irritated people in high places and pressure was applied, with the result that no American edition appeared, nor indeed a second edition from Weidenfeld & Nicolson, the British publishers. Today it is a much-sought book, commanding high prices. Nothing though could halt the continual use of that image of the Kray twins, nor any future images that accompanied their increased public prominence.

"That famous black and white David Bailey photo of the twins remains an icon, a last image of British gangland," as the crime writer Duncan Campbell noted. John Pearson, the original official biographer of the Krays, looked back in 2010 and considered what he hadn't been able to write earlier, adding information to things he could now place in perspective. "David Bailey's photographs had, as the phrase goes, 'iconised' them, and when sociologists started writing learned papers about them it was clear that they had assumed their place in the social history of the

Sixties. They were also something of a national obsession, and just as James Bond epitomises everything we take for granted in a secret agent and Sherlock Holmes is our ultimate detective, so the one word 'Kray' is embedded in our collective memory as accepted shorthand for the quintessential British gangster."

The script for *Performance* was worked on back in Paris, and also in St Tropez, the playground on the French Riviera for the jetsetters and the extremely wealthy, which had been enhanced by the presence of and allure given it by Brigitte Bardot in the Fifties. (Seeking the 'good life' and 'night life' in the south, seeing 'vie' flashing at you in 'Riviera', to cite Godard in *Pierrot le Fou.*) "We (Donald, Deborah and Anita) did go on holidays together. You know, on Saturday night, after clubbing, drive down to St Tropez" for weekends. Anita has remarked more than once that one time, when "Donald, Deborah and I all worked on it (the script) together" on the beach, a gust of wind blew it into the sea, and after rescuing the pages they had to iron them dry.

Because Donald gave few interviews, he rarely covered all the angles when he did. But in the long *Vague* interview he does say: "Anita had a lot of influence on the way that I saw *Performance*. And she's not often credited with it. (...) But in fact I became fascinated by some things that she was already deeply involved in, like Artaud theatre, Theatre of Cruelty, like she'd worked before with Schlondorff on her first picture. So I give her full credit."

Although perhaps *The Observer* went too far, in February 2008, when Anita was credited as the co-writer of the film, which shows how facts and myths can be built. Anita's observation on seeing the final film is telling: "I didn't even know all that gangster stuff. When I first saw it (in the film), it was the first time I'd even heard about it."

She also relates how they would often stop working on the script to discuss films. "There were days we didn't get much done on the script because we'd spent all day talking about movies."

Another anomaly, which is pointed out by Colin MacCabe in his book, revolves around a list of films Donald contributed to a *Time Out* poll in the Nineties. Amongst his favourites were films by Bertolucci, Godard and Buñuel, but only films by Eisenstein, Kurosawa and Kubrick dated from before *Performance*. There were no films from the period when he lived in

Paris. One might have thought one of the early films by Godard would rank. Or Cocteau. Most people, whether artists or the general populace, would have cited something from their formative years. Perhaps it was a bad day – another moment and the list would have been very different.

It comes as no surprise that Donald regularly stated that books were more important than films in his life. He credits his co-director, Nic Roeg, with being an ardent reader too, adding: "Nic and I had been friends for years. We both read the same books, which to my mind is more important than seeing the same films. Our initial inspiration came from Borges and Vladimir Nabokov's *Despair*, a story which makes a kind of ecstatic exploration of a character's fatal encounter with his double or alter ego – as in *Performance*. I was fascinated by the idea of murder which might also be suicide." Though we will return to that last sentence later, one wonders whether *Despair* was anything more than a nominal influence at first, whether it wasn't more of a trigger than a work actually taken on board, for, as the writer Paul Mayersberg points out: "*Despair* is about delusion. The character that Hermann picks up as a double, Fritz, bears no visual comparison."

Today our judgement might be blurred because, although Nic Roeg always wanted to make his version of the novel, it was Fassbinder who filmed it in 1977, with a script by Tom Stoppard and starring Dirk Bogarde as Hermann. Thus our own image, conjured from the deceptive skill of Nabokov's pen, has been superseded by images from the German director's film, as is so often the case when a novel is filmed. It then becomes virtually impossible to visualise the original novel for ourselves when we read or reread it. At one point, Nabokov, who leads the reader through a labyrinth of ways of seeing and understanding, has Hermann say: "An author's fondest dream is to turn the reader into a spectator." Perhaps he should have forbidden any film version to be made.

The novel is written in the first person and gives the reader no chance of knowing whether the likeness is simply in Hermann's imagination or whether his plan to murder Felix and take on his persona has any credibility. However, the film shows us clearly that it is all delusion on Hermann's part – at one point even he admits there is no similarity in their appearances. The only double is of the self, either employed with mirrors or by being outside oneself yet watching oneself, something that Hermann does from down the corridor, watching himself on the bed with his wife, as if both an actor on a stage and a member of the audience.

Donald never returned to live in London on a permanent basis. Each visit was usually accommodated with a short-stay lease on a flat, always within the world that he knew, never far from the King's Road, and quite often in Beaufort Street. His brother David, with his business and other involvements in the area, was always able to organise these residences. When Donald separated from Deborah Dixon in November 1967 and came to London, he abandoned many of his possessions, including his paintings.

The next phase of work on the script for *Performance* (still called *The Performers*) was set in motion when Donald renewed his friendship with David Litvinoff. They were old friends. They went way back: "I used to go around with David Litvinoff as a teenager. We hung around Soho together when I was still going to school. David was, apart from me, the most important person involved in the movie." An interesting claim. It was Litvinoff who brought his knowledge of London's East End to bear on the film, giving it a credibility and feeling that most films about the crime world seem to lack. "David was magnetised by the East End. He came from the poor end of a Jewish intellectual family that had got into the judge business. He had lived in the East End as a kid – he knew the real thing."

Perhaps Donald ran into him, or perhaps he found him through an earlier friend, Tim Whidborne, who lived in The Pheasantry on the King's Road, a Georgian building, part of the site where pheasants were raised for the Royal household in days gone by. Around this time, in 1967, other inhabitants in its apartments and studio spaces included Eric Clapton, Germaine Greer and Martin Sharp, whose *Oz* work and psychedelic posters can be seen as part of the collage work in the *Performance* décor. Sharp's place in The Pheasantry had been acquired for him by Litvinoff. Another of Sharp's friends from Australia, Philippe Mora, also lived in the complex and made a film, *Trouble in Molopolis* (1969), 'a gangster-Brecht-Cagney parody', which includes a scene with Litvinoff shot in that building.

I mention this because a world of myths has built up around Litvinoff. He was a poet who never wrote poetry. Such characters always create their work in the weave of other people. Litvinoff was no exception. He was the black sheep of his family, and whilst two of the other brothers worked hard and honestly, David had other ideas. "He was homosexual, loved low life, and tried to be a villain," is how John Pearson phrased it.

Litvinoff could give the right flavour to the script, giving the gangster dialogue an authenticity. He was also a source of contacts and arranged for Donald to meet various characters, among them the Krays, and then, south of the river, Tommy Gibbons at the Thomas à Becket pub, with its upstairs gym where James Fox was later taken to sharpen up.

It seems that Litvinoff didn't always remain on the best of terms with his friends on the east side of the city. It is acknowledged that the scene where the head of the chauffeur is shaved in the garage to give his master, the lawyer, a lesson in obedience to Chas' boss, Harry Flowers, owes something to an incident where Litvinoff got on the wrong side of his own connections, often said to be the Krays, and his own head was shaved. When he came round from his beating he found that he was dangling over the edge of a balcony, hung out to dry by his heels, blood streaming from a wound. It was "something to do with a gambler's debt at Esmeralda's Barn, a gaming room in Knightsbridge", in Wilton Place, according to Christopher Gibbs. This is not an uncommon way to terrify people. Vicki Hodge, the girlfriend of John Bindon, another actor in *Performance* with a villainous background, as we shall see, notes that "when I accused him (Bindon) of being afraid of his father, he picked me up by my ankles and held me over the balcony of a five-storey building."

Litvinoff had no visible means of income. He had no job, but had a way with words and an affability that allowed him to get whatever he wanted. Except that he took a shine to gambling and accrued debts of £3,000 or more at Esmeralda's Barn, the gambling room that the Krays owned. When Litvinoff confronted Ronnie with his problem, the Kray was only too keen to find a solution that suited him admirably. Ronnie agreed to cancel the debt in return for taking over the remainder of the lease on Litvinoff's flat in Ashburn Gardens, in Kensington, off the Gloucester Road, with the added proviso that he could also take over ownership of Litvinoff's young lover, Bobby Buckley, who also lived there. Graciously, Ronnie said that Litvinoff could continue to live there with them. That arrangement remained in place for 18 months. With a base in west

London, amongst the fashionable people of the time, and with Litvinoff providing a contact to that world, the Krays gained added respectability. It seemed they had struck a good deal.

As a result Buckley was made a croupier at Esmeralda's Barn. Other young pretty boys were also brought in to work there. Ronnie's former vice activity with teenage boys in the East End was resurrected, using Ashburn Gardens and Esmeralda's as focal points. The world that the Krays created and the ways in which people like Lord Boothby became trapped through their weaknesses did eventually unravel and become public. At the time, fearing libel action, two journalists writing about the Krays, Lewis Chester and Cal McCrystal, referred to them as "the two famous sporting twins" (they had been young boxing champions, and sponsored the sport) rather than criminals, giving them a respectability that was repeated so regularly that it avoided their thuggish side, at least for the time being.

The gambling den, Esmeralda's Barn, also attracted people like painters Lucian Freud and Francis Bacon. Freud befriended Litvinoff, liking him as a character and raconteur, and painted his portrait under the title *The Procurer.* Whilst Freud was not gay, he knew the set-up. For Bacon it was obviously no problem. He was interested in rough trade and the criminal fraternity from the East End.

Litvinoff was able to lend his hand and talking ability to merge this world with his friends from the King's Road. He was like a court jester, a jongleur even – "why not?" (a phrase that Donald uses often enough in interviews to be noticeable, and which I wonder is not drawn from a mannerism of Godard's, who uses a similar term, "pourquoi se gêner?", in his early interviews) – to a world that was young and rich, and had become the trendsetters for their generation. And when The Rolling Stones found themselves on the receiving end of society's backlash, with events like Redlands and the subsequent drug busts as the whip, their attitude to concepts of law and order went out the window. Unwittingly, society had given the Krays another step up; their world was now seen to be glamorous.

What better way for Ronnie and Reggie to be immortalised than to become the subject of books and feature in films. Their dress-sense and image had in the first place been shaped by old American gangster movies and yet now they were in turn influencing a British film with their style.

And *Performance* was not the only one. *Villain, Get Carter* and *The Long Good Friday* all followed, as did the Krays' own biopic with the Kemp brothers. None, though, was a patch on *Performance,* because none had that touch that came from associating with Litvinoff, who had not only shared his home with Ronnie, but had woven himself into a world that included many of the protagonists, from Donald Cammell to Mick Jagger to Christopher Gibbs, amongst others. For Ronnie there was no higher accolade than to be visited in prison by celebrities and, in this particular case, when the writer Francis Wyndham brought along James Fox.

Cammell said Litvinoff was "one of the great conversationalists and one of the great improvisers, what we call a 'chat artist' – he could chat fantastically in East End lingo."

Iain Sinclair, one of today's chroniclers of the East End, notes Litvinoff's life as "the slippage between high and low culture, between east and west of the city". Sinclair has listened to tapes of Litvinoff talking and says that he sounds a bit like Harold Pinter in the role of Goldberg in his own play *The Birthday Party.* For those not able to grasp that idea, they could try Sydney Tafler in the film version of the play. It might also help to have a look at Litvinoff's image in Lucian Freud's painting *Man in a Headscarf* (1954), originally called *The Procurer,* as noted above, but changed when Litvinoff took exception to being immortalised in that manner. Sinclair reports his performance on the tapes as "fast, ingratiating, ruthless, angered by some unintended slight. A grammatical error. An inadequate pause. An insult that can never be repaired. Litvinoff talked in inverted commas. A collage of customised quotations and compulsive puns."

"His energy and his violence were just incredible," said Deborah Dixon, quoted by Mick Brown. "As if his mind didn't fit his body. He could destroy anybody with words."

Pinter will return to menace us later. But it should be noted that one of the key factors in *Performance* is that it has almost no vulgar language, no swearing. Only once does Jagger say "fucking", and yet all the way through one feels that the language is overbearingly crude. That is because the very fabric of the language has been penetrated. They've gone right inside and rooted around for the violence within language itself. And that is Litvinoff, and that is Pinter. And it is something we will return to.

Litvinoff had a scar across his face, the result of being clever with his tongue. It dates from the time a couple of lads, probably connected to the Krays, visited him in his Kensington High Street flat, stripped him, shaved his head, tied him to a chair, razor-cut the corners of his mouth and hung him upside down over the balcony. Christopher Gibbs records that "David's version was that he found himself hanging upside down, cut from ear to ear, somewhere near the Derry & Tom's roof garden, hearing the CND marchers coming up Kensington High Street singing 'Corinna, Corinna'." This image found its way into another film, *Villain* (1971), made not long after, with Richard Burton as the Ronnie Kray figure. It's interesting to compare *Villain* with *Performance*'s opening scenes, for despite the presence of Burton and the writers Dick Clement and Ian La Frenais, it never gets to grips with the spoken language.

David Litvinoff had meted out similar treatment himself when he visited Nicky Cramer, the hanger-on who happened to be at Redlands during the infamous drugs bust. Cited as a possible snitch, Litvinoff visited Cramer, accompanied by John Bindon, and hung him out the window in a similar fashion after failing to extract any admission of guilt. Cramer was pronounced clean, and by all accounts decided to change some of his associations and vanished from the scene.

Litvinoff's own life ended at Christopher Gibbs' house, Davington Priory, in Faversham. He lived there for three years as its caretaker. But country life was not to his taste. As Marianne Faithfull writes, he "didn't want to get old, so he killed himself. He committed suicide at Gibbs's house on the Aubusson carpet – Chrissy thought that was frightfully poor form." There's the myth that it was a bloody affair, but it was more mundane – he overdosed on sleeping pills. All he left was a written note with instructions about the dispersal of his collection of blues tapes.

A rare photograph of Litvinoff appears in *The Ultimate Performance* documentary, with both Cammell and Litvinoff naked, Litvinoff holding Donald's penis. Though credited as "dialogue coach and technical advisor" on the film, his role ran much deeper. His presence threads through the film's fabric, although those texts claiming he wrote the script overstate the case.

And then *Performance* was written.

And though the French influences were ever-present and though the underground cinema also informed Donald's sensibilities, it was not an art movie that Donald had in mind. His sights were set higher. They were aimed at Hollywood, aiming to challenge and ultimately become part of that world. Almost a suicidal mission you might say. In Italy Bernardo Bertolucci was thinking along much the same lines. He wanted to embrace and use Hollywood, whilst at the same time challenging it. He was engaged on *The Spider's Stratagem*, followed quickly by *The Conformist*, the former drawn from a story by Jorge Luis Borges, *Theme of the Traitor and the Hero*.

Mick Jagger was kept up to speed on the script's development, but then he was in Donald's circle of friends. "Like a lot of movies it changed a lot from the original sitting around the kitchen version that it was, and then into the first script. By the time we came to do it I felt I knew it. I knew it almost as much as Donald knew it because it had become part of your life, you know."

Donald Cammell provided Warner Bros with a synopsis of *Performance* in October 1969.

Chas Devlin (JAMES FOX) is a young "villain" – a professional criminal – specializing in violence and the exercise of fear. In London, such men are called, by their own people, "performers" – a name that characterises their status as artists in their own group.

Chas' boss, Harry Flowers (JOHNNY SHANNON), refers to himself as a businessman. The structure and principles of this society, the Underworld, grotesquely reflect those of the "real" world of business on which they prey.

Chas enjoys his work and its rewards: Jaguars, predatory sex, the whole super-male fantasy of this ultimate man's world.

While he and his colleagues, Rosebloom (STANLEY MEADOWS) and Moody (JOHN BINDON), are methodically terrorizing the offices of a car rental company that Flowers plans to take-over, a lawyer (ALLEN CUTHBERTSON) is defending his client in the High Court on charges of corporation fraud involving the take-over of a small business by a big one.

The lawyer, mouthpiece of a rapacious businessman, and the gangster perform their separate authoritarian rituals – the hypocrisy of the one as absurd as the brutality of the other, and equally effective.

However, developing his case from ethics to actuality, the lawyer threatens to inculpate another man – "a guilty party" – to take the heat off his client. The man is Harry Flowers, notorious racketeer.

Chas is sent to warn lawyer and client not to involve "old friends". He deals with the adversary by constructing a vicious but appropriate terror-drama from the desecration of "property", material and human.

However, Harry Flowers firmly orders Chas not to take part in his next business operation – the wrecking of a betting shop with a view to persuading his owner, Joey Maddocks (ANTHONY VALENTINE), to be "merged". Joey is an old friend of Chas, and Harry's rule is "Keep personal relations out of business". Chas' pride is stung: he sees a reflection of his status, and moreover he has an obscure old score to settle with Joey. He disobeys Harry, and brashly delivers to him personally the humiliated new "partner".

Harry, recognizing rebellion by his "artist" against his allotted role, castigates him publicly for his primitivism and ignorance of modern methods; violence is necessary, but must always be bureaucratised, never individualised. Chas is "out of date".

Joey, seeing Chas fall from grace, feels free to avenge himself. Chas returns home to find Joey and a couple of mates of his waiting for him. They have systematically destroyed his flat. He fights savagely but is over-powered. Then Joey flogs him frenziedly with his own dog's leash. It is at the point of his deepest humiliation and subjection that Chas, by arousing a moment's pity in his tormentor, manages to break free long enough to reach a gun. With mindless inevitability, he carries his stoneage function to its logical conclusion and kills Joey.

The Flowers firm is shaken by this impermissible killing. Knowing that if Chas is caught, they will find themselves incriminated in a "gangland murder", they decide (with suitable corporate evasiveness) that the "mad dog" must be hunted down and destroyed before the police get him.

Chas flees, heading for the country. But in a railway waiting room, he overhears a young musician relating to his mother a dialogue he had with the landlord about finding a new tenant for his furnished room. He mentions the address. On an impulse, Chas changes his mind. He goes there.

Powis Square is a strange and faded area of London. The house, cavernous and baroquely crumbling, is the retreat of Turner (MICK JAGGER), retired rock'n'roll superstar. He, too, is, or was, an artist; he, too, is an outcast from a sub-culture he once dominated. His retirement is apparently voluntary. He is stuck. A curious fossil, his remaining audience consists of his girlfriend, enigmatic, ever-grinning Pherber (ANITA PALLENBERG) and his girlfriend's girlfriend, Lucy (MICHELE BRETON), a very young French illegal immigrant. A self-sufficient, affectionate, female-orientated, domestic atmosphere prevails. Cocooned in his female chrysalis, Turner is waiting – for what?

Chas, alien and battered, telling the garbled but just plausible story of a car accident and posing as a juggler (a show-biz crony of the previous tenant), is received by Pherber, who senses the aura of menace that emanates from the visitor, and possibly deduces that there has arrived on her doorstep the medium for a final effort from Turner towards recognition of himself.

Turner at first tries to eject Chas. Then he changes his mind. The new lodger installs himself.

Chas' opinion of his hosts is one of pure contempt. His disaster has not diminished the primitive sureness of his identity. He is without self-double. He sees his predicament as the opening to a new life; the fantasy of America, the Mecca of ultimate maleness. To this end, he needs Turner's help – to take a photograph of him for a forged passport. He explains he wants to "change his image" for his new act.

(Except that that is not what Donald provided. It was written up from the following.)

HARRY FLOWERS (John Shannon), London businessman, believes in old-fashioned free enterprise allied to modern methods. Take-overs and managers in particular, he swears by. Car-hire firms, small betting shops. . . . "small businesses, in this day and age, is against nature." Harry Flowers is a London mobster. He runs a firm; a lucrative protection racket.

He is proud of CHAS DEVLIN, his number one executive. Chas (James Fox) is the underworld's version of a P.R. man; a persuader, a polished practitioner of terror. What the trade calls in a term reserved for its top professionals, "a right performer." Money, mohair, Jaguars and sexual conquest are the goodies of Chas' good life, and above all the abundant opportunities he has to assert his superior qualities of he-manship in the ultimate Man's World.

Assisting Chas on his daily rounds of the "clientele" are ROSE-BLOOM (Stanley Meadows), who reads good books, and MOODY (John Bindon), who dislocates arms. However, when Flowers and his business partner DENNIS (Anthony Morton) order the wrecking of a small-time betting shop whose boss, JOEY MADDOCKS (Anthony Valentine) has resisted being "took over", Chas is firmly ordered to stay away and leave this routine little affair to be handled by Rosebloom. The reason is that Chas and Joey were once good friends – a relationship Flowers calls "double-personal". Chas, however, feels slighted, his pride has been stung, and moreover he wants to pay off some obscure adolescent score with Joey.

Harry's rank and file do a thorough job on the shop. Rosebloom is scheduled to pick up chastened Joey right after, but Chas, with shrewd timing, gets there first. He humiliates Joey before shipping him back to Flowers' office himself.

Nothing goes wrong. Flowers genially 'merges' Joey's business as planned, toasts are drunk. And then Flowers sends for Chas, and punctures his ego in front of all, telling him off for disobedience. Chas walks out. Joey feels better.

Chas gets home late, after a night of brooding and drinking. He is greeted by a glimpse of his flat, utterly destroyed, before Joey and two of his mates jump him. He fights savagely and hopelessly. Then Joey Maddocks takes his revenge with the relish of an old friend. He beats Chas with his dog's lead, forcing him to a deeper humiliation than his own. But Joey shocks even himself. He is moved to a moment's pity and Chas seizes his chance . . .

There is a gun hidden in his bathroom. Chas gets a hand to it, and according to his nature and the stoneage progression of pride and vengeance that is his ethic, he shoots and kills his friend with mindless inevitability.

"It was an accident," says Chas, on the phone to flabbergasted Harry Flowers, who has summoned a hasty conference in his early morning bedroom. The naked gang murder of a "little man" is good for headlines and very upsetting to the police. It's an outrage that rebounds on Flowers devastatingly.

"You're more than involved, Harry," his lawyer announces. "You're implicated."

Elusively but collectively, a decision is made. Chas the 'mad dog' must be found by his friends and put to sleep before the police catch up with him.

However, Chas has guessed what is in store for him, and he decides to flee from London to the country, to the village of a forgotten aunt. He is huddled in a station waiting-room when he overhears a conversation. A young musician is saying goodbye to his mother. He owes rent on his room, and his landlord is looking for a new tenant. He mentions the address in seedy Notting Hill Gate. On an impulse, Chas changes his mind.

He goes to the house. Cavernous and baroquely crumbling, it is the retreat of TURNER (Mick Jagger), retired rock'n'roll superstar. A curious fossil, his remaining audience consists of his girlfriend, enigmatic, ever-grinning PHERBER (Anita Pallenberg) and his girlfriend's girlfriend LUCY (Michele Breton), a very young French illegal immigrant. A self-sufficient, affectionate, female-oriented, domestic atmosphere prevails.

Chas, alien and battered, telling the garbled but just-plausible tale of a car accident and posing as a juggler (a show-biz crony of the previous tenant), is received by the household with successive degrees of ridicule, revulsion, sympathy and curiosity. Turner tries to get rid of him, then changes his mind. The new lodger installs himself. His opinion of his hosts is one of pure contempt. They are there only to be used towards his single end: escape. Needing a photograph of himself for a forged passport, he asks Turner to take one, explaining he wants to try out a new image for his act.

(At this point the accounts are merged, and Donald's is kept intact.)

The invitation to experiment on Chas' image seems to Turner supernaturally opportune. It is now apparent that he and Pherber know what, if not who, Chas really is, and that they, for their part, intend to use him. For in Turner's eyes, his lodger has assumed the proportions of a demonic figure, personifying the magnetism of violence that Turner knows was the core, or the cutting edge, of his own power as a performer.

The reason for his present predicament – his creative impotence – becomes clearer. At the height of his success, he had become aware of anomalous extensions of his art that led towards inchoate violence. He learned that the atavistic rituals of the performance with which he captured and manipulated his gigantic audience were capable of generating demonic forces beyond his control.

Whether Turner has lost this abominable gift or consciously rejected it, he recognises it in Chas in its pure form, despicable but seductive, and seized by the notion that Chas (this Doppelganger of his [crossed out in draft, with Chas written above]) can be made to disgorge the key to some monstrous enigma of human nature, he embarks with Pherber's connivance on the dissection of the guinea-pig that the underworld has deposited in his basement.

(Meanwhile, Lucy, repelled and frightened by the ominous aura in the house, goes off and leaves them to it. [Written with line through in draft]) A grotesque, admirably pretentious experiment begins its erratic course.

If the subject of it is tough, the methods employed on him are, after their fashion, equally so. Chas' prized virility and suspect sexuality are exposed to ingenious indignities (particularly in Pherber's hands). His image is changed in grossly literal terms. Drugged, defenceless, but stoically dignified, he slowly succumbs, wallowing with his hosts in a welter of abuse and tenderness, plagiarised literature and preposterous rituals, until he is ready for his final role: as solitary audience of Turner's final performance.

(Returning to the house. Lucy observes the results of Chas' ordeal with a youthfully candid eye; and changes her mind about the no-longer manly lodger. They share a common sorrow: they have to move on, they must get out. That night Lucy gives him quite casually all she has to give: a purple stone, a ring, a person. Chas accepts with grace. They talk about Turner, and Chas reveals his respect for that (-----ical?)* man. Then he goes upstairs to fetch Lucy her shampoo. (Chas) won't come back.

The morning is dark. There are visitors in the house, but Pherber sleeps on. Chas and Turner, washed-up performers, say good morning.) [A line is drawn through the whole bracketed section.]

* The copy is too faint here to discern this cryptic word.

4) they come and they go

WHENEVER anyone embarks on an adventure, they always hope that someone will pick up on their efforts, and part of any success can be about being in the right place at the right time. Sometimes accidental opportunities arise which can be capitalised on, as not everything successful needs to be engineered or manipulated. And even once you start attempting to control a situation, you cannot be sure everything will fall into place as intended.

In the early Sixties, when The Rolling Stones were starting to knit together, they found that another group, The Beatles, were already one step ahead and making their mark. In pop music's commercial world, the way to make a name for oneself is to find a niche, possibly as a contrast to other successful bands. It might all sound very calculating, but back in the early Sixties, before there were teams of image builders and advisors, there was no template. Bands simply fumbled around. Fortunately, the Stones had found a hustling manager in Andrew 'Loog' Oldham, who was making the right decisions for his boys, all slightly older than him, which was unusual in itself.

The Beatles were presented by their manager, Brian Epstein, as a wholesome bunch of lads, nice boys. What better way to respond than by adopting a bad boy image, generating animosity in the media between the two bands, irrespective of whether it was true or not. As Mick Jagger said later: "When you get the ball going they do it all for you, especially in this country. You don't have to do a thing, the media will pick up on it and exaggerate it beyond recognition. If they just get so much as a smell of a story they'll make it up or get a quote and turn it around to suit themselves. I don't have to tell you . . . the media needs a story and the bands need to be publicised.

Oldham had a stroke of genius in 1964 when he span the idea 'Would you let your sister go with a Rolling Stone?' It was first touted in *Melody*

Maker before being picked up across the media. 'Would you let your daughter marry one?' was another headline to enflame parents. The fire was being stoked.

Whereas The Beatles would have been welcomed into any family – "they make jokes, wear neat clothes, get along with royalty" – the Stones were perceived as dirty and unwashed. They were the type of lads who might "never wash their hands before lunch". The word 'morons' was too good to describe them.

Another trigger point for the Stones came in March 1965, when the band was coming back late from a gig and a simple everyday need had to be attended to. The Daimler in which the group and a few friends were travelling hurriedly pulled into a petrol station in Forest Gate in East London. Mick, Brian and Bill were all desperate to go to the toilet. Bill's bladder in particular needed to be relieved regularly, which was something of a joke in the band. However, the garage attendant refused them use of the facilities. According to some reports they were rude, although others claimed they were just desperate to relieve themselves, so they went outside and pissed against a boundary wall in the forecourt. After they departed the attendant called the police and in due course Mick, Brian and Bill were fined in court. Instead of letting the incident pass, the group used the story at every opportunity to gain publicity. It caught the public imagination, irritated the older generation and fuelled their bad boy image. Oldham "turned them into everything that parents would most hate, be most frightened by," wrote Nik Cohn. "Kids might see them the first time and not be sure about them, but then they'd hear their parents whining about those animals, those filthy long-haired morons, and suddenly they'd be converted, they'd identify like mad."

Hot on its tail came songs playing up the group's defiance, such as 'Satisfaction' (expressing lack of), and in 1967 the Stones released another outrage: 'Let's Spend the Night Together'. Jagger laughed at the time, explaining that in his world you were out enjoying yourself in clubs at night. It was during the day one was in bed, and young women were less than safe with them then, or words to that effect.

Even as the flames were being fanned they were invited onto the television variety show *Sunday Night at the London Palladium,* the height of each weekend's viewing. It was such a rarity to see someone even slightly rebellious on the show. What was the producer thinking? The finale of this family entertainment required the guests to stand on a revolving stage and wave to the audience in the theatre, and the families at home gathered around their television sets. The Stones refused to oblige. They thought it was outdated. They didn't see it as a big deal, but everyone else did, and the media went to town. It was as if the group had stuck two fingers up at society, who had graciously allowed them to sing their provocative song on 'their' show. No wonder no sane person would allow their daughter to spend time with these degenerates. And so it went on. This bunch needed to be put in their place.

As everyone knows, you should not confuse the private world of artists with their work. However, many fans, as well as society at large, often want to equate the two. Oldham worked on this blindness, as did the Stones themselves, by playing down their middle-class background, preferring to use them as "five shaggy hand grenades", as Marc Spitz terms them, to gleefully throw at the establishment. If it had been possible, Oldham would dearly have loved Mick and the band to have played Alex and the droogs in a film version of Anthony Burgess' novel *A Clockwork Orange*. This had been mooted, but Oldham later admitted: "We never had the rights. I believe if you lie enough it becomes a reality. In that instance, it didn't, but we had a great four or five months with it."

Where were the guardians of law and order in these simmering perturbations? Things were about to change with The Beatles after their manager's death and they had taken charge of their own image and direction(s), but prior to that you could still hear stories such as how Paul McCartney parked his Aston Martin badly in the street when visiting a friend, only for a young 'bobby' to knock on the door to enquire after the mis-parked car and, upon seeing McCartney, instead of reprimanding him, asking him to toss over the keys so that he could park the car properly.

The Stones themselves probably didn't have any great run-in with the police on a personal level, not at that time, but their media image as bad boys was having a successful effect on the general populace. Having nurtured and fed it they had to work with it, despite irritations and consequences that might affect them on a daily basis.

We all think we know Mick Jagger, but his image was set by Oldham, capitalising on the traits he had seen from the time when they'd first met.

Mick was to point out specifically in terms of his role in *Performance* that people think they know me, but they don't. Indeed, it is given added piquancy in the film with the identity question as a key factor for the two main characters: "Who are you?" "Do you know who you are?"

The fire was truly fanned one night in early 1967 when two young journalists opened the door and entered Blaise's in Kensington. There they found Brian Jones. These two, obviously news reporters with scant knowledge of contemporary music, approached Jones and found him affable, much to their surprise. They talked about various subjects as Brian sipped at his vodka and slipped down some bennies. When the journalists left, they thought they had caught Mick Jagger off-guard. They knew they could make trouble with a story that would help their careers.

The *News of the World* subsequently appeared on February 5, 1967 with an exposé about pop stars and drugs. Beneath a photo of Jagger it recounted how he took LSD. "During the time we were at the Blases (sic) Club, in Kensington, London, Jagger took about six Benzedrine tablets. 'I just wouldn't keep awake in places like this if I didn't have them,' he said. (...) Later at Blases, Jagger showed a companion and two girls a small piece of hash (marijuana) and invited them to his flat for 'a smoke'."

Jagger was furious. For a start he wasn't even in the country on the night in question. Besides, he would never talk about drugs to strangers, and wouldn't take any type of pill in public in case it was misconstrued. That night, during a previously booked appearance on the Eamonn Andrews TV talk show, he announced he was going to sue the *NOTW* for libel.

Robert Fraser advised Mick to let it drop, warning him that Oscar Wilde had made that mistake when suing the Marquess of Queensberry for libel, which had led to public scrutiny of his affairs, a trial, imprisonment, the slippery slope to his downfall, abandonment and death. Not that anyone was expecting this fiasco to go anywhere near that far.

And then followed the weekend that was to open up the whole idea of how publicity works and the way its effects can either burn down the house . . . or, if you're lucky, be turned to your advantage. Whoever controls the flames probably has to be a bit of a magician. That famed weekend at Redlands was to become the most instrumental moment in making *Performance* happen at all.

Keith Richards had invited Jagger and Marianne Faithfull to Redlands,

Deborah Dixon and Anita Pallenberg ironing dry the *Performance* script after its dip in the sea at St Tropez.
COURTESY OF DEBORAH DIXON; PHOTOGRAPH BY DONALD CAMMELL

Donald Cammell in his New York studio, with pet capuchin monkey, in 1959. COURTESY OF DEBORAH DIXON; PHOTOGRAPH BY NORMAN PARKINSON

Marianne Faithfull and Anita, bound for Tangier, in March 1967. DOVE/EXPRESS/GETTY IMAGES

Brian Jones. GAB ARCHIVE/REDFERNS

Christopher Gibbs in 1964. TOPFOTO/COLIN JONES

Richard Hamilton in his studio, with some of his *Swingeing London 67* series. HOMER SYKES

Robert Fraser at home in Mount Street, June 1967.
FRED MOTT/EVENING STANDARD/GETTY IMAGES

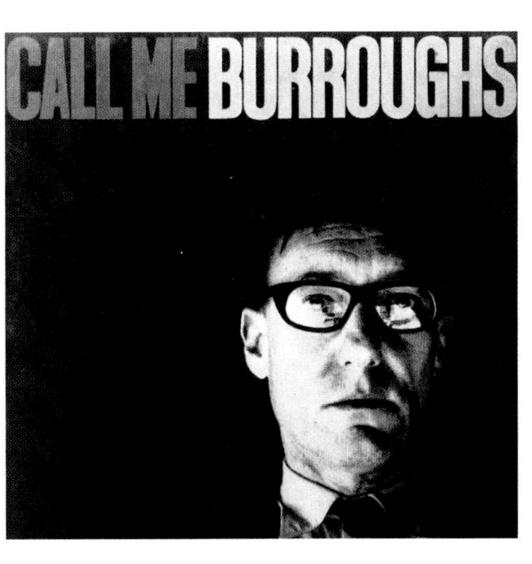

Cover of Doctor Burroughs' first vinyl album, 1965.

Ronnie and Reggie Kray with Judy Garland and her future husband Mark Herron in 1964. KEYSTONE/GETTY IMAGES

Harry Flowers poses for the camera in the Glass Bucket bar. WARNER BROS/PHOTOFEST

James Fox is charmed by Sarah Miles in *The Servant* (1963). MOVIESTORE COLLECTION/REX FEATURES

Ann Sidney and James Fox take a break during filming. BILL ROWNTREE/MIRRORPIX

John Bindon with his partner Vicki Hodge. MIRRORPIX

Donald Cammell in the co-director's chair. THEO BERGSTROM

Chas Devlin returns to the office after a day's work. THE KOBAL COLLECTION/WARNER/GOODTIMES

The Borges volume that echoes throughout *Performance*.

Anna Karina displays Godard's reading habits in *Alphaville* (1965).

The flowered kiss in Jean Genet's *Un Chant d'Amour* (1950).

Nic Roeg on set. THE KOBAL COLLECTION/WARNER/GOODTIMES

Mick Jagger has redecorating down to a T. WARNER BROS

his home in Sussex, for a small party. George Harrison and his wife Patti Boyd, Michael Cooper, Robert Fraser and Christopher Gibbs would be there too, though in the event the Beatle and his wife didn't arrive until late the next day, on the Sunday. And there were a couple of others: Nicky Cramer and a Canadian, David Schneiderman, 'The Acid King' as he was known, who would bring some tablets called 'White Lightning', which were a bit like acid.

On the Sunday morning, they all took the acid, and under its effects went down to the nearby beach and, later, in search of Edward James' house, where the owner's famous collection of surrealist art was displayed. As it turned out, they found it had just closed for the day, and they were unable to pull any strings for private admittance. As noted above, George Harrison and Patti came late but didn't stay long, having other things to do. Everyone else was still under the effects of the pills, each being in various states of coming down. They were all fairly relaxed.

Marianne felt grubby, sand and dirt sticking in her hair. She had brought no change of clothes, so she had a bath, wrapped herself in the large fur bedspread in their room, usually called a 'rug' in most accounts, and sat on a sofa.

At that point there was a knock at the door. Reluctant to answer the incessant banging, thinking it was fans seeking autographs, Keith's curiosity finally got the better of him. He was confronted by a man in a white trench coat with an army of uniformed policemen and women gathered behind. A search warrant was shown and everyone entered the premises and set about rummaging around. However, this raiding party was not a well-versed police squad trained to find drugs. This was just the local force asked to search for any scandalous drugs that these young people would be taking, acting on an unspecified tip-off.

Keith and his friends were still floating, euphoric, giggling. This visit by the local boys in blue seemed slightly unreal. Marianne parted her bedspread and flashed at a policeman, who turned red. She was approached to be searched by a policewoman. As she wore no clothes, she questioned the need. She flashed to the whole room, so that everyone was aware she was naked and there was nowhere to search. Marianne agrees she liked being on the stage, playing for the audience. She wasn't reserved or prudish, but neither was she acting the tart. She was just 'stoned'. All reports of the event come with different angles. The diamond is cut with different faces. Which are true and which aren't barely seems important now. After all, everything adds to the myths. (To see the evidence, the original fur spread, seek the Stones' video for 'We Love You', made by Peter Whitehead, which reveals Jagger as the naked person.)

Robert Fraser was found to have some pills, some of which were taken for tests. Mick's jacket contained a small lump of hash, which was ignored, but a phial of pills bought legally was taken away. When Schneiderman's attaché case was opened, crammed as it was with various drugs, he objected to any further investigation, telling the inquisitor that it was all unprocessed film, wrapped in foil, and if they exposed it a year's work would be ruined. The policeman apologised, left it alone and then found a small amount of hash and other things in his jacket, which satisfied him.

When they left, the haul was minimal, given what could have been found. But the raiding police were green and had not known what to expect.

Tony Sanchez, who worked for the Stones in various capacities – as driver, supplier of drugs and odd-job man – had contacts in the police who might be able to switch the heroin (in Fraser's case) for glucose, if the price was right. Sanchez said that the price for perverting the course of justice for Fraser, Jagger and Richards, whose premises it was found on, would be £6,000, though other accounts add or subtract a thousand. The money was duly gathered, "sufficient to buy a reasonable family house", as Sanchez observed, and handed over at a meet in a pub in Kilburn. After that everything seemed to go quiet. The bribe appeared to have worked.

And then the *NOTW* appeared with details of the raid, naming names, "every single detail", as if the reporter was sitting in the middle of the room taking notes. *NOTW* had set them up. Jagger would now be unable to continue with his libel case. *NOTW* had saved themselves a substantial payout, having realised that their incompetent journalists had confused the identities of Brian Jones and Mick Jagger.

The main suspect, as they were to discover, David Schneiderman, had left the country, eventually returning to the United States after meandering through various European countries.

Charges followed against Mick for unauthorised possession of four tablets containing amphetamine sulphate, Keith for allowing his house to be used for smoking cannabis resin and Robert Fraser for the unauthorised possession of heroin and eight capsules containing methyl amphetamine hydrochloride.

The media circus was set in motion; paranoia now ruled. The Stones were on tour and every step they took was regarded with suspicion. They were strip-searched each time they arrived at a country's border. However, the young were becoming enraged at this affront to their representatives. It wasn't a matter of whether you liked the Stones or not. Attacking the Stones was seen as attacking youth and the notion that the Stones were being made scapegoats began to take root, both here and abroad.

Keith and Mick thought the case against them wouldn't stand up. Marianne considered Mick very gallant to take responsibility for the pills she'd bought on holiday, and felt she should say so in court. Mick refused, telling her to say nothing: "We thrive on publicity like this, but it could kill your career stone dead."

On the day of the trial, the police raided Brian Jones, found drugs and charged him. There seemed to be a conspiracy afoot. This feeling was strengthened when Mick was found guilty, the judge having disallowed the deposition of Doctor Firth, who explained the nature of the pills and how he would have prescribed them if asked. Robert Fraser was also found guilty.

Mick and Robert were sent to Lewes Prison for the night, while Keith was allowed to return home to await trial in the morning. The following morning, Mick and Robert were seen in handcuffs, an image captured by a mass of photographers. However, unbeknown to those wishing to put the upstarts in their place, they had presented the world with an image that was soon to be picked up by Richard Hamilton, one of the artists Robert Fraser represented and had shown in his Duke Street gallery. More in due course . . .

At Keith's trial, the evidence was flimsier, so play was made of Marianne's fur wrap and the implication that an orgy was under way when the police arrived. Marianne was not named, but everyone knew the identity of the mysterious Miss X. That lunchtime in the local pub, it seems that two policemen added further fuel to the flames. They told their audience of gathered pressmen, trawling for gossip about the lewd behaviour in progress at Redlands when they raided, a story of how Marianne had a Mars bar inserted in her vagina, which Jagger was eating. This story has blighted Marianne throughout her life.

Keith stated from the dock that the *NOTW* had set up the raid to force the libel action to be dropped. This was reinforced when a witness said the raid had been undertaken on a tip-off from a newspaper.

And as for the controversy surrounding Marianne, when asked if a sense of embarrassment shouldn't have been in order given that there were eight men in the room, two of them strangers and the third 'a Moroccan servant', Keith responded: "Not at all. We are not old men. We are not worried about petty morals."

Keith was found guilty too.

Each was then given jail sentences: Keith a year, Robert six months and Mick three months.

The day after the trial all three were out on bail. The system had handled it badly, making martyrs of the accused and enhancing their anti-establishment credibility. Even so, the next step couldn't have been foreseen. *The Times*, prestigious and respected in those days, appeared with an editorial by William Rees-Mogg under the title 'Who Breaks a Butterfly on a Wheel?' which castigated the system.

"Mr Jagger has been sentenced to imprisonment for three months. He is appealing against conviction and sentence, and has been granted bail until the hearing of the appeal later in the year. In the meantime, the sentence of imprisonment is bound to be widely discussed by the public. And the circumstances are sufficiently unusual to warrant such discussion in the public interest.

"Mr Jagger was charged with being in possession of four tablets containing amphetamine sulphate and methyl amphetamine hydrochloride: these tablets had been bought, perfectly legally, in Italy, and brought back to this country. They are not a highly dangerous drug, or in proper dosage a dangerous drug at all. They are of the Benzedrine type and the Italian manufacturers recommend them both as a stimulant and as a remedy for travel sickness.

"In Britain, it is an offence to possess these drugs without a doctor's prescription. Mr Jagger's doctor says that he knew and had authorised their use, but he did not give a prescription for them as indeed they had already been purchased. His evidence was not challenged. This was therefore an offence of a technical character, which, before this case drew the point to public attention, any honest man might have been liable to commit. (If, after his visit to the Pope, the Archbishop of Canterbury had bought proprietary airsickness pills at Rome airport, and imported the unused tablets into Britain on his return, he would have risked committing precisely the same offence.) No one who has ever travelled and bought proprietary drugs abroad can be sure that he had not broken the law."

The piece continued in detail to explain how the judge had behaved, and to point out how the law was being misused in this case against Jagger. "It would be wrong to speculate on the judge's reasons which we do not know. It is however possible to consider the public reaction. There are many people who take a primitive view of the matter, what one might call a pre-legal view of the matter. They consider that Mr Jagger has 'got what was coming to him'. They resent the anarchic quality of The Rolling Stones' performances, dislike their songs, dislike their influence on teenagers and broadly suspect them of decadence, a word used by Miss Monica Furlong in the *Daily Mail*."

"There must remain a suspicion in this case that Mr Jagger received a more severe sentence than would have been thought proper for any purely anonymous young man." That is how the editor finished the piece. The immediate response was for other newspapers to offer support too. Eventually the *News of the World* admitted it had told the police in the first place.

Some time later, the trial judge, Judge Block, addressing a gathering of the Horsham Ploughing and Agricultural Society, tried to be clever, telling his audience how he regarded the law and the stand he had made: "We did our best, your fellow countrymen, I, and my fellow magistrates, to cut those stones down to size, but alas, it was not to be because the Court of Criminal Appeal let them roll free." His words didn't go unnoticed, finding their way to Fleet Street reportage, and condemnation from various quarters, not least because Brian Jones was on bail pending an appeal hearing.

On appeal, Mick's sentence was quashed, commuted to a conditional discharge on a technicality. Keith's, too, since the evidence was tenuous. Only Robert Fraser went to prison, serving four months of his sentence.

The next unprecedented step was for Jagger to be flown for an open-air, televised conversation outside London, a kind of round-table between him, the former Home Secretary Lord Stow Hill, the Bishop of Woolwich and William Rees-Mogg. In the event it was more of an unbalanced discourse, Mick labouring in shining armour to defend himself (and all youth, by implication) against the social evil of the establishment that the others represented. He didn't handle the debate brilliantly, but it didn't matter. It was more the case of one thing after another feeding the publicity machine.

The trial and its consequences hit the Stones badly. "Mick came up against the brick wall of reality," Keith said. Levels of corruption, which they had not given much thought to, suddenly appeared. Marianne's thoughts were that: "In the end, the assault on the Stones backfired because it had the ultimate effect of hugely empowering them. (...) No promoter (including the fiendishly ingenious Andrew Oldham) could have done more to mythologise the Stones. It transformed them from pop stars into cultural legends."

The Stones were now martyrs, and it was hoped that Jagger would reveal himself as a revolutionary leader by some on the left. Jagger didn't want that. The trial had cost a considerable amount of money and he wanted to get back to business. And yet he didn't want to lose the publicity that had accrued.

He needn't have worried. There was more to come, as Brian Jones was busted again. One event after another seemed to keep them in the headlines. It didn't matter that Brian wasn't jailed. The Stones were becoming rock'n'roll heroes, "more polarising, newsworthy and intensely interesting than The Beatles could ever hope to be", as Marc Spitz has noted.

Marianne's role was always as a performer. She had won the prize at *International Times*' launch party for 'the shortest/barest costume', dressed as a nun in a bottomless habit, without anyone being uncool enough to make a fuss. Her roles onstage and in film were not destined to go beyond anything but the temptress. But even so she seemed shocked by the effects she had. "My role was ambivalent and eventually had disastrous effects on me and my relationship with Mick. It was a horrible ordeal, but initially it created a bizarre bond between us. I took the poison-pen letters and all those dreadful things in the paper too hard. I was too young and insecure to have all that hatred directed at me and didn't know how to deal with it.

I turned it all on myself." From her perspective, she thought Mick survived it well. "Mick's attitude was much, much healthier. Like, 'Well, they're just idiots. I'm not gonna let this get in my way!' Which should have really been mine, too, but I wasn't grown up or secure enough to do that. Also I was slandered as the wanton woman in the fur rug, while Mick was the noble rock star on trial."

Who knows what makes a painting, a song, a book be regarded as a great work. Many speculate on how great works have slipped into partial or total oblivion for one reason or another. It is not necessarily to do with the work itself, but with other extenuating circumstances and contexts.

Mick as the singer was receiving most attention. Didn't Rees-Mogg focus his attention on Jagger, not on Richards? The singer of the band carries the image of the band. The singer will invariably be the focal point. Sometimes it is hard for other members to accept and it certainly seemed the case with the Stones, for Brian Jones just could not handle that he was not the star of the band. More philosophical musicians often say that the singer shoulders the brunt of the promotional work, with the result that their image becomes more public, making their manoeuvrability through society on a daily basis more difficult, whereas the more anonymous musicians are able to live more freely. At the end of the day, each band member usually receives the same wage for performing and recording. The only one to gain more is the writer of the songs.

Robert Fraser's gallery closed while he was in prison, but his secretary continued to maintain the office. Vast amounts of press cuttings arrived from the press clipping agency they employed to collect exhibition reviews. Every mention of Fraser's name warranted a snipping. Richard Hamilton hadn't treated local issues in his work for a while, but felt personal indignation about the situation regarding his art dealer, and went to the gallery's office to ask if he could take away the accumulations of cuttings. It seems that "there were innumerable reports of the same incident, each varying at the whim of reporters; colours of clothes, age of accused, food carried from restaurants to prisoners, police statements, judges' opinions, all were savoured to the utmost." This mine of information and misinformation was duly sifted through, and Hamilton started to make collages from them. And then he worked on a painting. Hamilton always liked the idea of treating all sources without any sense that one had any greater validity than another. A variety of pieces evolved as he explored the subject, but the image that was to capture the moment and pass into art history, being reproduced in all manner of books and on posters, is called *Swingeing London*. Hamilton said the title came from "a phrase that struck me very forcibly, a remark made by the judge in the case, who said, 'There are times when a swingeing sentence should be administered' – something like that, anyway – and only a few months earlier Robert had been very well represented in the *Time* piece (April 1966), which was called 'Swinging London'. So it was a pun on swinging London and the swingeing sentence."

The photo that Hamilton focussed on showed Mick, wearing a pale, velvety green coat, handcuffed to a smiling Robert Fraser. Here were two minor offenders being driven in a prison van and purposefully paraded before the cameras to set an example. They were handcuffed to each other as if they were violent criminals who might try to escape. With the cameras flashing they had lifted their restricted hands to cut out the light, rather than to prevent any photo being taken or to mask their identity. What they offered became a shining example of the misuse of handcuffs, the very opposite of the authorities' intention to humiliate them before the public.

Hamilton sought the original of John Twine's photo that was published in the *Daily Sketch*. This was enlarged and retouched. With the outline of his composition transferred to six canvases, Hamilton painted them "in contrasting texture, colour, intensity and style, some academically painted and others broadly worked, one with flat areas of poster-like colour". Afterwards, black pigment was silk-screened over the paintings.

Hal Foster, reflecting on Hamilton's life in 2011, asked what makes an image iconic, with particular reference to *Swingeing London 67*. "Somehow it stems from the present even as it evokes the past. Hamilton was a master at this spiking of the contemporary with the historical; he had an almost Warburgian ability to pick out the pose or the gesture that would both resonate across culture and reach back in artistic time."

While the above image was drawn from an event that had started in February, the following month in Marrakech (and two months before the trial), Cecil Beaton came across the Stones, and Mick Jagger in particular. Robert Fraser was with them, because they were out and awaiting news of whether they would be charged or not.

Beaton notes in his diaries how he first met Mick Jagger and the other Stones, "a sleepy looking band of gypsies", in the hotel lobby. Robert Fraser invited Beaton to join them for a drink.

"It was a strange group. The three 'Stones': Brian Jones, with his girl-friend, beatnik-dressed Anita Pallenberg – dirty white face, dirty black-ened eyes, dirty canary drops of hair, barbaric jewelry – Keith Richard in eighteenth-century suit, long black velvet coat and the tightest pants; and, of course, Mick Jagger, together with hangers-on, chauffeurs, and Americans.

"I thought at last an opportunity to photograph one of the most elusive people, whom I admire and am fascinated by, not determined whether he is beautiful or hideous.

"I was intent not to give the impression that I was only interested in Mick, but it happened that we sat next to one another, as he drank a Vodka Collins. And smoked with pointed fingers held high. His skin is chicken breast white, and of a fine quality. He has enormous inborn elegance," he observed in his diaries. Once they were in a Moroccan restaurant, "I was fascinated with the thin concave lines of his body, legs, arms. Mouth almost too large, but he is beautiful and ugly, feminine and masculine, a 'sport', a rare phenomenon.

"He is very gentle, and with perfect manners. He indicated that I should follow his example and eat the chicken with my fingers. It was tender and good. He has much appreciation, and his small, albino-fringed eyes notice everything. 'How different and more real this place is to Tangier – the women more rustic, heavy, lumpy, but their music very Spanish and their dancing too.' He has an analytical slant and compares everything he is seeing here with earlier impressions in other countries."

This haze of the first meeting came down to earth in broad daylight the following morning, by the swimming pool. "I could not believe this was the same person walking towards us, and yet I knew it was an aspect of him. The sun, very strong, was reflected from the white ground and made his face a white, podgy, shapeless mess, eyes very small, nose very pink and spreading, hair sandy dark. He wore Chanel Bois de Rose. His figure, his hands and arms were incredibly feminine. He looked like a self-conscious suburban young lady."

Nevertheless he photographed him out there. "He was a Tarzan of Piero di Cosimo. Lips of a fantastic roundness, body white and almost hairless. He is sexy, yet completely sexless. He could nearly be a eunuch. As a model he is a natural."

When *Performance* was in production, Sandy Lieberson had the idea to invite Cecil Beaton onto the set to take photographs and capitalise on his interest in Jagger. Warners were not prepared to fund such a shoot, so Sandy went ahead and paid for it from his own pocket. Beaton came on set three times and took photos, and was indeed photographed himself with the others. Whilst the results have been used, they never pushed enough buttons to join the great myths around the film. One can try to engineer these situations, hoping something will spark, but you can't always get what you want. But, you just might find . . .

5) casting in character, and versa

PEOPLE think they know who Mick Jagger is. This notion has been increasingly firmed up as the years have passed, as more information and images have forged the 'Mick Jagger' character in the public's imagination. Right from the early days each of us has formed our own personal image of him, the first impressions probably becoming the bedrock. It is not so easy, today, to cast oneself back to that time when The Rolling Stones were first marking out their ground and each member of the band was defining his own public character. Jagger has reiterated over the years, when referring to Turner, his role in *Performance*, that the audience always thought they knew who he was before they sat down in the cinema.

Though it is possible today to laugh at the image of the Stones "as louts, hairy brutes who were corrupting the nation's youth", if you were Mick, or any of the Stones, you had to maintain a line between public and private persona in order to retain your sanity. Mick hated doing interviews, as he felt it impinged on his private life, but it was a necessary evil that he found ways to handle. Marianne Faithfull, another who has suffered, being dragged along with various myths attached to her throughout her life, noted that for many years the press still "persisted in branding Mick as a degenerate, scruffy, smelly person." Of course that was entirely contrary to the real Jagger. "He was very clean, actually, always immaculately dressed and rather fussy and proper."

Images are part construction, part reality and part accident, as things that happen are sometimes retained whether one likes it or not. Jagger had changed his first name from Mike to Mick at the London School of Economics as it "seemed redolent of bourgeois young men with sports cars", as Philip Norman wrote in his biography of the Stones. He had also cultivated a mock-cockney accent, which he presented for his public image, but he also used it in the more refined circles in which he was starting to move as a way to create another mask there too, another form of privacy. It was as if he was testing the boundaries to which he could push those who wanted to befriend him. It wasn't until many years later that Mick consciously set out to display his real self on a wider scale with the television documentary *Being Mick* (2001), probably realising it was time, albeit perhaps too late, to present himself as a human being and not the caricature that the entire world had fixed in their brains.

To endorse the bad boy image, as well as for their own protection, Andrew Oldham started employing tough men as bodyguards for himself and the others. The idea that these men were drawn from the blurred edge of criminal associations set in early. Whether it is true or not, the Stones were leaders in this approach. There are many tales of those employed to look after them, perhaps as chauffeurs or general dog's-bodies, taking advantage of these young men casually wasting their money and themselves.

"I got impatient with all that courtier stuff, the chauffeurs and the bodyguards," Oldham said later. "It was like being back at public school. You had to be in Mick's house or Keith's house or Brian's house. It all started when they got involved with the so-called Society people – the Frasers, the Donald Cammells." He says that, but it was also noticed that Oldham liked the idea of being accompanied by a bodyguard who would "reflectively pat what seemed to be a bulge under his left armpit".

Whilst there was jubilation when they started gaining success in the early Sixties, there was a price to be paid. As the singer, Jagger became the frontman and would have to confront the internal conflict of usurping the supposed leader, Brian Jones.

Chrissie Shrimpton, his partner prior to Marianne Faithfull, notes how he used to stand before the bedroom mirror, posing and being sexy, looking for his image. "It was as if he were trying out different variants of the personality that seemed to go down so well in public, trying to find a version of it that was comfortable for everyday wear," she told Carey Schofield, an early Jagger biographer. It is easier to present an intimate image when you are working in a small club, but as time went by and the Stones moved into theatres, and then stadiums, where only a handful, if that, would ever see the nuances, the need to develop something more 'contrived' became imperative. As others have noted, a character has to be developed that is part actor and part mime, enabling the upfront performer to project in a situation where both his voice and words are drowned by the amplification.

While others might have cultivated the musician within themselves to hold up to the world, Jagger cultivated the Pop Art aspect of himself. No coincidence that a Pop Art image of Jagger flashes by in *Performance*.

It is only in recent years that he has decided the time is right to show his private side with *Being Mick*, to try to push forward an inkling of the real Mick Jagger, the family man. It might have been a marketing device, but it effectively showed what we expected, the human side of the man. Whether we cared or not by then is something else. But it was noticeable that he spoke in public with a normal voice, after a lifetime of presenting only his mock-cockney accent. Final footage in the car with his then-wife Jerry Hall reminds the viewer, and Jagger, who is holding the camera, that we are in their private life and it is now time for us to leave. There's work and there's life. "Let's go to life," Jerry says as the camera is turned off.

There is talk in various sources that Mick had a sexual relationship with Brian, however fleeting it might have been, and from then on Jagger felt vulnerable until Brian was removed from the band.

Ginger Baker remembers the early days when Brian invited him and Jack Bruce to a Stones gig at Cy Laurie's place in Windmill Street. "Mick was just standing stationary at the microphone singing. But Brian was leaping all about the stage, playing laying on his back and even jumping into the audience while he was playing. It was Brian, not Mick, who was the showman in the band."

Alexis Korner, who was also around in the formative stages of the Stones, recalls how Brian was so vital to the band, "because he had more edge to him than any of the others". Brian was the threat onstage, "he was the nasty one. I mean the whole nasty image of the Stones really started with Brian, not Mick. Because Brian was a bitch! You know, if you were talking of winning over audiences. That wasn't Brian's attitude. You broke an audience. Or an audience broke you. That was Brian's attitude. And he went out to needle people, to get them up, to really arouse them, so they really responded. He could be really evil onstage, Brian. You'd see him dancing forward with a tambourine and snapping it in your face and sticking his tongue out at you. In a nasty way. Not a schoolboyish way. And then he'd move back before you actually took a punch at him."

Brian was in effect Jagger's role model in the early days. Faithfull notes:

"Everything about Brian in those early days fascinated Mick. The way he behaved onstage, the way he walked, his style of dress, and especially his attitude toward music."

Though Jagger was intrigued by Jones' drug intake, and though he dabbled to a degree himself, he was mostly afraid of drugs, and just maintained a pretence of interest. Marianne said that Brian "was the first one into acid, and that was one of the reasons they laughed at Mick – because he was so straight and so conventional and terrified of hash or acid or whatever. He drank – not often – but when he got drunk he was truly awful. Obnoxious and awful. Belligerent. A cliché drunk."

And of course Brian also adopted that androgynous look first, attracting both genders with his stage persona. In an interview with Jonathan Cott in 1978, Jagger concedes that perhaps there's room for the androgynous type. "Anyway, all guys have a feminine side. But most girls don't really fall in love with a completely gay guy, even though they like the feminine side showing. And vice versa with men. They like a woman who combines things, too. They don't want someone who's either butch or totally helpless."

Despite the tendency to play it down, rock music lyrics of the period have a markedly misogynist attitude. Despite youth's new freedom, young men in the Sixties still reflected their father's generation in their attitudes towards women. Feminism was only just emerging, the female voice struggling to be heard. Feminism was represented by 'burning your bra', with much jocular comment attached. Those who came after still do not seem to realise how much has been achieved, how much young women today take for granted. The Sixties still had little regard for women, for their importance in matters outside the home.

That the lyrics that Jagger sang, as indeed did others, reflected a general repressive view towards women is no surprise. The answer is not "it's only rock'n'roll". And no matter how louche or romantic a figure Keith Richards still cuts today, his interviews are still peppered with talk of women as "chicks" and "ladies", even if he does perhaps have an equal terms relationship with his family and the other women in his daily life.

It's all very well covering songs written by others that use blatant or underlying misogyny, although no one is forced to cover them, but once the whole song is your responsibility, once you are penning the lyrics, then true colours emerge. When the Jagger/Richards composing team started, along came lyrics like 'Under My Thumb', which makes it clear from the very title that masculine dominance is being celebrated; 'Out of Time' with "You're obsolete, my baby" as its taunt; and 'Stupid Girl'. There was a whole period, and not just with the *Aftermath* album, that reflected a disdain for women. Marianne pointed out that the "overt misogyny of the *Between the Buttons* period reappeared in a disguised form in songs like 'Midnight Rambler' and 'Brown Sugar'. To me it was a further example of what Anita and I have often talked about – their hatred of women. Compelled to have them and can't bear them. Very English actually, a fear of the power of women."

Nevertheless, women fell over themselves to be in their company. In those early days the female activist groups were not developed enough to attack them publicly over their lyrics, though *Some Girls* did raise objections, albeit in the late Seventies by then. In the earlier days any criticism was easily sidestepped.

Going back to those early days, Jagger's partner of the time was Chrissie Shrimpton. "He can be sweet and caring," she said, "but he is also manipulative and possessive and extremely controlling. Mick is a master of verbal abuse. He has a vicious, vicious mouth. The fact is that Mick doesn't like women. He never has." Keith told Barbara Charone in his early biography: "Mick's attitude towards women is that they are cattle. They are goods – that's his basic attitude." "All women are groupies" is something that Jagger said himself. Whether these attitudes remain over the years is not my focus, even if various reports suggest some continuance.

Those very early days in the Sixties were spent on the roads, if possible. That was the way to build your audience. Perhaps it was the stress of continual touring and of women throwing themselves at the band that helped to harden their attitude. The Stones refused to take women on the road with them once they were out of the 'transit van' stage – they reckoned that most of the time they would be bored while the band were working, and all they could do would be wash, iron, cook . . . It seems that their songs were a reflection of an irritation with the environment of the road, also of a youthful naivety, what Jagger calls an "adolescence" on their part.

When Marianne Faithfull came into Jagger's life, and he fumbled an introduction by spilling a drink down her front, he realised that here was an intelligent woman who could help him to become educated. He had been a student at the prestigious LSE, but had left before completing the course. Initially Jagger placed it on hold for a year, though ultimately he never returned as the Stones had started to shape up as a viable proposition.

Marianne recounts that at the first meeting, when she and Jagger were left alone in a hotel room, she delayed the sexual conclusion by going for a walk in the park near the hotel. "I didn't know Mick at all, and my way of ascertaining whether he was all right or just a jerk was to ask him a lot of questions about King Arthur." After the interrogation, Mick asked: "Am I going to pass my A-Level, Marianne?" As Marianne succinctly stated: "It was quite ludicrous but that's how we were then. You would ask your date, 'Do you know Genet? Have you read *A Rebours*?' and if he said yes, you'd fuck."

Marianne Faithfull was just the type of woman Jagger needed to complete himself. Not only did she look serene, with that innocent convent girl education (always a fallacy) and that touch of class, being the daughter of a baroness (a distant relative of Sacher-Masoch was yet to give it that added piquancy), but she was also educated. And Jagger wanted to be educated too. He might have had a solid knowledge of blues music, but everything else was lacking. Reading James Bond as a schoolboy was hardly education. He was starting to attend art galleries, to read literature, but with Marianne he could stretch further. She would take him into that other world he aspired to; the classier people of society would be accepting with Marianne on his arm.

"You could see it on Mick's face every time they were at a party together," Donald Cammell said. "It was pure possession. 'Look what I've got, isn't it fantastic!'"

Marianne Faithfull taught him to "open up to a whole new world – theatre, dance, pictures, furniture, fabrics, architecture (...) I took him to the ballet for the first time and he loved it. It was a particularly fortunate time because he was just developing his dancing technique onstage (...) I thought he really must see Nureyev because what he was doing was so similar to Nureyev's style, and they even looked alike."

Marianne was not the only one who would tell him to read certain books, watch certain films or study certain paintings. Jagger had moved into a world of young educated men and women who had been brought up in a social milieu where education was not something you did to obtain good exam results so that you could in turn obtain good employment. There was no ulterior reason for being educated, the arts and your enjoyment of them was purely for the enhancement of your personal well-being. Christopher Gibbs and Robert Fraser were invaluable. If one of them told him about a book, he would acquire it, or send lists to his friend Miles at Indica Bookshop. He was quite open about it, and he wanted to learn.

If his look was camp or effeminate to the world in general, to his new rich friends he was just adding the aesthetic touch to his appearance that was indicated in the books he was reading. When they moved into 48 Cheyne Walk, the interior designer David Mlinaric brought that environment into line, acquiring "such exotic items as a Regency bed and a Louis XV bath (c.1770), which he bought in Ireland for £900", as noted by Bill Wyman. Gina Richardson, in her profile for the *Sunday Telegraph*, described the heavy drapes that kept out the daylight, with Mick and Marianne moving around amongst the carpets and tapestries like "children left in charge while grown-ups are away". It seems that what spoilt Jagger's presence for her was the way he slopped around the house in slip-on mules, "like a housewife".

Marianne does suggest that it reached the point where culture gained the upper hand. "Mick was never very interested in having sex. I always felt that whatever sexual drive Mick had, he used it up onstage and there was very little left over for his personal life." Though she did interject: "At any rate, it certainly didn't exist between us." So when they went away to "exotic places" like Morocco, and "we climbed into our draped, four-poster Moroccan bed for a siesta, Mick was only interested in reading a book and not in me."

Elizabeth Young, the arts and cultural journalist, notes in *Pandora's Handbag* that when she was at boarding school in the provinces, she bunked off and went round to the Stones' hotel early on a Sunday morning. "Unfortunately they didn't lasciviously rip off my school uniform in the Lounge Bar. They sent me down to the station to buy their Sunday papers which, I was disappointed to note, were all broadsheets."

Marianne also took Mick to the theatre. Indeed, he went to see her in plays, though she suggests she would have accepted more roles if she hadn't felt she had to play second string. William Gaskill, her director at the Royal Court, suggested that she "had the real actress's ability to transform herself into what was required by whoever she was with", but that if she wanted to act seriously, she would have to move away from the indiscipline of the pop star's life.

Jagger thought he should also extend himself into acting. But as Marianne's first husband, John Dunbar, noted, he wasn't sure how to go about it. It was one thing to take risks with musical ideas, a different matter in films. "He'd go way out on a limb when it came to making records. But movies – it was something he knew nothing about, and he didn't want to look foolish. The whole idea scared him. That's where Marianne came in. She kept propping up his ego, and gave him the confidence to at least give acting a try."

Though Jagger had been approached by various film people and offered a few scripts, his natural suspicion of outsiders meant he kept counsel only with those closest to him. "For as long as anyone could remember," Marianne wrote, "Andrew Oldham had claimed he was getting (or had) the rights to *A Clockwork Orange*, and everybody agreed there could hardly be a more perfect Alex than Mick." His friend Christopher Gibbs had co-written a script based on the Middle English romance *Gawain and the Green Knight*, with Mick lined up as the Green Knight. It was seemingly only going to be a matter of time, so Mick started taking acting lessons.

When his friend Donald Cammell, whom he had known for a few years, started to talk to him about a project that would become *Performance*, Mick took the plunge. "Donald was a fascinating guy," Jagger said in the documentary *The Ultimate Performance*. "Donald was a great talker, very erudite, very educated, very interested in the mysteries of life, hinging on the spiritual, but . . . he was very, very sensual, yet he had an aesthetic quality, a real mixture."

Marianne, a possibility for the female lead in the early stages, said that "Mick felt his role as Turner, the jaded rock star, would not be much of a stretch. Everyone would be playing themselves, more or less. What could be so difficult about that?"

Marianne's perception, looking back, is slightly different from what anyone else has said: "They were making a film out of what the public imagined our lives to be. It was voyeurism that got the financing for the project and has, subsequently, made the film into a cult classic. Warner Bros, I should think, envisioned a 'Hollywoodised' version of our circle complete with moral and retribution."

One wonders whether Donald Cammell saw that fine line in Jagger's performance between sexual power and violence at play. For some reason at that time Jagger saw his stage performance as a sexual interplay with the audience, despite the violence that had also been generated at concerts. James Fox commented how Donald "loved Mick Jagger's power over an audience". And that he was also "clearly fascinated by the power of the gangster world". Marianne recounted her own realisation of the inherent violence when she made the rare decision to go on a Stones tour in spring 1967. "I once joined Mick on tour and it resulted in the most horrendous incident of our entire relationship. After that I never went again." Nothing had been arranged. She intended to surprise him. "I went straight to the hotel and waited for him to come back from the concert. Evidently there had again been riots at the show that night. People had been trampled. Mick came straight from the concert to the hotel. I was waiting for him in my negligee in bed. The minute he walked in he was a different person, it was as if he were someone I didn't know. He was possessed, as if he had brought in with him whatever disruptive energy was going on at that concert. It goes both ways, from the performer to the audience and then it comes back at you magnified.

"He didn't say hello, he didn't even acknowledge me, he just walked over to the bed and began slapping me across the face. Not a word was spoken. I was terrified and I fled. He followed me and continued to hit me. He beat me quite badly and I didn't have a clue why." Her actual thought was that Mick had discovered she'd had sex with Keith, even though it was nothing dramatic. But she couldn't believe Keith would say anything. And Anita knew nothing either. "Nothing brought it on. It just erupted out of some inner turmoil, as if a demonic force had come over him. When it was over, it was like a hurricane that had spent itself and stopped. And we have never, ever mentioned it, so to this day I don't know what it was about. He never did anything like that again, he's not the sort of person who would."

While *Performance* was being set up, another offer came along that seemed interesting. It was an approach from the *enfant terrible* of French cinema, the *nouvelle vague*'s main figure, Jean-Luc Godard. This project was to be called *One Plus One*, though the film is also known as *Sympathy for the Devil*, and would not entail much more than the band being themselves in a studio, rehearsing and recording a song, 'Sympathy for the Devil', which would be juxtaposed against a political narrative. This was hardly a diversion. It was filmed and completed within months, making little impact on the preparations for *Performance*.

Marianne became Jagger's guide and advisor on how to develop the character of Turner. It was all very well playing a faded pop star, someone who had lost his demon, a recluse in a drug-ridden world, but that wasn't Jagger. If Jagger was going to appear in a film, he didn't want to fail. Cammell, and Nic Roeg too, once he was on board, suggested that Jagger had nothing to fear, that he just had to play himself. "The one thing this character could not be was Mick," Marianne said, certain that would be a bad idea: "You're much too together, too straight, too strong." Mick should think in terms of Brian. "You've got to imagine you're poor freaked-out, deluded, androgynous, druggie Brian," she told Mick, "but you also need a bit of Keith's tough, self-destructive, beautiful lawlessness." And, as Jagger himself noted in an interview, ". . . and Donald to some extent, though I don't think he knew it". Marianne says it was her idea that Mick should dye his hair dark like Keith's, and cut it like Brian's. "In the end he dyed it black, very black, a Chinese black, like Elvis's hair. (...) It gave him a strong graphic outline. His tights and costumes gave him a tinge of menace, a slight hint of Richard III."

As Marianne viewed the script it was an amalgam of stories told to Donald by Anita and others, mixed in with stories that Donald had gathered from personal experiences. The character of Turner that she saw and was helping Mick to shape up was "Vaguely tragic, a little pathetic, but still with an edge. He was the archetypal Sixties rock apocalypse character, a pre-Raphaelite Hamlet." And according to Marianne, what made it hard for Mick to draw much from himself was "that he was not dark enough or damaged enough", he was much too much of a normal person for any "truly bizarre fate to befall him". "Brian and Keith seemed, if not actually tragic figures, at least fated personalities, human beings with fatal flaws caught in the tow of deep undercurrents." When Marianne writes, albeit something like 20 years later, she says that the composite character that she was helping Jagger to form would be "two people who were extremely attractive to Anita and who were in turn obsessed with her". And yet until the last minute it was never envisaged that Anita should play Pherber, even though the part drew from her.

Ultimately Jagger had the idea "that people would take Turner as me". Though "it didn't really strike me as me. (...) You make these roles up on yourself and amalgams of other people."

As for the voice "and the way he talked, all lah-de-dah, up in the air, it was like Brian," Anita confirmed. "Brian was always a perfectionist in the way he was talking, choosing his words. He did want to catch your attention when he was speaking, to captivate you."

According to Christopher Gibbs, he saw Mick as "playing a role – a slightly kittenish role – somewhat absurd for those that know him well". And James Fox said: "Mick was absolutely not playing himself. He's not a drop-out, never was."

Not that they had a script for the second part of the film at that stage. It was more rough ideas, speculations, something that would grow "out of the relationships between the characters as we went along", as Nic Roeg said.

Jagger today, in a recent *The Word* interview, talking about the autobiographical input, ostensibly in connection with his new album but which applies equally to other matters, contends: "But hardly anything really is *that* autobiographical. We imbued it all with a sense of that, but it wasn't all real, although in some cases it can be. (...) A good novel's veracity can lie in an element of autobiography – it makes you believe that it's worth more than some facile play on words that were pulled out of the air. Certainly a lot of my songs are drawn from memories but they're a conjunction of things that I might not have even experienced directly. (...) Memory is just a spark for the writer; it sets you off into the imaginary."

Of course Mick wasn't to know that he would be one of the few 'stars' who would spend a lifetime in the spotlight. What would he have thought had he known that the film's cutting line "You'll look funny when you're 50" was to be a reality for a global audience to check out? There was always the idea that Marlene Dietrich or Greta Garbo were lurking ghosts in imagining the character. But Mick had also seen reclusive behaviour closer to home, amongst friends: Lennon out of town with his wife

Cynthia, feeling trapped in Weybridge (for a few years after 1964); Paul Getty, an infamous recluse, who moved from his house in Cheyne Walk to his places in Marrakech, Rome . . .

There was always a hint of Gloria Swanson as Norma Desmond in *Sunset Boulevard* (1950) about Turner. This impression was probably taken on board early, as Donald Cammell notes that Jagger should suggest to Chas, the intruder: "Why don't you go to a hotel?" as if Norma. That the intruder, once ensconced, becomes the key to unlocking the door to Norma's problems becomes one parallel. Others can be found with von Stroheim as her dog's body, protector and fan . . . a devotee. Perhaps of even more interest is the level of vainness that carries across from Swanson to Jagger in their roles. But the greatest tribute, a kind of homage, is when Turner performs for Chas, albeit briefly, mirroring Swanson's Chaplin routine for her guest, showing her brilliance has not left her, that her own demon still lurks and that perhaps she just needs someone more than her faithful servant, von Stroheim, to believe in her.

Ultimately Jagger has become adept at making and remaking another 'Jagger', the public one, someone he has managed to wear throughout his life. Shirley MacLaine remarks of her friend Elizabeth Taylor: "She did not see herself as 'Elizabeth Taylor' at all. She was much more like a Yiddisher momma, to be honest. She used to say she was going to have to be 'Elizabeth Taylor' and put on that show. That was the gig, after all. It's what she had to do."

Nic Roeg's interest in identity parallels Donald's, which is why they made this film together. Working with Jagger on *Performance*, and later with David Bowie and Art Garfunkel, must have helped Roeg to shape the ideas that he took further with *Insignificance* (1985). Even though he also lived in a film world, where actors on the screen and their real selves were very different, Roeg explored further this notion of identity and fame in *Insignificance*, using the characters of Marilyn Monroe, Joe DiMaggio, Albert Einstein and Senator McCarthy, real people who we all believe we have a tag on. The idea occurred when "an incident came up in my own life, and I thought, good God, nobody knows a damn thing about anyone. (...) They didn't know anything about each other. The Actress, The Ballplayer . . . Famous people are only perceived images; they're inventions, everything's an invention . . ."

"Because of being famous," the Professor complains, "everywhere I go people fall over themselves to be with me, like a troupe of clowns chasing an old automobile. Because of fame, everything I do develops into a ridiculous comedy." The Actress replies: "You're lucky. Everything I do develops into a nightmare. People keep throwing themselves in front of me and I daren't stop."

Before filming for *Performance* started, Jagger speculated on what lay ahead for him: "It's very much me. I'm going to make it if I can, different to me. I mean, he is me, the me on that album cover. He is supposed to be a great writer, like Dylan. But he's completely immersed in himself, he's a horrible person really. It's not supposed to be a comedy, but James Fox and I are gonna make it into a comedy. The cat I play is not really a pop musician, though. He's like me, he's a freak, just forgetting it sometimes. You go three months and you just can't make it, or you don't want to make it, so you just sit down. Just like me, but he's much more intelligent. That's the sort of cat he is: a really brilliant cat. That's difficult for me to do."

And while Mick was preparing his role, Bill Wyman was totting up the leader's bill: "a total fee of $100,000 plus 7½ per cent of the film's net profits."

By the time Mick Jagger and James Fox met, Fox was 28 years old, four years older than Jagger, and already a star leading the glamorous life. Dirk Bogarde summed it up in his introduction to James Fox's autobiography, *Comeback*: "James Fox was in the centre surrounded by glittering toys and Pretty People. It was the big breakthrough time for youth; or so it believed, and anything went, and anything did. Everything was possible, nothing impossible; it was all up for grabs and there was absolutely no sign of a tomorrow." Fame had arrived with *The Servant* (1963), a film that was undoubtedly seen by Jagger, and popular acclaim followed with *Those Magnificent Men in Their Flying Machines* (1965) and *Thoroughly Modern Millie* (1967). Fox met Jagger and the Stones in Rome in 1967, courtesy of Paul and Talitha Getty, when they were on that leg of their European tour. Fox and his girlfriend had just returned from a relaxed stay at the Getty's villa in Marrakech. "They had a beautiful walled home with a central courtyard richly floored with Moroccan tiles and a fountain. Off it were the principal living rooms, their walls, floors and ceilings covered with symmetrical patterns, inlaid with tiles or covered with Arabic velvet hangings." He continues: "The Moroccan lifestyle was rich and relaxing and, for hippy Westerners like ourselves, offered the perfect environment in which to get stoned." To elaborate: the "pipe filled with *kif* was passed around the circle. Its effect was to render all of us inactive. (…) We just gazed at the complicated patterns or watched the amused delight or intense concentration of our companions as another pipe was prepared."

Any doubts as to his drug experience are quashed in *Comeback*. "We not only used the local brew to smoke, but tripped with some powerful American chemical called STP; it offered a short trip which seemed to turn your mind into one of those kaleidoscopes children used to look into, where the patterns changed as you shook the little coloured grains against the angled prisms at the end."

Besides suspecting that his partner, Amanda, had had a dalliance with Mick, which didn't seem to perturb him, Fox enjoyed those days in their company. "Being around the Stones for those few days was like being on a trip. Night and day lost their identity. Events had their aura. People were bewitchingly interesting. I was attracted towards them and, having been drawn in, something was imparted to me also. I felt elite and powerful, high on energy."

That break and meeting the Stones had exhilarated him. He was ready to return to London to work and rented a flat near Marble Arch. "One day Mick came over and brought by a record which he liked – 'A Whiter Shade of Pale' by Procol Harum. We identified completely with this surreal song and its fugal sound. Our circle of friends were the beautiful trippers. We collected Arthur Rackham's illustrations, hung our rooms with Moroccan drapes and adorned ourselves with hats, scarves and butterfly brooches."

The people he had befriended were not from his former world. He recounted an occasion when he went with Mick and Marianne to a reception Dirk Bogarde was having for the film *Accident* at the Connaught Hotel. "We were the odd ones out in this rather respectable film people's circle. I felt distanced from the show-biz world. They seemed to be involved in rather false social behaviour and stagnant film ideas." The four of them retreated to the edge. "We sat on the radiators giggling and snapping amyl-nitrate capsules. Dirk came across and told me that if I wanted to do that kind of thing to do it in the loo."

Marianne's memory of the occasion was that she had gone with Mick to the party, which was essentially peopled with luminaries from the theatre world like Maggie Smith, Paul Scofield, Julie Christie . . . people who Robin Fox, her agent, represented. Robin Fox was, of course, the father of James Fox and his brother Edward Fox. They were another of the acting/theatre families, like the Redgraves and Attenboroughs. "You'd have thought a theatrical gathering of this kind would have been bubbling with witty repartee and wicked anecdotes, but one forgets these people are actors (poor darlings!) and generally nothing at all like the characters they play. Instead it was quite a stodgy bunch of actors talking shop."

Amongst this "terribly stuffy affair" she spied James Fox and his new girlfriend. However, it wasn't the beautiful young James Fox who caught her eye, but Andee Cohen. "She was an exquisite little thing, a vivid, fluttering creature, very thin and androgynous, with dark hair cut short like a boy's, and big, big eyes. (…) I adored her at once."

Marianne recounted how the four of them hung around together for a while, "long white nights spent lounging at each other's houses". James was fascinated with Mick "as if by some genie of mimicry and energy", while Mick in turn was taken with James. "Mick has always had a thing for upper-class folk," she said, "especially when he suspected they might enjoy a guided tour of rock slumming." But it ran deeper, because Mick was thinking of branching out into acting and he now had James before him to observe close up. "He wanted to see how James ticked."

Donald Cammell's friendship with James Fox had evolved on the shoot for *Duffy*. He had already intimated that there would be a future film part which he would direct himself. "He saw something in me I hadn't recognised," Fox observed, "something angry and violent. I was dissatisfied with being cast as a toffee-nosed layabout." Sandy Lieberson said that Donald had seen "a very below-the-surface steeliness".

The part of Chas as outlined in *The Performers* showed what Cammell thought Fox was capable of. "The role of a 'Front Man' is only to be found in the most sophisticated strata of crime; the criminal organisation. The Firm. To fill the role, it is not enough simply to be a giant thug (he will usually be accompanied by a bodyguard or two who admirably fulfil this role). A big firm (as opposed to a gang of casual tearaways) depends, like its counterpart in the Upperworld, upon its stock of goodwill (badwill?). To maintain this stock, respect – fearful respect – and, ideally, admiration (however qualified) must be maintained by Representatives of talent and ability. The man in charge of this department, working 'in the field', has executive status.

"To do his job perfectly, he need never use violence (though he must be capable of awesome violence, and be known to be capable of it – be known, ideally, to like it). He must, rather, physically and psychically, incarnate violence. Inevitably a certain glamour is involved. (He is a 'Performer' in the dramatic as well as the villains' sense of the word.) He must be a symbolic vessel, containing and projecting an aura of threat, of imminent violence that, if he is good, need never actually materialise."

It was *The Servant* that gave Fox the credentials for Chas, a character who was exactly the opposite; a villain, as opposed to 'a toffee-nosed snob'. Dirk Bogarde takes credit for discovering Fox for that role. He had switched on the television news only to catch the end of a play. The actor before his eyes was just the character Losey needed for *The Servant.* He phoned the director and told him to switch on his TV. Next day Bogarde phoned Robin Fox and asked after the actor billed as 'Maurice Oliver', only to discover that it was the agent's son, James. Bogarde wrote later: "Under the grace and breeding, the golden-boy innocence, I sensed (...) a muted quality of corruptibility. This young man could spoil like peaches: he could be led to the abyss."

Sarah Miles was the ideal choice for Vera, the sister, but they doubted whether she would come on board since she had been so successful alongside Sir Laurence Olivier in *Term of Trial* (1962) and this part was modest by comparison. To their astonishment, Bogarde and his companion found themselves sitting behind James Fox and his partner, Sarah Miles, at the premiere of *The L-Shaped Room.* They had not known that Fox and Miles had been together for three years, and they lived in Half Moon Street. Bogarde approached them and asked them to see Losey next day at the Connaught.

The exterior shots for *The Servant* were filmed in Royal Avenue, off the King's Road, opposite the house of the original novel's writer, Robin

Maugham. But the interior was shot in a studio. To create the right atmosphere, Richard Macdonald decorated it as a London club, with leather armchairs. Here was a claustrophobic set, a closed house, "an airless house". Just right for a script by a master of dialogue and sub-text, one who specialised in closed spaces, in environments where he could create a menacing atmosphere. Just right for Harold Pinter.

"Even though the character I was playing, Tony, was close to my own experience and temperament," Fox wrote, "I still needed to understand how to communicate that. We worked on simple intentions for each scene. Some were easier than others but in Harold Pinter's dialogue there is room for the sub-text and interior dialogue to be developed, and it was important to discover these layers."

Pinter's ability to convey the reality behind the spoken words, and his ability to pare them down to the essential, enabled Losey to explore the visual frame and work with Richard Macdonald's set design, particularly the core of the house, with the staircase, from which all the rooms branched off.

This film was instrumental in the careers not only of Fox, but of Dirk Bogarde and Joseph Losey as well. Its arrival in the cinema in November couldn't have been more fortuitous. The Profumo affair and the attendant scandal of a top Conservative politician telling lies to Parliament by denying a relationship with Christine Keeler, a prostitute, was just breaking.

Philip French reviewed the film in *The Observer*: "The film uncannily echoed the obsessive themes and occasions of the preceding months." No one had imagined that it would find a receptive audience, that it would be in the right place at the right time. For the previous six months, Losey had been organising small previews in an effort to find some supporters. As French noted: "The invitations were delivered orally or handwritten and usually a few persuasive people associated with the picture were there to talk about it afterwards. These screenings of what many initially thought a disturbing, obscure movie were fortuitously accompanied by the rumours and public disclosures of the Profumo affair that began in the spring with bizarre stories of a shooting outside a mews apartment and escalated through Jack Profumo's denial and resignation, Stephen Ward's trial and Christine Keeler's jailing for perjury. In a refracted way the events of the day were on the screen."

There's no way to account for how public events can bring success to a film. "*The Servant*, in its central action of seduction and betrayal, had uncannily pre-figured the burgeoning scandal (James Fox as Profumo, Dirk Bogarde as Ward, Sarah Miles as Keeler). And it suggested through its discreet orgies and the celebrated restaurant scene a web of corruption that extended into every corner of society – even the church."

Whilst Fox's mother, Angela, was furious about her son portraying such a degenerate playboy, she later congratulated Losey on his perception at recognising that aspect. As Losey told her, Fox couldn't have played the part so convincingly if there hadn't been some of it in him already. The family was to react in a similar fashion to James' role in *Performance*, though this time they tried to intervene before the shoot was completed.

Also of relevance is the way in which Sarah Miles talks about losing her relationship with Fox during filming of *The Servant*, when he went so deep into his part. "After shooting all day, Willy (James real name) would either go missing or arrive home wrapped so tightly in his character that I couldn't find him. I'd offer to help him unwrap the part and hang it up for the evening, but he'd get defensive and start clinging to it all night as well." And though she thinks she was to blame, she knew that: "If the relationship between servant and master was to reap dividends it was essential that Willy and Dirk were left alone. In their place I would have felt the same. We all put a great deal of hard work into that project, as well as risky soul-searching, but for their two characters the delving inward had to go even deeper, and it paid off a thousand fold in the finished film, the only place where it matters."

In 1968, James Fox went away to Peru for a break to explore the jungle, visit Inca settlements and go wherever the adventure led him. He was supposed to return to finish *Isadora*, but didn't reappear to complete a scene. Donald had told James that he would have a script ready by May called *The Performers*, with a role for him that "would involve my playing the part of a south London villain", the antithesis of his normal self. "I had to become a complete hood, someone who, to the drop-out society of the late 1960s, was a museum piece, using violence in an age of love, becoming a businessman in an age of laughing at the system."

On his return Fox set about his preparations. Cammell had arranged for David Litvinoff to help. Fox had also known Litvinoff for some years. He was "the greatest chat artist in London and could keep an assembled gathering of the unshockable in stitches for hours with his bravura performance, insults and spicy gossip".

Tommy Gibbons had been contacted by Litvinoff at the Thomas à Becket in the Old Kent Road. At that time the pub had a boxing gym upstairs, where the likes of Henry Cooper, one of Britain's few claims to boxing fame, trained for 14 years – the moment he knocked down Muhammad Ali, formerly Cassius Clay, towards the end of the fourth round in a world title fight in 1963 seemingly more memorable than the fact he was British, European and Commonwealth Heavyweight Champion. One of the seconds in the corner that night was Johnny Shannon.

"Well, I first got involved by a guy called Tommy Gibbons, who was a pal of mine who ran the pub in the Old Kent Road called the Thomas à Becket. And he rang me one day and said he had a couple of guys from a movie that wanted someone to meet an actor, take them around south London, meet the characters, take them round the pubs and he said he'd put my name in and it turned out the actor was James Fox." Not that Fox looked the part, even if he looked a character in another sense. "He used to dress very flamboyant: floppy hats, long hair, flowery scarves, all that. I suggested to him that the 'chaps' really don't walk round like that. That was it. He wore his nice suits everywhere after that."

Shannon trained boxers in the upstairs gym in his spare time. He had worked in the Covent Garden fruit market, in Berwick Street market and with newspaper wholesalers, as a night driver.

"They wanted someone to advise him on the Cockney speech in his script. I'd go through the script with him. I took him around the Old Kent Road, the pubs and clubs, and introduced him to some of the characters in south London. We taught James how to hold a cigarette right – the chaps hold it in a particular way; how to behave in a pub, call for a drink. James was accepted into that crowd lovingly; they thought he was great."

Not that Shannon ever referred to his acquaintances as villains or gangsters. "I know there were gangsters. But I don't know gangsters," he said in *The Ultimate Performance*. "I know the 'chaps', and the characters . . . it seems an Americanism, gangsters." ("They'll call us gangsters," says Dennis as he walks into Harry Flowers' bedroom. Much like a blinding left hand.)

"Well all the people that I knew and the people Jimmy met, and though they might be thought of as 'chaps', were all very nice people. They don't do anything wrong to their own. And Jimmy was regarded as one of their own."

Even talking through the build-up to the film, Johnny Shannon has a way – "placatory", I think that's the word for it. "Of course."

"He did a lot of exercises because he wanted to get himself fit and well for the job, for the movie. There was a time when he boxed one of the guys in the gym. This guy (pointing at Fox) has knocked seven bells out of the poor sod. The guy's nose was going bonk bonk bonk and blood was coming out of it . . . he loved it."

Donald had told James Fox to: "Go away and come back as Chas." Accounts vary of where he spent his time. But Fox says: "I decided to spend a week alone in a room in a hotel in Brixton, get a typical haircut and wear nothing but Cecil Gee clothes. I only spent a night at the hotel, but I spent a lot of time at the Becket, with Johnny and Tommy and Beryl his girlfriend, as well as in the gym and at the boxing venues at the Royal Garden Hotel."

Ann Sidney, the former Miss World, who had been lined up to play his girlfriend in the film, met James and they went out together.

But mainly it was about taking on the mantle of the hoodlum, the gangster, the villain . . . being with the "chaps" as Shannon insisted on calling them. There were two types of main villains in those days: those in the East End and those in south London. It's not that they were different, but they revolved around different personalities, as it were. South London was dominated by the Richardson brothers, Eddie and Charlie, whereas the East End was ruled by the Kray brothers, Ronnie and Reggie . . . the Twins. Fox was taken around, recalls meeting the Krays and others. Some were not out on the streets, but had to be seen at special times, 'visiting times', in the halls of the prisons where they were away on holiday at Her Majesty's pleasure. "And they were all unstintingly helpful. (...) On tape I listened to recollections of an actual revenge killing by the person involved whose name was not disclosed."

Another character, Jimmy Evans, who was to shape up as a role model for Fox's character, was also from the East End. We shall come to him in a while.

"By this time I was definitely looking the part. I became almost completely taken over by the role. I spoke, thought and ate like Chas." It's all very well getting into the part, but not everyone tests out the role by marching into the film production office in character and verbalising the office workers, a kind of practice run for what you see on screen at the car hire company. It terrified them. David Cammell confirms, as he was there at the time.

"If an actor can fill his mind with as much knowledge as possible about a part, it will help him to understand how his character would react, respond and feel in any situation. The rest is communicating it."

There is another story that Fox went out with some of the guys on a heist. Whether this was true or just a bit of mischief-making on someone's part, or a publicity angle from the production company, it adds neatly to the stories around the film, as if there weren't enough already.

The ability to switch on and off is key, as Sarah Miles pointed out. Marianne Faithfull wasn't so sure that there were enough people around Fox to support him once filming was under way. "In a sense most of the people in *Performance* weren't acting at all, they were simply exhibiting themselves. Real gangsters, real rock stars, real drug addicts, real sirens. With a trained actor there's a separation between what's going on on the set and what you do in your life, but most of the cast of *Performance* were amateurs. This damaged James the most, since he had no support from the other actors. One of the first things you learn in acting is how to share the weight, so negative energy is distributed equally. This protects an actor playing a very dark role from being pulled under, otherwise people would be cracking up all the time! It's called generous acting. James as a professional knew all about this, but no one else on the project had a clue, so he got really screwed."

But horses for courses. At the end of the day it's all about what is on the screen, as Sarah Miles also noted. It is one of the risks you decide to take. And what is on the screen is what Fox is remembered for. Kevin Jackson, writing on him, believes: "Fox's Chas is, I would contend, simply one of the greatest roles in British cinema: frightening to the point of the demonic, but also full of witty malice and flashes of dangerous intelligence. It's also an astonishing piece of social metamorphosis."

Sandy Lieberson thought afterwards that although everyone was affected by the film, Fox was really changed: "it had an effect on his life." He never returned to his former self. "Maybe this was an evolutionary thing, but you could say it was directly related to the film. It changed him."

James Fox has always said that *Performance* was his best role. One senses that Cammell had thought aspects of Artaud's ideas of theatre had been at work with Fox. "The essence of a 'total' performance is that the playing of a role becomes a transference of identity – a kind of 'possession'."

The other literary character that Donald was keen for both James Fox and Mick Jagger to take on board was the French poet, novelist and playwright Jean Genet. He presented both of them with copies of Genet's *The Thief's Journal*. Donald had initially come across Genet's work in New York, where he saw the first production of *The Blacks*, featuring his friend Roscoe Lee Browne as Archibald. But it was later in Paris that he picked up on the two novels in print in English, *The Thief's Journal* and *Our Lady of the Flowers*, which had been available for a few years from Olympia Press. By the mid-Sixties Anthony Blond in London was publishing them as hardbacks, and Panther and Penguin took them into paperback from 1966.

Donald was particularly keen for his two lead actors to take a note of the nature of violence as expressed by Genet. In an earlier draft of the script, he expressed it this way:

"Chas is the top 'Front Man' of Harry Flowers' firm. He's a criminal, a young thug, who's been picked for this key job by the professionals who run the business because he is what he is. In the first pages of *The Thief's Journal*, Jean Genet describes to perfection the essence of his kind:

"'Crime, I said to myself, had a long wait before producing such perfect successes as Pilorge and Angel Sun (...) it was necessary that a host of circumstances concur: to the handsomeness of their faces, to the strength and elegance of their bodies there had to be added their taste for crime, the circumstances which make the criminal, the moral vigour capable of accepting such a destiny, and finally, punishment, its cruelty, the intrinsic quality which enables a criminal to glory in it.'

"In a sociologist's view, psychopaths. But it is equally true that Mr Genet's vision is equally true, if not truer. Of course, he loved young men like this with a pure and powerful love. Possibly this is where it is, to coin a phrase, at. In any case Genet takes for granted the essence of Chas; which is, not to be violent, *but to be violence.* (Not to kill – a gun going off; but to threaten death – a loaded gun.)

"I give the name violence to a boldness lying idle and hankering for danger. (...) It unnerves you. This violence is a calm that disturbs you. One sometimes says: 'A guy with class!' Pilorge's delicate features were of an extreme violence. Their delicacy in particular was violent. (...) Even when at rest, motionless and smiling, there escaped from them through the eyes, the nostrils, the mouth, the palm of the hand . . . a radiant and sombre anger, visible as a haze."

Though Donald Cammell had wanted to direct one of his own scripts, he lacked the experience needed to ensure financial support for the project. He thought it might make it feasible if he brought on board one of Britain's best cinematographers, one with an impressive track record. That man was Nic Roeg, someone Donald had known for many years as they often mixed in the same social milieu. In his early days as a portrait painter, Donald had wanted to paint Nic's first wife, the actress Susan Stephen. "I approached him to be the cameraman. He said he didn't want to do any more pictures as a cameraman. He was now a director. And I had no qualms at all about saying, so what, we'll direct it together."

Nic was preparing *Walkabout* at that time, but delays having occurred, which was not unusual with film projects, he agreed to Donald's proposition. "We were perfect for each other, we could build on each other," Nic told Tom Milne and Penelope Houston in an 1973 *Sight & Sound* interview. A script came from Cammell, "just a few pages that Donald had written – a notion for a film about a gangster in London's underworld, and the relation of that specific kind of violence to the violence in human nature."

They were in sympathy with each other. Donald was filmed in 1983 talking about *Performance* for a documentary on Roeg's films, *Nothing As It Seems*: "Nic's curiosity was a very intellectual one, (...) he was curious about Turner. He was curious about the East End and the hoodlum milieu that I'd saturated myself in. But the curiosity that was more useful to him, and to both of us, was probably about the people he was working with. Characters he had not been familiar with prior to working with me and Mick. He had not been much in contact with musicians, with the

Sixties counter-culture, quasi-revolutionary characters with long hair and marijuana oozing from their pores."

Neither was to know that the less than common notion of a co-directing credit would provoke the perennial question of who did what. It was a question to combat, or bat aside, as the years progressed. It irritated both men to varying degrees. But it also added another token of magic to the cupboard filling with myths and mysteries around the film.

Cammell made it clear that he liked working as a team, and was against the idea of an *auteur* theory. Paul Mayersberg, in his *Sight & Sound* essay on working with Roeg on *The Man Who Fell to Earth*, said that they'd walk around a location, both contributing ideas, so who wrote what wasn't pertinent. Because Roeg gained recognition more speedily than Cammell, Roeg has often been given all or, at least, the major credit for *Performance*. But he has not derived any satisfaction from that. "The main thing about any collaboration is secrecy. Happily the secrecy has been maintained against all attempts at division. What would it gain people to know who did what? What is on the screen is on the screen."

In effect the two directors 'merged' their ideas and ways. Nic Roeg in another interview in 1984: "In a way all direction is co-direction since it involves a large number of artists. On *Performance* though we still had certain secrets, and Mick Jagger, who played the lead, sees the whole film differently to either Don or myself, because he knew things that we didn't, and vice versa.

"I like to allow for the random quality of everything. I am not one of those directors that thinks of his co-creators: 'Why don't you have a mind of your own and think my way!' All that grows from that approach is antagonism and awkwardness. Every person working on a film, from the scene painter to the lead actor, has their own expression and I allow for that. The director of a film is like a jockey and sometimes it is best to let the film have its own head and race off on its own. You can always pull in the reins later.

"Something may seem fine in the script but when you come to shoot it something else may offer itself as an alternative. If I never deviated from the original shooting script I feel that the end product would be sterile. I see myself as part of a team rather than the boss! I discuss things very closely with each member. They may have an idea that I've missed."

Nic Roeg was born in London on August 15, 1928. He was brought up in an environment of books and literature, which manifests itself in his work, his inspirations being literary, the allusions to the written word appearing at every turn. All who have worked with him over the years, whether scriptwriters or actors, have noted how books appear that might provide a fact, an idea, an insight.

Nic Roeg was 19 when he joined the post-production company De Lane Lea in Wardour Street. There he watched French films being dubbed into English. What caught his imagination was that when "running the films backwards and forwards to get the words right, I realised that film is a time machine. Film is nothing to do with the theatre at all – it has much more potential. The audience can be rushed out of their seats just to have a look at someone's watch, and then back again." Time shifting him. "I remember when *Last Year in Marienbad* was shown in England for the first time. It had a screening at the Cameo Polytechnic in Regent Street. It was an exciting time. But I remember people saying, 'Sacha Pitoëff walked upstairs, but when he walked downstairs he was in a dinner jacket. This man doesn't know how to make films.' But within 18 months commercials would be showing Mum putting a pie in the oven, and the next shot would be the cooked pie being put down on the table. Before all this it would have shown the family go out, then a subtitle 'four hours later' and so on. Resnais really excited me."

It's no surprise to discover that another inspiration in the early days was the British director Michael Powell, and his screenwriting partner, Emeric Pressburger. The narrative complexity of their films, the use of flashbacks and flashforwards in, for example, *The Life and Death of Colonel Blimp*, or identity issues in *Black Narcissus*, and the general overriding richness of colour. And this all at a time when realism was expected after the war. Here was a team that saw a way through using a romantic fantasy, building their world in a studio, rather than stepping out onto the streets.

Roeg started work at the bottom of the ladder as a clapper boy and tea-maker before moving on to camera assistant. His first real lesson came from an experienced cameraman, Joseph Ruttenberg, who was over from Hollywood to photograph *The Miniver Story* (1950) at the MGM studio in Boreham Wood. When Roeg asked what he was doing, Ruttenberg told the young clapper boy that he was aiming for "images that create the mood for the story". Roeg told him that he was contemplating taking a photography course. "Just stay on the set and watch and be a part of it; anything you want to know, I'll tell you." Roeg was also part of the camera crew on such films as *Ivanhoe* (1952), *The Adventures of Quentin Durward* (1955), *Bhowani Junction* (1956) and *Tarzan's Greatest Adventure* (1959). Then he worked as a camera operator on Fred Zinnemann's *The Sundowners* (1960) and on the second unit for the train crash sequence of David Lean's *Lawrence of Arabia* (1962).

He co-wrote the story for Cliff Owen's *A Prize of Arms* (1961), starring Stanley Baker, with Kevin Kavanagh, who would be unit manager on *Performance*. As others have noted, it is not so much a crime story, about a robbery, as a story where the occult seeps in, with one of the criminals having a premonition of events that will disrupt their plans.

Finally Roeg graduated to director of photography, and amongst his credits are *The Caretaker* (1963) and *Nothing but the Best* (1964) for Clive Donner, *The Masque of the Red Death* (1964) for Roger Corman, *Fahrenheit 451* (1966) for François Truffaut, *Far from the Madding Crowd* (1967) for John Schlesinger, and *A Funny Thing Happened on the Way to the Forum* (1966) and *Petulia* (1968) for Richard Lester.

Each step brought with it episodes of discovery. For instance, Roger Corman's adaptation of Edgar Allan Poe's *The Masque of the Red Death* is a sure sign of Roeg's interest in red. Corman himself praised the spectacular tracking shot of Jane Asher walking through a series of rooms, each coloured differently. *Fahrenheit 451* will crop up later. But again no one can fail to be struck by its use of red. Nor the disruptive process of time sequences to the narrative thread in *Petulia*, again as we will see later.

What becomes apparent is that the idea of non-linearity in the plots of Roeg's succession of films through the Seventies and Eighties at least has its grounding in his earlier work behind the camera. "Life isn't linear," Roeg says. "It's sideways." Not so much flashbacks and flashforwards, more what is going on in someone's head.

Johnny Shannon was caught off-guard one day when James Fox turned to him and said, "You know what Johnny, I think there's a part in this that you could play." Of course, having no acting experience, Shannon thought he meant some small part. "The scene where the chauffeur gets his head shaved. I thought, being bald, that was the part he meant – you know, give me a wig." He was not to know that Fox meant Harry Flowers, the boss, the character loosely based on Ronnie Kray. "He was talking about Harry Flowers – even better," is the way Shannon phrased it. He was not to know that he would shape the role so well that Shannon would become a reference for others determining what a shady character from the criminal world would be like in later films. Or that he would be employed to repeat the part, or variations of it, in films and on television for some years afterwards.

"Harry Flowers was supposedly a bit poofey, weren't he? I suppose I based it on a lot of different people, not on one particular person, although it was said at the time that they thought the Kray Twins."

Shannon thought he'd be entering a world where no one would accept him. But he had no need to worry: "They were all so nice, engineers, lighting men, the actors especially." Jagger recalled: "I saw him down Soho pushing a barrow one day. The next day I saw him on television in a play. He was doing the same thing. During filming he said to me, 'I'd thought you'd be a stuck-up little bastard, but you're alright!' "

I doubt whether when Donald asked Johnny Shannon to play Harry Flowers, or even later when he asked him, and the other gangsters, to strip for the 'Memo From Turner' scene, he had any intention of explaining the connection with Jean Genet. Donald's interest was in the ideas and atmosphere of Genet's work, not specific actions or direct references, though the titles of the works themselves, like *Our Lady of the Flowers* and *Miracle of the Rose*, are fairly blatant pointers, and seem to offer a spot of mischief given that *Performance* has characters called Harry Flowers and Rosie, or Rosebloom, and that Flowers' office is decorated with a bunch of roses, regardless of whether they are wilted or firm. If any of them had cared to watch Genet's own short film, *Un Chant d'Amour* (1950), they would have seen a convict holding blooms before his flies, along with other uses for flowers.

Flowers feature regularly in Genet's writings, Genet noting in *The Thief's Journal* that his own name is that of a yellow-blossomed broom. "Whenever I come across *genêt* (broom) blossoms on the heaths – I feel a deep sense of kinship with them. I regard them solemnly, with tenderness. My emotion seems ordained by all nature. I am alone in the world, and I am not sure that

I am not the king – perhaps the sprite – of these flowers. They render homage as I pass, bow without bowing, but recognise me." Another time, in *The Miracle of the Rose*, he states that an autopsy on a murderer would reveal a gigantic rose in place of his heart. Or in *Our Lady of the Flowers*, he talks of "members in full bloom", albeit lilies on that occasion.

Right at the start of *The Thief's Journal* he draws the connection: "*There is a close relationship between flowers and convicts*. The fragility and delicacy of the former are of the same nature as the brutal insensitivity of the latter. (My sexual excitement is the oscillation from one to the other.) Should I have to portray a convict – or a criminal – I shall so bedeck him with flowers that, as he disappears beneath them, he will himself become a flower, a gigantic and new one."

There are no illusions as to what *Performance* was to be concerned with. "*Performance* is a very decadent movie," Cammell said. "It isn't a moral tract. It's a poetic treatise on violence. Mick would probably be annoyed at this. But his dilemma was that he knew what he was trafficking in. He knew about power and violence. I mean, the Stones' music doesn't exactly radiate peace and love." James Fox could see that Cammell was interested in the relationship between the power of rock music and the power of the gangster. "He loved Mick Jagger's power over an audience. He was clearly fascinated by the power of the gangster world."

"Cammell wanted the real violence to seep onto the film and to possess his actors," said Kevin Macdonald, one of the makers of *The Ultimate Performance*.

When James Fox accepted the role, "In my imagination I thought, yeah, I could project myself into this Jack the Lad. They told me about these guys who were often very good looking, very athletic, very cold . . . performers . . . who'd go and put the frighteners on people and there were quite famous ones around."

James Fox's character, Chas, "was modelled on a man called Jimmy Evans". Donald Cammell recalled him as "a highly adrenalised character, very good looking. (. . .) He was a real East End hood and I was a bit frightened of him."

Jimmy Evans became involved with *Performance* through a connection he had made in Wormwood Scrubs: Robert Fraser. He recalls in *The Survivor*, his autobiography, that he was sitting outside a coffee bar in the

King's Road when a little grey Alfa-Romeo pulled up at the kerb and the driver called out to him to come over. It was Robert Fraser, whom Evans had met when Fraser was serving time for the Redlands drugs raid. According to Evans' understanding, Fraser had taken a fall for the Stones, receiving six months, which enamoured him to Evans: "I liked him for that." Fraser asked him if he would like to earn five grand. So Evans abandoned his cappuccino and climbed into the car. Fraser told him about *Performance*: "It's a gangster film and perhaps you could help with it."

They drove round to David Litvinoff's flat, where Cammell and Fox joined them. Having recently come out of the Scrubs, where the gym had been his focal point, Evans was soon doing press-ups with James Fox on the floor. Over the following weeks he says that, as he and Fox were much the same size, he gave James some suits.

"I have always taken a pride in my appearance. Just as I used to have top-of-the-range cars, I used to have plenty of smart clothes." The local police nicknamed him 'the Duke': "because every time we go to his home to give him a spin, loads of clothes come tumbling out the wardrobes," said a detective.

Evans also advised Cammell and the others on various points, such as where he kept a gun about his person. "I showed them the hip-pocket that I had stitched into each of these suits. It was made of shammy leather and that's where I used to keep a little Derringer or a little .22 or a revolver." He also advised on where he'd keep a gun in the house: "I always stick one in the laundry basket in the bathroom among the towels."

Evans also recalls that Cammell suggested they wanted Chas to be a little bit bisexual. When asked why, Cammell replied: "Cos a lot of gangsters are bisexual; Ronnie Kray's bisexual." That didn't go down well with Evans: "Name another one! Name one more. Because I know everybody who's at it. I know all the bank robbers, I know all the safe-blowers, I know all the cranks – and there's only Ronnie that I can say is like that."

Though Evans says he spent a few weeks with them, he refused to accept any payment. James Fox found a way round that, taking Evans and Litvinoff down to The Pheasantry to see Basil Ede who was painting in the basement. Fox asked him to give Jimmy "a nice water-colour". Ede gave him a bird painting (jays) that Evans still has in his possession.

Jimmy Evans was not a gang member, but a safe-blower of known repute. "I was not a gangster myself. I was a sole trader operating outside the gang structure." He knew the Krays, and was respected by them, though he calls them "Mickey Mouse Mobsters" in his book. He came to the attention of the media for two incidents. The first occurred in 1964, when he discovered that his wife was having an affair with George Foreman, the brother of the gangland killer Freddie Foreman. Jimmy visited him accompanied by a sawn-off shotgun and blew George's bollocks clean to oblivion, castrating him. Rather than accept this as acceptable behaviour in the circumstances, Freddie set about a vendetta with various consequences. Ronnie Kray's reaction was to send a message via Charlie Kray: "Tell Jimmy Evans he did well. That will show those south London mugs what the East End is all about."

The second incident, which connects to the first, revolves around the disappearance of Ginger Marks, a car dealer, which happened when he was out for the night with Jimmy Evans. Freddie Foreman tried to ambush Evans, but a mishearing took Marks to his death, as he had mistakenly heard "Ginger" rather than "Jimmy" when "Jimmy, come over here" was shouted from a car.

At the time the media didn't know the facts. Peter Watson, a crime correspondent for *The Sunday Times*, wrote: "No one even knows why he had disappeared – though it was rumoured that he had interfered in the disposal of the great train robbers' money and as a result had ended up being buried in a concrete flyover in London. It was also said at the time that £5,000 had been made available for his removal."

When Evans narrates stories about squaring up to people, he always notes his readiness to produce a gun from his pocket. Reach for a comb, and bring out a Derringer in his palm. As he said: "I ain't got the patience for all that fighting bollocks. I like something that barks here and bites over there." Albert Donoghue, the Krays' enforcer, wrote that "Jimmy Evans wasn't afraid of anybody – he was the most fearless man I ever met."

And Evans is in no doubt about his sex drive. His stepdad asked him what he wanted to do when he left school at 14. "I want to put my prick out the window and fuck the world. (...) I had too much energy. I had a huge sex drive, but I was also in a line of work which meant I never knew when my liberty or my life might suddenly end, so I packed every minute with intense, pleasurable experiences, usually involving women."

He expands on this when talking about his wife: "So there was me and my old woman. She had all the attention in the world. There was never a day when I didn't make love to her. Every day of my life. I'd take a bird home from a club, pump her, come home, wake up the missus and pump her. I couldn't get enough. I was a fuck machine. I loved women. And strangely enough, women liked me."

Jimmy Evans hadn't seen *Performance* until recently – the hardback edition of his autobiography in 2001 doesn't include any reference, only the paperback edition the following year has a chapter. However, his initial reaction, unsurprisingly, was to note that he wasn't "a poof" and thus further consideration was probably not worth pursuing.

Donald Cammell's overriding memory of him was: "very funny, very cold, very intense. And very entertaining."

And then there was Johnny Bindon: "a real psychopath of the greatest kind, a great actor, a great performer. Very excitable", is Donald's summing up of the man. Stanley Meadows, who played alongside him, said that: "Actors model themselves on screen gangsters." But not in this case. "John Bindon certainly wasn't acting. He'd been involved in collecting protection money. (…) He definitely had something on screen: this angelic smile and, of course, sheer physical presence." Johnny Bindon was the real McCoy. "He frightened the actors," Johnny Shannon recalled. He "used to wag his three-piece about. He loved all that. He was one of the 'chaps'. I never met him before *Performance*, but we knew all the same people. He used to enjoy telling these terrible stories about himself. People would laugh, but when he was out of the room people were horrified."

In October 1979 Bindon stood trial at the Old Bailey for the murder of John Darke at the Ranelagh Yacht Club in Fulham the previous year. He was coming to the aid of Roy Dennis who had been stabbed in the back by Darke, and in return he was attacked and stabbed in the chest. When Bindon rose from the floor he attacked Darke and killed him with a hunting knife loaned by a girlfriend.

It slid in "cold like an icicle", Bindon said, when Darke stabbed him. "I felt it go in. There was a pain and great coldness. It was like an icicle stuck there."

At that point, Darke "was leaning right over me and trying to talk to me. 'You are not such a big boy now Bindon.' I started to plead with him and held the wrist of his knife hand. He told me to let go of his hand. I let go because I was in no position to do anything else."

Once Darke was pulled off, Bindon took out a hunting knife. Darke came at him again. "I thought I was going to die." He says he struck out in the general direction, as his head was spinning, grappled and fought, and next thing they were separated. He had dealt him nine stab wounds.

Publicity at the time gave Bindon's profession as a tough guy actor who had appeared in *Hazell* and *Softly Softly*. *Performance* wasn't mentioned, which was probably just as well. He was cleared of murder.

In 1974, invited by the singer Dana Gillespie to holiday with her and some friends on the Caribbean island of Mustique, owned by millionaire Colin Tennant, he met Princess Margaret. She liked his humour and they struck up a friendship. The following year he was invited again, and was there for three months with his girlfriend, the model Vicki Hodge, the daughter of Sir John Rowland Hodge, 2nd Baronet of Chipstead. She remained his partner for 12 years.

"I've had this overwhelming urge to smash things since I was a kid." Though Bindon was brought up in Fulham in a working-class environment, he never blamed that background for his troubles as a hard man and villain. He just chose not to pursue learning at school, despite his father being a supporter of education. The film footage in *Performance* of children fighting in the street could easily have been a flashback to his upbringing.

He was known for standing up to school bullies. "I've got a useful pair of fists and I intend to use them if necessary. There's a lot of people out there who need characters like me."

Scraps with the law took him into petty crime and before long he had moved from borstal to terms in prison.

His screen idol was Robert Mitchum and he modelled his walk on the tough guy. As it made him look older than he was, it wasn't long before he was offered employment as an enforcer, collecting debts. The Krays had met Bindon in Wandsworth prison, introduced by Frank Mitchell ('The Mad Axeman'), whom he had befriended. Indeed, he was enamoured with Mitchell, becoming a trusted runner for him. Later, when the Krays had a problem with a man in Fulham who hadn't paid off a large debt, they invited Bindon to sort it out. "John did what he had to do," said Joey Pyle, a gang boss. "It was left to John to decide how to resolve the problem. It wouldn't be a kiss on the cheek, I can tell you that."

Ben Carruthers, a young American actor, whom Cammell had probably met in New York when the actor was filming Cassavetes' *Shadows*, met Bindon in London and suggested he might work as an actor. Bindon wasn't so sure. "It's just that anybody who acts is supposed to be a poof, and, if I get called that, there's gonna be a few more broken heads around. (...) In Fulham every tough wants to take me on! I don't want to fight, but that's all I've ever been inside for. At least if you're a thief there's a chance of getting something for nothing. But thieving doesn't appeal to me. This is the longest I've been out of jug since I was 11. If I can be a success in films, maybe I'll stay out."

It was through a writer he'd met in the King's Road, Nell Dunn, that Bindon got his break. She introduced him to the director Ken Loach, with the idea that he'd make an ideal 'technical adviser' for the film *Poor Cow*. The next thing he knew he was co-starring alongside Carol White, as well as being employed as 'technical adviser'. That break was not to be the end. Bindon wanted to move away from his associates and find a path in acting. It wasn't so easy when others were unhappy that he had not received his actor's Equity card in the usual fashion, accumulating bit part credits until judged worthy of membership. It slowed his progress.

Performance gave him another chance to shine. Roeg says that he was a "wild, naked talent; an extraordinary man; a totally unafraid person; people often mistrust that, mistake it for pugnacity". Bindon kept in contact, and 10 years later they met in the States, "shortly after his other problems. We were always able to pick up a friendly conversation. I had a very great regard for him. I liked his attitude of raw courage; he had an unencumbered attitude – people are so often encumbered by fear."

Bindon was brought in via 'technical adviser' Litvinoff. They knew each other from various haunts around the King's Road. In fact it was Bindon who had accompanied Litvinoff when he visited Nicky Cramer, who was believed to be the informer for the Redlands drugs raid. "They gave him a right hammering. He'd broken the golden rule and snitched, so he had to pay the price," one of Bindon's friends recalled some years later, offering another version, which is what you find when you research sources across the different social worlds. "John said Jagger was a little freaked out when he heard what had happened, but at least he knew it would never happen again."

Bindon was impressed with *Performance*, and always claimed it had left an indelible mark on him. He was a friend of John Porter, the bassist with Roxy Music for a while, later a record producer, married to Linda Keith, a former partner of Keith Richards. Bindon used to crash and relax in Porter's place regularly and talk, often about literature, for Bindon's father had always encouraged his children to read. "John kept banging on about how realistic *Performance* was. The trouble was that, if we were ever in a pub and someone gave me a hard time, he'd always want to beat them up and I had to hold him back. John thrived on the drama, but ultimately became a victim of it. There was always this rueful inevitability about John. He knew he was very capable, strong, sharp-minded and pretty intelligent with this incredible capacity for memory. But there was also much tragedy behind that ever-present smile. I think all the inevitability of his life had already kicked in."

"All the parts are villains but I'm not afraid of being typecast – after all, Humphrey Bogart was pretty successful and he didn't go helping old ladies across the street very often," was Bindon's philosophy. He played 'heavy' roles in TV series like *Hazell*, *The Sweeney*, *Softly Softly* and *Minder*, and appeared in such films as *Quadrophenia* and *Get Carter*.

But needing a change from acting he went into 'security', minding for his music and show business connections, working for Bowie and notably Led Zeppelin. Their road manager, Richard Cole, made it clear: "Bindon was always good value. Led Zeppelin loved him, especially their crazy bastard of a drummer, John Bonham. Bindon was a madman in the nicest possible way. He wasn't scared of anyone and it showed." The backstage incident that occurred on the US tour in July 1977 at the Oakland Coliseum culminated in the group's manager, Peter Grant, Bindon, Cole, and John Bonham being charged with assaulting the promoter's staff has become part of the folk legend of the band. Bindon's role meant that he wasn't allowed to remain long in that business.

But the other part of his life that adds greatly to the myths that surround *Performance* goes back to his time on Mustique. When he was invited there by his friend Dana Gillespie, he soon realised the place was rather secluded, a "sort of tropical paradise I'd only seen in the Bounty ads on telly", and that he was in select company.

Bindon was also not phased by stripping off, or revealing the size of his penis. From the age of 14 he had developed a party piece, a routine that he employed many times in pubs to parade his prowess, which was 12 inches long. "I'd hang five half-pint beer glasses on me manhood. Everyone would ask how it's done beforehand so I'd put them out of their misery and thread my old chap through the handles of the glasses."

On Mustique, Princess Margaret wanted confirmation of the rumours. "He jumped up and, with Princess Margaret and her lady-in-waiting in tow, walked along the beach," Vicki Hodge recounted. "Then he took out his appendage. The Princess examined it rather like a fossil. We all gasped. After a few moments, they all came back to the table. 'I've seen bigger,' the lady-in-waiting said. 'You may have seen bigger,' John said, 'but you don't know how well I use it.'"

The secret life of Bindon and his visits to Kensington Palace, alone with the Princess, entering discreetly with the collusion of her staff, is also legend. Bindon vowed never to talk about the relationship or what went on, though there are suggestions that he didn't quite keep to that pledge.

This was reinforced when an incident that terrified Bindon occurred as he returned to his Chesham Mews home. He was approached by four men and knew immediately they were MI5 officers. They guided him into the back of a black Rover coupé and, as they drove out of the mews, a police car moved aside to allow them through. That action in itself scared Bindon, knowing the degree to which the operation was being cloaked from prying eyes. On the drive around London, they put the frighteners on him, warned him off from ever talking about his relationship with the Princess. "Bindon was freaked out by that visit from the spooks," a friend revealed. He was scared because he knew those men meant more business than any villains.

Bindon's favourite phrase was: "I think there must have been a little misunderstanding."

Initially, Marianne Faithfull was in line for the part of Pherber, which would have been convenient, as she could have lived out a romance with

Mick before the cameras, playing with whatever image they wanted to project of themselves. Marianne was gaining major acting experience, initially in the theatre with Edward Bond's adaptation of Chekhov's *Three Sisters* in April 1967 and also Bond's *Early Morning* in March 1968, both at the Royal Court, and then in film with Jack Cardiff's *Girl on a Motorcycle* (1968) opposite Alain Delon. However, she was pregnant and was delighted at the prospect of having another child.

Although Anita Pallenberg was involved in the writing of the script, it was not envisaged that she would play the part of Pherber, even if there seemed no more natural contender. Right from the start, in its earliest incarnation as *The Liars*, it looked as if the character was shaped around her, describing Pherber as "very direct, spontaneous, pithy, funny, rather arrogant, ironic more by accident than design, and at the same time elliptical and evasive when it comes to any questions about herself – sort of automatically secretive". Anita had already started to work in film, first with Volker Schlöndorff's *A Degree of Murder* (1967) and subsequently in *Barbarella* and *Candy* (a cameo), both released in 1968. As *Performance* approached its shooting date she was also to discover that she was pregnant.

When *Barbarella* was proposed, Keith had asked Anita how much she was being paid, offering to match it for her *not* to do the role. His insecurity, and the fear that she might become involved with another person, made him blind to the idea that there might be more to life than being a rock chick, and that people like Anita (and indeed Marianne) needed something more.

Anita did not come on board *Performance* until filming had started. An earlier choice for Pherber was the American actress Tuesday Weld, who had started her career in films before her teens (and had been considered for the part of Lolita in Kubrick's film). Whilst she had built up a reputation in these young roles, she wanted to move on. Weld had arrived in London. Donald wanted Deborah to meet her, to see if she felt Weld was the right choice. As now seems apparent, Donald wanted the film to convey some of the atmosphere of his recent life with Deborah. It was not just a matter of bringing belongings from the Paris home onto the set, but also of having the right feeling between all the participants. The choice of Weld was undoubtedly aimed at giving it an acceptable chance on the American market. In the event, Weld was having back problems and, stretching out with Deborah, lying across her back, she flipped herself over and landed awkwardly, breaking her ankle. She was taken to the nearest hospital by Deborah and David Litvinoff. Deborah recalls accompanying Weld to Heathrow in a wheelchair and putting her on a plane to America.

Deborah says that Donald had always wanted Anita to play the part. Perhaps Anita was reluctant to step into such an incestuous role, something that she could see Donald was conspiring towards.

Loulou de la Falaise was also known to Donald and considered for Pherber. She was later to marry Thadée Klossowski and become a designer at Yves Saint Laurent. She had no film experience, and suspecting that she hadn't much of a chance and wouldn't receive the support of the financiers in Hollywood, she left town, seemingly for New York.

The part of Lucy was also originally destined for another actress, Mia Farrow. She hadn't even arrived in London before she had to withdraw, having slipped over in New York, breaking her ankle. There was enough warning here for Donald to ask Michèle Breton to step in. Michèle was more than just known to Donald; she had lived in Paris with Donald and Deborah Dixon in a *ménage à trois*. "Troilism was one of his (Donald's) main obsessions. Young girls was definitely the number one obsession," stated Myriam Gibril, his partner immediately after *Performance* had finished shooting. Deborah and Donald had met Michèle on the beach in St Tropez. "She was a peasant from the hills around St Tropez – her father was a garagiste. She was a great sexual catalyst in the film – very beautiful, very bright, no education at all. She was very good with Jimmy. She was about 14 when Deborah and I met her, and then we took her back to Paris and she was already destined for a bad end." Though why Donald should add that final remark is not known. Mick Brown tracked her down not that many years ago in Berlin, and found her alive, but not feeling good about her experience on *Performance*. It was also fanciful that she was only 14. She was actually 16, according to her account with Mick Brown, when her parents sent her packing from the family home in Brittany with the idea that they never wanted to see her again. Though the publicity office at Warner Bros gave out her bio as: "At age 15, she left Grenoble, where her parents, both university teachers, had moved from Deville la Rouen, where Michele was born. Then, she went to St Tropez, stayed with her grandmother, lay around in the sun and became fascinated by the film people there."

In Paris she did some fashion modelling. It seems from the earlier versions of the script that Breton had always been in mind, or perhaps Donald was using Breton as a model for the character, not exactly thinking she could realistically be given the part.

"She represented that image that Donald was so in love with – that young girl who is totally uninhibited, no hang-up whatsoever," said Sandy Lieberson, adding: "A strange little creature, totally androgynous-looking – the way Donald liked them." That look was to become instrumental in the manipulation of identity confusions in the film. That she was 17 at the time and Cammell had to falsify her age to gain the necessary work permit finds its way into the film when Lucy refers to her attempt to obtain a work permit in order to stay in this country.

Michèle had no major acting experience, though she did have an uncredited role in Godard's *Weekend*, as part of a group, and another role in an Italian RAI television series *L'Odissea*. She came to London and embarked on a crash course in English to prepare for the role. What becomes interesting, with hindsight, is that these two female roles should have been destined for anyone else but Anita Pallenberg and Michèle Breton. It seems as if the characters were drawn up with them in mind, integral to the story. They certainly were fated to play the roles. It's not that Tuesday Weld and Mia Farrow would not have created something intriguing, but it would have been a different film altogether. Farrow's early fame in the soap opera *Peyton Place* might have been one reason to approach her, particularly with the idea of her waifish image, emphasised as the series developed when her hair was cut short. Her role in Losey's *Secret Ceremony* (1968) might give us some idea of what she would have looked like. Though our most memorable image of Farrow is probably in Polanski's *Rosemary's Baby*, that film was not released until June 1968. Polanski was a friend of Donald's and might well have suggested her. Polanski had initially wanted Tuesday Weld for *Rosemary's Baby*, but the studio suggested Farrow, who was a bigger star, and in the end Polanski cast her without a screen test once he saw that she had a nervy edge.

Marianne noted what I've tried to reflect: "the symmetry of the characters in the film mirrored rather too uncannily the relationship between

James and Andee, Mick and myself. Michèle Breton had short hair and a boyish, skinny little body like Andee's. Not as lovely, but the same androgynous look."

Donald's brother, David, was already established in the film business. After reading history at Trinity College in Cambridge, he had formed an award-winning company with Hugh Hudson, later joined by Robert Brownjohn, called Cammell, Hudson & Brownjohn. They had already had their successes making commercials for television and the cinema. Hugh Hudson went on to direct *Chariots of Fire*, amongst others, and Robert Brownjohn gained fame for the style he brought to the title sequences of *From Russia with Love* and *Goldfinger*. David Cammell agreed to come on board as associate producer, and set up the film's production office on his company's site, separated from the rest, "across the courtyard in a wing of the studios" in Shawfield Street, off the King's Road. Effectively, David was running the show, in control of budgets and schedules, finding the locations and drawing on his contacts, along with Nic's, to find a crew that was experienced, but he would also bring in young technicians who would have a good feel for the ambience of what was about to be shot.

David's relationship with his brother was one of typical healthy rivalry. As he joked, they got on very well together "because we mainly lived on different continents". But in those early days they moved in the same circles around the King's Road. He speaks of David Litvinoff bringing him a coat one time, only to discover years later when collecting the coat at a dinner party that another guest used to have a coat just like that. Litvinoff was famous for his redistribution of possessions to those he thought more needy. Donald had already been involved in developing one of David's storylines for what would become *The Touchables*. David would always be able to find places for Donald to rent when he wanted to stay in London for a period. He was the ideal person to find the right locations for filming. "One of the reasons why the film is as good as it is, is that I produced it, and I produced it in the way no other film was made before, when we did it all on location."

Three key locations were found. For the exterior of Turner's house, number 25 Powis Square was used, though the number was changed to 81 for the benefit of those living there. Not that that has hindered it from featuring as a Notting Hill reference point on tours of the area today.

The second was at 15 Lowndes Square in Knightsbridge, which would become not only the interior for Turner's Powis Square home, but also the place to build the set for Chas' flat. It had not been easy to find a suitable house. Most that might have been suitable had been converted into flats. And then David recalled a house in Lowndes Square where he had lost an unhealthy amount of money in a game of poker. The place belonged to the father of that game's organiser, Captain Leonard Plugge, something of an offbeat businessman and a former Conservative MP for Chatham. He lived nearby in Dolphin Square.

When they checked it out, Donald recalled: "It was perfect; the faded splendour of its cavernous reception rooms, the ancient lift jammed in the basement, the stone staircase curling up to impenetrable gloom. On the walls hung innumerable paintings in various stages of disrepair." David found that Lenny Plugge "was only too pleased to get a pittance by renting it off. The whole place was festooned with paintings – the Plugge collection – and one condition of renting the house was that we should insure them for £2 million. I thought they were a bit dodgy and they were in rather battered condition. There was a Rembrandt, a Rubens and a Velasquez, and several were signed by Rembrandt as well as Rubens. Anyway, we removed the paintings, wrapped them in blankets and put them upstairs in the caretaker's flat. The caretaker was a strange sort of dog's body who wandered around brandishing a luger. And there was another appalling creature who lived upstairs with him, a mongol whose bed we had to fumigate when we discovered that it was festering with lice. He took rather a shine to me and used to follow me around all day. Mr Plugge, who was about 85, was also staggering about. He went to the opera every night, wearing an ermine coat, although he was completely broke and was always being hunted by creditors. He was never seen without a pretty girl on either arm, and would totter up the stairs as we were filming, telling them he was going to get them into the movies."

There was more colour to come when David Cammell was awoken early one morning by the police in connection with the missing Plugge art collection. David initially thought it was a prank by Litvinoff or someone, "but it turned out to be true, the whole lot had disappeared. Then some of the film crew remembered that the caretaker had been looking rather flush and had bought himself a new motor car recently. We discovered that he had whipped the whole lot. He was on the run for about two weeks, and was finally arrested at Paddington station. He then rang up and asked me to stand bail for him. I told him that he had caused me more anxiety than anyone else on earth, and I hoped that he rotted. We found out that he had sold the paintings at auction – £3,800 for the entire lot, which rather blew the lid off the fabulous Plugge collection. Then the next thing was that the woman who lived next door complained about what she called our ice-cream van. She called me in and said did I realise that there were more titled people living in Lowndes Square than anywhere else in London except Eaton Square. She said we were lowering the tone, and she put an injunction on us and stopped us filming. We had a lot of money at stake, so we had to get a vacation judge back to hear the case, which went on for two days in the High Court. It turned out that the house had been mortgaged twice over and old Plugge had no right to let it out at all. The Sun Life Insurance Company was delighted – it was a heaven-sent opportunity for them to get rid of him. In the end Plugge agreed to give up the remainder of his lease – there was only 18 months left to run and it was a full repairing lease, so he was well out of it. And we were allowed to carry on so long as we behaved ourselves."

The third location was a vacant house at 25 Hyde Park Gate, a few doors down from Winston Churchill's townhouse. There they shot the scenes for Turner's basement, kitchen, garden and greenhouse. It was demolished almost directly filming had finished.

Other locations will be noted as we proceed.

Before the cameras roll, a quick summary of the film, as Donald Cammell relayed it some years later for Paul Joyce's documentary on Nic Roeg: "It's about an experiment conducted by an artist, Turner, a hunt, a search, for his own lost creative talent. He believes himself to be at the end of his career. He's a man in despair. And then destiny brings him his mirror image, Chas, the man who sees what he was, what he could be again. Chas arrives by accident, by chance, in his house. The predator arrives at the house of the artist, the barbarian arrives at the house of the intellectual.

The intellectual sees in him, after first trying to reject him, sees in him the mirror of himself, of what he could be, of what he once was. And he embarks on an experiment with drugs, and uses the remaining fire of his song, of his poetry, to get inside this other being's head, to merge with him."

6) always three on sunday

ON May 7, 1968, Ken Hyman, the executive vice-president of Warner Brothers-Seven Arts, announced that: "Mick Jagger has been signed to make his motion picture dramatic acting debut in *The Performers*." Shooting was scheduled to begin on location in and around London from mid-July. A month later, the details were more precise. Shooting was to start on Monday July 29, and the film would be called *Performance*. For Donald and David Cammell, six weeks before filming, there was an upset when their father died.

As it was proposed to shoot the film chronologically, Mick Jagger was told that he wouldn't be needed until early September, and then for six weeks, from 8 am to 7 pm each day. Marianne was expecting their baby and left town, moving to Ireland, where they found a house in Tuam, County Galway, a place to which Mick could fly each weekend.

In a couple of pre-filming interviews, one with Jonathan Cott for *Rolling Stone*, Jagger talked about his feelings on acting as opposed to singing onstage. "They are both just projections of your ego, which you're not supposed to have, but you can't do without. You certainly can't act without it. (...) This character in the film has this fantastic ego thing, which is all right 'cause I can make that. If people get the feeling that you are out there with them, and if you come on strong, then you'll make it. It's just a matter of looking confident, being confident and believing the part, then it's cool." And to Helen Lawrenson, who was to use the interview later in *Esquire*: "I question my motive: why should I be doing a film at all? I hope I'll enjoy doing it and I hope it may use another part of my brain that's been lying dormant, but maybe I'm just doing it to promote my own ego. It's all hung up in every direction."

Mick's time on set was to be longer than outlined. He started on Monday September 2 and finished shooting in the Lowndes Square house on Friday November 1.

Nic Roeg, who was used to shooting under studio conditions, with all the attendant business of prying eyes and endless justifications to the powers-that-be, was in a luxury situation. "We were left alone. We were in this void. With a freedom that nobody was checking up on. How often could that happen? Now you have 18 people on the set questioning whether someone raises their fork or not." Donald too, talking about his relationship with Nic, in an interview before the cameras, said: "We spent all our time together – evenings, lunchhours and so on – talking about how we were going to do a scene, how we'd do a set-up, do a shot. I rehearsed all the actors and Nic used to come in and watch rehearsals. He'd come in and see . . . always had to wear a blue blazer. One of the rules of the set was that Nic had to wear the blue blazer and tie and I had all the gear, you know. Getting on the set I would pass the ball completely to Nic, with the camera crew, because there he was in his element. I would block the actors and he would block the camera and it worked great."

Perhaps Donald had taken his cue from *La Collectionneuse*, for as his brother David pointed out: "I think Donald wanted to create an atmosphere so that the film itself would evolve with its own momentum. (...) Originally Donald had planned to move the principal cast into the Lowndes Square location and actually live there for a week, rehearse and get to know each other."

That wasn't to be. Not that the main protagonists didn't know each other intimately already, and certainly they lived near enough to each other. Donald had rented a studio flat at 30a Old Church Street this time.

Nevertheless, as Annabel Davis-Goff, who was responsible for continuity, remarked, the house "was more like somewhere we all lived rather than a set. Not only because we worked such long hours (...) but because it was such an interrelated group." The camera room was in the basement – "the source of many refreshing early morning gin and tonics" – and the all-purpose room on the ground floor, while "we took occasional naps on parts of the set that lent itself to that".

The idea that it was a family, even if the cast and crew didn't mix too much, comes across from David Cammell. He felt that "once they were installed on the set, they did begin to play off against each other both behind the camera as well as in front of it. And that's what gives it that authentic quality."

Any idea that this was a nine-to-five job is ably dispelled by Annabel. She notes that Nic Roeg sent her and the camera crew "to the Balthus exhibition at the Tate and told us to think about light sources". They also "used to see every movie that came out. Always three on Sunday (our only day off). Art house and Leicester Square." She recalls, too, that Donald and Nic took Michèle Breton to a screening of *The Red Shoes*.

"Donald and Nic worked together in an immensely positive way," Sandy Lieberson stated. "It was Donald's concept. He wrote the screenplay, but the interpretation was a collaboration." As Nic Roeg saw it: "Donald and I had an absolute identification of interest in every scene."

Nic is very clear that what makes it work all boils down not to a love of photography but rather to a love of film, "and the telling of stories through film". There is a distinction between cinematography and photography which he learnt by working on the studio floor, not by going to film school, something Roeg seems to look back upon with relief, "in a way". You make the movie through the cinematography; "it's the scene that must be served."

With *Performance*, Nic commented in a 2002 interview: "Of course, you must plan everything very carefully before you start, but then you must be ready to let go – to be ready to trip over the gold at your feet. Certainly, we tripped over plenty of things in *Performance*, but that's what made it such a great experience."

But as he had said many years before in his 1973 *Sight & Sound* interview: "When we went on the floor each day, though, the scenes were exact; we knew the intention, and the artists knew the intention, so they had an influence in a subjective rather than objective way, insofar as their behaviour patterns would take shape." One thing which amused Roeg enormously, and that has become one of the myths of the film, was that "there never was a final script, and it was a marvellous stroke when Warner Brothers flew a man over to stop the film because we weren't sticking to the script. Show us where we're straying, we said. 'Well,' he said, 'I haven't got a copy here, but they tell me . . .'"

While he was trying to make *Ishtar*, his next project, Donald did an interview in 1972 with *Cinema Rising*. As noted earlier, Donald was against the *auteur* theory, his opposition being that: "It's a way of trying to demonstrate the view that cinema is an art form, and that therefore there must be a single creative mind controlling the artefact, through to its ultimate form. It's a way of justifying movie-making, socially and culturally.

"But leaving aside the reasons for the concept, I think it's contradicted by the facts. I think that many of the greatest artefacts – things that have moved people most throughout history – have been collectively produced. You don't even have to look for examples: the whole of Egyptian culture, arcane cultures generally. Today in tribal cultures, the vast majority of the products are collectively produced. The hang-up is the concept of one ego necessarily controlling the production in order for that ego to be expressed; the notion that the expression of an ego is the final goal of any artwork, that this is what it's for. I think that an artwork expresses itself, that the creators involved will all see in it their own egos, each one individually satisfied when looking at the final work. My analogy is with contemporary music, where people go into it collectively, and their egos are satisfied collectively and individually. Look at Mick and Keith and their confréres: they see in their work as The Rolling Stones what they each wanted to say. Working in the film medium is ideally suited to interaction of different heads; it's the ideal medium for all the good functions of collective work."

7) other inquisitions

SOME might not like the idea of an intertextual world being created, "a mosaic of quotations", as the French semiotician Julia Kristeva referred to it in the late Sixties, when the currency was earning its keep in intellectual circles on the Left Bank in Paris. A weave of references from different disciplines would be used not to pepper an empty idea or to disseminate interpretations, but to give a sign of a culture or the imagined universe of its creator . . . to evidence the creator's reading, if not library, in other words. The term, 'intertextuality', might have been new, but the notion of textual interaction, under other names, had been around in literary theory for years.

In film terms, a relevant contemporary reference for *Performance* is Jean-Luc Godard. He is a good example of a filmmaker whose films "have become increasingly fragmentary in construction, are composed of scores of references, allusions, quotations, anecdotes, and news items", noted Paul Mayersberg in an article about Godard in 1966. So much so, in fact, that his films can be regarded as collages, or "a cultural mosaic". A classic example, one that could figure highly in a study of references for Godard's accountability in *Performance*, would be *Pierrot le Fou* (1965), with Céline, Chateaubriand, Rimbaud, Michel Simon in Renoir's *La Chienne*, Picasso . . . that just being a scratch on the surface of the intellectual adventures through that film. One might even go further and suggest that *Pierrot*'s montage veers towards genuine cut-up cut-ins.

Even though Godard shows a passion for quoting, right from his early films he has always felt reproached for such a course. "People in life quote as they please, so we have the right to quote as we please. Therefore I show people quoting, merely making sure that they quote what pleases me." Bertolucci supports that viewpoint when he says: "I make quotes because the films I have seen form part of reality, like the people I've met, the countries I've travelled in, the winters of my childhood, the summer holidays."

What happens if you do not recognise the quotes? When is a quote not a quote? If no one recognises the references, then it becomes a buried quote, and is then perhaps not a quote. Do others have to recognise a quote for it to be one? Or does one have to wait for the filmmaker, or the author of the text, to reveal it?

Roland Barthes, a literary theoretician of the time, notes in *The Pleasure of the Text*: "I savour the sway of formulas, the reversal of origins, the ease which brings the anterior text out of the subsequent one." One of his pleasures was that meanings accumulated in the most random ways, an unpredictability that is found in life. An idea that other theoreticians, such as Michael Riffaterre, disapproved of, feeling that the intertextual is only acceptable if the structural identity is maintained, if there is a "centring text" to retain its "leadership in meaning".

This leads to a writer regarded as being at the centre of Donald Cammell's thinking with *Performance*, namely the Argentinian Jorge Luis Borges. He wrote a few film criticisms, one of which was on Welles' *Citizen Kane*, which he regarded as a "labyrinth with no centre", a "chaos of appearances" that leads to no resolution, at least for those within the narrative, though for the viewer the 'rosebud' mystery that is the premise of the film is answered. *Performance* is a film without resolution. It is kept open, purposely, to offer each reader possibilities for interpretation, its wealth of references clarifying rather than distorting this purpose.

When reading Kafka, another writer whose work goes through mazes of thinking, Borges "felt I could recognise his voice, or his habits, in the texts of various literatures and various ages". He then lists, with explanations, Zeno's paradox against motion, a fable by the ninth-century Chinese writer Han Yu, Kierkegaard, Browning's poem 'Fears and Scruples', a short story by Léon Bloy, and another by Lord Dunsany. "If I am not mistaken, the heterogeneous pieces I have listed resemble Kafka; if I am not mistaken, not all of them resemble each other." Borges wants us to see the significance. "Kafka's idiosyncrasy is present in each of these writings, to a greater or lesser degree, but if Kafka had not written, we would not perceive it; that is to say, it would not exist." Reversing our usual understanding of moving from the past to the present, he suggests going from the present to the past. He wants us to see with the time paradox "that each writer *creates* his precursors. His work modifies our conception of the past, as it will modify the future." Of course, while Borges is suggesting that Kafka makes his own precursors, it is in fact Borges who has made them by showing us this list of precursors that we might never have noticed except for his, Borges', reading.

8) fairly bursting at its seams

PERFORMANCE is not so much a violent film as a film about violence. This can be traced through every scene, read on as many of the levels as one wishes to read the film. Even when the scene has a surface appearance that conveys a 'peace and love' atmosphere, violence seems to be underlying, with the scene used as a counterpoint to highlight our awareness of the violence at work elsewhere.

The period in which the film was made, after May 68, would suggest that social tension was active, in the air, even if the fictional occupants of the house are cut off from society, and all the occupants of the house in film shoot terms were absorbed in making a film that focused them and made them somewhat oblivious to what was happening elsewhere, abroad in particular. (Television and media reportage in the late Sixties was not as blanket and all-pervading as it can be now, if it chooses.) Though we had come through a 'summer of love' in 1967, and although a wash of hippie liberal thinking had been in the air for the preceding few years, there was also a substantial amount of violence apparent in life as in the arts.

The link of violence with The Rolling Stones goes right back to their beginnings earlier in the decade. Alexis Korner made it clear, as noted, that Brian Jones baited the audience, banging his tambourine in their faces, for example.

Whilst Jagger tends to relate that his stage behaviour is more about taunting the audience in a sexual manner, he has still noted his aggression and the way the audience responded well before *Performance* was filmed, well before the death at Altamont hit home hard. "I get a strange feeling onstage. I feel all this energy coming from the audience. I feel quite violent sometimes. I quite often want to smash up the microphone or something. I don't feel the same person onstage as I am normally."

There have been countless reports about the violence that was stirred up by the Stones' performances, the continual riots and the destruction in the music venues across Europe, often leading to their shows grinding to abrupt halts midway through. In his 1968 interview with Miles for *International Times*, Mick, obviously a bit stoned, was asked how he felt when an audience riots at a concert, if he picks up on any energy. "Yes! Wow! Tingle with it! The energy's great. I mean, they give you *so* much energy, just don't know what to do with it man, and it lasts too, every performer has felt that. It's just the way you are, the way the energy is, I don't really know why . . . I know I try and do it, and then, I never went onstage with the idea of keeping everything cool. I never wanted it to be peaceful, even if I did before I went onstage, soon as I got on there and felt what they felt, I've wanted to make, I mean, they were totally in control, as much as I was. I mean I was in control but they were also."

One time in Zurich, a man leapt onto the stage and attacked Jagger before anyone could pull him off. Mick was hurled to the floor and stomped on. That shook him.

"Mick was an animal" after performing, Tom Keylock said. As noted earlier, Marianne talked about the time she waited for Mick back at the hotel. When he entered the room "there was a froth of spittle around his lips. His eyes were violent. He was making sounds, guttural sounds, and he was completely unintelligible. He was a berserk stranger. He picked me up and slammed me against the wall, several times." Once he had calmed down, he behaved as if nothing had happened, never spoke of it again.

Keylock thought that the gap between the Jagger onstage and off was wider than people understood. "You could see him becoming Mick Jagger, doing exercises, psyching himself up, staring into space, while the others more or less just turned up."

The bands at the time didn't have enormous banks of speakers to assault an audience – that started as the Sixties were in full flight, courtesy of Cream. But groups could still create aggression in their music. During early live performances, The Who did a version of 'Smokestack Lightning' which ended with Pete Townshend smashing his guitar into the speaker, and invariably destroying it on the floor, running up higher replacement bills than their wages at that point. The destructive element became part of their act, eventually built into their own song, 'My Generation', giving them an anthem that could be grasped and used as a convenient weapon with which to build their fame. "From valueless objects – a guitar, a microphone, a hackneyed pop tune – we abstract a new value. We take objects with one function and give them another. And the auto-destructive element – the way we destroy our instruments – adds immediacy to it all." Townshend admitted that one influence had been his lecturer at Ealing Art School, Gustav Metzger, the artist known for his destructive artwork.

In October 1966 there was a Who 'happening' on *Ready Steady Go!*, based on 'Theatre of the Absurd' ideas, as their managers used in the hyped-up publicity for the show. It was certainly chaotic, with a typical Who finale, their first on live television. The visual splendour of the smoke and destruction was impossible to transfer to the EP they released, the record consisting mainly of re-recorded numbers, some of which were never played on the show. Goodbye 'My Generation'. Hello, the Ferrari. Or should that be: Hello, the Bentley, the Aston Martin, the Rolls-Royce . . .

Once Jimi Hendrix was in town, and his Experience was formed and in operation over the final months of 1966, there came another level of violence and aggression, with or without damaging a guitar. Violence as much as tenderness was expressed in the sound of Hendrix's music, though there was no getting away from a later number such as 'Machine Gun' for his assault on the results of violence both personal and societal.

Gustav Metzger, a shy, retiring artist, sought to be more social by instigating a project, DIAS (Destruction in Art Symposium), that attracted attention mainly for degrees of violence and 'obscenity' not seen before in London. Though other artists had contributed quieter approaches to destruction, attracting polite police interference, it was the artists from Vienna, Otto Muehl and Hermann Nitsch, whose 'actions' caused offence. Naked people, usually women, were variously bound, covered with flour, margarine, raw eggs and paint as they writhed on the performance space, or, in Nitsch's case, carried out 'actions' with 'crucified' carcasses of various animals, lambs mainly. In their different ways, Nitsch and Muehl related their violence to the recent past, as well as to the violence of society and the Vietnam War.

Without embracing all the arts, or indeed all aspects, another relevant development in terms of *Performance* can be found in theatre. There was a level of violence not just in the actions onstage but in the use of language. Leaving aside Harold Pinter for the time being, there was the Austrian-born German writer Peter Handke. Born during the war, in 1942, he emerged as the *enfant terrible* of German literature in 1966, adept at both publicity and handling the attention he received, in particular for his play *Offending the Audience*. Four actors as actors, not role-players, faced the audience and for an hour regaled them with what was happening there and then as a theatre experience, which eventually turned into an attack on the audience through a barrage of 164 abuses, treating the audience as necessary participants in the staging of the production. The occasion finally ended with a cordial: "You were welcome here. We thank you. Good Night." This was not an anti-play, more one about the dependence and acceptance of theatre as an institution, as one critic observed. It was also a great success, with numerous theatres abroad staging the play. Whether it was interpreted as the author wished was another matter, and not for our concern here.

In his 'rules for the actors', Handke offers 16 to be obeyed, starting with: "Listen to the litanies in the Catholic churches." Seventh on the list is: "Listen to 'Tell Me' by The Rolling Stones". He was particularly interested in the actors, called 'speakers', absorbing the rhythm/beat of the Stones, to understand how to drive forward the short and sharp sentences.

Like other activities which were part of the Sixties revolution, Handke is specifically saying that his speaks-ins, as he calls them, "do not want to revolutionise, but to make aware". That was very much what the Sixties was about, though not everyone saw it that way.

Whilst a lot of anti-theatre features levels of verbal abuse and aggression, Handke's play seemed to be a cut above its precursors. One thinks of Alfred Jarry's *Ubu Roi* (1896), or various Dada events (following the First World War), or Eugène Ionesco's *The Bald Prima Donna,* one of those prime plays bracketed as the 'Theatre of the Absurd' (its author had initially wanted to end this, his first play, with the massacre of the audience). Others might also cite the Vienna Group of writers (which started in the Fifties), particularly Gerhard Rühm and Friedrich Achleitner, whose work, called 'concrete poetry', often broke down language because Handke's play was specifically about words rather than pictures or images. And yet another aspect of contemporary performance was taking place in the art world, under the name 'actions' in Vienna (rather than the term 'happenings' used elsewhere). Through the Sixties, these 'actions', as mentioned, mainly dealt with extremes of sexuality, visceral activity and indeed violence. The leaders in this field were mostly men, like Otto Muehl, Hermann Nitsch and Günter Brus, though one should also include the female artist Valie Export. Handke, too, was born in Austria and went to university there at Graz, though perhaps surprisingly he studied law, not literature. But then again his use of language in *Offending the Audience* was made up of words with precise meanings, typical of the world of law. Again, if words are the key in this piece, then we have to bring in another Austrian, the philosopher Wittgenstein, as another influence, for his "acceptance only of that reality which can be verified by the physical senses".

Another pivotal moment on the stage in London occurred in November 1965 when Edward Bond's play *Saved* opened at the Royal Court. Whilst the play was attacked by most critics – "loathed" is the word its director William Gaskill used – it attracted attention because it was staged in defiance in its uncensored form, using the conditions of a 'theatre club' production, since the Lord Chamberlain's Office had refused to issue a public performance licence unless two scenes were rewritten. However, this tactic didn't stop prosecution, or it being found guilty, though ultimately *Saved* was instrumental in having the redundant practice of theatre censorship removed. Whilst particular obscenities were excused, the main cause for the furore was the park scene in which a baby in its pram is taunted, abused and finally stoned to death by a group of 'louts'. I put that in inverted commas because Bond, as well as its director Gaskill, would argue that they are not any different from the rest of us, and that is in part the aim of the play. "I think what's marvellous about *Saved*," wrote Gaskill in the programme for its second season in repertory, "is that Bond shows this absolutely clearly – he shows you a sequence of scenes which cover a wide range of people's existence – both of ordinary life, their love affairs, their home life, *and* their acts of violence. When the mother hits the father with the teapot it is meant to be an action as violent as the killing of the baby. When Himmler ordered the destruction of Lidice, there are famous descriptions of the way he said goodbye to his wife and kissed his children and to him there was no inconsistency between an absolutely warm sentimental home life and an act of extreme brutality. I think unless you can relate one to the other – unless you are prepared to comprehend both as part of the problem – you will never ever solve the problem or begin to

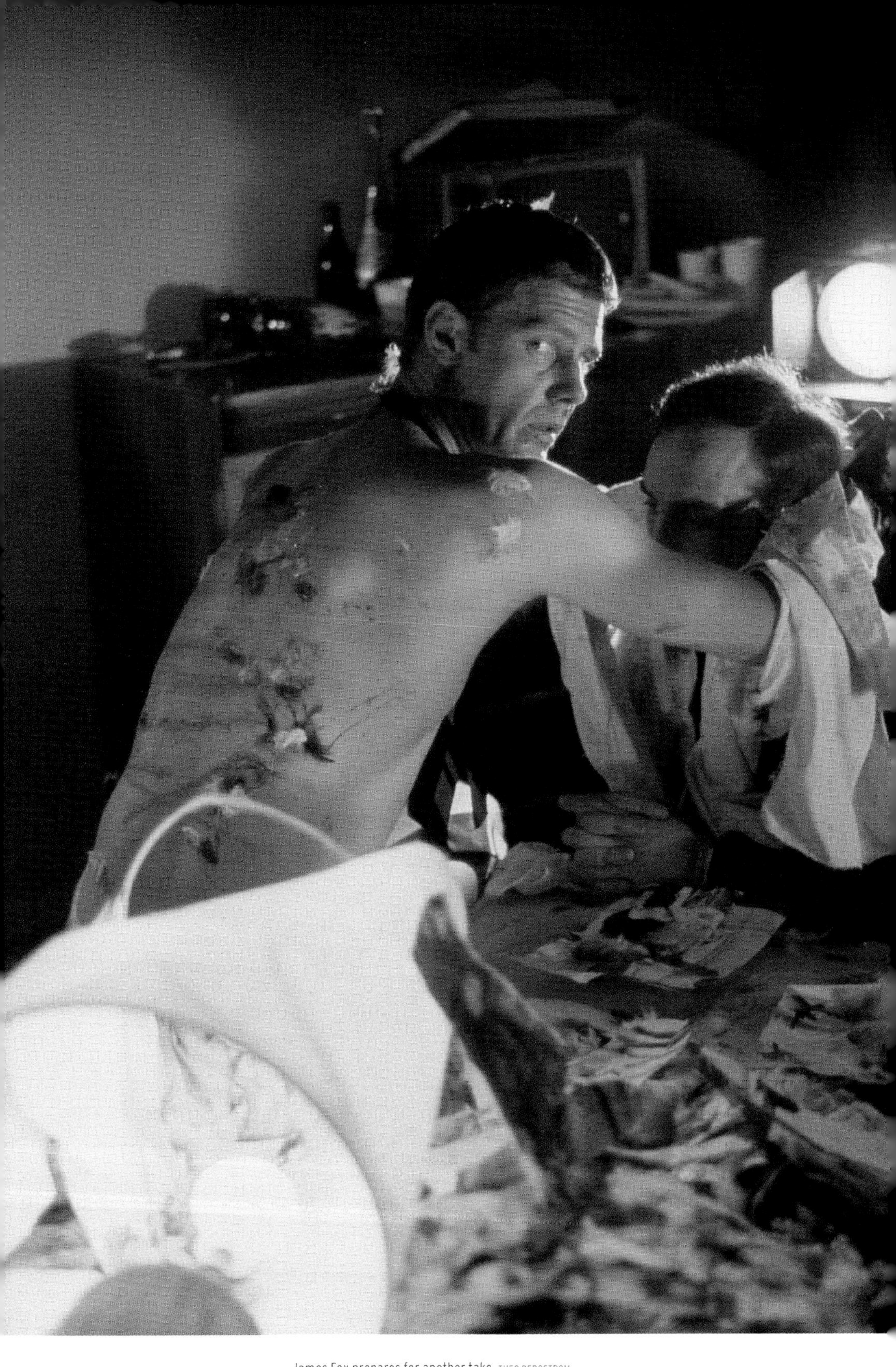

James Fox prepares for another take. THEO BERGSTROM

Redecorating Chas' flat. WARNER BROS

Joey Maddocks' boys set about their revenge. WARNER BROS

Pherber applies red to Turner's lips. ANDREW MACLEAR/HULTON ARCHIVE/GETTY IMAGES

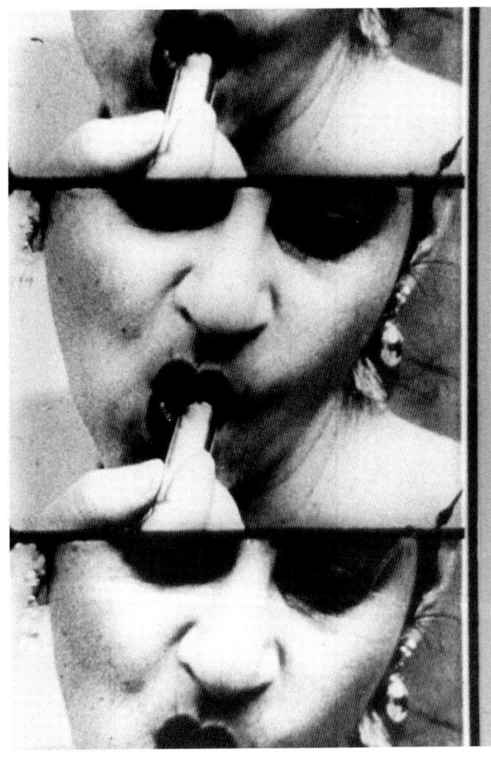

Lipstick has its scene in Jack Smith's *Flaming Creatures* (1963).

Antonin Artaud in *Les Cenci* in 1935. ROGER VIOLLET

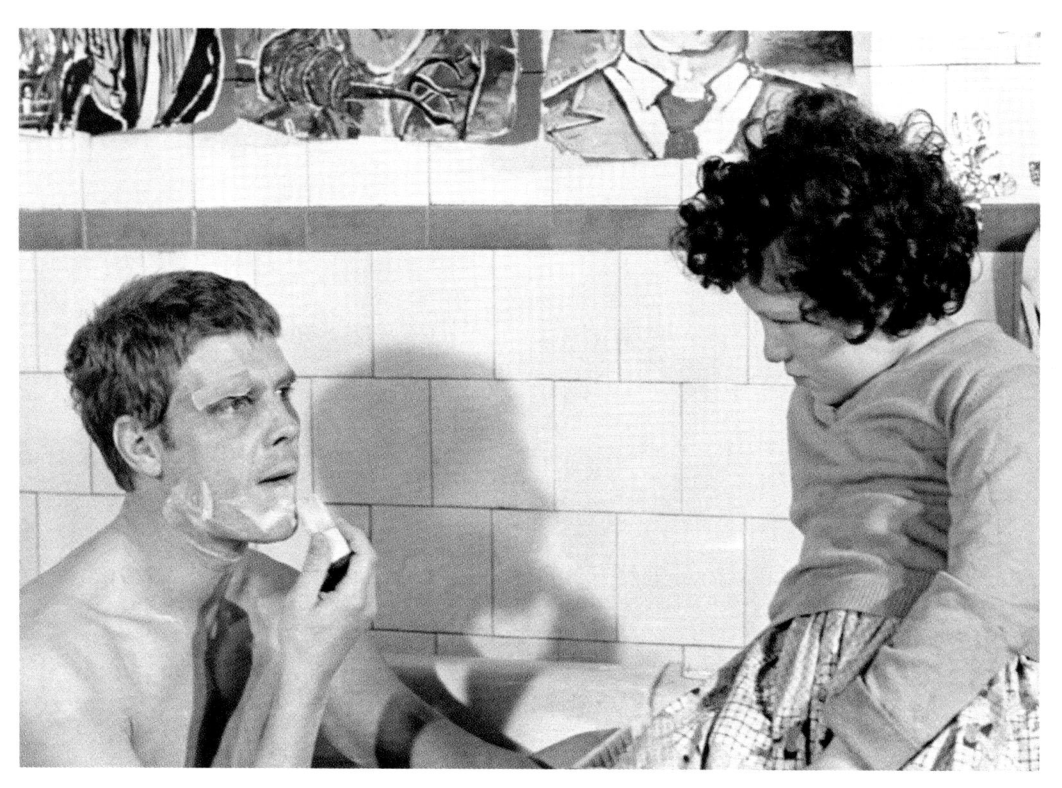

Lorraine watches Chas as he cleans up. KEYSTONE FEATURES/GETTY IMAGES

Turner, Pherber and Lucy have more to do than clean up. THE KOBAL COLLECTION/WARNER/GOODTIMES

Turner picks up Chas' conclusion: "I just… you know, perform". THE KOBAL COLLECTION/WARNER/GOODTIMES

Turner shows his skill as a juggler of words. WARNER BROS/PHOTOFEST

Chas realises the identity of his landlord. WARNER BROS

Pherber is not so keen on Chas' colour change. WARNER BROS/PHOTOFEST

The search for a new image begins. THEO BERGSTROM

Turner watches over Chas being dismantled. UNITED ARCHIVES GMBH/ALAMY

Jagger searches for another route. WARNER BROS

Pherber on the Persian carpet. THE KOBAL COLLECTION/WARNER/GOODTIMES

Jagger uses his Polaroid between takes. BARON WOLMAN

understand it. I think Bond understands that more than anything – that you cannot isolate the act of violence as one of horror."

Penelope Gilliatt's initial review in *The Observer* was notable for its defence of the play, making a very pertinent point: "Though the vernacular language may make the play look like 'a slice of life', a phrase that is used to mean a very inferior slab of theatrical fruit cake, the truth is that the prose is skilfully stylised. It uses a hard, curt unit of dialogue, a statement of panic masquerading as an attack, hardly ever more than five or six syllables to a line. People don't elaborate; they stab in the dark, the dagger turns into rubber or a wisp of fog, and the bad dream has already left them behind."

What Bond wanted to show with his play, his ideas about violence and that society itself is inherently aggressive because society is basically unjust, was probably not understood at the time. "There is no way out for our sort of society, an unjust society must be violent."

As we've seen, Marianne Faithfull's relationship with the Royal Court began when she played in Edward Bond's version of Chekhov's *Three Sisters* (April 1967) and then in Bond's own *Early Morning*, directed by William Gaskill, in March 1968, a play that was not without its own scandal, with its depiction of Queen Victoria and Florence Nightingale (Marianne) as lesbian lovers. The second Sunday night performance was cancelled after police pressure, the licensee of the theatre withdrawing permission for it to be staged even in club circumstances. It seems that 'her indoors' at Buckingham Palace was quite fond of her great-great-grandmother and let it be known that "enough was enough".

Away from the theatre with its proscenium arch, there was an underground theatre in the making, both here and in America. Jeff Nuttall's The People Show was active in underground London during the late Sixties, and written about in *International Times*, even if it was not seen by all the protagonists of *Performance*. Two seminal examples of early shows when Nuttall was a key component are worth citing. The first occurred in the basement of Better Books in the Charing Cross Road during early 1967 and was called *A Nice Quiet Night*. Of course it was anything but. Jeff notes in an article (in *Unit 10*, Tony Elliott's forerunner to *Time Out*, edited while he was at Keele University), 'Thoughts of chairman me': "I have a trick of writing what I know of performers' secret problems into the script and constructing the show around them. In *A Nice Quiet Night* I did this for Laura and it worked to such a degree that Laura was crying for hours after each performance, but what a performance." What Nuttall was referring to was the point in the piece with Laura Gilbert hanging upside down from a butcher's hook, next to the carcass of a side of beef that had been allowed to hang for a couple of days, but not to the point of being maggot-ridden. The echo of Chaim Soutine's use of a hanging carcass was obvious, as indeed was the visit of Hermann Nitsch for the DIAS 'action'. Mark Long and John Darling were in the process of baiting Laura when a member of the audience stood up and called for a halt to the performance. He was a psychiatrist and said that Laura was being harmed. That might well have been true, but Laura was keen to pursue this action. In fact, Jeff says she was interested in "audience assault". Mark turned on the intruder and set about insulting him with a string of abuse: "Who did he think he was? What right did he have to . . ." to such a degree that those present thought it was a set-up, some audience participation. But it wasn't. The assault on Laura was eventually resumed with renewed aggression until she was left devastated at the end. I understood it took her an hour or more to come down after each performance. Whatever your views on the matter, this is what was happening in London at the time.

Nuttall writes in his memoirs: "Her insistence on continuing with the piece made the show a ritual testing ground for all of us. I got letters calling me a bastard. We knew we were into something very serious, something slightly beyond any of our warring contentions, a certain weird collective magic . . ."

Another time, shortly after, in August 1967, the audience at another show, *People Show Number Sixteen* at the Arts Laboratory in Drury Lane, was ushered into four cages made from old bedspring bases and chicken wire. Once they were locked in, the performance began. Besides the assault with noise, and with poking bits of cloth drenched in disinfectant through the netting of the cages, at some point audience members were taken out and interrogated at a table with a torch shone in their faces.

The People Show, who were always termed 'experimental improvisionary theatre', came about through the meeting of actors with Jeff Nuttall and Laura Gilbert, both artists. Jeff drew on his interests in painting, collage and assemblage, as well as the influence of the Happenings in America by Allan Kaprow and Robert Rauschenberg. For Nuttall it could not last on that level. In effect, the others were not aggressive enough: "they were concerned with *theatre*, with communication, entertainment, character, message, plot, presentation and they were not concerned with aesthetics, musical values, abstraction, except as possible props, effects, something to bolster something specific."

Anyone wanting to know the true spirit underlying the arts at the time would do well not only to read Nuttall's counter-culture criticism, *Bomb Culture* (1968), or various contributions to *International Times*, but also to seek out one of his novels, such as *The Case of Isabel and the Bleeding Foetus* (1967), or to read about *My Own Mag* and his relationship with Burroughs, whom he published.

Mention has been made of Anita Pallenberg's connection to The Living Theatre, with whom she had some involvement earlier in New York, before they felt they had no choice but to expel themselves from their homeland in 1963 and become a travelling theatre, mainly around Europe. During 1967, when Anita was filming *Barbarella* in Rome, some of her social time was spent in the company of the troupe and their two founders, Julian Beck and Judith Malina. As a result, any of Anita's friends who visited were also introduced. The knot tightened to the extent that when The Living Theatre came to London, a number of them stayed in Robert Fraser's Mount Street flat, much to the chagrin of Paul Getty, who was staying there when in London.

The Living Theatre was formed in the late Forties, based primarily on ideas around Antonin Artaud, whom Judith called "my madman muse", and his concepts of theatre as explained in texts which were published in English as *The Theater and its Double* (Grove Press, 1958) in order, in Artaud's words, "to restore to the theatre a passionate and convulsive concentration of life". What has always been difficult in trying to work with Artaud's ideas is that Artaud himself was never able to put them fully into practice, as those around him in the Thirties would not extend their boundaries far enough. In a way, The Living Theatre, and others, have taken on and explored the territory he mapped out. Beck and Malina, with their travelling hippie troupe, were able to live and work in a more communal sense.

In 1964, the first piece of theirs that truly created Theatre of Cruelty was called *Mysteries and Smaller Pieces*, but it was their version of *Frankenstein* that became their tour de force in Artaudian senses. It used as source material Mary Shelley's novel and various Frankenstein films to weave together fragments of the tale "through three acts of ritual, myth, dreams, nightmares, hallucinations, magic, legends, prisons, ancient sciences, and contemporary civilisation".

A key essayist of the period, Susan Sontag, wrote in *Theatre and Film* (1966) that "the source of the idea of art as an act of violence pervading cinema and theatre is the aesthetics of Futurism and of Surrealism; its principal texts are, for theatre, the writings of Artaud and, for cinema, two films of Luis Buñuel, *L'Age d'Or* and *Un Chien Andalou.* (More recent examples: the early plays of Ionesco, at least as conceived; the "cinemas of cruelty" of Hitchcock, Clouzot, Franju, Robert Aldrich, Polanski; work by the Living Theatre; some of the neo-cinematic light shows in experimental theatre and discotheques; the sound of late Cage and LaMonte Young.) The relation of art to an audience understood to be passive, inert, surfeited, can only be assault. Art becomes identical with aggression."

She pointed out the danger of it becoming a convention in itself, "reinforcing rather than challenging the deadness of the audience". She was adamant that "the depth of the assault" must mean not "diluting" Artaud. She noted that no work in the theatre had captured what Artaud's writings express, "the demand for a totally open (therefore flayed, self-cruel) consciousness of which theatre would be one adjunct or instrument".

When Peter Brook offered a disclaimer to his company's work on Artaud's Theatre of Cruelty, which culminated in *Marat/Sade*, Sontag suggested that whilst Brook might have thought his work was trivial in on Artaudian senses, she didn't. Another essay in 1965, a review of Brook's staging of Weiss' *Marat/Sade* at the Royal Shakespeare Company's Aldwych Theatre in London, has her note that "Weiss does not present ideas as much as he immerses his audience in them. Intellectual debate is the material of the play, but it is not its subject or its end. The Charenton (madhouse) setting insures that this debate takes place in a constant atmosphere of barely suppressed violence: all ideas are volatile at this temperature."

This, too, was taken on board in October 1966, with Peter Brook's anti-Vietnam production, *US*, staged for the RSC in London's Aldwych Theatre. Brook clearly saw it as a full-scale assault on an English audience's nerves, prejudices and emotions, for the theatre "has one precise social function, to disturb the spectator".

The reason why his company was able to do this play was that Brook had brought over Jerzy Grotowski, the Polish director, to work with his actors some months before, working on their own selves as actors, getting down to the "fundamental problem of what that something is that stirs in a man when he is doing what is called acting". What still resonates from that production is Adrian Mitchell's poem, 'To Whom It May Concern', its accumulating repeat motif at the end of each couplet, until it ripens and rips out: "You put your bombers in, you put your conscience out, / You take the human being and you twist it all about / So scrub my skin with women / Chain my tongue with whisky / Stuff my nose with garlic / Coat my eyes with butter / Fill my ears with silver / Stick my legs in plaster / Tell me lies about Vietnam." Fortunately Mitchell's own haunting rendition of it is preserved in Peter Whitehead's *Wholly Communion*, a recording of the 1965 Albert Hall Poetry Reading.

All these works tell us that man is an aggressive creature, that to describe our violence towards each other as 'animal', 'brutal' or 'bestial' is wrong, as man is almost the only creature/vertebrate (the exceptions are some rodents) who "habitually destroys members of his own species", who takes "positive pleasure in the exercise of cruelty upon another of his own kind". Though we might recoil in horror at various atrocities we read about in the papers or see on television, we know that each of us harbours "those same savage impulses" which can lead us to murder and other acts of violence and aggression.

In *Performance*, this is what Jagger seeks to fire in himself, to pump himself up so that he can again take to the stage. Not love and peace, but an unleashing of the aggression that is his demon.

Aggression is a word that, as the psychiatrist Anthony Storr says, is "fairly bursting at its seams". We expect it to be good and bad. We use it as a positive for competitiveness in sport, or indeed for the challenges of business in the workplace, as much as we do for the violence of the villain or the soldier. We deplore one, yet we need the other to survive. As Storr says: "When a child rebels against authority it is being aggressive: but it is also manifesting a drive towards independence which is a necessary and valuable part of growing up. There's nothing wrong with 'attacking' problems."

Cut.

9) nothing is as it seems (1)

A JET fighter streaks across the sky, a thunderous sound assaulting our ears. A black car slices across the screen, across "England's green and pleasant land", but we are not destined to spend our time in the countryside. We are city bound. The black car, a Rolls-Royce, pulls up outside a Surrey country pub, The Black Swan. Pulls up again. The Black Swan, Ockham. A couple 'making love' flash at us. We will accept fast editing cuts, but not a shot repeating itself. This is not real. This is a film. "I am a film." It couldn't be clearer. Ingmar Bergman's *Persona*, two years previously, had made it apparent from its opening frames that we were watching a film, an artifice, when it showed the mechanics of a film, the source of the light, the projection in operation. There is to be no mistake. I am a film. And, what is more, this is going to be an assault on your senses. This is to be a living experience. You'll either love it. Or hate it. You might throw up. Or you might sink back, settle into your seat, into a world where the pleasure of the text is paramount. This is *Performance*. The title is lined up on the edge of a mirror, the back of the mirror. We are being framed for Antonin Artaud's total theatre in film terms.

The jet fighter was a high-performance plane. One of those in service at the time, like the English Electric Lightning F.6, climbing fast, sound crescendoing, something in the region of an impressive 36,000 feet in less than three minutes from break release, shooting across the sky at speeds of 1,300 mph. This is a class act. But this plane is not British. It's probably an American fighter, perhaps footage from a test model for the F-15, thrusting and streaking across the sky, its vapour trail leaving a temporary scar on the clear blue.

The car that claws and scratches its way across the screen is a Rolls-Royce. Who is the owner? We are not going to know for a while. The windows are blacked out and, even though the camera zooms in on the window to "have a look", we learn almost nothing. All we know is that it is around lunchtime, for the pubs at that time, whether countryside or otherwise, did not open until mid to late morning. The chauffeur eats his pie, a quick bite, as he shines the bonnet, almost to mirror satisfaction. He is proud of his owner's car, his car. Perhaps a bird has decorated it en route. If this is to be the lawyer's car, coming in from his home in the 'sticks' for a day's business in the courts, it is strange that he will be arriving halfway through the morning, for the courts start earlier. It's as if this is another day, the previous one, or the one after. Yesterday. Tomorrow. Time sequences are shifting, are going to be roughed up, thrown around a little.

But we barely notice. There is sex on the screen. We have to be attentive because the images are coming fast and furious. The editing is 'blink of an eye' material. We don't want to miss something revealing. A man, looking pretty handsome and fit, is bedding a young woman. They seem to be enjoying themselves, but then again perhaps not. They seem to be performing for each other. There is violence. Pleasure comes from the violence. A whip is produced. He has it wrapped around her neck and seems to be half-strangling her. He certainly slaps her around the face, playfully, for he is not going to damage her face. He can only achieve satisfaction from violence. The young woman returns the pleasure, scratches and claws at his back a bit more than playfully; they must be her own nails.

And then it is over. We miss the climax, if indeed there was one.

Or perhaps there was, because the flashes cut the bed scene across the bonnet of the Rolls-Royce coming full on at us with its mascot, the Spirit of Ecstasy, also known as 'the Flying Lady', clearly evident. The commissioned figurine for Lord Montagu's Rolls-Royce Silver Ghost was based on a young woman, Eleanor Thornton, his secretary, made by Charles Sykes; the initial version with her fluttering robes had one finger held to her lips, and was called *The Whisper*, which related to the secret relationship between the secretary and Lord Montagu. This was later adapted as the mascot taken up for general use by Rolls-Royce.

We are treated to the tea-maker alarm sounding off. It is a quarter to three, not in the morning, the afternoon. First meal, breakfast. Straightaway we notice the dialogue is going to be sharp. We had better be astute. We can expect craft and sub-text. This is a world where Harold Pinter has had an influence, carved his name into the woodwork. His early play, *The*

Birthday Party (1958), springs to mind, the breakfast ritual, before the menace arrives in the shape of the visitors.

When Dana speaks to Chas, for those are the names of the couple we've watched perform, it's almost like the opening of *The Birthday Party*. If the film scene was extended, you could imagine it developing in a parallel fashion. In Pinter, Petey returns home for his breakfast after his first stint on the beach preparing the deckchairs. "Is that you?" his wife Meg asks, knowing it is. "Yes, it's me," he replies. She puts her head through the hatch: "Are you back?" He affirms. "I've got your cornflakes ready," she says and brings them to the hatch for him to collect, take to the table and eat while reading the paper propped up before him.

No sooner does he start spooning them into his mouth than she asks: "Are they nice?" "Very nice," he responds, as always. "I thought they'd be nice." This is the way Pinter unravels his characters, tells us so much through astute observation. Meg sits and watches him eat, then asks, as usual: "You got your paper?" He doesn't look up from reading, affirms. "Is it good?" "Not bad." "What does it say?" "Nothing much."

"You're up," Dana says. As with Pinter, we are all liable to make such obvious remarks. "Cornflakes or Rice Krispies?"

Dana is not Chas' regular girl. She makes that quite clear as she pokes around in the kitchenette for breakfast, mutters "confirmed bachelor, aren't you?" Is this the first time? It could be the last time, I don't know. Oh no, he says he'll pick her up later. Or, perhaps. She can't get him to confirm a time. He wants her out, he wants to tidy up.

And though we might suggest scratching of backs as some form of sado-masochistic pleasure, each era has playful sexual peccadilloes. Love bites might be in fashion at one period. Scratching backs at another. 'Stray Cat Blues', on the Stones' *Beggars Banquet* album, recorded just prior to filming *Performance*, tells of a man with a 15-year-old groupie, later reduced to 13 on live renditions: "I bet your mama don't know you can bite like that / I'll bet she never saw you scratch my back."

There is the whip to account for; we'll bear that in mind. Not everyone has one at the back of the wardrobe.

Dana's a singer. Another performer. We notice Chas smokes Lark cigarettes. His entertainment revolves around performers. The door of his wardrobe swings shut, its mirror reflecting tacked-up photos of Frank

Sinatra, a boxer and a model girlfriend, amongst others. His chest of drawers bears reminders: a 'Talk of the Town' programme, a publicity sheet for Sammy Davis Jr and friends, and an invitation card to the Scotch of St James, a nightclub where villains like the Kray twins and their associates had been known to mix with the new rock and pop stars of the times, similar to the Ad Lib, Speakeasy, Blaise's . . . Chas couldn't care a damn about Dana's singing. She was just sex for the night. He makes that clear as he hustles her out the door, their next assignation left in the balance. In fact when Dana leaves the flat, she leaves the film. Her part was brief, perhaps briefer than it might have been. Perhaps a substantial amount was left on the floor, along with her clothes. But Ann Sidney has no regrets. "It made sense in establishing the character of Chas, as far as his main desires, his wants, where he was going, the fact that he had no respect for women." Initially the part was pencilled in for Vicki Hodge, Johnny Bindon's partner at the time, keeping it all in the family, but the actor's union, Equity, wouldn't allow it.

Chas needs to tidy up. He is quite fastidious about his appearance, and the state of his living conditions. Everything has its place, whether on the side dresser, with his pen, watch, cuff-links, money, etc laid out in orderly fashion when he undresses at night, or his underwear and clothes neatly folded away in drawers or hanging in cupboards. Or his magazines and papers on the coffee table in his living room.

The set for Chas' place was constructed in the drawing room at Lowndes Square. There's something familiar about this flat. It seems to have echoes of an image that we know. It is not a direct copy of an image, but it is certainly a kind of 'homage', though Cammell said he didn't like using the word homage when questioned about his use of the artist Francis Bacon. "It's very easy to say homage. Every time one copies someone you say it's an homage. So I copied some of, maybe not literally, but I copied in my heart." This flat bears a resemblance to the world depicted in Richard Hamilton's art, particularly the famous collage *Just what is it that makes today's homes so different, so appealing?*, made for This Is Tomorrow, the 1956 exhibition at the Whitechapel Art Gallery. This Is Tomorrow was an interdisciplinary group exhibition, drawing together artists, architects, graphic designers and musicians, a way to bind fine and applied arts. The collage was made as a catalogue illustration and for use on the poster.

The show is often regarded as the key to the birth of British Pop Art, with Hamilton's contribution putting him at the forefront, though he always refused to be left holding the Pop Art baby, whether as its father or grandfather. He had more to do than be stuck with a label.

After the Redlands bust the *Swingeing London* image created by Hamilton, using the press cuttings from his art dealer, Robert Fraser, made his name even more noticeable to the circle around Cammell, Jagger and their friends, as is evident from Hamilton's involvement with The Beatles around this time. He produced the artwork for their next record, *The White Album*.

Just what is it . . . has become *the* founding image of British Pop Art, with its living-room scene, cold and sterile, a reflection of and genuflection to the new religion of modern consumerism and the use of gadgetry. The work lifts quotations from sources like advertising and popular culture, what Hamilton labelled as "self-confessed plagiarism". One cannot fail to notice that the ceiling of the image is a view of Earth from space, whereas the ground is sand in a faraway exotic country, hardly divorced from the opening and closing images of *Performance* itself. "My 'home' would have been incomplete without its token life-force, so Adam and Eve struck a pose along with the rest of the gadgetry," Hamilton said. His 'ideal home' beings are a Charles Atlas-type bodybuilder and a derivative Marilyn, taken from an erotic magazine, both posing for the viewer. Only here in *Performance* we have our own British Atlas, a fit man, who wakes up in the morning, does a few limbering squat exercises, flexes his arm muscles by locking his hands and pulling them tight. And here is our Marilyn, Dana, played by Ann Sidney, the former Miss United Kingdom and Miss World.

But that's only half the picture. The kitchenette, the whole view of the bathroom, the living room, all with their pale blue, white and cream colours, link through to Hamilton's other paintings from that era, termed *Interiors*. But these are not direct copies, they are a continued sense of homage, and have a direct relationship to the adverts and publicity that inspired Hamilton. This is acknowledged by the further use of such composed establishing shots throughout the early part of the film, until the point when Joey Maddocks decides redecoration of the flat is in order and brings in his mates with their paint and tools to do the work. At that point, Roeg's establishing shots and angles bear no relation to the Hamilton framings in its earlier fastidious stage. Thus, here, as we see Dana moving around the kitchenette and the living room, we know she is the advertiser's idea of the ideal woman, not dressed as the housewife doing her daily chores, but as the woman who doesn't look like she soils her hands, dressed in smart casual clothes, or still wearing the clothes from the night before.

This is the future, the look based on America, the land that Harry Flowers and his associates aspire to in a theoretical sense, "progress", even if they do not wish to move there. America, the land to which Chas will later want to escape.

America, for Dana too, is also the place she aspires to, the American Dream, as her voice is being wasted where she performs now, in London.

The red light is on.

Why should Dana dab a red spot of nail varnish on her face? This is a disturbing use of red. We understand red will be a featured colour in this film, but surely applying red lipstick would do the job, if indeed she is making a beauty spot. But she isn't. It's a mistake, a distraction, for it is removed after that moment. It's a painterly gesture, a red in the mirror's reflection. We will have to watch it spread.

As they both go about the routines of dressing and applying various deodorants and make-up, there is no sign of showers or washing as one would see today; perhaps we must reason that the viewer has had their quota of nudity already. All they need are mirrors to watch what they do, and to prepare their images. Mirrors at every turn . . . "for narcissistic purposes".

Jimmy Evans says he was a natty dresser. The dress sense in *Performance* is not quite on the same level as that of Ronnie and Reggie Kray, both very conscious of their attire, adopting the dark blue suits of one of their heroes, the film star gangster George Raft. Sharp suits, white shirts and tightly knotted slim silk ties were the order of the day, not only for themselves but also for their associates. "Never anything out of place. That was what it was all about," said Tony Lambrianou, one of their boys. He was proud when either Kray would comment, "I do like that suit, Tony." Ronnie couldn't stand anybody looking flash, even though he developed quite a taste for jewellery: a large gold ring, a gold bracelet watch and diamond cuff-links. Their biographer, John Pearson, in a recent book that fills in details left aside in his earlier classic on the boys, notes: "They wouldn't dream of fighting anyone, still less of killing him, unless they were wearing ties." (A point to bear in mind when Chas goes about his killings.)

This is what performing is all about. And we are moving fast. There is information to be offered. We still do not know where we are, or whom we are with.

Doors and other things are continually closing at the start: a wardrobe door, a bedside drawer, a car door and car window, all can be seen as links for editing purposes, but equally they can be seen as a statement on life being about closing doors, enclosures, whereas later on it's about opening the doors (of perception). We need to keep our eyes wide for any openings.

And as yet we've not had time to pick up on the fragment of the first song on the soundtrack, Randy Newman singing 'Gone Dead Train'. It will have its time eventually. After all, it was layered in afterwards, when the film was completed, when there was a question mark over the "empty cellar" and the "train is done gone dead", to quote the original blues number with the same title.

"Morning, Rosie," Chas says as he climbs into the back of a Rover Coupé. As it pulls away we see a white Jaguar parked nearby in the parking lot. Chas has driven his car there and transferred to the company car. But is this morning? Perhaps it's similar to the idea of breakfast as the first meal, no matter what the time of day. It is afternoon as morning: 3.20 was the time on the clock when we last saw it. Morning starts late. Everything is topsy-turvy here. Vice versa to the life of the majority.

Chas calls him Rosie. His name is Rosebloom. We've yet to meet the boss, Harry Flowers. These names don't necessarily show an interest in horticulture, or the proximity of the Chelsea Flower Show. We are running alongside references to Jean Genet, a world with homosexual preferences. But Chas is Chas Devlin; nothing untoward in his name it would seem.

Riding around in black cars, there is a sense of death understated. But as noted, Chas has a white Jaguar parked to one side, or we will recall that it is his, once we've seen the film a few times, and again, having watched the film before, we know that the final car ride will be in a white Rolls-Royce. We would naturally think this is unusual, unless the final ending is some form of bid to be on the side of the angels, or some form of spiritual transcendence. The reverse was shown in Orson Welles' *The Lady from Shanghai*, where Rita Hayworth starts out dressed in white, or almost white, showing she is on the side of good, but as the film proceeds she moves towards black, so that the final shots are heavily laden with death and doom.

There is some pace involved in these opening sections. And we haven't stopped. We can't stop. We can catch up later.

The question is, once they set out on their 'morning' business, will they find workers in their offices? Better get a move on and go directly to those who might still be at their desks. Unless this is another day, of course.

Rosebloom and Moody engage in chat as they go about their routines, like most of the working populace, their attention drawn to the previous evening's viewing on television, when the family were gathered around the small screen in the corner. At that time it was unheard of for a house to own more than one television, which was positioned in the living room, as it was the family entertainment. There were only three channels: BBC1, BBC2 and ITV. BBC2 was first treated to the use of colour in 1967, whilst the main channels – BBC1 and ITV – went to colour in 1969. The Beatles' *Magical Mystery Tour* was originally shown in black and white on Boxing Day in 1967, and repeated a few days later in colour on BBC2. That a film so obviously reliant on colour should have to be offered first in black and white seems unimaginable today. Moody, played by Johnny Bindon, talks about the disgraceful sight on television the previous night, the level of violence not being acceptable. One step further and he'd be a subscriber to Mary Whitehouse and her brigade for the 'clean up TV' campaign, another thorn in the side of society at the time. The criminal fraternity can be extremely moral on some fronts without realising the contradictions in their behaviour.

Rosebloom, seated next to him in the other front seat, agrees that it is a disgusting situation, or at least says the words without much show of emotion, as will be his way throughout.

Then reality steps back in. "Where to, Chas?" Moody asks from behind the wheel. "That car hire garage." We have yet to see these three men at work. We are not sure what their business is exactly, that it will be violence, on a daily basis.

We have gained little clue from their language. Swearing is out. To use 'fuck' in its adjectival form might be prevalent (and even accepted) in just about any environment today, but in the late Sixties it was not. One used restraint. One allowed other words to convey aggression. And if one had limited vocabulary, one placed an emphasis on other words, innocuous words if need be, in such a way that you made good words sound bad. Though here, when Moody almost has a brush with another car, he abuses the driver, "you bastard foreign female", managing with those few words to show a level of denigration that hits the nail on the head at each count for him.

So far women have played no role, other than for Chas' sexual entertainment – I'm not sure that 'pleasure' is the right word. Here the unseen woman is the bad driver, which was accepted fare for the time. Women were intended as passengers, not drivers. No bus or taxi would be driven by anyone but a male. The reasoning went along the lines that women would be distracted, would turn their head at the sight of a dress shop window display, and other such nonsense. Women were incapable of focussing on the road ahead, and thus would potentially cause an accident. This sounds like a terrible indictment, but it was how things were to a certain extent.

In order to remind us that dress sense is important, and that our three men are businessmen, not thugs, Rosebloom tells Moody that he is not dressed properly: "put your tie on". You cannot go about daily business dressed scruffily. Bindon puts it on as they prepare to make their entrance.

Chas and his two associates, Rosebloom and Moody, are 'enforcers', a term used in a similar fashion to the police. They enforce the law, the law as writ, or spoken, by the higher echelons in their community. As Ronnie Kray, or the Kray twins as an entity, are noted as the role models for this aspect of the film, it might be a good idea to devote a few moments to one of their enforcers, Albert Donoghue, their right-hand man for many years, who turned against them later when the game was up and the courts were in business, their business. He had been asked to take the fall for Frank Mitchell's murder, but didn't see fit to.

Donoghue's job was to do the 'milk round' on a Friday, going to see their 'subscribers', collecting the weekly 'pension', as protection money was named. The Firm, as the Krays' organisation was called, was much like any other business. Every morning they met at nine at the Krays' home in Vallence Road to discuss any information anyone had "got from the night before", and then planned the day's business, "who to visit, who to use, who to take, who was going to drive".

Donoghue outlines other 'missions', like when a robbery has taken place and they try to muscle in on the rewards, for a one-off payment: "If he says, 'I'm not going to give you any money,' you don't jump all over him there and then. You come back to the Twins and you say, 'He's not going to pay.'" In that case you take three or four of the guys "and you give him a talking-to. You send him to hospital for a couple of days and then you talk to him again."

But in general, with the normal 'clients', direct violence was not the way to conduct oneself. "You never threatened people or smashed the place up. You'd say, 'Look, you're opening the gaff, and we're looking after it. So where do we come in?' Then the club owner would offer, say £50, and there'd be a bit of haggling until an agreement was struck."

Donoghue emphasises that straight pubs or bookmakers were out. "We only collected off crooked people, or off people who were dealing with crooked people." As he saw it, the sums were not colossal, "but a tenner in the Sixties would be worth, say, £150 today. So as my total weekly collection was around £200, it's as if today I'm walking around with £3,000 cash in my pocket every Friday." His own 'pension' was £25 a week, "but Reggie would give me 10 per cent of any other business we put together, so that would bring me in another £50. So I was picking up £75 a week in all from the Firm in those days. That's around £1,200 today."

That was the reality of the Firm, "hustling day-to-day, night after night", not the way they've been written and spoken about, "the three known murders".

Basically, as Donoghue puts it, they were all "just parasites. Thieves' ponces. (...) We'd find out who's just had a tickle and go in. It's a despicable form of crime, nothing to be proud of, but we didn't even pretend to have pride in our craft. We weren't top-notch master criminals. We were just bloody thugs, simple as that. Leeches."

Cab companies were easy pickings. Once you'd taken them over, you'd phone other cab companies in the area and let them know who's connected to the company, so they didn't interfere. One method to debilitate a rival was to get the drivers called out on 'scrub calls', which means that they would arrive at the address to find nobody there. By threatening rivals that you would 'disconnect your wiring', business was booming. In one deal that Donoghue did as a private enterprise, away from the Krays, the owner of the cab company "was giving me 60 per cent, but his turnover was so much increased that he was probably getting twice as much money himself. I did the man a favour. I did myself a favour, but I saved his business. Look at it that way. Today, when they bring these big guys in to big companies – management consultants – they do the same thing. They nick a bit, don't they? Far more than we thugs ever did. So, business consultant I was, already."

The entrance of Flowers' men into the car hire firm had been tried out earlier, while James Fox was fitting himself out for his role, taking on board the necessary traits, marching into the film production office of Goodtimes Enterprises, flexing his muscles to see how convincing his act would be. He succeeded. The women in the office were terrified. No one seemed to recognise him as Fox. No one said: "it's him, it's him, that's the one, innit?"

Successful intimidation is all a matter of stance, injecting fear into others without the need for overt violence. Here, everyone cowers, holds their breath. We note that the car hire workers are mainly women, as is to be expected. Poking and prodding and knocking a few files around does the trick. But just to re-enforce that business is intended, one large action is needed. Moody removes a vital piece of equipment from the wall, a radio transmitter, and allows it to crash to the floor, deriding it as "obsolete". What helps to heighten the sense of aggression throughout this scene is the use of computer noise as an irritant, at a level to pierce our eardrums.

A film that Donald Cammell had asked Jagger and Fox to see when it opened in London in December 1967 was John Boorman's *Point Blank*. It vibrated with violence, even using clear comic effect to emphasise the violence, something *Performance* hoped to mirror. That approach is seen when Boorman has Lee Marvin as Walker become a prospective buyer at the car business of the man he wants to gain information from. Big John doesn't pay enough attention to Walker, as a pretty female client has caught his eye, so Walker asks to take the large convertible for a ride. He drives off the road beneath the Los Angeles freeway, where Walker coolly and casually smashes the car back and forth against the concrete pillars, gradually reducing it to a heap, his victim wrecked too, abandoned to listen to his company's commercial on the local radio, the only part of the vehicle still fully operational.

As the enforcers go about their daily business, the lawyer, Harley-Brown, has arrived in court, which is, in this case, for filming, a large function room in Chelsea Old Town Hall, on the King's Road. Here, he proceeds to address the court, more particularly the jury, outlining how legitimate business is about merging big companies with smaller companies: "I say, merger, gentlemen, not takeover – words still have meanings even in our days of the computer." His presentation has a direct parallel with the world of the criminal organisation that is represented by Harry Flowers. Indeed, the reason he is standing there is because his client, Mr Fraser (a most unlikely comparison to Robert Fraser, but probably a private joke lurks somewhere), is involved with Harry Flowers, and has run into a spot of bother on procedures. The lawyer states that he does not intend to mince his words but to name names, and states that Harry Flowers should be in the dock, not his client. This idea does not go down too well with Flowers, who wants a quiet life. For him, "business is business, progress is progress". The lawyer believes that too. It just seems that they have different ways of comprehending that notion.

They both believe in mergers. And mergers are what we will see employed regularly.

There is a clever use of editing, so that scenes 'merge': a sentence started by Chas in one environment is finished by the lawyer in court, as a way to concertina scenes and ideas. Annabel Davis-Goff, responsible for continuity, recalls that one day when shooting the courtroom scene, Nic "gave the actor a whole page of dialogue rewritten the night before – difficult to learn and full of semi-meaningless legalese". As expected, the actor, Allan Cuthbertson, fluffed it a few times. Nic had given it to him "assuming he would have difficulty learning it, and wanted the times he broke down, looked lost, or even swore". Even if *Performance* has gained its longevity partly as a result of the re-editing of the film's first stages, it would still be intriguing to see the version that was twice as long in the first part.

When the barrister starts, he addresses the jury as "gentlemen of the jury", which is a correct observation, for they are all male. It's not that women were not called up to serve on juries, but there must have been various procedures at the time that restricted them. One recalls that in 1967, when Hubert Selby Jr's *Last Exit to Brooklyn* was taken to court for obscenity, the judge ordered, using the Sexual Disqualification Act of 1919, that the jury had to be all male because there might be some embarrassment in the jury room if men and women had to discuss the book together, particularly, one might hazard, the gang rape in the 'Tralala' section.

To emphasise that this is an all-male world, the next scene, for the shot dissolves the jury, or perhaps the word is 'merges', with the audience at a private Soho club watching seedy films. The film being projected features flagellation, a young woman having her panties lowered and then being flogged on the buttocks with a cat o'nine tails, lightly and playfully.

Behind the small auditorium, in fact a viewing theatre in Wardour Street, not a stone's throw from a real porn club, Chas sets about intimidating the Maltese owner for his 'pension'. There seems to be some resistance, but not enough to warrant destruction. A healthy punch or two and the 'clientele' is back in line. Healthy sex in the back room is noted too, with pin-up pictures of naked women on the wall. (Another 'normal' pursuit in operation that we will see pinned on the wall of the garage where the barrister houses his Rolls-Royce.) The Maltese with his limited vocabulary seems to be unaware of the ambiguities of his words, accusing Chas of "bleeding me white" as he hands over the money and calling the whole procedure "British justice", only for the camera to remind us that a flagellation scene is being screened close at hand and that the British justice system being admonished is called '*le vice anglais*' abroad. This type of 'perversion', as it was termed in the literature of the day, was also the mark of a good public school education, very much the world that the barrister himself, with his snooty voice, indicates he was reared in. Not that all flagellation and birching were the prerogative of a public school eduction; for the rest of the populace our state school punishment was usually restricted to caning on the hands, rarely then on the buttocks.

There are two women in attendance in the cramped conditions of the club, working as waitresses, servicing the customers with drinks.

The Argentinian writer Jorge Luis Borges makes his entrance in *Performance* in the hands of Rosebloom, who is waiting outside the private film club, seated in the back seat of the Rover, reading a copy of Borges' *A Personal Anthology*. No one would believe that a villain would ever be seen reading a literary book of this nature.

The hardcover book in Rosie's hands here – one that reappears twice during the film, once in Turner's hands, and finally resting behind a painting in Chas' friend's home – is not *Labyrinths* or *Fictions*. These were the two most common paperbacks available at the time: the former in a New Directions edition, imported from America, until Penguin issued it in 1970, and *Fictions* in a Calder edition (Jupiter series, 1965) with a photo of Borges on the cover. *A Personal Anthology*, which appeared not long before the film went into production in 1968, also featured a portrait of Borges, the one that recurs at the end of the film.

This is a film and we have to appreciate the double edge of the dagger being used. Books have appeared in films, often to dress a set, to lend an academic or learned atmosphere to a scene. Sometimes the books are for real, whilst at other times they are a fake display, just covers, or painted 'flats' as in the theatre, particularly if there are a huge number of them, a veritable Library of Babel right out of Borges' writings. Both Cammell and Roeg were deeply aware of the films of Jean-Luc Godard, where the use of books was almost a fetish. Sometimes books are held up for us to see the covers, as Karina does with Paul Eluard's *Capitale de la Douleur* in *Alphaville*, and other times they are read aloud to offer ideas. Magazines appear even more frequently.

Paul Mayersberg has a neat way of saying it in conversation when he calls it "elite product placement". His impression is that "the notion of inarticulate people, gangsters, reading sophisticated, so-called literary fiction, comes from a cross-cultural idea that Godard developed in many of his films of the Sixties where ordinary people and shop girls and soldiers are looking at fiction that they could not possibly have read". So that if "you put something in that is completely unlikely, improbable, if not impossible, you suddenly realise you are watching a film". What becomes interesting for Mayersberg in his reading of the situation is that by offering a Borges book to be displayed and used by the characters, Rosebloom in this case, "you would have to know about Borges, who was well known in literary circles" but was not known generally. Whereas "if it was Godard it would be Racine". In *Performance* "they don't quote Shakespeare. And they don't quote Dickens, and there's no reference to Thomas Hardy or George Eliot. In other words they are not from the past in that way, they are current culture, current counter-culture, even fads. They are not to do with what Godard was doing, which was to relate to a school, an academic past. Every child in school would have read Balzac and Racine and so forth. Maybe they didn't pay attention to it, but they would have read it, it would have been a set book, but what happens with this film, what was chosen was the current tastes of the makers of the film."

Roeg, of course, in this, his first film as director, even if sharing the director's seat, is continuing his relation with on-screen books which was the very subject of Truffaut's *Fahrenheit 451*, a search-and-destroy operation of all books. And not long before he had been photographing *Petulia* for Dick Lester in which there is a two-second shot at the Roller Derby of a disinterested teenager in the audience, presumably dragged there by a parent, who is oblivious to the action, casually reading *3 Lives* by Gertrude Stein, recognisable in the glimpse because of the distinct orange cover of its Vintage Book edition. To quote its back cover, extracted from the Stein academic Donald Sutherland: "Gertrude Stein in this work tried to coordinate the composition of the language with the process of consciousness." Was that careful addition from Lester, Roeg or another hand?

The idea that Rosebloom should read Borges while he waits for Chas to finish business is amusing, not only because of the contents of the book, particularly 'The South', which we will return to. I would suggest that if one wants to tap into a notion of the real world, there is another side to the blade, for it is a dagger. Already we have noticed that the back sill of the company car has *The Times* and *Illustrated London News* in prominent view, hardly the reading matter of these three men, one would surmise.

But something happened in that period in our prison systems. At one time the only activity one really had in prison to occupy one's time was sewing mailbags, and perhaps reading a newspaper or popular paperback, as well as being given a bit of exercise. However, there came a point, a time of reform, when these activities were expanded to take in grander ideas of education, working and exercising. Gyms were developed so that the incarcerated could keep fit. Other skills were encouraged, not only so one would be paid, but also so that one could learn a craft or skill. And education took on a serious purpose. Libraries grew and visiting teachers were drafted in to aid the inmates in their studies. Opportunities were given to those who had poor upbringings, and had never previously had a feasible chance of being educated. With years ahead of them, they read, studied and worked through a series of exams, culminating in university degrees for some. By the Sixties there were ex-villains emerging into the daylight who had degrees in literature and sociology, two favourites, the latter presumably because the prisoners could try to understand why they had gone down that path in the first place. Thus someone like John McVicar or Walter Probyn would publish books such as *McVicar Himself* and *Angel Face*. Others would follow over the years. And so men who had been deprived of learning started to become learned. Thus there is an implication here with Rosebloom reading Borges, if one wants it, that Rosebloom had been inside and acquired a taste for higher reading material than the mass market product.

In the synopsis Cammell provided for the financiers he introduces Rosebloom as someone "who reads good books", and Roeg in an interview suggests that "the intention was in fact to try to hint that he might be Harry Flowers' brother. Why does Harry Flowers put up with Rosebloom? Maybe because he's his brother." No other signs seem to develop that idea.

The Hit (1984), a decade or more later, wouldn't exist without *Performance.* The gangsters, whether those sent to kill Terence Stamp, or indeed Stamp himself, owe to Chas and Harry Flowers' boys. When *The Hit* opens we see Stamp lying on his bed in a witness protection flat, reading, or at the kitchen table reading, the book knocked aside by the plain-clothes cop, as we are to discover, jealous perhaps that Stamp reads and is en route to court to grass on his former friends. Why will he grass? Because he doesn't want 10 years in prison. Again, why? Has he been there before? That would be the implication. Perhaps he had already served a long stretch and that has given him the habit of reading. So the 10 years he spends in Spain, once relocated, is a strange freedom, because it is akin to another sentence, where he is cut off, house bound to a degree, spending his time reading, the wall of books a witness to the fact.

In public the boys refer to each other by different names. For the Maltese film club proprietor, Chas is Mr Molloy. I'm afraid there's only one Molloy. "How right you are." But rather than going down that

Beckettian path, we should look closer to home. Donald was, in fact, looking around the cramped filming space, thinking of a name to add, and looked straight at the cameraman, Mike Molloy.

The final stop of the night, accompanied by his two associates, sees Chas intercept the barrister, Harley-Brown, who is accompanying his client, Fraser, to the club (the Garrick is suggested in the script) after that day's appearance in court, for it is an ongoing trial. The chauffeur is calmly blocked by Moody from interfering as Chas passes and moves towards the back door of the Rolls. The chauffeur offers a telling remark to Moody, perhaps instigating his coming fate: "All right, let's keep our hair on, shall we?" This whole scene is a past event, as noted by an intercut remark set in Harry's office where the boss asks Chas if he'd got to see the lawyer guy, and is told: "it'll be straightened out in the morning." As yet we don't even know what he's talking about, as the time sequences shift back and forth quickly.

Chas' professionalism ("He's a nutcase, like all artists, but I can rely on him," as Harry reminds us) lies in his ability to adjust the levels of care with which he meets the various forms of resistance to his demands. Here there is no need for recourse to a physical roughing up in the street, words will suffice. The accused in court, Fraser ("an old pal and an old partner" of Harry Flowers, at least as Chas puts it to him), understands and says nothing to ruffle the hair, but Harley-Brown has too many chips on his shoulder. Chas has to take that extra thrust to try to cut him down to size – "Shut your 'ole, Mr Counsel" – when he refuses to quieten. Confirmed by Rosebloom, who repeats "'ole" and points into his mouth. The use of holes is a motif that recurs, right up to the final one, death itself.

But whilst Chas tries to be calm about it – often using a wink here, a nod and a wink even, as later with his old pal Joey Maddocks, to try to smooth the situation – the barrister is insistent that he's in charge and cannot be intimidated. "Are you threatening my client?"

Chas pushes again. "You bet I am, poncey."

At least he can make sure Fraser knows his place: "Do you follow me? . . . eh? . . . boy?"

Harley-Brown refuses to learn. His social standing does not allow him to be subservient to anyone. Chas calmly holds his cool and takes the final step to warn him. He inches his nose closer to the barrister, waiting for a response, and sniffs at him. He already knows the man doesn't smell right, as the saying goes. This is more than that. This is the need to assert the pecking order. An animal might sniff at another to hold it on tenterhooks, but with humans it is also a class-ridden gesture, the sniffy upper-class person who sniffs at the worker, literally and metaphorically. Chas has reversed the role and offers the ultimate menace of sniffing at the barrister.

This gesture, however, has another importance, for it brings to our notice that considerations of smell are part of the 'total theatre' experience on offer. When *Performance* was first released in America, a couple of key reviewers suggested the film stunk. It was meant in a pejorative way. But, in fact, it is to the credit of this film that we can smell it. We will not be surprised if we smell, or think we smell, joss sticks or incense once we gain admittance to Jagger's home later. Didn't the police at the Redlands drugs raid enquire as to why incense or joss sticks were burning, their conclusion being that it was to mask the smell of hashish or grass being smoked? Here we are being made aware of an angle that is to have a pay-off almost immediately in the following sequence.

In the film version of Pinter's *The Birthday Party*, the ending matches up to the beginning when we see the two menacing men, Goldberg and McCann, arrive at the seaside in their grand car. They are leaving and they are taking the guest, Stanley, with them, although where and why we have no real idea. Petey doesn't want them to take him. Goldberg comes back, goes up to Petey, looks at him for a moment, "studies him" it notes in the script, and says: "(*insidiously*) Why don't you come with us, Mr Boles?

McCann: Yes, why don't you come with us?

Goldberg: Come with us to Monty. There's plenty of room in the car.

Petey doesn't move. The men leave, taking Stanley, who is compliant."

The straightening out "in the morning" arrives. It is early, the paperboy and the milkman deliver early, as they've always done in this country – the crack of dawn. The chauffeur leaves the Queen's Gate Mews home, the London residence of his employer, and crosses to the garage. We note there is a smattering of red, cars carefully chosen and parked: a red Lotus Elan, an E-Type Jaguar, an MG, a mini . . . five in all.

Harley-Brown's chauffeur is grabbed, gagged and bound to a chair as he steps into the dark garage. Then he is made to watch the punishment meted out on his boss' property, as well as becoming the recipient of attention himself.

Chas sets about pouring concentrated sulphuric acid from a large stone jar across the Rolls' polished surface, "a gallon and a half". Concentrated sulphuric acid, as any schoolchild knows after enduring chemistry classes, burns into a material and produces clouds of fumes that one certainly shouldn't inhale. Chas pours and we smell the fumes. Our olfactory cells are touched. Or so we imagine.

As mentioned earlier, Jeff Nuttall's People Show regularly created works that had an unreasonable smell about them. In fact, the audience was assaulted by it. The piece *A Nice Quiet Night* included a side of beef that had been hanging in the basement space in Better Books for some days, so the performance smelt throughout. The piece *People Show Number Sixteen* at the Arts Lab had rags soaked in disinfectant stuffed into the mesh of the cages in which the audience was trapped. One member of that People Show troupe was Mike Figgis, who later, as a director in his own right, notably used smell in his film *Liebestraum* (1991), Kim Novak recalling her husband coming home from a night out, remarking about her husband's fingers, "I could smell cunt on them." That shocked the audience, and before that, the film company. When we sit comfortably in our seats we do not wish to be assaulted by senses of smell, whether acrid or delicious. It is sufficient that the visual assault be kept under control. And the aural one.

Not to leave Nic Roeg out of the picture, Harold Pinter made a pertinent comment, filmed in 1962 on the set of *The Caretaker*, on which Roeg was director of photography. Squeezed for the interview into an attic room, with a bucket catching water through the leaky roof, Pinter answers a question about why he wants it filmed on location, not in a studio, despite the cramped conditions. "A studio is a studio. It's large and hygienic. This is a room, it smells like a room. This house smells like a house. And I like the smell."

Performance is about cultural references; the makers cannot help but bring them in, one after another. Not always direct references. Not always overly intentional. But if you were living in a cultured, and even counter-cultured world, at that time, the idea of taking on board what was vibrant around you became part of your way of life, your way of being.

Thus the manner in which Chas goes about pouring the acid over the

Rolls, and the manner in which it is filmed, is almost a dance. But not just any dance. It is akin to the dance that Jackson Pollock made as he painted, as he poured and trickled paint onto his canvas on the floor, as he flicked and spattered paint from the pots with the sticks he used instead of brushes. There was always the intent to have a rhythm to the process, a theatricality, Pollock becoming an 'actor', wittingly or not. We have the evidence. Hans Namuth's 1950 film showed him going through the process. "I want to express my inner feelings rather than to illustrate them," Pollock comments on the soundtrack. The image is going to be the result of the painter's encounter with the canvas, using whatever tools and materials he deems necessary. "On the floor I am more at ease. I feel nearer, more a part of the painting, since this way I can work around it, work from four sides and literally be *in* the painting. This is akin to the Indian sand painters of the West."

Pollock was not just for the art specialist. His actions also hit the media headlines as abuse was heaped on his work, compared to the mess of a child or a chimp. Or further, "Jack the dripper". Certainly there is violence in his art; he was not a man at peace, as we know from the biographies.

Even if I align Jackson Pollock painting and dancing around the canvas, I also know that the material here is not paint but acid, and greater care is needed because of the destructive nature of the liquid.

At that period in London there was a master of the use of acid for artistic purposes, Gustav Metzger. His work involved stretching nylon across a support, plate glass, or a framework, and painting, spraying or flinging nitric or hydrochloric acid at it, the effect being that the nylon burnt and tore. This he did in public performances. Metzger was involved with a group of artists, as noted before, who came together in 1966 to present the Destruction in Art Symposium, sponsored by the ICA.

And no sooner does Chas finish reworking and refashioning the paint on the surface of the Rolls, and we are shown the texture of the damaged car, than Chas, Rosebloom and Moody set about refashioning the chauffeur's head, offering him a haircut. This is not to be a neat back and sides, however, or even a careful removal of the hair to turn him into a skinhead (though the shaven head concept didn't really shine until the following decade); this is a further exploration in the use of a visual texture.

While there are a number of other artists whose work springs readily to mind, one in particular is Tàpies, for whom Donald Cammell had shown an interest earlier and the review of Cammell's exhibition in New York pointed out the relationship of his work with the Spanish artist. This allusion here to Tàpies would be solely to the texture of his canvases, not to specific paintings or even to any of the signs or vocabulary that he had built up over the years.

And there appears to be another reference that might slip into our gaze, the direct influence of the British artist Mark Boyle. He was gaining credence at the time not only for his 'liquid light shows', primarily with the Soft Machine, starting at the UFO Club in London, where he virtually held residence, but also for his *Journey to the Surface of the Earth* and allied explorations. These were studies of the Earth's surface; he travelled to sites with his assistants (his wife, Joan Hills, and children, later known as the Boyle Family) and reproduced an area six feet square exactly, creating a multi-sensual presentation by collecting materials, filming and photographing, taking surface casts with Epikote resin, going to extraordinary lengths to capture the exactness of the spot chosen at random, a dart thrown at a map on the wall, a dagger at the door.

In the script it says: "Tiny trickles of blood rivulet downwards from razor blade nicks unintentionally caused by bumps, pimples, etc." These were in fact filmed, as nicks couldn't be avoided in the situation, and though left in at various edits, were finally removed by the film censor, who felt they might give people ideas.

For all the art references and the appreciation of the close-up textures of the damaged car and the chauffeur's head, this scene also drew very specifically from David Litvinoff's own experience.

It is totally in keeping that our friends should arrive with a cut-throat razor to do the job. But as they also brought along the shaving soap, and the brush, this indicates that they are old-fashioned and conservative in their shaving etiquette – no razor-blade device or electric shaver for them. Again, the cut-throat razor is being lined up for a future appearance. Rather than keep our hair on, as suggested earlier, now it all comes off. This is also a joke on the youth of the day, with their long hair, dirty and unwashed, "you name it". And already an undercurrent set in motion with the coming, the eventual arrival of the one with long hair, Mick Jagger, the star of the film, its raison d'être.

There is another touch in this scene that helps us to understand how *Performance* has a different frame of mind from most other films. As Chas goes about shaving away at the scalp, painting with the razor would be an apt way of viewing it, he is obviously thinking. Contemplation is something we have seen before, for instance in the back of the Rover en route to work, a few moments of reflection, a gathering of psychic energies before he steps into action. And in his bed, contemplating his partner giving him sexual pleasure, fellating him we presume. As Chas draws the blade across the head, Moody, a chat artist, continues his banter, and is told to shut it. Yet he still continues: "Hair today, gone tomorrow."

Chas explodes, goes ballistic. "I said shut your bloody hole." Chas is an artist. Harry Flowers says he's an artist. Even if a "nutcase, like all artists". An artist concentrates on what he is doing. Distractions and irritations are not put up with. Anyone who is not an artist imagines one can merrily paint (for example) with noise and distractions around. After all, we read about or know that artists have music playing in their studios as they work. They might well do, but it is mainly not listened to. It is a background noise, a fill-in. Painting requires concentration; all art requires concentration.

Those on set knew what they were dicing with when it came to John Bindon. His character was called Moody after all. Billy Murray, who had an uncredited part as one of Joey Maddocks' workers, Steve, another character with the know-how in razor use, recalls that when Fox told Bindon to shut his hole, there was a look on Bindon's face as he viewed Fox. "We all knew then that John had been there in real life." It wasn't a good idea to go out drinking in the pubs with Bindon after a day's shoot, because, in all likelihood, a punch-up would ensue sooner or later. "It was like a living nightmare," one of the cast said. "John might have been used to such real-life violence, but it terrified the rest of us." One day he arrived on set with a matchbox. "John had this matchbox in his hand which he kept shaking around," Billy Murray recounted. He was asking "D'you want to know what's in it?" "There was a thumb in it. Some guy had stuck his finger in Bindon's mouth during one of the fights and he'd bitten it off at the top joint and it was still in the matchbox." The story went that the victim had been phoning Bindon's mother all night asking for its return so the hospital could sew it back on. It might have horrified the cast, but then they didn't know this was a fiction that Bindon had dragged around with him since he was a kid. No one ever looked in the matchbox to verify his story. Bindon was full of such tales. He even entertained Princess Margaret with his banter. Legends.

Fox seems to have taken his cue for the response to Moody's banter from John Boorman's *Point Blank*, from the scene where John Vernon as Reese snaps when counting the stolen money. He finds it falls short of his expectations and knows that it means he will need to limit the number of payouts, to eliminate his partner in crime, or, more likely, someone he had an earlier homosexual relationship with (this is given credence by the way Walker later empties his revolver into the mattress of the bed he had expected to find Reese lying in).

Point Blank has become a quiet cult film, mainly because of the presence of Lee Marvin as the cold killer who sets about trying to collect on the money that is rightfully his. But unlike other American gangster films, this was directed by a British filmmaker, John Boorman, even if it was based on an American novel, *The Hunter*, written by Donald Westlake under his Richard Stark pseudonym. Stark wrote a series with Walker (called Parker) as the protagonist. He was one of the Fifties and Sixties crime writers, like Day Keene, Harry Whittington, Jim Thompson and others, who were interested in writing crime fiction from the perspective of the criminal mind, having no interest in police procedures. *Point Blank* is often thought to be about Walker on the Rock, Alcatraz, thinking back, betrayed, as he lies dying from his gunshot wounds. Whether the film is a series of flash-backs, the idea of Marvin as a cold killer (who died on the Rock, as Angie Dickinson says, meaning emotionally, though literally can be understood) was one of the attitudes that Cammell wanted Fox to take on board.

As in so many scenes, the mirror plays its part. Always for narcissistic reasons at this stage. Here it's a hand mirror, to enquire if the chauffeur likes the haircut that Chas the barber has treated him to. "Trendsetting, what?"

Musically the film is lining up for Jagger's arrival, the method here being the car radio that Rosie switches on for us to hear a Mississippi Delta number, as the DJ informs us.

Back in Harry Flowers' office, arrangements are being made to bring Joey Maddocks' betting shop into the fold, to join the consortium, a merger. And it's the word 'merged' that Harry will reiterate to Joey once he has been brought into the group. Not "took over". It is not a matter of whether Maddocks is interested or agrees; it is a matter of how he comes on board. It seems strong-arm tactics are needed, something even more direct than we've seen to date. Unfortunately, Chas is not allowed to be part of the operation because of a personal relationship between Joey and Chas that goes back some years. Harry Flowers reminds him: "Your relations with Joey was double personal, right?" Their relationship is not stated blatantly, but there is no doubt that there was a homosexual bond between them at one point, one that has left a bad taste all round. Perhaps it was when they were youthful boxing contenders. It seems they fought each other. Perhaps Joey came late, rose fast, edged Chas off his perch. We see a blinding flash of Joey's left jab coming at the camera, us, poking us in the face, poking Chas' memory. "Keep personal relations out of business."

Which is probably where Harry met Chas, as boxing photos as mementoes adorn the office wall. Perhaps a touch from Johnny Shannon's life too, why not?

Once again we see the future, with a flash of Mad Cyril throwing a dustbin through the front window of Joey Maddocks' betting shop on the Fulham Road.

Flowers is aware that he's needling Chas, but he pushes on regardless. Whatever occurs is going to be as much his fault. There'll be something to pay. They live in a world of tensions. They court these tensions. No matter what they say.

And now we understand Harold Pinter. It's not the pauses, the silences, but the application of pauses and silences. White paint, not bare canvas.

On the wall behind Harry's desk is a large mirror, used for narcissistic purposes, of course; Chas preening and grooming himself in it when given the chance. All mirrors in the early stages of this film are clearly for this purpose. Only later will they take on a deeper meaning. There's also a mantelpiece on which to place, temporarily, a canvas of a man on a horse. This is no classic though, no Stubbs, no Van Dyck, or any landed gentry image of possessive power. Harry Flowers might wish that it were so. The suggestion is that it is a portrait of Harry Flowers on a horse, perhaps his horse, to reflect the circles he moves in, or would like to move in. When the Krays moved upmarket, they acquired a Victorian mansion on the edge of Bildeston in Suffolk, and part of the status of being in the country was the use of horses, shotguns . . . the activities that come with country life. At least you aspire to it, imagine you are doing it, being part of it. This painting is a poor effort. Chas might be an 'artist', but Harry is just a boss, with little aesthetic sensitivity.

Just as Harry Flowers wishes to be part of the horsey set, so there is a sense that he belongs to the Freemasons, or perhaps another organisation, something to do with magic, initiation rights and signs. He toys with his desk implements as he speaks, places the pens to present a directional power sign. We don't know what it means, but it won't be the last time we see such signs in operation.

There is a sense of glamour in aligning Harry Flowers with Ronnie Kray: as former villain John McVicar wrote: "There is in Ronnie's face the will to kill. It is the face of someone who is going to taste the ultimate power of deciding, according to his own whim, whether others will live or die." Yet there is nothing in Harry Flowers that lets us see him as evil or a killer. He might be the boss, deaths might result, violence aplenty, but we do not see him, or imagine him, walking into a pub and shooting another villain in the head. Chas, though, is a different story.

Ronnie, not Reggie, was the one who enjoyed his violence the most, whether listening to someone else's tale, always asking to hear all the details, or administering it himself, smashing somebody with whatever was at hand, hammer, bayonet, axe . . . and, once finished, saying, "hold that!" and walking away.

Harry Flowers delegates. He is a businessman. Ronnie and Reggie were not businessmen. They had no idea how to run a company, or let someone else run it for them at the top level. They only knew how to create terror, how to obtain the money and then spend it. To survive as a criminal enterprise requires keeping your face out of the media, out of the public eye. Ronnie and Reggie courted attention. If you go around trying to be famous, as happened, in the end you not only become famous, you become infamous. Philanthropy can be a good thing, as they say, but you can get too much of it. You can be flash with it, contributing to boxing matches in aid of medical research, handing van loads of gifts to old people's homes and handouts to bereaved locals, the money obtained through menaces and extortion, milking it for the publicity so that you come across as the 'good boys'.

When the night's business is finished, Harry lets the window blind up to show that it is a new day for the outside world, whereas for them the day has ended. This shot is in Mount Street, the street in which Anita resided during shooting.

Again we are let in on a play on words, the vase of red roses by the window having died but not been thrown out. A sign of the bad times to come. Dying flowers, fading rose blooms. Death in a vase. (Although they had been shooting on the set for three days, Nic decided to film them that way, knowingly.)

With the new day, Chas is determined to re-arrange his affairs. He removes a gun from behind a tile in the bathroom wall. Jimmy Evans had indicated keeping weapons in the bathroom, behind a tile, in the laundry basket among the dirty washing, accessible.

Chas tucks the gun in his belt. He could have had a secret pocket made, as Evans suggested. Chas squares up to the mirror. Though he is looking at his appearance, this is the first time we sense that he is looking at himself and saying: "Who am I?" and responding, still, with "I know who I am." He plays with the band ring on his middle finger. Is this a friendship ring of some kind? Something that bound him to Joey in earlier times, perhaps? We will never know, for it has been removed by the next shot. A brown ring, an amber ring perhaps. Something simple. To wear a ring on the middle finger of the yin hand is said to represent the ability to tell right from wrong. Perhaps even a sign to give one the authority to determine that difference and act on it. Chas is perhaps on the point of going through to the other side – of the mirror – in search of the truth, of questioning his identity. If there is a Jean Cocteau moment, this might well be it.

While Chas is organising his life, preparing himself for tidying up, as baited by Harry Flowers (when I say no, I mean yes), straightening his flat meticulously, obsessively, to the degree of compulsive disorder, his nemesis' property is being re-arranged, its frontage destroyed, its interior redecorated.

It is interesting to note that the police detective who investigates the disturbance the following morning should have a scar across his cheek, one normally administered to villains. To recall that Litvinoff had a scar after a razor incident. Derek Raymond reminds us in his autobiography, *The Hidden Files*, that: "Small-time grasses usually got off with a smiler – that's to say, one corner of your mouth continued up to your ear with the help of a razor to show people that your mouth was too big; you could never get work with villains again." What had this officer of the law done to receive this reward? Another versa moment added as a touch.

Given the level of jokes and references to be found, one could also surmise that the lavatory bowl left in the destroyed premises in the Fulham Road, a vacant antiques shop opposite Chelsea football ground, is a reference to Duchamp's urinal rather than a sign that Maddocks' betting shop business is going down the pan unless he agrees to the business proposition and joins the "associated group of companies", the democratic organisation run by Harry Flowers. This might seem far-fetched, given that the urinal is not in pristine condition, though it does bear a signature, metaphorically, of its source, as Chas confirms when he walks in and thrusts a Burberry coat into Joey's chest before taking him away to visit the prospective proprietor, "acquisition of". Before Cammell left Paris he was involved with artists who didn't think he was a good painter, by all accounts, which means that they were not particularly enamoured with his technical skills, but preferred art that had either abstract qualities or 'ready-made' characteristics. Not that I'm "making actual allegations", as such. "I can't do that. What I mean, I got no proof, have I?"

As Harry Flowers and Joey Maddocks, accompanied by Dennis and Jack from the business, come through the door from the offices upstairs, we see the nameplates for the companies registered at the address: South African Development Ltd; Presto Repossessions Ltd; Sportsmen's Management Assoc; Daisy May; Toy & Shoe Factors Ltd. All of them, except possibly the last, could easily fit Harry Flowers' business interests, and could well be just his, not shared space with other companies. One should not be surprised that Harry has interests in South Africa. Whilst the Kray twins are generally used as reference for Flowers' set-up, one should realise that south of the river, based in Bermondsey, was another notorious group of villains led by Charlie and Eddie Richardson. The Richardsons had business interests in scrap metal here, but they also had developments and investments in South Africa.

Though we have seen the exterior of the second floor office, the idea of the nightclub being below does not exactly fit into any spatial sense we might be forming. And yet, according to Chas, the bar, and, through logic, the nightclub, are downstairs. It is only fitting that the four should approach the bar through the back curtain, and across the nightclub stage. They are hardly performers in the same league as Chas, but they command the stage and that is how they intend to conduct themselves in what will become a confrontation with Chas.

As is to be expected from this seedy nightclub and bar, the women in sight are rather down-at-heel companions or hostesses, wallflower props to the male environment. The walls are covered in publicity photos for cabaret artists who might have sung in the club, or have visited it after hours for a nightcap when working elsewhere. Even the mural painted above the benches is a cheap pastiche of a Parisian *fin de siècle* cabaret, albeit English-style. Called the Haycroft Club in the script, The Glass Bucket on the screen, it was ironically another place in Wardour Street, The Latin Quarter. But no one grumbles. They seem to like the comfort and lack of threatening behaviour. Even Rosie, earlier seen reading the lofty literature of Borges, is shown in Godardian sign-setting mode quietly reading a Marvel comic, confirmed by specialist Kim Newman as *Strange Tales #168*, which came out in May 1968. *Strange Tales* paired two features, often as try-outs to see if either could sustain their own series. In the event, after this issue, both Doctor Strange and Nick Fury, Agent of SHIELD, had their own titles. It has been commented that comic fans thought the creators of Doctor Strange must have taken drugs, for the experiences parallel those obtained when "high on mushrooms".

The Kray twins showed their arrogance in court at the Old Bailey, Ronnie Kray telling Judge Melford Stevenson: "If I wasn't here now I'd probably be having a drink with Judy Garland." That lack of respect for the system and authority was sure to see them taken down a few pegs and taught a lesson. Their time was lengthened not just to fit the guilty verdict for murder. Interestingly, the reason they were in the dock in the first place was because they had, in their turn, killed George Cornell and Jack McVitie, whom they judged as having lacked respect for them.

And that is precisely why Harry Flowers decides to take Chas down a peg or two. "He enjoys his work . . ." might be an accusation levelled at Chas, but Harry is guilty of precisely the same abuse of his position. He knows there is animosity between Chas and Joey, so he sees fit to keep that tension active, baiting Chas with Joey smiling broadly over his shoulder.

"Who do you think you are?" he asks Chas. "The Lone Ranger." A poor choice, for though he was our Fifties childhood television hero, he never acted alone. He might have galloped about on Silver, his white stallion, but he always had his faithful sidekick, the Native American Tonto, beside him.

In fact, Harry knows who he is, shifting ground, and offers "Jack the Lad", qualifying that he's a special performer all right, but he has to remember that "you're bloody working for me, you berk", by which he means not him, but "the business". In fact, Chas has to remember that he's just a "cog". And you'd better not forget it, "boy".

But Chas knows who he is, at least today he knows who he is. "I know who I am." But does he, for then he says: "I know what I am." Exactly. As he will find out before the night is through. He had looked in the mirror. He had contemplated it. Today he is still sure of himself. He does not need his confidence shattered, his illusions betrayed. Not today.

Oh yes, he says, he enjoys his work: "I get a load of kicks out of it." Then he sees the opening. "Putting a little stick about. Putting the frighteners on flash little twerps," indicating Joey gloating over his new boss' shoulder. He will get the upper hand and then depart. He bites his tongue, waits for the moment. The punch line is being set up. He concludes: "You push the button on that . . . thing", which he directs at Joey. Thing. Not human being. Flowers ignores, or tries to deflate. Or misses the point. Flowers probably knows that he's read it wrong. But he's the boss. He's entitled. Joey is not a human being. "He's a lying slag, he's a grass . . ." And he is more. Something really did go on between Chas and Joey, once upon a time.

There is a strange shot as the scene ends and the image of Harry and Dennis dissolves to the next sequence. Just prior to Chas' arrival home at the crack of dawn we see inside his flat, situated in The Grampians in Shepherd's Bush, ostensibly. The set though was built in Lowndes Square. Chas is somewhat drunk, the worse for wear, as they say. But this shot is not a glimpse of the destruction or the re-decoration occurring in his flat, but a brief whiteness. It is not a blank canvas as such, not a pure whiteness, but as if a blank canvas is leaning against a wall. Or a bit of an alcove, awkwardly composed. There is no obvious reading. It is only momentarily shown, with Harry and Dennis left as a faint and lingering image, slowly fading into the pale. This seems to be the secret shot of the film. A pause before the mayhem? An oblique pause, not a Pinter pause, but a painterly pause. A sign that we are about to move on, we are about to enter a perverse world, something with echoes of obliquity as found in the work of Balthus, or his brother Klossowski. It is an open question.

The scene that ensues, that is supposed to be Joey Maddocks' payback time against Chas, is a source of ideas and information that we can barely keep abreast of. It is given its atmosphere and sense of heightened violence by relating to contemporary art in a very blatant fashion. The walls receive red paint, thrown from a tin, thrown at random. We see the hits. "I hit," says the Dutch painter, Karel Appel, in terms of his action of throwing paint against the canvas. "I don't paint. I hit."

The paint hits. The fight gets under way. Chas is smacked hard in the face as he walks in the door. Blood will start to appear. But equally it could be paint. You cannot throw red paint around a room without splattering yourself. And then closer still. To enhance the fight the camera is in there too, in the thick of it, fighting for its place, shooting loose. Fragments. A montage of.

And we are left in no doubt that Francis Bacon is in on the act. Not because we see any images of his work, but because we see the reflection of known shots of his studio, of his disorganised painting environment, the result of a fight between Bacon and his materials, Bacon and his demons, discarded tubes, brushes and photos, used to fire his imagination, all crumpled and trashed across surfaces and studio floor. Boxing photos in the main; one with Shannon as Flowers behind Chas. Indeed the shots we glimpse of the floor here in *Performance*, taken from above, are so paint splattered that it is as if the art director has chosen to pay homage to more than just Bacon. Having already mentioned Pollock, there is an echo of his studio floor out at his home in East Hampton on Long Island, another famous image and location for art tourists today.

This image of a painter's battlefield is capitalised upon with white splatterings, the white of feathers, feathers everywhere, as if shaken from slashed pillows. As the men hit Chas, you think he's having the stuffing knocked out of him. And that thought is immediately confirmed as feathers float down through the air. Feathers stick to the sweat on Chas' body as the scene progresses, and we have flashes of Northern Ireland, the tarrings and featherings, still part of our thoughts at the time.

An arm appears, spray painting black on a dark red wall. Elsewhere. Decorating. Jagger. At least we suspect it's him.

Bacon's work starts with chance hits, what he called "an accident", which were "involuntary marks" upon the canvas that he then found ways to develop as an image. That was how he achieved the rawness he sought, speaking directly to the nervous system, both of the painter and the spectator.

Donald had wanted the fighting actors to "just let things *happen*" (as Pherber will stress), which didn't go down well with Anthony Valentine, playing Maddocks. "You cannot Mickey Mouse fights, because somebody will get hurt." Instead of it being choreographed like a ballet, they had to go in there and "do it", Cammell insisted. The original take included two boxers from the Becket. Valentine arranged with Fox for a basic opening gambit to set things rolling. Fox wasn't overly worried. He could handle himself. He had been educated in these things, schooled in these matters, down the Becket, out with the 'chaps'. He was fit. Don't worry about me. Valentine said Fox "was as hard as the Rock of Gibraltar" after three months of working out at the gym. But damage occurred. One guy had a broken nose, the other cracked ribs. They had to bring in replacements for other takes. One of these was Billy Murray. Even for the filmed violence one senses that there was an underlying real violence. Tensions were being exploited on both sides of the camera.

Valentine recalled in an interview for Mick Brown's book that "Don wanted me stripped to the waist and oiled up. For me, playing the part was a question of 'show me the marks, show me the lights and I'll act it for you' – but, please, don't give me all this crap about being oiled." Either Cammell didn't explain, or didn't know at that point, still improvising the scene, feeling his way, that he would have had images to exploit which would echo the relationship of Joey and Chas as boxers. Chas' boxing images lay as photos torn and crumpled around the floor. It could have been a poetic possibility, whereas Valentine admits he was "a bit too prosaic" in his understanding of the film.

If blood was drawn, it wasn't noticed to any great degree. The red paint did the cover up. Godard's influence was at work. "There's a good deal of blood in *Pierrot le Fou*," said one of the *Cahiers du Cinéma* interviewers to Godard. "Not blood, red" was the response.

Tony Lambrianou, who was there when McVitie was killed by Reggie Kray, noted the blood in that flat. "It was absolutely everywhere, soaking all over the place. It was like someone got a bucket of red paint and threw it over the floor."

Although one can note the violence in the painting activity of Jackson Pollock, Karel Appel and Francis Bacon, the result on the wall has overtones of Clyfford Still (who hated the idea that a painting had to be stopped by the limitations of the edge). Tàpies too, this time the red cross on the wall is encroaching on his vocabulary, not just the influence of its texture. These resonances, although left in the hands of Nic Roeg, are drawn from Cammell's sensibility as an artist. Having been in New York at the turn of the Sixties he would also have come across that world of 'happenings', which also seems pertinent to the fray under way.

'Happenings' derive from a painterly experience, painters breaking out of the two-dimensional mould, adding objects, activating art into a live experience, with a heavy input of theatre and theatricality. In New York there were Pop artists like Jim Dine, Claes Oldenburg and Red Grooms, alongside Allan Kaprow, who coined the term. And it didn't have boundaries limiting it to one art form. Philip Corner and LaMonte Young were both also active in music. Without taking too many examples, one could draw a case for the acid painting of the Rolls-Royce as a 'happening', an 'action'.

No one says it has to be a live event. It can be filmed and edited, so that the document made is the 'happening', which is equally viable. We are talking flexibility of rules, to the degree of no rules, to the extent that each 'action' or 'happening' is distinct from any other. Oldenburg's birthday party film springs to mind. Or again Hermann Nitsch and Otto Muehl with their visceral 'actions', and the films that Kurt Kren made which went beyond documentation of their work, becoming films in their own right with their fast editing style.

Amongst the debris is a photo of Chas holding Henry, the white bull terrier, the reason for the presence of a dog lead, retained as a memento.

While Joey uses the lead to flagellate Chas, Steve brandishes his razor. "Shall I decorate 'im? Eh Joey?" Shall I? Echoes of Ronnie Hart, in October 1967, holding Jack 'the Hat' McVitie in a hug round his neck, shouting to Reggie Kray, knife in hand, "Do him, Reg, go on, do him."

Not that the Krays would use a razor. If they were cutting someone's face or buttocks, they'd use a knife or sharpened cutlass. Ronnie used to say: "Razors are old-fashioned and strike us as babyish. You can't put no power behind a razor."

One of John Bindon's old friends, Billy Murray, took the uncredited part of Steve, Maddocks' worker. As a teenager in the East End his desire to act was met by funds from the Krays, who paid for him to go to the East 15 Acting School, because they "liked his attitude". Later he had long-running television roles as a corrupt policeman in *The Bill* and as a villain in *EastEnders*.

Joey whips Chas. He hopes he is gaining his revenge. It wasn't so much the whipping that was objected to by the censor, but that it was intercut with Chas' opening scenes with Dana, where his sado-masochistic pleasures were first displayed. Versions that are available now have some of this footage.

When *Marat/Sade* was staged in 1964, the scene that caused the most objection was the whipping scene. Peter Brook had decided to interpret Weiss' script in which Sade is whipped by Charlotte Corday by using her long hair as the instrument, while Sade recites points about the Revolution, and the nature of human nature. Brook wanted to retain the emotional, to highlight the erotic experience.

There still seems to be some question as to why flagellation has become so instrumental in this film. The fact that '*le vice anglais*' has such international recognition, that the amount of literature on the subject is overwhelming, with its presence in Victorian literature bulging at the seams, and that it has a large following right up to the time of the film, and since, does have its grounding in our public school education. That Cammell and his associates had this background is hardly the issue. That Cammell should find that Marianne Faithfull has blood ties to Leopold von Sacher-Masoch, whether discussed or not, could only have added fuel. Why the character Chas Devlin, a working-class lad of Irish descent, should have this leaning is none too clear. But life has these strange anomalies, many of us finding traits or complete lifestyles that seem to run counter to our upbringings.

Roeg is quite convinced of the importance of the visual. He has no qualms. "Thought can be transferred by the juxtaposition of images, and you mustn't be afraid of the audience not understanding. You can say things visually, immediately, and that's where film, I believe, is going."

The objection that Jimmy Evans had to the film, or more accurately to the fact that Chas' role draws on him, is the word scrawled on the wall. "Poof", it reads. Poof, in red. Evans will accept that Harry is a homosexual, because Ronnie Kray was homosexual. Not gay. There's a difference. Words have meaning even . . . "I'm not queer," he used to say. "I'm homosexual." Homosexual he might have been, but you didn't call Ronnie a poof. That some of his associates might have done is one thing, but you didn't say it to his face, or allow it to get back. The usual story is that Ronnie heard that George Cornell had called him "a fat poof", so Ronnie walked into the Blind Beggar pub on Whitechapel Road, pulled out his 9 mm Mauser and shot him in the head. Others say there was more to it than that, stating that Cornell saw Ronnie approaching, and sarcastically remarked: "Well look who's here." After Ronnie withdrew his gun, Cornell looked at him and said: "You ain't got the bottle." After such a comment, the reason for pulling the trigger takes on another meaning.

By all accounts the fight sequence was cut to ribbons. As was the juxtaposition of the whipping received by Chas from Maddocks with the sado-masochism of the opening sex scene between Chas and Dana. This footage is also accompanied by the original scene's 'easy listening' music, suggesting that whilst Maddocks is administering the beating, Chas is merging both as pleasures. It has backfired on Maddocks. Perhaps it is also relevant to note that the pan to the word 'POOF', scrawled in red paint on the wall, is Joey's attempt to remind Chas that he is homosexual, and that any images in his mind are an aberration on Chas' part (as is the photo of the woman seen prior to the pan). Joey refuses to accept that he has switched sides. In their world you cannot be both. Such a merger he despises.

In an earlier cut, before Warners insisted on the removal of some lines, as Joey whips Chas, he demands that he spells out who he is – "I am a little poof" – which he precedes with the excised lines: "You always was a dirty little boy. A nasty perverted little boy."

The censors did not like the relationship of sex and violence. There was another shot that was removed, certainly in Britain, though earlier showings in America suggest it still existed. The initial version I saw one afternoon in a viewing theatre, before its release, had a close-up shot of Chas' shoe. Across this shoe was drawn a cut-throat razor blade, slowly . . . as Joey dies, a last act against his old friend. An action that Chas could simply have stopped, but allowed to continue. The pain was his pleasure. Others have noted that they've seen mention of that image, but perhaps never saw it. I think the reference is clear once seen. There is absolutely no mistaking that it was a reworking of the razor cut in Buñuel's *Un Chien Andalou*, the slicing of the eye. This image made a strong impression in the Sixties, with Buñuel's film often shown in other environments, such as clubs like UFO, alongside underground movies. It was convenient because there was no sound, and the images throughout made a good backdrop to the psychedelic experience during the night. One could go further and note that Polanski uses the razor idea for *Repulsion*, his opening titles running variously across a close-up of Catherine Deneuve's eyeball, until the final credit 'directed by Roman Polanski', which draws itself neatly right to left across the centre. (Deneuve, too, uses the razor for murderous effect later in the film, though after the first slice across the back of the landlord's neck, its use is conveyed more through Chico Hamilton's percussive sounds than in any openly visual assault.) Cammell was a friend of Polanski in Paris at this period. Polanski was very influenced by Surrealism, mainly the paintings of Dalí and Matta, but Buñuel was the main film one. And particularly in *Repulsion*, which is a homage.

The removal of the slicing across the shoe just prior to the film's release negates the foundation laid at the opening of *Performance*: the jet streaking across the screen, the sky, and the Rolls-Royce initially cutting across the screen, albeit in the opposite direction. Perhaps the shock of the jet, the jolt of the noise, is more of a surprise to the viewer who is just settling back to watch the film, only to be greeted by such a blaring sound.

The use of the razor is not a total surprise. Chas has wielded it with the chauffeur, and Steve has threatened to decorate him already in the scene. And yet, the removal of the shot from the film as we know it today is probably a good thing. *Performance* is not a Buñuel tribute. This image is too blatant, does not "fit in". *Performance* is a violent film, on just about every level, so a viewer squirming from the image of razor-cutting would be unnecessary. As a result of the withdrawal of this image, a few other shots where blood is seen seeping from the shoe, leaking onto the floor, as at the cafeteria in the railway station, have also been trimmed.

But that doesn't detract from the importance of the eye. We can't fail to notice that from time to time the characters talk directly to camera, to us. And at Chas' crucial shooting scenes, the viewpoint is always the gun being shot at us, us, us . . . to echo Flowers. We are the targets as much as those on the screen at each occasion. It is an assault on the whole nature of watching film. It is one way to remind us that it is a film. There is another way of drawing us in and asking for our viewpoint, as we will see shortly with Pherber.

Jagger at home in his living room. The place is now redecorated. He is relaxing. North African music sets the atmosphere.

"Say it! Say it! Go on . . . Say it!"

Who are you?

Chas knows.

"I . . . am . . ."

Chas falls unconscious. Or so they think. He knows what he's doing. He knows who he is. He's a professional. He's a performer. Watch me perform.

While Steve goes to fetch water to revive him, Joey comes over to gloat at his conquest. Only to find that Chas lifts his head, looks him in the eyes, winks, responds and retakes control of the situation.

Though his wrists are bound with a torn shirt, he muscles the two adversaries aside and reaches for a gun, another gun, this one hidden beneath the dirty laundry basket – the nod towards Jimmy Evans, a place he'd use or did use . . . personally.

With the gun in his hands everything changes. The electronic low note that sounds in our heads modulates upwards to increase the tension. Chas pulls himself up, regains his stance. He knows who he is. He has known all along. It is just a matter of telling the cowering Joey Maddocks, that "thing", who is fast realising that his life is about to be switched off.

Joey tries a way out.

"Do you remember Mick?" Who's Mick? We don't want to answer that one.

As Chas lines up his response, he tells Joey who he is. Or, indeed, what he is. "I AM A BULLET."

He cocks his gun and fires, shoots the ex-lover hidden beneath the sheet he has drawn up to hide beneath, as if that could stop anything.

The screen goes red. Is RED. This is the end. Joey reappears, risen again briefly from his shroud, and states, incredulously: "Look what you done."

A flashback in black and white suggests that two kids fighting in the street are Chas and Joey, a childhood memory, remembered by either. Or both. Or is that Mick? Or were they fighting over Mick?

In an interview in 1972, Donald said there was a 'secret movie' within *Performance* itself, "a childhood dream, or nightmare", which has come to be interpreted as the two seconds of the street fight, taken from Carol Reed's *Odd Man Out* (1947), where two boys have a brawl watched by a number of others. It cannot be as bland, as literal as that: two boys fighting.

Odd Man Out is about a criminal on the run, after he has killed a man as he escapes from a robbery. There is a spiritual element to the film with Johnny (James Mason), wounded and aided by his girl, Kathleen (Kathleen Ryan), heading for the ship that will take him away. As the police close in, Kathleen fires the gun at them knowing it will bring on a return volley, killing them both. However, the spiritual journey of those final hours suggests that the end is not the end, but a stage towards a transcendence. It is perhaps this link to *Performance* that is cryptically spoken of by Donald as the 'secret movie'. Though one wonders if another 'secret' overtone, a personal angle, is related to Reed's opening and closing shots alongside Harland and Wolff's Belfast shipyards, harking back to Donald's heritage, as a descendant of the Cammell Laird shipbuilders. Another personal echo for Donald would be James Mason, for whom, he says in interview, he had "a soft spot". Whilst he had met Mason on the set for *Duffy*, Donald also had a strong liking for Kubrick's film *Lolita* (1962), in which Mason played the role of Humbert. It might also be worth bearing in mind that *Odd Man Out* is a keen favourite of Polanski.

On another level, taking into account earlier drafts of the script, when Chas is making phone calls from the telephone box as he tries to determine which way he should go, phoning Harry, then his friend Tony who works in Covent Garden, he then makes a third call. Though the scripts have slightly different scenarios, they share one common feature: the call is made to 'an old queen' who feigns pleasure at hearing from Chas after such a long while, adding that the moment is not exactly conducive as he is not alone. This is untrue, as the script makes clear that he sinks back into his bed, alone. The idea that Chas does have a homosexual background is given no ambiguity in those versions.

Of course, if Anthony Valentine had agreed to go about the whipping bare-chested, he might have seen the boxing allusion but he would not have known that Donald was a fan of Jean Cocteau and that it fitted in well with the artist at work stripped to the waist in *The Blood of a Poet* (1930), a film that has undoubtedly been a torch to many gay filmmakers in the years since.

It is too late. He's dead. "You're dead, Joey."

And as he grovels at Chas' feet, the mess of the Bacon studio image stronger than ever, we hear a voice.

"You can stay. Yesterday . . . till . . . tomorrow."

Whose voice is this? We would believe it is Joey's. Distorted perhaps, in his dying gasps. But it is an older voice. Has it been lifted, cryptically, from *Odd Man Out*? There is no trace. A father? A guardian? A teacher? It sounds like someone in authority, with the command of Alec Guinness in the delivery. It's a mystery.

This is where the razor cut existed.

Then he's dead.

Perhaps there was more to the razor cut. Chas chose not to stop it. The pain was his pleasure. Equally, he could have taken on the mantle of the martyr, the Christ figure, wanting atonement for his sins. Perhaps that was too much. You can go.

Steve is coming round in the bath. He peers across at what has just happened in the other room. He expects to see Chas, but whom does he see? He sees the back of a head. Mick Jagger's head. Framed in the doorway of the bedroom, reflected in the bathroom mirror. As Steve focuses on the sight, the camera zooms in on Jagger from behind, naked from the waist, giving us that overtone that Cammell wanted. It zooms in until it becomes the back of a head. This is the entrance of Mick Jagger. After the teasers, are we about to see the real McCoy? Not yet.

But what does it mean? We are being asked to ponder, then forget.

Steve is ordered out of the flat. Chas prepares to depart, grabs a few necessities, the one shirt not slashed to ribbons, some money stashed away in the bathroom. Would he take all of it? Would he leave some? Later we will ask ourselves those questions. He turns the dead body over, removes a memento from the pocket, something useful, a pair of dark glasses.

The phone starts ringing. The place is a shambles, yet he thinks to switch off the electric fire. Old habits die hard. He ignores the phone, leaves it to irritate, and contemplates his next move, for a second.

As Paul Mayersberg pointed out, with regard to a moment in *The Man Who Fell to Earth*, as Buck Henry is thrown to his death, the phone is ringing in his office: "It just rings . . . the unanswered phone that might be nothing . . . or it could save you. If only you answered it, you could get out of this."

We have seen three shots of Jagger. Three shots and a verbal. Remember? Mick. What do they mean? Particularly the final shot, the zoom in on the back of his head. We know it is Jagger's head, and hairstyle, because we know Jagger is the star of the film and we haven't seen him perform yet. But this is a film. We are not supposed to confuse Jagger and the character he will play. It is only the back of a head, it could be another, even if we've seen a gangster world where the main characters sport the shorter, groomed hairstyle of the day. This is long-haired stuff. Perhaps it's a girl? Could be.

We are talking 1967 and 1968. During this period anybody with hair that long, down to the shoulders, or even shorter, was regarded as 'long-haired' in the pejorative sense. It was a daily occurrence to find yourself taunted and made fun of as you went about your life. "Excuse me, miss. Oh, sorry, I thought you was a girl." You smiled. Or not. You got pissed off. You became oblivious. Habit.

Is this a boy or a girl? Of course we know it's Jagger.

James Fox recalls that earlier in 1968, in New York, his "mildly hippy appearance" attracted the editor of *Vogue*, who commissioned Irving Penn, one of the top photographers, to take a shot of the back of his head for the magazine. "She particularly liked the way my hair grew."

Normally the idea that is linked with seeing someone from behind is that we are being watched and do not know it. We are vulnerable, and let's not forget it. "It's a cruel vantage point, isn't it?" says Nic Roeg. "You always know there has to be someone behind watching the person you cannot see. People are often most interesting at their most vulnerable."

Roeg used that effect later in *The Man Who Fell to Earth*, in particular the incident in the pawnshop when the old woman behind the counter is able to look at a mirror strategically placed and see Bowie's head from behind. She can see what the face shows, and she can see what he can't see of himself. She can make her own judgement on how to treat the customer.

Where does this idea come from? Before *Performance* Nic Roeg had worked with François Truffaut, and was very impressed by the French director on many levels. One particular point that struck him was Truffaut's liking for seeing his characters from behind. In fact, in *Fahrenheit 451*, when the composite portrait of the main character, played by Oskar Werner, is seen, it shows side shots and a central photo of him from behind. Roeg asked Truffaut why he was fascinated with the image of a person from behind and was told: "I always like going into the projection box on the first night – mostly because I don't like to sit in the audience to see what they're feeling. But also because I like to watch the back of their heads – I can tell more about how they like it from there than if I sit among them."

This goes further. Truffaut learnt a lot of his skills and craft from Hitchcock. Indeed, he produced a book of interviews with Hitchcock, a classic in itself. So it is not unreasonable to suggest that Hitchcock also has a say in the matter. A particular example would be the first scene in *Notorious*, where Cary Grant is introduced, almost in silhouette, the camera placed behind the actor's head as he watches Ingrid Bergman drink and entertain. All we see is the back of his head for the whole scene, almost like having a member of the audience obscuring our view of the screen. (Which would also be part of what Hitchcock wants you to take on board.) Whilst Cary Grant is a star, his entrance is held off. And it is only with the next scene that the camera pans round to show his face.

Godard should also be taken into account briefly. In a film like *Vivre Sa Vie* (1962), which I'll use as an example because it returns later, it can hardly go unnoticed that as the couple talk during the opening bar scene we watch them from behind, see the back of their heads. The image is registered, but the intent is different because Godard wants the viewer to focus on the sound, the dialogue.

That brief shot of Jagger that registers and passes, that serves the studio, who were desperate for Jagger to appear on screen sooner than a linear narrative would allow, becomes another loaded image.

Chas had thought to drive out of London. But no sooner has he crossed the river than he decides that, though the hour is early, it is not too early to call for help. He phones his friend Tony to see if he has any ideas. Without serious contemplation he phones his mother. It is true desperation, for a professional like Chas will know that Flowers will locate family and friends and apply the pressure. Chas will have done likewise in the past, or would do if the circumstance arose. And yet, knowing that, Chas still walks into the trap. It is fate. It is a death wish. Many criminals are picked up on the run when they take shelter in their home patch, or with relatives, because they are incapable of living incognito outside a particular framework of places, people and habits. Being holed up in a room, or even a flat or house, is not much better. Sooner or later they step out into the air, freedom . . . with the chance of being caught.

Meanwhile, Harry Flowers' home life has been disturbed. He is lying in his bed at home, filmed in the penthouse of the Royal Garden Hotel in Kensington, his young man for the night in the bathroom sprucing himself up. The associates are arriving. Harry is not pleased with the bother, though deep down he knows he encouraged it. His star performer has become a liability and he knows that too. He would prefer to bury his head in the sand, metaphorically, and hope that by the time he comes up for air all will be neat and rosy.

Not long before, Harry and Dennis had been talking in the nightclub about the future, about organisations in the States, indicating that the Mafia is the new world, progress. And now, a few hours later, Dennis walks in using the Americans as an example of what not to aspire to. "They'll call us . . . gangsters!" Make no mistake, at that time the British villain was a criminal, a robber, a thief, a thug . . . anything but a gangster. The Kray twins had their minds set on being linked to the Mafia, a 'desire' to be gangsters, but they never attained that level.

Whilst the threat of the police is voiced, as yet they are not a relevant part of the film, never will be. All we have seen of 'law and order' is a detective sergeant with a scarred face who checks out Joey Maddocks' damaged premises and suggests that unless he makes a signed statement containing allegations against Harry Flowers, nothing can be done. In fact, he concludes before departing: "Looks like you've got a war on your hands, Joey." Nothing to do with us. It's a private matter. Even a family matter. And that suits the police. That the policeman openly talks about who did it, in the same way the police did about the Krays and others of the time, indicates there was little desire to do anything directly. Backhanders were common. It wasn't until the Seventies that Scotland Yard had its first major scandal, the first round of cosmetic surgery carried out for public consumption, and various high-ranking officers (Commander Drury of the Flying Squad being the highest) locked away. The rest were swept under the carpet, keeping "the filth", as Steve refers to them, out of sight for a while.

Steve's flight is the other occasion when a policeman shows his face. It is almost a reference to *Dixon of Dock Green*, a series about a famed homely bobby that originally graced our television screens in the Fifties and made us all feel loving towards the police. Steve, fleeing from the flat, destined to raise the alarm, is ordered to stop in the street. "Don't you bloody move," says our friendly bobby on the beat from the other side of the road. Steve could easily outrun the copper, who could only blow his whistle, but somehow, in that era, it was felt you might as well face the music. After all, Steve's done nothing wrong. His boss has been murdered, and he was just a worker in the shop. He might have been a bit of a tearaway, but not a villain. Since those times, anyone in that situation wouldn't have slowed, let alone stopped, when challenged by such an ineffectual looking character as this policeman.

Another side of Harry Flowers is now being revealed. His partners are male; he has a young man in the bathroom cleaning himself when we join the scene. Though it has not been overly stated, it seems one can assume at this point that Dennis is homosexual. And probably Rosie, too. Dennis has made his entrance, tossing off his coat and taking a stance that begs no questions. Rosie has come in with him and not only has a delicate touch, tapping a lamp to make a faulty bulb reconnect, but then directs a mouth spray into his throat. We realise now that his name, whether Rosie or Rosebloom, might well be female in origin, for good reason. And that any layering of ideas that we might pursue in relation to the writings of Jean Genet is going to be apposite.

This emphasis on homosexuality in relation to the criminal fraternity in this film has not always gone down too well. The actors have played along, laughed about it, but Jimmy Evans was none too pleased, as noted earlier.

Albert Donoghue doesn't see it the same way. No one would deny that Ronnie had his preferences. "He didn't hide the fact that he was a homosexual, he liked the young boys – I mean young men not children – and they were known as his 'prospects'." But Donoghue doesn't see him as standing alone. "Ronnie wasn't the only gangster I knew who preferred men to women. There's half a dozen villains I can name who were queer, and they weren't shy about letting anybody know about it. Even in the Sixties this wasn't anything unusual."

Of the main characters only Bindon is ready to show his manhood and proclaim there's nothing wrong with me. I'm a man, a real man. A man all the time.

Little things add to this matter of cleaning up after the event, whether in the bathroom, where Shannon will end the sequence, or the throat, in the hole, as Rosie refers to it regularly, spraying it clean. Or Dennis sucking fresh mints: Polo, the mint with the hole.

All these turnabouts sound simple and corny and punning, but the film works in this way too, layer upon layer of references so that your mind is constantly working, attentive, laughing at it, with it, keeping you – the spectator – on your toes, keeping a level of lightness as counterpoint to the violence being piled on wave after wave.

And whilst the film started with a jet streaking through the blue, here in the bedroom, the power has deflated; the jet that Dennis toys with is a silver ornament that turns into a cigarette lighter. A poor substitute for the forceful expulsion earlier.

All to indicate that they have to clean themselves of their problem: Chas. Bindon is the one who voices what needs to be done with a sick animal: put it out of its misery. Our misery. The misery of "this terrific democratic organisation". Right, Joey? Ah, he's no longer here. He's already departed.

A sequence of signs to reinforce the need for cleaning up: tidying everything away is in progress. On the streets of Wandsworth where Chas is jammed in a telephone box, the council sign outside states: "This is a litter black spot. Keep Wandsworth tidy." Chas has to be got rid of. Tidied away. Killed.

He knows his fate. Told to wait by Harry, he draws with his free hand, doodles on the telephone directory, doodles a man, and then loops a noose around his neck, drawing the armature, the gallows, to finish the job. Realising what he has unconsciously drawn, he scribbles to erase the image, and hangs up the phone. Fate has called the shots. He knows that. Hello, hello, Harry? He still thought Harry would understand. They go back. Hello. Hello. Anybody there? The ultimate book of communication reveals the loneliness of this distance runner.

With fate showing its hand unconsciously, it comes to mind that the Swiss artist Giacometti would always scribble and doodle in the cafés or anywhere he rested for a few minutes. In recent times archives have turned up his 1963 drawings of Christine Keeler made across the top and margins of *France-Soir*, the photograph and article beneath reporting on the Profumo scandal in London.

Not only does Chas' drawing have the style of Giacometti's work, but the telephone box is also filmed in a way that emphasises it as the type of armature that one finds in Giacometti's (and Bacon's) art.

And as Chas scribbles it out, obliterates it, the passing truck freezes, the image ends, crash. Chas knows his fate. There is that inner scream, that Artaudian cry, a screaming Bacon Pope, all pouring forth with that truck ending.

These are not fancies. The way Roeg frames his shots shows that he is aware of all these echoes and potentials.

Chas' fate is sealed. He will go to Aunt Mary in Barnstaple, termed 'a village' in earlier drafts, which will go down well with the town's inhabitants. He will be traced there. He puts his mother's safety in jeopardy, not that his mother knows exactly what he does. He's just in a spot of bother and needs to go away for a while. "Now behave yourself, mind," every mother's message to her son, whether he be called Charlie or whatever. He's a good lad really. I don't believe anything I read in the papers. Violet always turned out her boys, Ronnie, Reggie and Charlie, looking smart and presentable, clean shirts laid out each morning.

Red is still the order of the day. If there's one consistency in this film it will be red. London likes red. Red telephone boxes. Red double-decker buses. Red chairs at the station. Chas goes about changing his identity, changing his hair, lacquering a mix of a cream, an antiseptic tube that he snatched as he left his wrecked home, with the remnants of a discarded tin of red paint, spreading the last traces of his redecorated flat on his head.

What is he thinking? He might look cool, but he's pushing all the wrong buttons. "Wouldn't you?" William Burroughs might drawl.

Cut in Jagger spraying his red wall with black. Cut in more than once. We can only use the name 'Jagger' for we know nothing more. Mick sprays the wall that we saw earlier. He is not covering it with black, but building a frame, an armature, painting edges to it, even though it's only at the 'T' stage. An empty frame even. Can he fill it? Or is this symptomatic of his condition? Giving it a shadow existence. There is a move towards Mark Rothko.

Not that Jagger was necessarily thinking of artworks as he painted the wall, or that his movement was to do with action painting in the way it was with the acid painting of the car. But there is a correlation and comparison of movements. Again Jagger is not using a brush, but a modern way to cover the wall, or indeed a canvas, handling a spray gun.

Whether there is a conscious relationship, the one that springs to mind relates to Mark Rothko. The colours, the red, can probably match a Rothko canvas, and the black fits. But do they fit? Is this a feeling? Seeing a Rothko is about feeling, emotion. We enter into a Rothko, initially through its vastness, for many are as big as the wall in the film. When Rothko held his first major exhibition in London in 1961 at the Whitechapel Gallery, people were simply driven into awe and silence, "beyond words". Many said they went expecting to make derisive remarks, but on entering the gallery they became overwhelmed, "sublimely full", as one recalled, "and yet entirely – shockingly – empty".

The music is getting upbeat. Jagger is going to arrive in full flow, we imagine. He will perform.

Chas heads for Paddington station to take a train to Barnstaple, "change at Exeter". With time to kill, he heads for the cafeteria. There seems to be no attempt to conceal the spatial arrangements. We see out the window and there is a lonely railway siding. In fact this was filmed in a buffet at Olympia, an auxiliary station used when exhibitions are staged in the nearby halls. This is not the first time that disorientation on this level has not been worried about. It's a purposeful misaligning of space, not a slip of continuity. The bear moves around in Turner's house, Chas' rooms shift dimensions, the exterior of Flowers' office in Mount Street does not appear to be above a nightclub, whether the Raymond Revue Bar or any other.

A chance meeting across a cafeteria table of a red-haired villain and a guitar case takes Chas in a new direction. For the first time he has made a decision that will take him into uncharted territory, a way that leaves few traces, except for the taxi driver and the few people in the street around Powis Square as he strolls towards his destination, people who might or might not read the newspapers (the *Daily Express*, the *Daily Sketch*, the *Evening Standard*, the *Daily Mirror* . . .) and pick up on the photos that will surely appear in the popular press. "That's him."

His saviour is a guy who looks like a double for Jimi Hendrix (with the bearded touch of Eldridge Cleaver, prescient for Jimi's future Black Panther interests), a recent arrival in London, who is taking the place by storm, particularly among the musicians, turning up to jam at virtually every hot nightspot. Here he goes under the name of Noel. Not Father Christmas, though he may as well be. A godsend under the cloak of Noel Redding, even if the guy playing him was called Noel Swabey. (Not to forget that Jimi's younger brother was called Leon, not that anyone would have known at the time.) It's a joke and more. The saddest joke is that the voice was later dubbed by Ian McShane, a good English actor who likes to play criminal parts, among other cheeky chappies. Other voices would be dubbed, particularly for the American market, but today it seems that the DVD available has no dubbing except for Noel. Revenge on Hendrix, revenge for daring to change music so dramatically. Flash bastard. We'll pull him down a peg or two. Society doesn't always change in the ways one thinks or hopes it might. Nothing is as it seems.

At least they left him with images of women plastered across his guitar case, kept his libido intact with true credentials. Women flit by. A young woman brings Chas his drink. A young girl peeks in the window, the first of two youngsters, this one looking remarkably like Lorraine: "a prescient image, an echo of what's to come", as Annabel Davis-Goff remarked.

Noel's mother is there. She will help him on his way, just as Chas' own mother has given us context for his life.

Whilst Noel gives any stray ear the information that his flat is temporarily up for rent while he goes to Liverpool – another joke, this one at the expense of The Beatles, hitting the Brits below the belt – it is the mother who sets the image we are to have as we turn Mick Jagger into Turner, the painter of inner landscapes, who we can finally pin a name to. Or soon, anyway. "That Turner. He's a drug addict. He's peculiar. He's a hermit. He can't face reality. That's what it is." Now we know who we're dealing with.

One must remain bemused that his mother is called Mrs Bono. As we will learn, the music for the film was supposedly to be supplied by Jagger and his friends, the Stones, whereas circumstances forced the filmmakers to turn to others, people who already had a hand in The Rolling Stones recording catalogue, with Jack Nitzsche at the core. Jack of course worked with Sonny Bono . . . Sonny and Cher, another couple who landed on our shores and had a blast at the charts before going in different directions. Sonny was 11 years older than Cher. Is some form of statement being implied? Or just another whimsy for the amusement of those involved?

We have seen Chas' girlfriend and every other female used and marginalised. We have yet to see how the women in Turner's house will be presented. And here, at the pivotal point of the film, to whom do the men turn at their hour of need?: their mothers.

Whilst there are no conspicuous female references in the art, the literature, the cinema . . . there is the real presence of both Buffy Sainte-Marie and Merry Clayton in the music. Both women are far from decorative, and the film would be poorer without them. And though we have not stepped into the house, when we do we will discover that the part of Pherber will be central. She will present all the roles that women are required to provide. She will be the controlling agent, the instigator at the core, the magician who engineers the manoeuvres, physically and mentally.

We have already seen that this film would not have shaped up as it did if it hadn't been for the very real presence and input of Anita Pallenberg, Marianne Faithfull and Deborah Dixon. Outside the personal, the Women's Movement was building its base. Germaine Greer's *The Female Eunuch* was on the typewriter.

10) nothing is as it seems (2)

CHAS enters Powis Square accompanied by Ry Cooder's blues playing on the soundtrack. The idea seems to be that the location, in the heart of Notting Hill, is an area where black people live, mainly West Indians, alongside others who can't afford more than these poor, run-down conditions. In the few shots we see outside the house, the black presence is shown on the peripheries. We have seen already a black show-girl in the wings at the club, a black garage attendant watching at the car hire firm. And we have seen that Noel has his place, in the basement. Though the film is about violence, and though Notting Hill had under-lying racial tensions at the time, this is allowed to lie dormant for the time being.

Only when we step inside the house – with the faded gloom of its retired and reclusive rock star, Turner, whose finances are starting to dwindle – do we see the truth of the black situation. Not only has Turner made his money exploiting black music, but also he has kept a black musi-cian as a pet in the basement. At least that is how it comes across. And if you don't like that image, try "my son", the term Noel uses when recounting his story about Turner to his mother. Soon we will hear the racial tension boil; soon we will be awoken by The Last Poets. But will it be treated as real or faux rage?

Chas is dropped off by taxi and walks towards 81. This is not the real number and the address is only used for its façade. Chas is about to step through the looking glass, to go into the mirror. And as he does so the film splits in two. When he enters this new world, though not 'the New World' that Dennis had talked up, despite nominal contact with the outside world, there is little evidence that this will be a thriller, that the 'chaps' who work for Harry Flowers, the media or the police are looking for Chas, and closing in. The world he steps into is outside time. It's as if the clock will stay still when the outside world is excluded. (Further, the idea of Cocteau's world through the mirror in *Orphée* resonates.) There is no television, no hint of radio, not even a telephone "up 'ere". The only contact is via the payphone in the basement that Noel used. Other requirements can be brought in by Mrs Gibbs and Lorraine, the daily cleaner and her daughter.

Polanski was one of Donald's friends in Paris. Just as *Repulsion* had impressed itself on Donald, so Polanski's subsequent film can be seen as having a bearing. *Cul-de-sac* (1966) is primarily about two gangsters, one injured, on the run after a bungled robbery, who find their way to the isolated home of a reclusive and effeminate man and his attractive young French wife. These two gangsters would seem to be successors of Gus and Ben from Pinter's *The Dumb Waiter*, and Goldberg and McCann from *The Birthday Party*. They also need the use of a phone to contact their boss. The overtones of Pinter (and indeed Samuel Beckett's tramps), both acknowledged, are to the fore as Jack MacGowran and Donald Pleasence are cast in key roles, both actors having high credentials on how to perform Pinter and Beckett on the stage.

Much has been made of the idea that *Performance* is in fact two films, as if the two parts do not connect properly. And yet a film from a few years earlier, that had a profound effect on those interested in European cinema, was Antonioni's *L'Avventura* (1960). On a boat trip to an island one of the women vanishes. As the search continues in vain the film changes course and focuses on another woman, Monica Vitti, her relationship with a man becoming the narrative focus. The split in two is meant as a new direction, a new world. Not long before *Performance* was filmed, Antonioni had been in London making his Swinging Sixties film, *Blowup*. One of the key scenes, a drug party, was shot in Christopher Gibbs' home in Cheyne Walk. Gibbs will be instrumental in the décor that lies behind the door of 81 Powis Square, the house that Chas is about to step into.

In effect, though *Performance* appears as a two-part film, it is one film with a mirror in the middle that both reflects and joins the two parts, with the question of identity floated through the first part to be inverted and explored, or exploited, in the second part.

The decayed façade of the property was of no interest to the owners. It merged with the rest of the neighbourhood, made its occupants fit in. An area where the West Indian population had a stronghold, courtesy of the era of the unscrupulous landlord Peter Rachman, was now being frequented by hippies, with Portobello Road in close proximity. These occupants could draw thick curtains to exclude the outside world. Their interest was the exploration of the mind, whether by books or the use of drugs.

It's worth noting, as a subtext, that Brian Jones lived in Powis Square with a girlfriend for a while in the early Sixties.

On arrival at number 81, Chas rings the bell and glances around. The morning's milk has been delivered. Also on the steps are a carton of cream, a tray of mushrooms in potting soil, and four Mars bars. The latter caused some comment, as they were a quite tasteless and hurtful reference to Marianne Faithfull and the Redlands drugs saga. Whose idea was it to place them there? Whose sense of humour was in full swing? It seems that it could have been the idea of the set dresser, who thought it would make a good joke. When Nic Roeg saw them, he asked for an explanation, as he had little idea of their pertinence. They remained. At the time no one really contemplated how much of a legend the whole Mars bar saga would become, how one of those bars would dog Marianne's life and enter the mythology of the times. Even as recently as March 2011, Marianne related to *The Observer*: "I've hated being associated with that famous confection. I don't eat them and I never have, and what is said to have happened just never did. So I have no good feelings about it whatsoever. It's meant the loss of my feminine self." Note that she doesn't actually soil herself by naming it directly. Keith Richards is the most recent commentator: "How the Mars bar got into the story I don't know. There was one on the table – there were a couple, because on acid suddenly you get sugar lack and you're munching away. (...) But the bar as a dildo? That's rather a large leap. The weird thing about these myths is that they stick when they're so obviously false. Perhaps the idea is that it's so outlandish or crude or prurient that it can't have been invented."

Why someone should want to take a confectionery that most of us treasured from our childhood and give it that twist is sad for those who invented the tale. There are people within the police force and within society who have a warped mind. That is how the Stones and their friends thought about it. For many of us, who were born just before the war ended, or just after, growing up in a time of rations, a Mars bar was a treat.

You didn't necessarily eat it all in one go. You might slice it and eat it over a couple of days or more. Sweets were a treat, not part of the daily diet.

The tendency is to think the Mars inclusion was a mischievous gesture by Donald Cammell, either to annoy Jagger or to please him. One feels sure that Jagger would have gained more pleasure from the idea that Noel, as the tenant in the basement who has echoes of Hendrix, is below while they were on the floors above. It has piquancy, for when Hendrix first came to London in 1966, Jagger suggested that Marianne should go to see him play. She did, at the Seven and a Half. She noted that he was good, but that he hadn't got his persona together: "he wasn't yet the voodoo chile." A few months later when Jagger and Marianne went to see Hendrix at the Speakeasy, Hendrix came off stage and squeezed in on the couple's seating, turning his attention to Marianne, propositioning her outrageously while bad-mouthing Jagger. Mick tried to ignore his behaviour and chose not to cause a scene. Marianne left with Mick that night.

Another touch of the set dresser's humour appeared in the station cafeteria scene where a box of Cadbury's Roses (another treat of the period, something you would buy on Mother's Day, or when visiting home) is sitting on the table with Mrs Bono. It was part of the running visual gag around Rosebloom and roses.

Once Chas steps into the house a shot is offered of him standing in the entrance hall, with the initial unnerving idea that he has stepped into a horror scene, a notion encouraged by the addition of a few suitable bars on the soundtrack. This moment appears to be a fixed shot, until suddenly the camera moves, suggesting that there is in fact someone watching Chas, a regular occurrence for Roeg in his subsequent films, always noting that we are all being watched, whether we know it or not.

As production designer for the first time on a set, Richard Macdonald took the opportunity to build a spiral staircase in the studio for Losey's *The Servant*, "right up to the top where it ends in an absolute blank trap in the room of Vera. And to the bottom where it ends in a trap that opens onto Royal Avenue in the snow," Losey recalled. Because it was constructed, it could be explored for vantage points, angles, power positions, it could be used to link all the rooms for interplay. Whilst *Performance* was based in a real house in Lowndes Square, the staircase was still employed as the spine to return to before going into a different room, a different burrow. It even had a real additional offbeat touch with the top of the house inhabited by its caretaker and his companions.

Chas has to live by his wits once he enters the house. It is Lewis Carroll's Wonderland, full of puns and associations. Looking around the basement room, he sees an image of James Dean on the wall, way before the viewer knows the poster is present, and introduces himself as "Johnny Dean" to Pherber, the young woman there to receive the intruder. Though he says that Noel is "an ol' friend", she knows he is not. Yet on reporting upstairs she tells Turner that Johnny Dean, the new lodger, is close with Noel. "Actually, he's obviously very, very deeply involved with Noel." She sees danger in Chas, and she sees herself as a temptress, a seducer, the spider maintaining the web. Albert Donoghue, the Kray's enforcer, said that women are drawn to people like him: "it's the aura of danger, violence and evil that captivates even very attractive, high-class women."

Whether as a participant, or a viewer relaxed in our seat, the world is to become one of shiftings. Anita Pallenberg as Pherber stretches out on Noel's bed. She is dressed in a second-hand red fox fur coat, bought as a present to herself with money earnt from a modelling assignment in Paris in 1963 or '64. She wears loose trousers beneath. But with the next shot, from Chas' perspective, she suddenly has no trousers. She flexes her legs, and reveals them as bare all the way to the top. But this isn't only Chas' viewpoint and imagination, for we also find her desirable. Thus a full shot of the scene from the side shows her still with bare legs. It's a distancing moment, a twist to disorientate us, to confuse reality and fantasy. Pherber also adds to our mental torture by rubbing and plucking at the fur around her pubic area.

To add another layer to this important sequence of shots, it now gains relevance in terms of the Mars bar inclusion, for Marianne at the time of the raid was wrapped in a fur rug. And legend has it that she flashed it open for all to see, both her friends and the raiding police, in a mischievous way while on the sofa, and then again as she was going up the stairs accompanying the policewoman who wanted to search her 'naked body' for any drugs concealed about her person.

In the earlier draft, *The Performers*, Pherber was susceptible to the 'juggler' who had "dropped from a Fellini film into the basement . . . his pockets full of tinsel money, his eyes full of knives". She knew he was leading them somewhere, but not where exactly.

The labyrinth that was this house's construct was not all located in Lowndes Square. Beneath the staircase, the basement room was filmed at 25 Hyde Park Gate. One needs to keep one's wits about one. Like many a labyrinth, there are doors that can be peered into but not entered. At least Chas found the right room eventually.

The mix of images in Noel's burrow takes in art like Peter Blake's *Doktor K. Tortur*, the political with Martin Luther King, cinema with James Dean and *Bonnie & Clyde*, as well as psychedelic and music references with Dylan, Jim Morrison and others. Many of the images collaged here, and upstairs on the screens in the big room, relate to a world found in the art of Martin Sharp and his *Oz* work, alongside that by Nigel Waymouth and Michael English, known as Hapshash & the Coloured Coat. When George Melly visited the latter in their studio, he noted that their work showed no attempt to conceal the sources, "almost a collage of other men's hard-won visions: Mucha, Ernst, Magritte, Bosch, William Blake, comic books, engravings of Red Indians, Disney, Dulac, ancient illustrations of treatises on alchemy". The imagery in Noel's room and upstairs is an extension of that principle, as indeed are the references in the film. Boxes within boxes within boxes. Borges is an influence that runs deep.

Back upstairs, Pherber collects her film camera, an 8 mm, and shoots her reflection in the mirror.

Anita had had no intention of being on the shoot of the film. She had been involved in various sessions writing and talking through the ideas for the film. The character of Pherber was drawn on her, closer than any other character, right from the initial stages, but the role had been lined up variously for Marianne Faithfull, then Tuesday Weld . . . It was only once shooting was under way that Donald had to resolve the crisis of Weld's broken ankle and asked Anita if she would play the part. He had been impressed by her acting in Volker Schlöndorff's film *A Degree of Murder* (1967). Anita would be ideal for his film. His hunch was right. As Germaine Greer observed at the film's release: "What she brought to *Performance* was not a performance, but herself."

Pallenberg's problem was that she was pregnant. She wanted to have the child. But in the end she decided to have an abortion, and defer having children.

Keith was none too pleased that Anita wanted to do the film. He offered to cover whatever fee she was receiving. He was worried that Anita was about to step into a role that required having a relationship with Jagger, as the script had been talked about enough during its preparatory stages. He knew only too well that close proximity between the two was tempting, for Jagger and for Anita. He'd been there already in that game with her as regards Brian. The other twist was that Marianne had been helping Mick shape his part, with Weld or someone else as Pherber. "What I hadn't anticipated was that Mick, by playing Brian and Keith, would be playing two people who were extremely attractive to Anita and who were in turn obsessed with her."

No one has suggested where the name Pherber was drawn from, or why. Most of the names have relevance, even if only as private jokes. Pherber was a name that was in place by the end of the very first outline. That Donald and the circles he moved in were discovering Tangier and Marrakech, that the Berbers were the inhabitants, and indeed that stories around the Berber prostitutes with their genital tattoos were intriguing to them, suggests that it stems from that source.

Anita knew what she was getting herself into with Donald. He was an extremist, "he would have it all or nothing". She had been involved sexually with Donald earlier in Paris. It has always sounded like she never hit it off with Jagger, something that probably offered itself as a challenge. In later interviews she often cites that Mick was in love with Keith, that Keith was the man Mick wanted to be, more casual, not so uptight. These stories and their fluctuations are part of The Rolling Stones' story, and have helped to feed the *Performance* legend too.

The art director was John Clark. He had recently worked on *Secret Ceremony* with Losey, filming not far away at Debenham House in Addison Road, with its turquoise ceramic tiles and green-glazed bricks, an Arts and Crafts nightmare, or splendour. The house in Lowndes Square was the opposite; they could start from scratch. Clark was asked to work with others. David Litvinoff was helpful in providing details for Chas' flat that they constructed there. But for Turner's house, Jagger asked if Christopher Gibbs could have a hand in the décor, as he had been involved in decorating his new home at 48 Cheyne Walk, and before that had shaped Jones' home environment. Christopher Gibbs thought it was quite magnanimous of a true professional, like John Clark, to let him become instrumental. As Gibbs recalled, he "was really nice about somebody coming in who didn't know about anything except what he wanted it to look like, and he wasn't a bit unfriendly. Then I had Donald's girlfriend working with me, Deborah Dixon, a beautiful Texan girl who I liked very much and who is a very good friend of mine still." Though Deborah had separated from Donald, he wanted her participation, he wanted "Turner's house and accoutrements as well as the costumes to correspond to an aesthetic we had shared". To that end she brought many objects from her home to decorate and be used: "silver goblets, Derby plates, Persian mirror . . ."

The earlier draft, *The Performers*, acknowledges what Donald sought, specifying that Turner's bedroom should be "decorated predominantly in the Gibbsian Moroccan manner, furnished with strange and beautiful things." Gibbs saw his brief as being to make a setting in which Jagger would be comfortable, drawing on his experience of knowing Mick well. Whilst he had decorated 48 Cheyne Walk with plenty of Moroccan splendour, it also mirrored his own tastes and the environment at his home a few doors along from Mick's, described by one observer as "a dreamlike vision straight out of the Arabian Nights". As far as the set was concerned, "Lots of things were chosen for the glitter of the surface or the sumptuous appearance . . . antique Moroccan things, ancient Persian carpets, tapestries, those enormous Japanese plates." But not everything was brought in from abroad. Some of the silks came from Ulla Larson, who had a stall in the Chelsea Antiques Market on the King's Road, for which she received a name check from Lucy as the Myers twins leave after their failure to sell Turner the Magritte painting. And Gibbs notes: "I was making some things and hiring some things from film-hire places." Gibbs was ideal for the role, being a man with refined sensitivities with regard to everything that concerned him. He describes himself as "an enthusiast, a chaser and scholar of a rich diversity of works of art and man". For him the idea of stepping into the ephemeral world of a film set was a delight, "spinning all that up and inventing it as you went along: the great thing about that world is the immediacy of it, the accidents and the sudden mad demands." The overall effect had to be "something mysterious and beautiful and unexpected, exotic and voluptuous and far away from pedestrian; some hint of earthly paradise". It was expressed another way by John Clark: "When you went into Lowndes Square you took one breath and you were stoned."

There was probably a good deal of truth in that if one believes the reports of the hash being brought onto the set. As with any of the underground environments, as noted by George Melly when he visited Hapshash & the Coloured Coat, you felt that you "had tumbled into a world where time operates at a different speed".

Props were always an important part of the set. Annabel Davis-Goff recalls that Jagger asked "for the entire run of *Country Life*" as part of the props, which stuck in her mind, though they don't seem to have found their way into any final shot. For Nic Roeg: "props have their own life." They create credibility and depth of feeling to the space. "When you go into someone's house, what do you do? I head for the bookshelves."

When care is taken with the props it is annoying to lose them. Tony Sanchez says in his famous account of his time with the Stones that Anita would put props aside and ask him to smuggle them out under his coat. "Once it was an Oriental headband with a snake twined around it; another time it was the bust of an Egyptian god." Donald knew what was going on but didn't want to upset Mick or Anita by complaining. But it had to stop. A scene would be half-completed and a prop would vanish overnight. Sanchez says that Donald whispered in his ear one day that he wished people would leave his props alone, and from that point on he refused to carry out Anita's assignments. Another account indicates that Donald banned Sanchez after suspecting him of stealing a gun being used as a prop.

Whilst it is noticeable that the rooms and the viewer's eye are crammed with detail, there is also an important idea that things do not sit still. Not only do small props move around, but also large ones, adding to the notion that not only is time shifting, but spatial arrangements are being manipulated too. This is only to be expected in an environment where the characters are half-stoned. How better to avoid the tired cliché of staggering characters, or glazed eyes, or woozy camerawork. How much better to keep shifting the viewer's perceptions, perceptibly and almost imperceptibly. Nothing is as it seems.

The white polar bear skin that moves around the rooms might well have its origins in the décor of the famed decadent Robert, Comte de Montesquiou-Fezensac, immortalised both by Proust's Baron de Charlus in *A la recherche du temps perdu* and by Huysmans as the reclusive aesthete, des Esseintes, in *A rebours* (Against Nature). To set the scene, we follow the poet Stéphane Mallarmé into the Comte's home in the rue Franklin. As recounted by Robert Baldick in his biography of J.-K. Huysmans: "It was late at night when the poet was shown over the house, and the only illumination came from a few scattered candelabra; yet in the flickering light Mallarmé observed that the door-bell was in fact a sacring-bell, that one room was furnished as a monastery cell and another as the cabin of a yacht, and that the third contained a Louis Quinze pulpit, three or four cathedral stalls, and a strip of altar railing. He was shown, too, a sled picturesquely placed on a snow-white bearskin, a library of rare books in suitably coloured bindings, and the remains of an unfortunate tortoise whose shell had been coated with gold paint." Mallarmé was amazed. "He went away in a state of exaltation," the Comte wrote later, and related "to Huysmans what he had seen during the few moments he spent in Ali-Baba's Cave."

It has to be borne in mind that most of *Performance*'s main protagonists had good backgrounds, if not privileged and moneyed backgrounds. The world of the dandies and dilettantes was never far from view. That James Fox should be playing a character with working-class roots, the very opposite of his own, was no accident. This frisson was part of the mosaic.

Not only the bohemian set, but the hippies too, the 'peace and love' brigade, many of whom lived around Notting Hill and its neighbouring areas, were not exactly poor. Few were of a real working-class background. When you watch footage of Pink Floyd being interviewed from that period, it is clear from the plummy voices where their origins lay. As Barry Miles notes, Pink Floyd, for all the promotion of them as the face of the Underground, were actually just a band trying to make it through an opening that had cropped up for them. Only Syd Barrett seemed to share any of the Underground's ideals, and of course Syd became a casualty. Not that everyone generally didn't speak better in those times, articulated more clearly. That Jagger should choose to create another mask, with his mock-cockney voice, is fascinating in hindsight.

Whilst the first part has been a mosaic of the external world, sliding images and time back and forth, requiring us to keep our visual wits about us, now the mosaic becomes internal, withdrawing into sensations of the mind and intellectual reflections.

When Pherber moves upstairs with her camera to rejoin Turner and Lucy, the third member of their household arrangement, who are asleep in bed, we expect to see a peace-loving sexual scene evolve, far from the violence of the opening sexual sequence between Chas and Dana some 30 minutes earlier, for this new environment has all the signs of a Sixties hippy pad, with its mixture of North African and Middle-Eastern cloths draped for their colourful splendour, and the soundtrack reminiscent of Moroccan music. The conjured smell of this scene, as other scenes, will be of incense burning, even if we cannot see it at this point. And indeed that is what we will experience, after Pherber has reminded us that she has an 8 mm camera and intends to shoot some film. And 'shoot' is the operative word, for she takes up the stance of a gunman, rests the camera across her left arm, aims and fires. This play on the word 'shoot' will continue; shooting a needle into her buttock later, whilst Chas shoots his gun for a second time in that same room, just after he has told them he has to "shoot off".

This terminology is not far from the unintentionally violent language we all use in our lives. Anita has regularly recounted how she "hit" on Brian Jones at that initial meeting with the Stones. She saw herself as his groupie. It might well be sexual spiel, but it's the language derived from the criminal. If you're hit, you're dead.

Once Pherber has finished filming beneath the covers, she lays aside her camera and joins in the love scene with Turner and Lucy. For a few moments we relax into the sight and play mind games with what is going on before our eyes. The opening scene with Turner is a stark contrast to Chas' opening scene of violence with Dana.

Whilst this is going on in front of the canvas, behind the scenes another scenario was being played out. Keith Richards and Anita didn't live in London; they were based at Redlands, on the south coast. For the eight-week duration of the shoot, starting from September 5, it was arranged that Anita and Keith would rent Robert Fraser's flat at 23 Mount Street for £30 a week, as he was moving into another one further up the road at 120, Kenneth Tynan's old flat. Though that was the agreement,

Robert never moved out and, effectively, as Anita pointed out, "all we really rented was Christopher Gibbs' four-poster bed".

Keith spent some of his days playing guitar and working on songs for a future album, and the rest of the time in Robert Fraser's company. This was a double-sided blade, for Fraser had a heroin habit, and was instrumental in both Keith and Anita obtaining their drug habits. And he was also instrumental in creating a bad atmosphere between his friends. The intent might not have been malicious, but the results played out over many years.

In the film itself jealousy has no part, in fact it is dismissed whenever signs of it appear from Chas' lips. But it was part of the construct behind the camera.

As might have become apparent, the world of the people involved seemed to have its fair share of those who enjoyed manipulating others. Donald was as much a part of this game as anyone else. He probably thought he could use it effectively as an explorative device for the good of the film. By creating one tension it might develop other tensions that could be fed upon. This can work with actors, or indeed non-actors, but it's a fine line being trod, a large element of risk is likely.

Keith would work at the flat, writing songs that were destined for *Let It Bleed*, and at other times would sit in his Bentley parked outside the shoot in Lowndes Square. A world of myths has been constructed around this aspect of the film. Robert Fraser would go into the house and bring back stories to bait Keith, comments about Anita and Mick. He knew the script called for sex scenes to be shot right from the first days. Time in bed, time in the bath. Day in, day out. Though Anita was an actress, to some degree, she hadn't the discipline of the drama school approach on how to handle yourself on set. Keith was raging with jealousy outside. Fraser and others suggested that not only was sex happening on set, being filmed, but it was continuing below in the dressing room. Donald added to this, recounting what went on some years later, in the 1988 interview with David Del Valle, though what he said at the time of making *Performance* might be another matter. "The relationship between Mick and Anita was real. They became lovers, even though she was Keith Richards' lady. I'll never forget Keith Richards' Rolls-Royce parked across the street from the location, keeping an eye on his paramour. Jagger simply took Anita under the house for sex. Keith would come on the set looking for hanky-panky, not realising that he was standing about three feet above the action!"

Anita had to return home from a day's shoot to confront tensions and stories. As Anita said: "It was very difficult for me. Keith and Robert were both so cynical and sarcastic, slagging off the movie every day. I'd come home from filming and they would be slagging off Jagger, slagging off everything. I got quite confused. (...) In that period drugs seemed to be the biggest happening. The bathroom was the most important place. First you'd shoot up, then you'd puke, then you'd feel great. For me though, it always fizzled out because next morning I had to go to work. It just didn't seem real. I don't know what opinion Robert had of Donald Cammell and the film, because Keith thought it was rubbish. Although I think Keith liked the finished film, but we never really talked about it."

Whatever the reality, the stories abounded. After the fact, stories changed and the confusion developed further. A few years later one set of stories was told, later still further stories, and today Keith writes in his autobiography further reflections. But what happened at the time will always be blurred.

Keith knew better than to go into the house. He couldn't jeopardise the band. Donald banned Fraser from coming anywhere near the set. Sandy Lieberson summed it up in a filmed interview: "There were all kinds of psychological little games going on. They were all tremendous games players, particularly Donald."

Another angle is that Anita had Mick under her thumb. She was in control of the Stones in some respects; she wielded one form of power. It was always suspected, and then admitted, that she had sex with Jagger, off set, and that really everyone involved in the relationships felt betrayed.

But years later, in various accounts, Anita denied having sex with Jagger. And so the story seems to go on.

And then later Donald, in his 1992 filmed interview, seems to play it down. "They were a little unruly. The unruly one, and I'm sure he doesn't mind me mentioning this now, was Keith . . . who got extremely annoyed at what he thought was going on in the house."

But what about sexual chemistry on the set? This comes up when discussing many films and we as the audience either sense something from the film, or read about it in gossip columns. Film is an illusion and what might look like a wonderful, romantic scene could have taken hours to shoot, with any sexual ardour dampened by a whole crew watching, often bored and wanting the take to be right. Undoubtedly relationships do evolve, and might be noticeable on set. Bogart and Bacall in *To Have and Have Not* exude it, and they felt it. Whereas Fred Astaire and Ginger Rogers are said to have gone through 'six years of mutual aggression' despite the wonderful on screen relationship in their series of films. Other times people point out a relationship between a lead actress and director that is expressed through a direct look at the camera. But is the Jagger and Pallenberg story a myth created by Cammell, a bit of trouble-making, as has been suggested, or a real relationship, or fling, as Keith suggests, going off to screw Marianne to compensate?

Jagger has kept quiet because officially there is no biography, and thus no admittance, or denial. Only rumours. Collating the reports in books and articles from different factions, a sizeable amount after all these years, many feeding off each other, is one thing, asking people now to look back is another. Many have agendas to follow today that they didn't have earlier. Putting aside the archives, recently I heard a version that I'd not come across before, but which sounds quite plausible. Mick had no intention of having sex with Anita during the film, because of his loyalties to Keith and the band, among other reasons. But when the crunch came, he broke his resolution, and did have sex, for how long is not said, once or more. After that he was angry, angry with himself for his weakness. In other words, he's human. Even if she might have expected better from him, according to Marianne: "The only person who was never out of control and might have showed some restraint was Mick. But poor Mick was on a bit of a high wire himself. He was somewhat cowed by Donald, who had a ferocious temper and would go off like a firecracker, unleashing blistering tirades. Mick found the whole process of filming very bewildering. Compared to performing in a rock'n'roll band, it was excruciating. The repetition, the retakes, the out-of-sequence performing to thin air. Mick was losing control!"

Amongst the takes that Keith has now on that historic moment, there is the point that whilst he didn't really know the truth for a long while, he claims: "I smelled it. Mostly from Mick, who didn't give any sign of it, which is why I smelled it."

Paul Mayersberg, who has explored sexual relations in his screenplays, as in his novels, feels: "The most dangerous thing you can do is get involved sexually with another person. That's the thing that is going to cause you more pain than anything else you can do in your life, I think. There's plenty of anguish, there's plenty of bad memories, but there's also the actual instant blinding pain that can only come through encounters." You can flirt, you can be friends, but as soon as you have sex together, life changes irreversibly. Your relationship will always be different. It is a mark of how essential is our sexual being. We know this will happen and yet we still let it happen.

Because the film was shot chronologically, to see what would 'happen', what would evolve, this bed scene was part of the first days shoot in the Turner house, probably as a way to break down the characters and make them relax together. Or perhaps it was a bit of mischief on Donald's part. It is not easy to film sex scenes, particularly with non-actors. Just as Cammell didn't want the fight scene to be staged, so he wanted the sex scene to be filmed in the same way. Shoot and see what 'happens', and anything that goes awry can be sorted out later. Cammell was striving for the pornographic, whether of violence in the fight scene, or the sexual in the bed. "If we have learned nothing else from Genet, we can be sure of this: his result may have been art, but that's not as important as his intention, which was pornography," was a thought put across by the writer Kenneth Tynan in his introduction to the book *Dirty Movies*.

Anita reminds us that Donald "loved to play mind games. He liked to twist your head around. Wind you up. Mostly sexually. Sexual perversions. He would egg you on to imagine situations, fantasies and all that stuff."

In a sense what Donald was hoping to capture were ideas he had heard about The Living Theatre, mainly from Anita. But Julian Beck and Judith Malina's troupe were a way of life, not something from which one could conveniently extract ideas.

The scene was shot under the covers, as much for effect as anything. Nic used a 16 mm wind-up Bolex. "It was like a porno shoot," Anita recalled later. "There was a camera under the sheets and there was all kinds of sex going on, but I put it down to method acting." There were naked bodies, there was caressing. Whether there was actual penetration or not, there is no proof. Just allegations. Again, a jokey remark – "How was it for you?"

– that Cammell made to Nic as they emerged from the hot tent with the lights filtering through, is given distorted weight. You read it as you want, and everyone is happy.

It seems very little 'pornography' is in evidence from the out-takes, according to David Cammell. The lab that was processing the film was Humphries. The clapper loader suggested to David that a note be added to the camera sheets to make sure that one specific female technician was kept away from the footage in case she took umbrage at the content. In the event, of course, this particular woman did view the print and reported it to the manager. Next day, David Cammell received a phone call and went round with Sandy Lieberson. The managing director and chairman had the rushes on the desk, with a hammer and chisel next to them. They said that they could leave themselves "open to prosecution under the Obscene Publications Act" and then duly proceeded to destroy the print with the tools "in front of our eyes". The gesture made, the can with the negative was handed over, and they were asked to leave by the back door so that no one would see them carrying the can. Cammell took it to Technicolor and they printed it off.

(If the real film was having processing problems, where was Pherber expecting to process the home movie she was shooting for herself in the film?)

To give some perspective to the display, or not, of genitalia, and the speed with which censorship issues were changing, James Fox had been party to the handling of the censor, John Trevelyan, only a few years before with *The Servant*, the film that had brought him into the public eye. The scene in question was one of cunnilingus, or apparent cunnilingus, for nothing is actually seen. Sarah Miles as Vera is seducing James Fox. She is seated deep in an egg-cup chair, her feet dangling over the side, the same side, with Fox on the floor kissing her. There was nothing explicit about it, only an implication of cunnilingus, the camera pulled back behind the chair. It was the first time it had been presented on British screens, and the censor allowed it because Losey was the filmmaker and Harold Pinter the writer. Trevelyan had seen the script in advance and discussed the scenes where possible confrontations might arise.

It had occurred a few years before in Louis Malle's *Les Amants* (1958), resulting in the censor being set to work. But again it was all implied, the camera panning away from Jeanne Moreau's body to leave the rest to the viewer's imagination. You might be forgiven for not easily verifying these facts, for the new bible of truth, the internet, suggests cunnilingus on film first occurred with Roeg's *Don't Look Now* in 1973, or Jaeckin's *Emmanuelle* in 1974. Besides seeing *The Servant* for oneself, Alexander Walker's *Sex in the Movies* (Penguin, 1968) has a two-page spread of six frames from the scene as evidence.

Cunnilingus did not go away. It raised its head again in 1968 on the London stage, at the Royal Court, not surprisingly, with the staging of Michael McClure's *The Beard,* a short play with just two characters, Billy the Kid and Jean Harlow, its verbal duel rising to a physical climax with Billy on the floor between Jean Harlow's spread thighs. Again controversy was raised in the press, though the theatre was given club restrictions to proceed. Reviews of the time gave the impression that cunnilingus didn't even have a word in English. One referred to it as "a genital kiss by the man on the woman". Another wrote: "He plunges his head into her satin lap in an action so private that it still, apparently, lacks an English name." Really? 'Gamahuching' in Victorian sexual literature like *My Secret Life* has a healthy history, and cunnilingus dates back to 1887, with Havelock Ellis using it in 1905, and Gershon Legman writing the first book on the subject, *Oragenitalism*, originally published in 1940. This has a point because in 1972, Donald Cammell was working on a film version of *The Beard*, with Mick Jagger announced to play Billy the Kid. "What scared him was playing an American mythological character, when he has this uncertainty about looking absurd. But I saw it as a great comedy and I tried to make a change and be absurd. I wanted him to be not the demonic Mick, but the Mick I know very well who's a very humorous character offstage."

At the time, films could be seen in Paris in which sexual permissiveness had gone further, even if it were titillatory, the films originating from France, Italy, Denmark and Sweden, all straining the boundaries of nudity or bed romps. Unlike *Performance*, most did not seem natural, except perhaps Vilgot Sjöman's *I Am Curious (Yellow)*, which appeared in 1967 and ran the censorship gauntlet for its display of nudity, pubic hair and staged sexual intercourse, but mainly because the young woman is seen kissing her lover's flaccid penis.

One example of the bounds that were acceptable in sexual terms in radical movies in Europe at the time is *Quiet Days in Clichy*. It was based on Henry Miller's book, set in Paris, written in 1940 and published in 1956 by Olympia Press, but not filmed and released until 1970. Or attempted to be released, for copies were seized and it was banned and unavailable for many years in England, the United States and Sweden at least. This film, which is blatantly about having sex, and which brazenly tries to transgress by repeated use of the word 'cunt', does show sexual behaviour, even if today it seems rather passé in the way in which its characters behave. Its spirit of liberation is felt and accepted, its director Jens Jørgen Thorsen being primarily a Danish prankster and situationist. The film reflects Miller's creed of living life to the full in Thirties Paris. Though the bath scene in *Quiet Days* is sexual, even if appearing more of a sad affair than the intended *joie de vivre*, it's hardly a bath scene, more a way to stage nakedness. Unlike *Performance*, which has a true bath scene, as will become apparent.

One wonders whether the presence of Kenneth Anger in London, and his friendship with those involved around *Performance*, didn't lead to discussions and showings of underground movies of the period, including those pushing at the sexual boundaries, particularly a film like Jack Smith's *Flaming Creatures* (1963) or Warhol's early films. Not that Donald wanted to replicate them, rather that he hoped to venture into that terrain. Not that he wanted to show a penis creeping over someone's shoulder, or casual fondling of genitals and breasts . . . features of *Flaming Creatures*. "A treatment of sex which makes us aware of the restraint of all previous filmmakers," said Jonas Mekas.

Though Cammell wanted the scene to go as far as he thought he could take it, he also had a star in Mick Jagger who would determine ultimately where the line was drawn for himself and his image. He might never say anything publicly, but he would know how to handle the matter, eventually. Nothing is black and white rather than nothing is true; everything is permitted. I also use the above references because notions of Hollywood are distinct counterpoints, despite their underground category. *Performance* might often be termed a glorified home movie, but it is still a glorified Hollywood home movie, breaking the conventions and rules in some ways, but coming in on budget and time, which is how Hollywood views everything at the end of the day. It is a product after all.

Film is about glamour, sex, violence, stardom . . . ultimately about Hollywood. We must never forget that in terms of this film. Donald would not have fitted into the Zanzibar ethic. He would never have fitted into the European art film ethic, for while *Performance* plays against Hollywood in various ways, it also relates to it. And aspires to it. Overall, Nic would not have tolerated underground film ethics, though in terms of different scenes, he would explore whatever approaches seemed viable.

What is important though is that the sex scene seems to happen of its own accord. In fact many of the scenes have that naturalness, as if the camera had dropped in on peaceful activities in the daily life of the Turner household, letting the camera run Warhol style, "a treat for the senses" to use Sontag's comment on *Flaming Creatures*. And indeed, when she notes that Smith's film is more about "intersexuality" than homosexuality, we can see here with *Performance* that this is virtually the same, as only Pherber can be said to look female; the blurs at the edges, the merges and ambiguities that result from editing here (as indeed in the later bed scene) giving us this thought. "The film (scene) is built out of a complex web of ambiguities and ambivalences, whose primary image is the confusion of male and female flesh."

For Paul Mayersberg, sex in a novel allows the reader to imagine the scene as they want, something that cannot be accomplished on a screen. He suggests that the closer one gets to the subject, the more viewers turn off. "Is it something about film that is meant to appeal to a wider audience, and the more specific you get about a relationship in order to understand it, the narrower the field of appeal is? So a sexual encounter that appeals to certain people won't appeal to others. So if you find out what the origin of a sexual relationship, of an emotional relationship is, then it starts to wear off in its appeal to a wide audience because it turns out that it's something specific: the colour of her hair, the fact that she didn't wear a bra, the guy has a big cock."

Film needs a more general view to encompass the needs of a wider audience. "The truth is that film doesn't do well in describing emotional relationships of a sensual kind because they are always so personal and close and detailed and even fetishistic that they don't communicate on the screen. You don't like the actors so you don't want to see the film, whereas in a book you become that person. So you can become a person whom you don't like.

"In a story you can go on fucking all night so long as you can stand it or want it. On a screen you cannot have a scene of sex that lasts very long because people get bored or irritated. Why? Because they want to go and do it themselves. Because they want to be part of it and can't because it's a film, actors. My feeling is that voyeurism as a mode of sexual encouragement doesn't work on film except as a quick flash of something. It never works so that it just stays in your mind as an image. It doesn't work as a way of thinking or living. You cannot go on watching something on film in a way that you can in a book. So it occurred to me that the sort of scenes that were missing in films were the kind of scenes you could actually sustain intelligently in a book without being repetitious. And those are the scenes that everyone said you can put dots there, you don't need that. Scenes of explicit sex. Why if we're spending our lives in explicit sex isn't it a suitable subject? How can you go on doing it for a whole night, and it turns out it's boring. It wasn't boring when you were doing it so what makes it boring or upsetting or whatever?" The more the film can work with glimpses, the more the individual viewer can endorse and fabricate to suit their own pleasures. That this threesome sex scene in *Performance* shows no sexual play in anything but mild caresses, that it is over and gone quickly, is probably what makes it work.

We also have in the back of our heads that this is Mick Jagger, rock star, not Turner the character, and that he is in bed with two women, and that it is a *ménage à trois*. While it might be a fantasy of many viewers, up there on the screen it can obviously be an everyday occurrence for people like Jagger and other rock stars. It has always been noted that Donald Cammell favoured threesomes, and that Brian Jones was pleased to be part of that situation. And we also gather that Anita Pallenberg and Michèle Breton had been in a *ménage à trois* with Donald and Deborah at different times. Part of this reality was being transferred to the screen in *Performance*, with Jagger as Donald "to some extent, though I don't think he knew it", Jagger later remarked.

Going further, there is also the question of bisexuality that runs through this set-up. As I've shown, or indicated, almost every one of the main protagonists had a bisexual nature, or had a bisexual side they were willing to explore at various times in their early lives. Perhaps this should be recognised as acceptable in life. Unlike homosexuality, there is no commonplace pejorative term to taunt the bisexual person. Bisexuality is a lifestyle, not because one is gay or not, but just part of the love situation. Though for many people it suggests depravity and decadence, the psychiatrist Charlotte Wolff believes that human beings are aware of their double nature, of the maleness and femaleness they contain. If, as Freud says, their bisexuality is unconscious: "it is unconscious only because society has made it so with its labels of *normality* causing men and women to suppress their other side." Though people may feel what she calls their "bi-gender identity", most do not live it out in sexual relationships with both sexes.

Roeg has been kept out of this picture, but he notes, when shooting *Bad Timing,* that Art Garfunkel came up to him "and said he realised he was really playing me. But I told him that he was only part of it. I challenged him to decipher when I was wearing the trousers and when I was wearing the dress."

One film that would reside in the fabric of Cammell's life as well as in his thinking for this film is Truffaut's *Jules and Jim* (1961). There is a distinction to be made between a *ménage à trois* and troilism. Troilism or threesomes are a situation, an event, whereas *ménage à trois* is a household arrangement, a living condition, and does not necessarily mean that sexual relationships are part of the set-up.

'Onward, Christian Soldiers', sung by an eight-year-old cockney, takes us from the bed scene to Chas catching up on sleep in the basement. Lorraine, whom we had seen arriving with her mother, the 'daily', has discovered Chas in Noel's bed. "Who's been sleeping in his bed?" In fact it must have been a surprise, for not only will she ask Chas about Noel, but she had commented on arrival: "Oy mum, when's Christmas?" Not only the play on words, but the continual layerings that familiarity with Pinter's use of dialogue and working methods would prepare us for. Chas can relate to her, and responds positively when offered a cup of tea. He is soon to be pulled up, reminded wryly of his own profession, not as a juggler, but as a 'performer'. "D'you want to earn a bob?" She does. And before he knows it, his request for her to pop out and buy some turps so that he can remove the paint from his hair has moved from a bob to two bob to five bob, and then cut back when seemingly pushed too far to 'half a dollar', a playful use of our money system to switch currencies and the implications of the British/American references employed repeatedly. Nine-year-old

Laraine Wickens was given the part after she had been hanging around the production office demanding empty bottles on which she could collect the refunds. It was a way of earning a bit extra for a child in those times, more particularly if pocket money was non-existent.

Chas must wonder what he has stepped into. He had only just accepted Pherber extorting a high rent and extras from him. And now a child. Home from home.

The idea that Jagger should then move from three-in-a-bed sex to a prolonged bath scene with the two women in his spacious octangular bath, "with seventeenth-century Japanese dishes" and "tiles designed from a Persian carpet", also seemed to offend.

That we should see them cleaning themselves after sex is a good contrast again to the earlier post-sex Chas and Dana scene. There is a further irony, which is probably one reason for using the scene, in that the Stones were regarded as 'filthy', the letters pages to newspapers regularly reminded us at each outrage connected to the band, people suggesting they have their hair cut, given a bath, etc. That Brian Jones, known to the others in the band as Mr Shampoo, washed his hair twice a day, right back to the early Edith Grove days, makes it something of a joke.

After the film was finished, Jagger commented that he thought his character Turner's posturing was funny: "Too much intellectual posturing in the bath when you're with two women is not a good thing – that's not to be taken too seriously! It made my skin go all funny!"

But stay in a bath they did, filming for some days. At one point someone from Warners arrived, "stood, his Macintosh over his arm, expressionless on the edge of the set", and then expressed dismay that even the bath water was dirty. Nic commented that only dirty people wash.

What is successful about the bath scene, as with the bed scene, is the naturalness of the participants going about their ablutions without any sense of coyness or embarrassment, or any particular sense that they were covering up or trying to avoid angles for the camera. This is unusual, whether for mainstream, art house or underground films. In most films featuring bath scenes there is either a conspicuous use of bubbles, or a sinking of bodies beneath a high water level. Here it is hardly sexy, not played for its erotic contribution. If anything it has the sense of children at play in the bath. There is a movable yellow duck in view too, as in all good homes!

It's noticeable that in *Duffy* there was a large sunken bath in the father's country mansion suitable for a number to bathe together, and in *Secret Ceremony* another – where Elizabeth Taylor and Mia Farrow go through the usual coy bath scene routine.

To continue the gender ambiguities, one has to notice that, unlike in the published script, the dialogue in the bath does note the slippage: after Turner remarks that he doesn't want any more bums in his basement, Pherber sets the ball rolling by referring to Jagger as female, with "A juggler, madam."

Turner: I don't want her. I don't want her.

Pherber: You'd love her.

Turner: Yeah, you might like her.

Pherber: You'd love him.

Just like the naturalness of their bodies, they slip in and out of genders as easily.

Marianne Faithfull noted that Mick came home early more than once and found her in bed with another woman. He was astonished at first. "I did have girlfriends and I did have affairs with them," said Faithfull. "Mick knew about my girlfriends. His attitude was that he'd much prefer me to have a girlfriend than a boyfriend. Same as I preferred him to be in bed with a man rather than a woman."

Can an echo be found in Sartre's famous play *Huis Clos*, often translated as either *In Camera* or *No Exit,* neither offering a full understanding of the title, but which most understand by its oft-quoted line: "Hell is other people"? This play, set in hell, revolves around three people, a man and two women, and is an intellectual exercise in their existential position, locked in a room with only the company of the others and their issues, sins and memories to occupy their time, to torture each other . . . for eternity.

In *Performance* it is interesting to wonder whether it is hell, purgatory or paradise (on earth) that our three characters reside in. It would appear outwardly to be a kind of paradise, a freedom to do as they want, the opposite of Sartre's position for his characters in *Huis Clos*, and yet, as we discover, Turner would prefer not to be there, but to recover his demon and return to a life in the outside world. Chas offers the possibility of a way out.

Sartre wrote his play at the end of the war, with the Gestapo as the threat at his door, living a hell on earth. Turner's hell on earth can be changed if he jumps on the similar intruder, Chas, whom Pherber has admitted, and enters him to seek out his demon and thus escape through the open door.

Perhaps Turner, like Inez in Sartre's play, does face up to his situation, helped by Chas, who supplies the bullet, confronting his responsibility and his suffering, enabling him to step through the door and assert his existence, or as Sartre puts it: "Life begins on the other side of despair."

I use this reference because Sartre's play, as indeed his novel *Nausea*, has had a lingering life, alongside Camus' *L'Etranger* (*The Outsider/The Stranger*), and was a subtext to much intellectual thinking throughout the Fifties, Sixties and beyond.

When Chas first phoned Tony, his mate, he was at home in bed, which is strange for a commission agent at the fruit and veg market in the old Covent Garden, where an early morning start is the usual. But we are getting to notice that perceptible and imperceptible shifts occur in time and space. I am a film.

Though Chas understands that the outside world is seeking him, no great panic is conveyed. It's as if we are through the looking glass and this now is the real world and earlier is elsewhere, another world, something from the past. Time has moved on.

Chas has turned his nose up at the dirtiness of the basement, something he describes to Tony as "you know . . . on the left (. . .) long hair, beatniks, druggers, free love, foreigners . . ." to which his friend smirks, reading the opposite meaning. But Chas knows. "I'm determined to fit in", as he will tell Turner soon enough. Whatever he feels, he has to use this as his base for the time being, as it's such a good "hidey-hole", down the burrow, underground, to mix our Alice references, which is in order, as everything else is mixed in this labyrinthine work under construction.

As Cammell wrote in the earlier draft, *The Performers*: "He has gone to earth in a ridiculous and, to him, despicable burrow; but for his purposes it is perfect. Every instinct and insight of his agile brain into the workings of intellects among the Firm, and (though he fears them less) the Police, tell him that this house is, of all unlikely hideouts, the very last that the hunters would suspect."

Not that he has seen the owner of the place as yet. Chas is still 'below stairs'. He will make his entrance afresh, this time wearing his camel hair coat, as if this is business, not that he intends to 'enforce', but perhaps he intends to 'perform', or to emphasise to us at least that he is still a performer, as that coat goes with the job, his uniform.

As always, the idea that we are being watched is conveyed. This time by Turner, we imagine, from the second floor, as Chas climbs the stairs. In a while he will spy on Chas from inside the room, from behind the screens, resonating in tone and manner to a scene in *The Caretaker*, shot by Roeg remember, when Alan Bates, as Mick, stands aside behind another door on the top floor to watch his brother and the tramp come up the stairs.

"In you go, dad," Lorrie says to Chas as she ushers him into the big room. The first thing he sees is a polar bear, as a spread, as a rug, one of nature's killers, and though we all have sympathy for the animal, it is still a vicious killer. Here, killed. Dead. A spread. And the music starts through the speakers. An assault of sound, the sound of black music. The Last Poets with 'Wake Up, Niggers'. The overwhelming music presence in the film will be black and ethnic, though it will mainly be conceived, played and produced by white musicians. Only The Last Poets are total outsiders, approached for a work they had already produced. Anita is the one who apparently recommended these proto-rap artists, and permission to use the song was made by Jagger in person, with the record company. It appears he didn't actually meet The Last Poets. The Last Poets were Jalaluddin Mansur Nuriddin, Omar Ben Hassan and Abiodun Oyewole at that period. They were formed in the aftermath of Martin Luther King's assassination in April 1968. "The Black Power movement was building and I had to become a part of it," says Oyewole. They drew their inspiration from the poet LeRoi Jones (who changed his name to Amiri Baraka), who had moved into Harlem to form a black arts movement after Malcolm X was assassinated.

Their use of the word 'nigger' is key, a taunt to stir their fellow black men into action, to incite them to become street-fighting men. They are the modern-day version of the troubadour, the jongleur, Villons of the streets of urban America. The group's name derives from the South African poet Willie Kgositsile, who fled from apartheid to New York. In a poem he read at the East Wind workshop in Harlem, he said: "This was the last age of essays and poems, and that guns and rifles would take their place, so therefore, we are the last poets of this age."

While their cries resound in his ears, pounding as an oral dagger, Chas walks around the room, casting his eye over the array of instruments and tapes, a musician's home space for working on ideas, complemented with its desk space, sitting areas, books and images spread around. As the music ends, "the Grim Reaper" its final words, Chas looks at the mirrored ceiling and sees Turner standing behind the screens, as if on cue.

The day that Jagger arrived on set, there was a sense of apprehension among the crew, many of them having already formed an opinion based on the media image that had been built up over the years. They were in for a surprise. There was no grand entrance, no prima donna on display. Jagger, it is reported, came in quietly, showing right from the start that he was a fresher and that he expected to learn. The scene of his meeting with Chas was their first to be filmed. It was rehearsed and shot a half-dozen times, no retake being Jagger's fault. Mike Molloy recalled that when one of the grips was hammering small battens of wood ('termites') into the floor, Jagger asked what he was doing. "Nic Roeg's getting into some very complicated shots and you're going to have a lot of moves to make. The wood's like marks so you can feel them with your toes and you won't have to look for chalk marks or anything like that." Jagger said he didn't need them. They were removed. And he never missed his marks or his cues.

No sooner has Chas met Turner than he puts his foot in it. Something drawn from personal experience one would expect, whether from Jagger or his friends, with their newly acquired wealth, expensive houses and Persian carpets and rugs. Chas drops cigarette ash to the floor. "That carpet is 200 years old," Turner points out. How many times has Jagger said that to someone dropping ash, or worse, about to spill coffee or alcohol? At least he looks after his possessions. We wonder what happened to Brian Jones' Persian carpets. Or Keith Richards'. Though the latter was wont to tell the story about the policewoman at the Redlands raid who was standing on the edge of his floor cushion. He asked if she'd "mind stepping off that Moroccan cushion, because you're ruining the tapestries". At which the cop stepped off and apologised. Not Chas. "A valuable antique, is it?" Holding his ground.

Being in this room is the first time we realise that upstairs is a sealed environment. Though Turner draws the big drapes, the windows are already curtained on a lighter basis. Much like Jagger's place in Cheyne

Walk it seems. "I don't think we had any daylight in Lowndes Square. It was hermetically sealed, yes, I think Nic shut all the windows," recalled James Fox, thinking back about the set. That only added to the intimacy. "We were all very, very close friends so we knew each other terribly well, we trusted each other," Fox confirmed.

As Turner introduces himself, he switches on the full lighting, breaking the murkiness of the set whilst The Last Poets play. The lights that flicker into operation are fluorescent strips of white light. They are not fixed to the ceiling, or any wall fixture. They are free-floating, movable. One will be used later as a dancing tool, a spear of light, but for the moment they are arranged, leaning against the walls.

Again they are consciously employed as art references. In the Sixties when minimal art opened up in different directions, the American artist Dan Flavin worked with light. Unlike others who were part of the kinetic art movement and used light in motion or changes in luminosity, Flavin was interested in obtaining the ordinary ready-made industrial fluorescent tubes and working with them in a space. There is a temptation to see them as sculptural works, or paintings with lights against a wall, but he explored the space by modulating corners or by making free-standing works in a room.

"Flavin is an activist among pacifists in art," said the critic Gregory Battcock, explaining how he had moved away from working with the accepted concepts of sculpture and painting, taking them to a new level of thinking. What he creates "is the phenomenon of the piece's existence in a particular location, at a particular moment in time". Much depends on the natural light, or lack of, in the space. By using fluorescent light he was taking light away from the 'source' of illumination, usually singular and radiating from a point. Fluorescent strips obliterated shadows, could be used to surround, making his work attain "a high degree of artificiality and unnaturalness".

In a journal entry in 1962, Flavin makes it clear that sentimental notions of immortality are to be ignored as motivations: "I can take the ordinary lamp out of use and into a magic that touches ancient mysteries. And yet it is still a lamp that burns to death like any other of its kind. In time the whole electrical system will pass into inactive history. My lamps will no longer be operative; but it must be remembered that they once gave light."

As noticed, Roeg seems to be responding to discussions around Artaud, exploring different ways to use light, overexposing, filtering, discolouring and desaturating, whatever could be pushed further.

Turner tells Chas he can't stay, he will have to leave, setting in motion a cat-and-mouse game. "But the thing is . . ." Chas casts forth. The thing is that he has his luggage, his stage gear, and it all will be arriving direct from the Continent.

Turner returns, or rather pokes his head around the screen near the door. "Why don't you go to a hotel?" The idea was to conjure up Gloria Swanson as Norma Desmond in *Sunset Boulevard*, Turner as the recluse who does not want anyone intruding on his territory. Cammell was clear on that. That's why he gave him the line. "It's the sort of remark an ageing bitch would say to a lesser mortal."

Indeed, one might have an inkling that Jagger had studied Gloria Swanson, adapted his entrance as a counter to Swanson's grand sweep down the stairs. Here Turner is making his grand entrance, his public entrance, for a public of one, Chas, even though his public is actually us, because this is a film, we know that right from the start. And we are regularly reminded of it with cinematic and photographic tricks. But rather than swish down a staircase, he swishes into the room; rather than make grand gestures, he dips his fingers into the bowl, licks them, minces his way in, disorientating us, disorientating Chas. Not playing for the crowds, playing for the clouds, for that is where we are left momentarily, wondering which cloud he is on. Knowing he will tell us to get off of my cloud when he sees fit to say it. This is the image he wants you to have.

Prior to his appearance, we had seen Turner applying his face for the day, having lipstick painted on by Pherber. Or perhaps it is an acknowledgement of *Flaming Creatures*, where lipstick application is a key action. Or perhaps he was just preparing for his role to meet his guest, a mixture of images, for though he enters wearing an ornate dressing gown, shuffling in slippers, he peels the gown off to perform, looking like "some medieval court catamite" as one visitor recorded. Just right for the dialogue that ensued. Another time it could have been interpreted as vampiric, or demonic.

Or indeed in another twist, as a ballet dancer. "I thought he really must see Nureyev because what he was doing was so similar to Nureyev's style, and they even looked alike," Marianne said. She took him as often as it was possible. Mick became "obsessed" with Nureyev. "I remember one particularly, it was a ballet he had made for himself called *Paradise Lost*. At the climax he dived like a cannonball through a drawing of a huge pair of bright red woman's lips that resembled a vagina – they looked very like Mick's lips actually – breaking the paper."

It has been remarked by Jagger, as much as by others, that he kept his lipstick and make-up on away from the set, and that he had a period where he overindulged in that look, daily. And yet, Jagger is keen to make fun of James Fox for adopting the mannerisms of Chas, for living out the life of the criminal persona for the duration of the shoot.

Jagger had at least seen a few gangsters in his time. As the Krays moved in on the West End, so they turned up at nightclubs. As did the Richardsons. Whether he met any personally, their presence was usually felt. Anita and Keith had certainly seen the Krays in Tangier. They recount walking along the beach and seeing "these two strange beach boys walking along, dressed in suits, looking like the Blues Brothers. It was the Kray twins. (…) They'd brought a touch of Southend with them, handkerchief knotted on the corners over the head and trousers rolled up." They were there for the sun, and Ronnie's pursuit of young boys.

The Stones were no strangers to having hard men around them, one or two steps away from being villains perhaps, who might be all lightness at times, but capable of doing damage when required. As the Stones, as a group and individually, were to find out to their cost. Nevertheless, the romance of villains, or pirates, never fades.

The wordplay that will evolve between Chas and Turner is hardly a duel, though there is a violence lurking beneath. It was a bit like Muhammad Ali boxing, jumping around the ring, ducking and diving without actually throwing a punch, or touching the other boxer. Intimidation, in one respect. The master of this in dialogue is Harold Pinter, and this is why his name keeps recurring. So many of those involved either had worked on scripts that he had written, or had seen his work enough to have been influenced. How to hold a conversation without getting anywhere, but in fact getting somewhere. Both Aston and Mick in *The Caretaker* run rings around Davies, the tramp, a game called 'put on', where you are talked to in riddles, and you understand what is happening but are unable to respond. McCann and Goldberg do it to Stanley in *The*

Birthday Party, too. Whilst you can see you are being poked at, you cannot see the reason for it, not until it is too late. Likewise, the audience is left stranded too, in a sea of implication and confusion and helplessness. At one point in *The Caretaker*, the tramp is so confused, his only way to respond is to say in despair: "Listen! I don't know who you are!"

Peter Hall, directing Pinter, notes that it is like juggling, "particularly in the repeated phrase, the catching up of a phrase and repeating it over three sentences, keeping it up in the air, like a ball".

To take another turn, to refer to Artaud before we come to him. In London in the early Sixties, Peter Brook, along with Charles Marowitz, ran an experimental theatre workshop, the Theatre of Cruelty, to explore Artaud's ideas. Paul Ableman wrote some scripts, published as *Tests*, an example of which (from *Spine*) shows how language was taken to be used as a tool of violence.

1. Spine.
2. Spine.
3. Dogma.
2. Dog.
3. Spice.
4. I called once.
3. Spice.
4. I called.
3. Spice.
. . .

Having introduced himself as a juggler, Chas carries his injured hand like a beacon to display his misfortune.

There is an irony in that, not many years before, in *Thoroughly Modern Millie*, Fox saw the opportunity to juggle in the film, and "practised for six weeks with three tin plates" to learn to do the bit of business.

Knowing that juggling in a physical sense is out, tested by tossing two balls to him to watch Chas let them bounce off him and fall to the floor, Turner sets about a verbal juggle, pursuing the connection between juggler and jongleur, merging their interests.

The jongleur in medieval France, and also a joglar, was a performer of texts, a storyteller, a reciter who committed texts to memory. Though he didn't necessarily write the texts, unlike a troubadour, it wasn't totally unknown for him to do so. Primarily, though, he was a performer, and his activities extended to being a musician, a juggler, an acrobat or tumbler and, indeed, an actor. The relationship to Jagger and a contemporary rock band on tour is not lost. Joglars were often better received than troubadours, because many were closer to the people, coming from a lower class than the troubadours. A juggler too is not all that one imagines today. In history, a juggler was a magician, something of a sorcerer, one who deceived by trickery.

So whilst Turner juggles and spins the words, he merges their identities, and also reveals their underbelly. He knows Chas is a fraud. He couldn't juggle his way into a spotlight. But he is intrigued. Turner performs for him, and then realises it is too easy. He can be erudite, can mix references, invent references, create an imaginary world, leave a marker of a master of that world (what George Steiner calls Borges' "anti-world, a perfectly coherent space in which his mind can conjure at will") by nodding in a reference to a Borges story, *Tlön, Uqbar, Orbis Tertius*, about an attempt to wriggle an imaginary land into the reference books over centuries of intrigue and manipulation. There is no intrigue. Fourteen balls! He can go. He cannot stay.

Davies in *The Caretaker* is not bright enough to know where the line is. He fails. He is told to leave.

Turner withdraws. "I don't like music."

Even one-handed Chas can spar. "Comical little geezer. You'll look funny when you're 50." That might hurt, but Turner rides with it. No, he doesn't. He doesn't want him there. Not until he says: "I'm determined to fit in. I've got to fit in." "That bad, is it, eh?"

He's still running through the cogs, the permutations, until Chas throws out another jab, another lifeline. He doesn't know who Turner is?

That makes him a challenge. That excites Turner, sets him ticking. This character is from another world. He has no knowledge of him. He can stay. On a daily basis. Yesterday till tomorrow. Words start recurring, reflecting, coming through the mirror.

This is a film that one can repeatedly say has pivot points. If there are too many pivot points then perhaps we should call them key points. But pivot is more appropriate, because that reflects the nature of the film, turning on itself continually, keeping us at the edge, giving itself an edge.

How can anyone say that once inside Turner's house the film slows? Whilst the first part is physical and external, the second is mental and faster; nothing encumbers the flight of the imagination.

The act that Jagger offered during that period is available for all to see. Recorded in December 1968, just after *Performance* was filmed, though not released for almost 30 years, *The Rolling Stones Rock and Roll Circus* shows the Stones running through a short set including 'Jumpin' Jack Flash', 'Parachute Woman', 'No Expectations', 'You Can't Always Get What You Want' and 'Sympathy for the Devil'. That is one flashback we can have. Another is internal, a Seventies or Eighties memory of an *Observer* or *Sunday Times* colour supplement, with a projected impression of what Jagger would look like in his mature years, showing a balding man, probably based on a photo of his father, Joe. Getting it wrong.

Turner's image has slipped. This guy doesn't know who he is.

"Do you know who you are?"

He does.

But he doesn't know who Turner is. That's a jolt to any star. Faded, but not forgotten, is forgivable. Faded and forgotten is unforgivable. A jolt to his identity.

In the outside world, Chas himself is a bigger star for a few days, his 15 minutes of fame, if only the rock star had a television or read the papers.

That Mrs Gibbs or Lorrie might have seen the papers is left aside. Or that anyone from the taxi driver to the people in the street would recall is similarly left aside. This is a film. We are focussed on the relationship in the house; the outside world, though brought in, even if only nominally, is not relevant.

But Turner doesn't need to know who Chas is exactly. Our viewpoint from behind the folding screens shows imagery of Twenties Chicago gangsters. Romantic images are not the same as the real thing. But it's desperate, "it's that bad". Turner agrees. It works both ways. Vice. And versa.

Though we have seen mushrooms in the tray on the doorstep, it is from this point that mushrooms, whether for eating as part of a meal, or as a hallucinogenic, will start to inveigle their way into daily business. Pherber is outside tending and picking not only the edible but also the magic mushrooms, the fly agaric, the *Amanita muscaria*.

Chas is watching her. As they have been watching him, so now he is watching them, through the barred windows of the basement, a protection against people breaking in rather than the occupant breaking out.

Performance is ready to take forward another key factor, the use of red. Nic Roeg had been party to the use of the colour in something of a dominant fashion in Truffaut's *Fahrenheit 451*, with its fire engine and environment. And in Corman's *The Masque of the Red Death* with the red figure of death, who brings death in the form of a redness, a film swept with red, from blood, to wine, to lipstick, to roses, to dresses, to windows, to the red-haired Jane Asher, who escapes the redness, and the red upside-down cross branded into Juliana's breast. Tobe Hooper talks about how he used red in his films, going back to *The Texas Chain Saw Massacre*, taking it further than an intellectual function, using it as a subliminal presence to heighten our reaction to the film. "I build and construct (the film) in such a way that it's a mathematical method, not just in the rhythm of the cutting, but in the content of what you see, what you feel, and when you feel it. About halfway through a show, or even earlier, the accumulation of and the way the images have been presented begin to open little trap doors in the mind . . . there are messages . . . And when all these things accumulate at the moment of impact, they make the impact powerful . . . and pure."

As Chas goes about applying turps to remove the red paint from his hair, he suddenly realises who Turner is. His reflection on the reflection in the mirror catches sight of the Albert Hall concert poster that hangs on the basement wall. He confirms the identity with Lorrie, who comes to keep Chas company. Her comments on "old rubber lips" affirm that the confusion of Jagger and Turner is being painted in here too, in the film itself.

Bringing a young girl into a film like *Performance* is tempting fate. Laraine Wickens was nine years old at the time. Because she has moved away into another life, it is difficult to pursue various rumours of her behaviour on set, best summed up as being a bit of a minx. There is nothing shy about her. On set she was as mischievous as she appears. In the scene where Fox is in the bath, Laraine wasn't lacking in being forward in her reactions and remarks, though barely a trace is perceptible in the finished film.

Jagger for one got on well with her; a photo of them on the set confirms this. But Jagger has always said that he likes children and taking care of them, whether his own or others, which *Being Mick*, filmed in 2001, reaffirms.

Mrs Gibbs, her mother, is probably a jokey nod towards Christopher Gibbs. Mrs Gibbs is the daily who comes in to clean and 'do' for Turner and his friends. She asks Chas: "Would you like me to do your room now?" An in-joke? Because Gibbs has done the décor upstairs, but, looking around the basement, it really needs someone 'to do' that too.

A new scene in the kitchen looks as if it will just be about preparing a meal, with some mushrooms freshly picked from the greenhouse. But this scene opens with the two women talking about an electric connection, Lucy trying to put together two parts that are the same, two females, rather than a male and female which will slot together, adding an observation on the homosexual and bisexual nature of the tenants. "That won't fit in, look, it's all holes."

When we rejoin the scene, Turner is seated in a kitchen chair, reading out loud from Borges, the same book Rosebloom was reading in the car, *A Personal Anthology*, with a portrait of the Argentinian author on its cover.

If we read in public we are often aware of what it is we read. We might not want to be seen publicly reading a book of politics that is contrary to our viewpoint, in case those around align us with that viewpoint. In *Performance*, Jagger is reading Borges in the kitchen, as Rosebloom was in the car. This is a film. Would Jagger have wanted to read anything but an erudite book? In a 1981 backstage interview Jagger was asked what he read. He is not being pretentious, though it might sound so out of context. He admits that he cannot read heavy books on the road, just light fiction, as anything is better than watching TV, though he says he likes something substantial by his bed, such as biographies, because you can pick them up and put them down. And when asked what he's reading at the moment, he says a biography of Bernard Baruch, the American financier, and tries to explain a bit, not apologise for his heavy reading, before suggesting he'd better go and get ready for the show. (An aside: one wonders if Jagger ever picked up on Baruch's acknowledged favourite book: Charles Mackay's *Extraordinary Popular Delusions and the Madness of Crowds*.) Julien Temple, another director who's worked with Jagger, notes: "Not many people in music are very stimulating, but he'll show a serious knowledge of the history of Central America or very early German cinema, or the decline and fall of the Roman Empire."

And, not to be forgotten, Turner is reading out loud to the two women and, of course, to us. The idea of reading to others while they work has a history in itself, though there have been periods through the centuries and in various cultures where it has been forbidden, the notion that those being read to would rise above their station by gaining more knowledge than was necessary. Know your place. As children we are read to, even after we know how to read. We enjoy the bedtime story, or hearing another read to us, even though the freedom of the tone, speed and intonation is taken out of our hands. It can become the subject of a book itself, like *La Lectrice* by Raymond Jean, made into a film in 1988, where the reader (played by Miou-Miou) was paid to visit homes and read 'stimulating books' to a stream of listeners, often leading to other adventures. And of course it can be one way in which the blind can obtain information. The pertinence in *Performance* is the reference to Borges, who was blind in later years, and had to have a reader on a daily basis to read him his favourite books.

Turner is reading a particular story, an account of a man who meets gauchos, or gangsters, by chance one day. Turner is setting up his own story, doing research, finding relevance in his world of books. The story that he is reading 'The South' is chosen as prescient for our story, the film. The main character, Dahlmann, a city dweller, is travelling south to a family house in the country to recover from a stay in hospital. The train stops short, in the middle of nowhere, and he goes into a bar for a drink. There he is taunted by a group of gauchos, one challenging him to a knife fight. He has no knife of his own, he is a city dweller. "From a corner of the old room, the old ecstatic gaucho threw him a naked dagger, which landed at his feet." (Bear this in mind for the Old Man of the Mountain, coming up soon.) Dahlmann is not adept at using such a weapon. But he takes up the knife and the challenge and steps outside knowing that he will be killed.

This not only foresees the position that Turner will face with Chas when confronted by his challenge, and which he will accept and provoke so that Chas shoots him, but it also relates to the 'secret' film, *Odd Man*

Out, where the young woman, Kathleen, fires at the police in the knowledge that they will fire back and kill her and the man.

What also figures in this story, though not mentioned, is that Dahlmann is not actually travelling south, but is experiencing a fever as he lies dying in hospital, for he had bumped his head on an open door as he hurriedly climbed a staircase to collect a book he had acquired, the *Thousand and One Nights*, and though the person he had gone to visit was shocked to see the blood on his forehead, or was it red from the freshly painted wood on the door, he had not tended to the wound properly, septicaemia occurring and thus necessitating hospitalisation. The suggestion is that he is dreaming, for it becomes more confused as he thinks he is two men at one time, that he would rather go south and meet his death with a knife than die in a hospital bed. "He felt that if he had been able to choose, then, or to dream his death, this would have been the death he would have chosen or dreamt." This has its echo, too, in another film that has been mentioned, *Point Blank*, which many interpret as being about Walker (Lee Marvin) in the process of dying, casting his mind back through events. And so we enter a Borgean labyrinth. Nothing is easy. Nothing is as it seems.

To pick up on Godard's *Vivre Sa Vie* again, towards the end there is a sequence where Luigi reads to Nana from the 'The Oval Portrait' by Edgar Allan Poe, a very Borgean story about a painter who works on a portrait of his wife, only to find when he feels he has captured her 'lifelikeness' that the wife he turns to eulogise with, who is sitting for him, is dead. This occurs before the scene when Nana herself is gunned down as she is handed over in a deal between two pimps, an event that we could see coming, not only because of the Poe extract, but because earlier there was a gunning down in the street outside the café near where Nana worked as a prostitute, and because in another scene she goes to the cinema to see Carl Dreyer's *The Passion of Joan of Arc* and we watch the extract where Artaud as the monk prepares Jeanne d'Arc for her death, which Nana watches in tears as Maria Falconetti weeps on the screen. The story outside the story is that Anna Karina, who plays Nana, was the wife of Godard at the time, and their relationship was drawing to a close, so Godard is in a way exploiting the personal situation for his own ends.

This idea of bringing in other books, films and art as references for a homage might be okay for some directors, but both Cammell and Roeg are of the opinion that they are there to reinforce the film's own ideas, otherwise they should not be included.

Pierrot le Fou, which started out as a Lolita-type story, is a key Godardian reference for Cammell – shown later in his film *White of the Eye* (1987), with a repeat of *Pierrot*'s dynamitic ending. It opens with Jean-Paul Belmondo reading aloud in the bath from Elie Faure's *Histoire de l'Art* to his bemused young daughter, forewarning us of what will be repeated within the film, in the same way as the imitation of Michel Simon from *La Chienne* foretells what will happen. *Pierrot* could be seen as a labyrinthine film, one that might be interesting to map out on tracing paper and overlay on *Performance*.

This idea that one story or reference calls up another is what Donald said he liked about Borges. "The phrases and words in his stories call to mind other stories that bring to mind other stories and yet it all happens in a very brief space of time. That is my idea of a movie."

Turner is interrupted in his reading when a fly hits him in the eye. It could have blinded him. The reference to Borges' blindness is gone in a flash. As is the idea that the gauchos in 'The South' had thrown bread pellets at Dahlmann to taunt him into action in the first place. Besides the continuation of the playfulness of language that we saw upstairs, this takes a twist, or a turn, into a reference to the mushrooms, not the mushrooms being prepared for the meal, but the hallucinogenic mushroom, fly agaric, which is being cultivated in the back garden too.

The fly in the eye, or 'I', which spins through our reactions instantly, is there and gone. Pherber and Turner are focussed on the story, on the issue at hand. "Why?" "Because you are afraid of him?"

It is just such brief flashes that make filmmaker Horace Ové stress that *Performance* understood the Sixties, whereas *Blowup* didn't make it for most of us who were there. With *Performance*, "There was a simple little thing there when Mick Jagger was talking and a fly was flying around in the room and the soundtrack came up, and I think it hit him in his face (…) that was so fucking psychedelic, that piece of observation. Yet a lot of filmmakers could look at that and not even know what it fucking means, but what it means was that everything was exaggerated under LSD, right into the fly, the spider, the flower."

"Why?"

"Because you are afraid of him."

"Right. And he's afraid too."

"Of you?"

John McVicar didn't have much time for *The Krays* (1990), the Kray film with the Kemp brothers, but he did see one line of dialogue, when Ronnie Kray said: "It's fear. I realised that ages ago. If people are afraid of you, you can do anything. The glamour is the fear."

Chas makes his connection to the outside world, catching his friend Tony, not in the market this time, nor at home, but in the boxing gym, the Thomas à Becket to be exact. He informs Chas of the need for a new photo to make up the false passport, so that he can be smuggled aboard a freighter and shipped to the land of opportunities, direct to the big city, New York. But first, he needs to change his image. Filming at the gym had its glamour too, for when the crew arrived at the Becket, they found Henry Cooper, the British heavyweight champion, training for a title fight with Karl Mildenberger.

Before Chas goes in search of more coins for the payphone, he peeks inside the cupboard in the hall, and sees empty painting frames. For one reason or another, the subject, the paintings themselves, are missing. Unusually, a sequence follows to resolve that question. The doorbell rings, and the Myers twins appear, carrying a painting by the Belgian surrealist René Magritte.

The question of which painting should come through the door had raised a few problems. Any painting they chose could easily be reproduced and serve the purpose. A René Magritte was mooted. They wanted a real one. Nic says: "We knew a couple that had one, but they wouldn't lend it to me." Robert Fraser was a good friend of Alexandre Iolas in Paris, Magritte's dealer, but it didn't come from that source. Paul McCartney did own some Magrittes, acquired from Iolas via Fraser. Jagger noted how Fraser "was always trying to sell me Magritte, which would have been a fantastic buy. I just didn't have the money." This was noted in the narrative.

Magritte's *Not to be Reproduced* (1937) would have been an obvious choice, with its figure seen from behind reflected in the mirror, as the back of his head, the same view as the one we see before the mirror, whilst the book on the mantelpiece, Magritte's favourite, Edgar Allan Poe's only novel, *The Narrative of Arthur Gordon Pym of Nantucket* (in French), is reflected correctly. The idea that we should reveal reality or truth, and define who we are, is scuppered by Magritte. The painting is a portrait of Edward James, the collector of surrealist work, who commissioned it. I expect it would have been housed in his home near Chichester, not far from Redlands, a place that was known to many of the main protagonists on the film. It could be reproduced. But Roeg was insistent that they needed a real Magritte.

In the end they rented one, for £60 a week, from the Brook Street Gallery, a painting called *Portrait of Alex Salkin* (1945), a Belgian lawyer and collector of Magritte's work. It should not be read as having a deep significance, even if the subject, Salkin, looks a bit like Harry Flowers, or indeed more like the Borges portrait on the cover of *A Personal Anthology*. But that was mere coincidence. What was important was that it was real, not a reproduction. And to have a real painting on the set was treated with awe by everyone. As Roeg remarked later: "When the man came and put it up, the whole atmosphere changed; something came out of it that was worth re-photographing."

For the narrative, the Myers twins are sent away with the painting minus its frame, which Turner kept, and stored in the basement cupboard.

We are left to read something into the fact that the painting is removed and the frame retained, an irony that plays with the philosophy of Magritte's work.

Turner cannot buy a Magritte, it is far too cold. Turner is a man who has lost his demon, who seeks the Artaudian cry. Money or not, it doesn't speak. We hear nothing. Magritte doesn't want us to hear anything. It is an image. It is a question of illusion and reality with Magritte. Its greatest presence is its absence. We know it was in the house, and that it will appear in Chas' fantasy, Chas who never saw the painting itself. And at the end, Jagger's emptied body will be in the cupboard among the frames, beside the one that held the Magritte. We think of what is not there, that absence. That is enough for us to bear, no need for any image to add to the layers.

The irony of taking a painting for its presence as a valuable object lies in the fact that we are not tempted to read it for its meaning, which is precisely how Magritte would want it. "If one looks at a thing with the intention of trying to discover what it means, one ends up no longer seeing the thing itself, but thinking of the question that has been raised." We have no reason to think when we see it. We have to just look. A conflict with everything else in the film? Do we just look at everything, try to understand nothing? And yet if we look at the violence in a flat manner, at face value, do we not feel repulsed? It is because we try to understand it, to rationalise, that we accept it and don't blandly vomit over our neighbour's shoes. You can only vomit if you are not involved in the film. You should have left long ago.

Chas goes upstairs in search of money for the phone. Just before he opens the door to the kitchen, there's a crash on the other side. A knife has been thrown at it, not for the first time judging by the series of holes on the door. Do they read the story of the gauchos and their knife fights regularly in the kitchen?

At home in Chelsea, Jagger was known to stick a note at night with a dagger bearing instructions to be woken up without fail at nine.

Again, we move directly into word games, using cockney terminology, which keeps understanding clearly to a British line of thinking. Have you got sixpence for the phone? No response. "Can I use the blower up 'ere?" The word 'blower' being a phone. He is not to know they have no phone. "We haven't got a blower up 'ere." Turner drops his 'h' to get into step. But in putting his hand to his ear, Turner suggests Chas' hair, and switches the inference to hairdryers. Pherber picks up and asks what he's done to his hair, as the colour has changed. Turner responds, swinging it away again. "He's blown it." Blown his cover, everything. This quick spin, without much to hang onto, takes us into the comedy routine that can be seen with Beckett's tramps in *Waiting for Godot*, which in turn fed off quickfire routines in Marx Brothers' films.

When it comes to language, Turner is adept at duelling, or sparring, with Chas. This time he has on board his 'lover', as Lorraine has informed Chas, not his 'secretary'. Chas is now faced by a double image as they flick thoughts at him, suggesting where they saw his act previously, poking jabs, or thrusts, to see where the point will prick. At one point Turner goes into the future, suggesting 1969 as the time, and Pherber repercusses the confusion and nonsense by harking back to the crashed Ferrari, suggesting a Bugatti, a car way back in the past.

Against the ropes, Chas offers the time and place when they caught his act. But no one is interested. The contest had finished without him knowing.

Chas brings up a change of image. He wants to know if there's a Polaroid camera about the place because his agent feels it's "time for a change", a different look. He receives the response that such a dubious request deserves. "Yes, no," says Pherber. "Yes, no," says Turner.

We now hark back and refer to the earlier use of the back of the head shots, but this time looking over the shoulder, echoing an earlier shot when Chas looked over the shoulder of Harry and combed his hair in his mirror. Here the frame employs superimposition and mixes the images of Chas and Turner, indicating that identities are about to be re-examined, beneath the pretext of a change of image. The reference that also crops up is to Bergman's *Persona* (1966), though the image here is not created with the same intent as Bergman's, or in precisely the same way. Bergman's method is much simpler, aligning the two women, one behind the other, for us to perceive them as fused. There is no technical trickery. Bergman just wants to indicate a momentary merging of their personalities.

Red is the key that unlocks the door to Artaud as Turner notes Chas' hair related to Van Gogh's red hair. Alongside Cammell's acknowledgement of the role of Borges in his thinking for this film, the other key reference is the French poet and theatre theorist, Antonin Artaud. Although he was known in the Sixties, there was not a great deal available in English translation. *The Theater and Its Double* was readily available from Grove Press, well distributed. Although John Calder in Britain was to publish the first volume of the *Collected Works* in 1968, the book that was available and that could be purchased in good counter-culture bookshops in San Francisco, New York, London, Paris . . . was the *Artaud Anthology*, edited by Jack Hirschman, published by Ferlinghetti's City Lights Books in 1965. This was virtually the bible for anyone interested in Artaud, because it took extracts from his work across the span of his life, including the important later works. In the *Artaud Anthology* there is one key late work, *Van Gogh: The Man Suicided by Society*, that is the text that Donald Cammell specifically read, in that edition. Not just any edition. Donald was mainly reading in English. Whilst a general reading of the book is obviously in order, the reason I cite the Van Gogh text begins with the relationship to Chas' red hair. As seen, Chas had dyed his hair red, using antiseptic cream mixed with red paint, and then once installed in the basement, removed it with turps, the resultant scarlet red liquid streaking down his face. It is no good seeking the French edition. The *Anthology* version gives us: "I see the bloody red face of the painter coming at me . . .", followed by "canvasses, brushes, his own red hair, tubes . . ." And then, on the facing page, Artaud explains that the motif of the candle on the chair "tells a great deal more under Van Gogh's brush than the whole series of Greek tragedies, or the plays of Cyril Turner, Webster, or Ford, which, incidentally, have never been played". Cyril Turner, you ask. You cannot fail to halt if you are half-literate. Who is Cyril Turner? Has someone gone mad? Then you cast your mind through literary history and, of course, it strikes you, like it struck Chas when he saw the poster of Turner and recognised the image as Turner/Jagger, "old rubber lips". Turner is a mistype for Tourneur, Cyril Tourneur, the Jacobean dramatist. There is no way that Cammell didn't catch that snag in the text, taking on board Turner as the name for his character. And while we are about it, Cyril is lifted from the good laugh he must have had, Mad Cyril fitted in just right. One can run with the interpretations and conclusions as one wants if one reads the full text. There is a possibility that Turner was written instead of Tourneur, on purpose, because Cyril's father might have been called Turner, but it would be so unusual given that Cyril Tourneur is known now almost exclusively for his play, if indeed it is his, *The Revenger's Tragedy* (1607). And Artaud cites him, because Artaud had listed Tourneur's play as one of the few that he wanted his theatre to stage.

The Revenger's Tragedy did not receive its first professional production until 1966, when it was staged at Stratford-upon-Avon, directed by Trevor Nunn. One of the reasons it had been dismissed over the centuries relates to the idea that Tourneur had other possible employment as an assassin, a hitman. The text itself was dismissed as "a product either of sheer barbarism or of some pitiable psychopathic perversion". Reading reviews of the Stratford production helps one to understand why Artaud would have wished to take on that experience. The first edition of Artaud's *Van Gogh*, published by K Éditeur in 1947, was collected in Vol. XIII of the *Oeuvres Complètes* in 1974, and is clear in its use of Tourneur. No other English translation since has deigned to write Tourneur as Turner. And before anyone asks, this is not a Borgean reference in itself, only found in my copy of *Artaud Anthology*. Read *Tlön* . . . to see what I mean.

One might have thought that Turner related to J.M.W. Turner, though there is barely any relevance to connect them. Turner was the painter of light, the great landscape artist, but the landscape here is inner landscape, the world of hallucinogenics. Though a good trip through Turner at the Tate and elsewhere is worthy of research, there is nothing more than a faint echo.

During this scene, where the language slips and slides, like the eel that wriggles from the tank onto the table and that Chas automatically pops back in its tank, there are other sleights of hand, a sense of magic. Harry Flowers was seen toying with his pens on his desk, not tidying them, but aligning them in a directional manner, as if from some form of magic belief. Turner does the same with the knives on the table as he talks, directing the points at each other, then turning them away. To add to this magic, there is film magic, one second a tin of lychees is there, a second later it has vanished. Or versa. Whether these are intended as signs for merger or takeover, or the nature of sexual identities, is not clear. Anita recalled that there were "little ritual things, things that had to be there, like certain books always had to be there and then when we were in the kitchen there was this thing about the way we lay the forks and the knives. That was all part of Donald's little magic things."

The tin of lychees is not the only appearing and disappearing act. The knife that is suddenly withdrawn from the door seems to belong to a knife thrower, materialising out of thin air.

Though there is a toying with magic, and a number of the participants were interested in magic, perhaps in a faddish way, there is also the lurking presence of the underground filmmaker Kenneth Anger to be accounted for. Anger was a frequent visitor to London for some years, and had befriended Jagger, Cammell and others, his desire being to involve any number of them in his projects, which he was partly successful in accomplishing. Anger was initially drawn to Cammell because of Donald's father's connection to Aleister Crowley. Though Donald had been raised in a house in which magicians, metaphysicians and spiritualists came and went, he had moved away from the influence, a form of youthful rebellion. Later he appeared to have taken a more wide-ranging interest in magic, seeing its connection to rituals and tribal cultures, that would also attract him to a poet like Artaud.

Many thought that Anita dabbled the most, though she too relates how one time when they had a car crash, she and Keith put it down to the presence of "a load of books and things and objects of Kenneth Anger's in the car", and after phoning Mick, they carried out a "ritual fire burning". "That was just panic, and to be safe. I mean, some people do have the power, if you practise it a lot, you can do it." She was referring to Kenneth Anger, whose presence brought elements of fear with it. Jagger too had shown an intellectual interest in magic, reading assiduously through the books bought from Watkins in Cecil Court. At one point, when Anger tried to get his attention by throwing copies of William Blake's poems tied to bricks through his windows in Cheyne Walk, he gathered together all his Eliphas Levis and other books and burnt them on the fire.

"It was an absolute nightmare," recalls Pallenberg. "Donald was a real prima donna – going into fits of fury, screaming, shouting and trying to put all of these mad, deviant, perverted sexual scenarios into the movie. Nic Roeg would spend seven hours lighting one shot. We'd sit huddled together in the basement, shivering, getting stoned and waiting for scenes that we would eventually do maybe 28 times." Anita seems to have been the most vociferous when it came to making remarks about the long wait for a shot to be set up. But the point was that Roeg's photography had to be done properly to work. When you are chasing images, a series of fragments, a mosaic, it takes time. There is no going back at the editing stage when you want an extraordinarily packed image and it is just not there, or looks mundane. "And the film will be lost on the audience because the power of the images and the montage of those images and connections has to be visceral at all times," Paul Mayersberg notes. "If you let that go, then the film will go, because it consists of images. It doesn't consist of a narrative."

Waiting to film can be a tiresome activity. Jagger, Fox and Pallenberg have talked at various times about the experience, the mind games at play, the tensions being exploited.

Anita would be playful, baiting Fox to take drugs. "He refused to take a mushroom or acid. I kept on taunting him. In the morning when he had some coffee I said I'd put some acid in your coffee. Really childish stuff because I was a brat, you know." Fox never denied "popping pills" or "smoking pot", but "I never did LSD or cocaine or heroin." In general, Anita admits that Fox was a challenge to her. "James was such a professional, so we were all a bit intimidated by him, so we stuck more together, me and Mick stuck more together, me and Mick against James." James would be "like studying his script and we'd be walking around smoking joints. Just the opposite. Just to annoy him."

Donald remembered the baiting that went on. "Mick is a ruthless tease and he worked on Jimmy for two or three days probably before Jimmy had a complete crack-up and was totally impossible, couldn't work anymore, said this is it . . . he was going to lie down and die." James said that Mick had "tortured" him, according to Donald. "And he said, 'I'd lay one on him you know.' He was so built up and pumped up, he'd been boxing every day in his character. He could have carved up anybody on the set."

Fox, being the professional, saw it as a positive way for Jagger to behave. "As a character Chas was anathema to Turner, and as I got into the part some of this rubbed off between Mick and myself. For example, he and Anita would tease me with love play while I sat waiting to film in the house in Lowndes Square, or when it came to the interview scene between Turner and Chas, Mick would offer me a drag of a joint. I would hesitate and he would say: 'trying to give them up, are you?' or something like that. Whereas previously, Mick and I had shared some ironical attitudes, now he in his character became harder, more cynical, more isolated. I believe his performance as Turner was thoughtfully constructed and that it is too little acknowledged for the piece of acting it was."

When Peter Hall talks about directing Harold Pinter, he offers an understanding that could be seen in the way Jagger was working on Fox in the dressing room, whether he was totally conscious of it or not. "I think at the base of a good deal of Harold's work is the cockney game of taking the piss: and part of that game is that you should not be quite sure whether the piss is being taken or not. In fact, if you know I'm taking the piss, I'm not really doing it very well: and a good deal of Harold's tone has to do with that very veiled kind of mockery. Now, actors can't play veiling until they know what they're veiling, so we play mockery, we play hatred, we play animosity, we play the extreme black-and-white terms of a character.

That stage of rehearsal is very crude, but it's a very important stage, because unless the actor understands what game he is playing, what his actual underlying motivations are, the ambiguity of the text will mean nothing. People who think that all you've got to do in Pinter is to say it, hold the pause and then say the next line, are wrong."

Jagger was learning how to make it happen, even if he was not the consummate performer that he would have liked to have been at that point, as Altamont was to reveal. "It's about if you get completely lost and you're on the edge, whether it's in any kind of performance, of any kind of art form, people will be riveted by that because they will want to see you perform in a transcendental state, not just go through the motions."

Knowing how to switch from the boredom of waiting backstage to making one's entrance has to be got down to an art if one is in a band of the Stones' magnitude. There are preparations before going on, just as there are ways afterwards to come down from the cathartic experience of the show. Mark Fisher, stage designer for tours, says: "One time, I was standing talking to him (Mick) beside the stage, before he went on in some giant stadium, pouring with rain. (...) Meanwhile, the percussive opening of 'Not Fade Away' was beginning and he became more and more distracted, then disappeared into a trance, spun around and marched onstage. It was like watching a witch doctor or shaman transporting himself from the everyday world and into this private ecstasy."

Cammell, meanwhile, thrived on the friction. "Donald wanted my character to wind everyone else up, which I was more than happy to do," Anita recalled. "It was not a harmonious shoot, but that's what Donald wanted: chaos, paranoia and grief." But Donald, too, fell prey to those games, as they slipped from his control. His brother, David, recounted: "There was one point when I got a call to say Donald had walked off the set and disappeared. And I shot over there. I had a big convertible car, and I just cruised around the streets. By a miracle I found him up in Knightsbridge on a pavement. I persuaded him to get into the car and we had a chat and I took him back and he decided to go on shooting. It was something to do with Mick teasing James."

In the Eighties, when James Fox returned to acting, he recalled the shoot. He had started to doubt his lifestyle, and the situation only exacerbated it. He felt himself withdrawing from the environment. "I was always pretty scared of Anita Pallenberg; and I remember going with her to the German Food Centre in Knightsbridge for a sausage and thinking 'this girl is mad and terrifying and this isn't anything I want to be connected with.' They were going one step further than he was prepared to go. He was asking himself, "Who am I?"

It was during this shoot, with the waiting around, and then going home to an environment at Robert Fraser's flat, where he was still in residence, that Anita started taking heroin seriously, as already noted. She had thought the others hadn't noticed, but they had, and the call back to shoot the scene injecting herself with Vitamin B12 was a sign of their recognition.

David Cammell says that Donald was "fairly abstemious, he didn't drink very much, he didn't get very spaced out. He didn't overindulge in anything, apart from sex probably."

Friends and visitors to the set filled the waiting time. Cecil Beaton was hired by Sandy Lieberson to take photographs. This was paid for from Sandy's own pocket as Warners refused the expense. He visited three times, on October 3 and 9, and then November 1, the last time with Geoffrey Sawyer as his assistant, according to the four pages of 'visitors to set' list.

Other photographers were allowed on set. Journalists, too. Ray Connolly in the Saturday edition of the *Evening Standard* on October 5 talks about his visit to interview Jagger. He starts by noting that the interviewer before had been summarily dismissed by Jagger with three words: "Yes . . . Sometimes . . . No." Looking down the visitors' list, that would mean it was the journalist for *Photoplay* who received two minutes, as the two other interviewers that day were distinguished and their interviews are known. Connolly runs through his interview with Mick and Anita, who recount how bored they are, waiting for the hour to come to sign off and go home. Anita seemed in a cheery mood though: "The film opens with a blue film: and then we come in and it really gets going."

Chas is led upstairs to the lion's den by Turner, where he and Pherber set about unravelling the identity of their visitor. They know from the start what they are dealing with. The first Polaroid image has an uncanny resemblance to Harley-Brown, the lawyer, echoing or reflecting the earlier alignments of the business world with the criminal. The costume relates to an acknowledged image of the gangster world as perceived in

American movies, images that we've seen in Turner's workroom. In the earlier script, *The Performers*, Cammell made it clear that the collages are the handiwork of Pherber, images of archaic gangster violence, and that dressing Chas up is a "verisimilarexactitudinous reproduction of true 1928 Chicago Loop District style". Not that either Turner or Pherber will say it directly, nor Chas. All he can offer is that it is not the image he seeks, this one makes him look "dodgy".

Whilst Chas is being peeled like an onion, Turner offers the contrast of a decadent look, something from the world of Oscar Wilde, Aubrey Beardsley . . . lying on the floor before the burning logs, a cosy corner of the room. This must have had echoes of Jagger with his friends such as Christopher Gibbs spending evenings talking about literature and philosophy as they sip fine wines, and smoke joints. Charles Baudelaire, in his *Intimate Journals*, offers the definition: "The Dandy should aspire to be uninterruptedly sublime. He should live and sleep in front of a mirror." Whether large or small. With Chas focusing on his image, Turner too is aware of his own image, the hand mirror noting his narcissistic side.

The next photo is a mirror reflection. Chas and his double. But still it bears the gangster look. He will have to face it. He has to tell them he needs something more like . . . "a sort of passport size", Turner proffers.

Both Pherber and Turner change clothes themselves as they lead Chas through the process of dressing up and down in clothes taken from the racks. The two residents of the house know full well what is required, but they want Chas to reveal it for himself. Chas bares all, in fact, bares his back, which is starting to fester, and become septic. Pherber, the woman of the house, the mother, nurse, cook, 'secretary' and lover to Turner, steps in to treat the wounds, washing and coating them in antiseptic creams. Perhaps Chas has left it too long. Perhaps a doctor should be called. Dr Burroughs is suggested. For a shot or two. This is a reference to the writer William Burroughs, a play on his character Dr Benway, who appears in various texts, starting with *Naked Lunch*.

"Call Dr Burroughs" could have easily played on *Call Me Burroughs*, an album of Burroughs reading extracts from two novels, *Naked Lunch* and *Nova Express*, recorded in Paris and released by The English Bookshop there in 1965. Limited supplies found their way across the Channel to London, to shops such as Better Books in the Charing Cross Road. That dry voice drawl as the needle moved through the vinyl groove: "Drove all night, came at dawn to a warm misty place, barking dogs and the sound of running water. 'Thomas and Charlie,' I said. 'What?' 'That's the name of this town. Sea level. We climb straight up from here ten thousand feet.' I took a fix and went to sleep in the back seat. She was a good driver. You can tell as soon as someone touches the wheel." Those opening words and voice become indelibly ingrained on first hearing. That slow drawl that states "I am a recording instrument" has had no equivalent since this author bought a copy almost 50 years ago. Emmett Williams on the sleeve compares it to "a slow but faithful old Ford, with out-of-date St Louis plates (...) hell-bent for interplanetary travel".

Naked Lunch had been published in Paris by the Olympia Press in 1959. Though Burroughs' style of writing was fragmentary, this book was not composed using the famed 'cut-up technique' that became attached to his name. Both books from 1960, *Minutes to Go* and *The Exterminator*, used cut-ups, followed by the fuller works, *The Soft Machine* (1961), *The Ticket that Exploded* (1962) and *Nova Express* (1964). And though Burroughs is often credited as the writer who discovered 'cut-up', like some form of Columbus, he was in fact only its most conspicuous exponent, and has never denied that it was Brion Gysin who brought it to his attention. In late 1959, Gysin had noticed while trimming mounts for his drawings, slicing with a Stanley knife on a pile of newspapers to protect the table surface, that some of the cut texts of these sheets when read across pages from another text made some interesting and often hilarious combinations. He knew that this jarring of one text against another, one image against another, was old hat in art terms, almost 50 years old hat in fact, when Picasso and Braque were getting their collages under way, but he wasn't aware of it in literary terms, even if there were precedents in Tristan Tzara, Marcel Duchamp and other surrealist activities with language. He showed Burroughs later that day, and they set about cutting newspapers together along with works by Rimbaud and Shakespeare. They also folded pages and read across the results. "Cut-ups establish new connections between images, and one's range of vision consequently expands."

What initially appealed was the way it liberated the author from his control mechanisms. Later, Burroughs would have to rationalise this for those who removed any form of literary quality from writing in this manner. "The cut-ups are simply random at one point. That is, you take scissors and cut the page, and how random is that? What appears to be random may not, in fact, be random at all. You have selected what you want to cut up. After that, you select what you want to use . . . You can't always get the best results. Some cut-ups are interesting and some of them aren't. There is the important matter of selection to consider. (. . .) Sometimes I have cut-up an entire page and only got one sentence from it."

What was also important was that it compared to a liberation of the mind, in fact had a parallel with normal daily life. "Every time you walk down the street or look out the window, your stream of consciousness is cut by random factors. (. . .) Somebody is reading a newspaper, and his eye follows the column in the proper Aristotelian manner, one idea and sentence at a time. But subliminally he is reading the columns on either side and is aware of the person sitting next to him. That's a cut-up."

And another effect that found favour with Burroughs was seeing that, by cutting one text into another text later in a manuscript, and then writing it into an earlier position, he could move the future into the present, or vice versa. "Perhaps events are pre-written and pre-recorded and when you cut word lines the future leaks out."

Relinquishing the fixedness of time and space in this manner was what appealed to both Nic Roeg and Donald Cammell. Gysin had become a friend of Cammell, having met him in Tangier. And through him, Cammell and his friends met Burroughs. Marianne says Anita went off to talk with Burroughs in the Tangier hotel as she was "obsessed" with him. Burroughs ignored Marianne. She was regarded as empty-headed, though years later, in 1987, they formed a friendship. Women for Burroughs were regularly treated like morons. Marianne forgives him.

"The fold-in method extends to writing the flashback used in movies to enable a writer to move backwards and forwards in time. Characters and themes are carried over from one to the other, moving back and forth in time and space, making repeated trips through the same space but in previous times." Though Burroughs could say that, it wasn't until he met Antony Balch in Paris in 1960 at the Beat Hotel in rue Git-le-Coeur that he put it to the test. *Towers Open Fire*, a text that found its way into *Nova Express*, was the basis for the film that was shot in 1962–63 in Paris and Gibraltar, with Burroughs in the lead. There is no story as such, and no dialogue. The budget was minimal, and the soundtrack added in London in 1963 and released in 1964. Though the censor asked for the removal of "fuck" and "shit", a scene where Balch is masturbating remains in its entirety because the activity was not seen for what it was. The Paris Pullman showed it alongside Tod Browning's *Freaks*. It also had airings at the Times Theatre, Baker Street and the Piccadilly Jacey. Today it is viewable on DVD or on websites like UbuWeb.

Footage for another film, to be entitled *Guerrila Conditions*, a documentary on Burroughs and Gysin, was filmed but not completed. This footage became a component of the film, *The Cut Ups*, which used footage from other short films. Balch left the editing to a film technician, playing no part, only giving instructions on how it was to be cut and assembled. Four reels of film were cut into 12-inch lengths and assembled with no attempt at artistic judgement. The finished film opened at the Cinephone in London's Oxford Street in 1966. The audience loved it, or hated it. Many left expressing disgust, to which the staff responded that it had a U certificate, "nothing disgusting about it, nothing the censor objected to".

Brion Gysin saw Cammell in Paris often. He probably explained the cut-up techniques and might well have suggested that Donald see Balch in London, just knock on his door. Balch lived in the same house as Burroughs at 22 Duke Street, St James for some years. If Donald had visited, Balch would have shown him the films in the screening room he'd set up. Roeg saw *The Cut Ups* at the Oxford Street run, rather than at any private showing.

Burroughs' presence in London had a much greater influence on counter-culture at the time than on literature because he was doing interviews and writing for *International Times* and the underground press, and films such as *Towers Open Fire* and *The Cut Ups* were being shown at UFO and various underground events.

Chas is too fit to need the doctor. Pherber will sort it out. She has a medical kit to end all medical kits, to fix all ills, containing, according to *The Performers*' draft, "an unrivalled collection of 80 per cent used-up tubes of antibiotics, sun-creams, and theatrical make-up; baby lotions, hypodermic syringes, an unrivalled collection of pills, a foot-bandage, a Balinese opium pipe, Hong Kong aphrodisiacs, baby food, pornographic pictures, spare parts for a Japanese miniature hairdryer, and so forth."

Unbeknown to him at that point, the mushrooms Chas has taken include *Amanita muscaria*. While the effects are awaited, Turner changes into something simpler, something more appropriate to become Jagger, the blues player, picking at a guitar. Jagger made it clear that he wasn't intending to do a 'number' and make it a musical. He would perform a song, or two, if the plot required it. This wasn't going to be 'rock star makes a film', this wasn't going to be a Presley movie. Roeg commented: "Jagger said in effect 'screw the contract, I'm not going to get up and sing a song, it has to come out of the film', so the two scenes where he sings are essentially part of the film. He's got to sing at that point, but it was terribly difficult to find that point." The earlier draft, *The Performers*, suggests that a blues would be playing on a record-player, not that Jagger himself would perform it.

In a shadow, with his back reflected in a wall mirror, Turner plucks, simply, but violently, at two songs by Robert Johnson, one of the great blues singer/musicians. 'Come On In My Kitchen', like many of Johnson's songs, is not a clear narrative, working more with emotional intensity, but it could be seen to be about love, infidelity and betrayal. There is also the idea that Jagger was aware that Johnson sung in a high voice at times, imitating a female voice, and that the initial line "Come in my kitchen", with its metaphorical illusion to a woman's vagina, fits in well with the mosaic of gender blurrings weaving through the film.

The other snatch is from 'Me and the Devil Blues', which relates to an earlier stage, given that it references the devil, and the idea of layering allusions to demons and devils would be part of the reason for choosing Johnson in the first place, as much has been made of the idea that Johnson sold his soul to the devil at the famous Crossroads.

"Hello Satan, I believe it's time to go" is directly relevant, even though the film's ending hadn't been lined up at that point.

There is also the fact that Johnson was an itinerant musician, a walking musician, which fits in as an overlap with the notion of troubadour, jongleur. Johnson recorded these songs in 1936–37, died young at 27, poisoned by strychnine, possibly from a bottle of whisky tampered with by the husband of a woman he had been flirting with. "Have you got a drop of Scotch?" Chas asks. "No, sorry."

Chas is starting to unravel, with a little help from his friends, nudging at his buttons . . . He rides into sight, silver bullets in mind, the Lone Ranger, reveals his first layer, his change from Johnny Dean to Chas Devlin . . . and Turner switches to a quote from John Lee Hooker's 'I'm bad like Jesse James' . . . he mentions Jesse James, it being okay to align Chas with a notorious bank robber at this stage, as all he perceives is that he's a gangster.

Then Turner calls Chas "a striped beast", a tiger, that animal that Borges holds dear. For Borges it's that sign and energy that keeps him writing, pursuing the illusion that the written can become real, that the written sign, the written tiger, the dreamtiger, can become the real tiger out there in the jungle. That the impossible can be achieved can become an obsession, an obsession that can only reach its end through madness. He thinks Chas still has that "striped beast", that demon if you like, because later Pherber will suggest that Turner saw his demon as "just a beautiful little freaky stripy beast . . . darling", slipping away . . . then gone. But before Turner can pursue it, Chas has risen and seen the light.

Chas is aware of the mushroom's effects when he sees the light change, a simple candlelight (but not on Van Gogh's chair), before he moves to the mosaic tabletop. And yet, as if to reveal his mentality, the underlying instincts, his first thought is to ask how much it will cost to buy the table.

Roeg was adamant that the way to film the drug experience was not to go "psychedelic". Fancy camerawork is superficial and dates a film. Because they have bored a hole into the nature of their exploration, a simple dazzling effect, with a touch of music, is enough. Roeg: "I have reservations about translating drug experiences onto film. In *Performance* I kept it more simple. No light shows or strobes. (…) It's hard to translate a drug experience on film without falling into cliché."

Jagger told Beaton, when they met in Morocco, that he should take LSD. "One's brain works not on four cylinders but on 4,000. You see everything aglow. You see yourself beautiful and ugly, and other people as if for the first time."

One of the problems with mushrooms, as I understand it, is that they are unpredictable. Even though Turner wants to know how much Pherber has fed Chas, quantity is not the real factor, but quality. Mushroom potency is variable. And that's not taking into account the variable factors at play in its user. What they might get from trying to bore in, from trying to open the doors inside the skull, is anyone's guess. At least the exploration had an inner intent. Henri Michaux, an explorer through the terrain of mescaline and other hallucinogenics, sought to discover not the product of thought, but the process of thought, the mechanism that makes knowledge possible. Another poet with an interest in drug usage, Michael McClure, sees his mushroom experience as different from other hallucinogens: "It opens you up so that you feel internally deep inside, and all around you, the utterly human and humane." And whilst perceptions are distorted, this is not as certain as the inner experience. Michaux's expansive writings and attempts to capture the experience on paper with words and drawings are voluminous. He found that: "we inhabit a self that has no identity and no name, we live in a *there* that is a *here,* within something that we are and are not." As Michaux notes, you have to remember that it is "maltreatment" by an "invading poison", and who knows what each mind will do when confronted. "I found myself all at once at a good altitude, climbing fast, fast, fast . . . I had become a strange aeronaut."

Turner explains that by boring into his head, he wanted to see how he ticked. But they have to take one step at a time, because Chas is getting lost. His former self is coming through, he responds to being called Chas. He repeats words and ideas from earlier.

To convey that the journey is labyrinthine, the scene occurs in front of the tiled wall of the bath, with the heightened idea that Chas can fall into it, like Alice into the burrow.

Borges likes to use the image of the labyrinth, to avoid the word 'maze', because you feel the word 'amazement', whereas with labyrinth "you think of Crete and you think of the Greeks. While in maze you may think of Hampton Court, well, not very much of a labyrinth, a kind of toy labyrinth." He is thinking of a more substantial labyrinth, one that could encompass the world, a Library of Babel that could accrue.

Cammell and Roeg are quite content if you pursue the original legend of the labyrinth, the one that Theseus entered without losing himself, finding the Minotaur to destroy, a parallel for the narrative under exploration.

It is a mental labyrinth because one image does not run into the next, you have to retain the information, balls in the air, and bring it to mind at other points. The film needs you to be attentive, probably to re-view it. To make your own labyrinth.

Borges also reserves the mischievous right to say in an interview with Georges Charbonnier: "I amused myself with the idea, not of losing myself in a labyrinth, but in a labyrinth which also loses itself." Our trip does not necessarily have an end, a closure, but is an adventure in which we choose our paths.

So whilst the film as a whole has labyrinthine structures, there is the box within the box of Chas' labyrinth, as the drug bores into him, as he falls into the bath, to make the clue to labyrinths easier, and shifts into his mind in search of the demon. To slay or retrieve, or just to look at?

This is the aspect of Borges that Cammell had wanted to reflect. And I use 'reflect', because the mirror is used as well, not to step through, in the Cocteau fashion, the Lewis Carroll fashion, as we are already there, but in another fashion, turning it over and over to spin the self as desired.

Nic Roeg states, like Cammell, that he detests homages. The inclusion of Borges or anyone, the allusions to any person or any art, are there to add to the fabric of the narrative. Borges liked detective stories, which didn't mean he wanted to solve the crime, or solve a mystery. The mystery is interesting in itself, the process of detection, the journey through the labyrinth. As Borges showed with *Tlön, Uqbar, Orbis Tertius*, the journey into exploring the mysterious appearance of four pages at the end of the *Encyclopedia Britannica*, one particular copy, leads to other multiplying references. But as with any journey through a labyrinth, one has choices to make, taking courses that lead to further choices. This is the fun of the art experience, to go counter to resolving and closing doors, drawers, holes . . . to open them, open up the imagination to the possibilities that can enhance one's own being.

This is one of the reasons why the décor of the house never seems to sit still, why whole rooms appear to be re-arranged, not only objects that move around from one shot to the next. Nothing is as it seems.

This is a journey chosen by Cammell and Roeg, where their overlapping interests merged, and which is why it makes nonsense to try to define who did what . . . precisely. It is of no consequence. This is an adventure that is offered to the viewer, something to sit back and enjoy as a mental stimulant, a drug of a different order. The fabric of the content is bound into the fabric of the film is bound into the fabric of the viewer's experience.

Around this period there was also another interest, a way into the brain, a boring into the head, called trepanning. Not that it was widespread, but the few who did go down that route were documented in the underground press.

Daniel Richter's *Residu* magazine, with a supplement, *The Mongol Review*, in Spring 1966, and *Transatlantic Review*, in its Winter 1966/67 issue, the latter with editorial involvement by Heathcote Williams, both contained long texts with Dr Bart Huges on his experience of 'brainbloodvolume', and how to achieve the same effect that people experience when they stand on their heads for a period each day. He said that a comparable high could be made permanent by making a 'third eye', by boring a hole in one's head. Finding no one willing to drill into the top of his skull, Huges had to self-trepan, an option not open to many others. In counterculture reading of the time, any idea of boring into one's head, as Turner expresses in the film, carries an echo of this. John Lennon is known to have been interested in the idea and talked with Huges, but he recommended that for Lennon it wasn't necessary, as he was creative enough already.

There are people who have been accidentally trepanned in a car accident or similar, who have noticed a resultant heightened condition. There is also a history of trepanning going back to the Incas, as it has been known for centuries that it offers a way back to the vitality of a youthful mind. The clue is given in that we are all born with holes in our heads, the plates constructed so that the baby can squeeze through to the outside. After birth it takes some months until the soft spot, the fontanelle, closes up. Until then the heartbeat is visible on a baby's head. As Huges sees it, "our mind loses its pulsating vitality" at that time. "Our brain suffocates inside our own skull." Huges' intent to "expand consciousness" was as much for its enjoyable side as for gaining more mental energy.

Now that Chas has brought to the surface his profession, and how he goes about performing, Turner wants to know more. He knows a thing or two about performing, about the mechanics. He's been there, but he's lost it. He thinks he needs to go to the edge, he thinks he can articulate it, but he can't go there.

"The only performance that makes it, that really makes it, that makes it all the way, is the one that achieves madness." Turner sees that nutshell.

This line is not something directly attributable to Artaud, but something that has been derived from reading Artaud, and indeed lies at the heart of Artaud's own experience. Whether in the *Van Gogh* text, or other texts, or in his ideas about theatre, his Theatre of Cruelty, exploration at limits was achieved through living on the edge, not through any fabricated activity. In the *Van Gogh* text, Artaud talked about madness, which might have led to Cammell writing his line. Artaud wrote: "And what is a genuine lunatic? He is a man who prefers to go mad, in the social sense of the word, rather than forfeit a certain higher idea of human honour. (...) For a lunatic is a man that society does not wish to hear but wants to prevent from uttering certain unbearable truths."

"Artaud is one of the great, daring mapmakers of consciousness *in extremis*," wrote Susan Sontag. Right at the beginning of the cited anthology the reader can grasp Artaud's state 20 years earlier, in 1923, from his first letter to Jacques Rivière, the editor of the *NRF*, who had rejected Artaud's poems, leading to an extraordinary correspondence that the editor wanted to publish. Artaud explains his state: "I suffer from a frightful disease of the mind. My thought abandons me at all stages. From the simple acts of thinking to the external act of its materialisation in words. Words, forms of phrases, inner directions of thinking, simple reactions of the mind – I am in constant pursuit of my intellectual being. Hence, whenever *I can seize upon a form*, however imperfect it may be, I hold it fast, it makes me suffer, but I accept the fact in the fear of not dying entirely."

Sontag notes that Artaud "wants the theatre to address itself neither to the spectators' minds nor to their senses but to their 'total existence'." She recognised that we can be inspired by his writings: "One can be scorched, changed by Artaud." But there is no way of applying or staying true to his ideas. Even he couldn't apply them.

He was seeking a Theatre of Cruelty, where the notion of 'cruelty' was not a violent behaviour, but the need for the cruelty it requires of the actor to bring out the truth. To do this the text, and language, is not enough, it cannot be trusted. It had to be opened up with gestures, groans, shrieks, cries . . . And the staging itself couldn't be bound to a normal setting. Nothing is sacred, everything is permitted. Everything has to be turned inside out. And vice versa.

As the Sixties got under way, theatre and happenings took on aspects of what Artaud suggested, many because of the practioners' direct readings of *The Theater and its Double.*

David Cooper pointed out in his book, *Psychiatry and Anti-psychiatry* (1967), that Artaud's arguments with his psychiatrists in the hospital in which he was incarcerated always ended with his need to conform or else they would dish out more electro-shocks. "He had more to say relevant to madness than all the textbooks of psychiatry, but the trouble was that Artaud saw too much and spoke too much of the truth. He had to be cured. It is perhaps not too absurd to say that it is very often when people start to become *sane* that they enter the mental hospital."

Michel Foucault's *Madness & Civilization* was published in English in 1965. This work gained wider readership alongside the first books by Roland Barthes and Claude Lévi-Strauss, those other French intellectuals gaining vibrancy amongst the counter-culture. Foucault's book uses Artaud's state as an example of madness. Donald might have read the book, or talked about Foucault's ideas with others, as it was certainly a subject that pre-occupied his own personal state of being. As Foucault sees it: "(Artaud's) madness is precisely the absence of the work of art, the reiterated presence of that absence, its central void experienced and measured in all its endless dimensions. (...) Artaud's oeuvre experiences its own absence in madness, but that experience, the fresh courage of that ordeal, all those words hurled against a fundamental absence of language, all that space of physical suffering and terror which surrounds or rather coincides with the void – that is the work of art itself: the sheer cliff over the abyss of the work's absence."

Donald would have heard more about Artaud from Anita, who went to Rome in spring and summer 1967 to work on *Barbarella.* There she renewed her relationship with the people of The Living Theatre, whom she had known in 1961 in New York. The troupe was steeped in the ideas and writings of Artaud; *The Theater and its Double* was its bible. When they came to London, many of the troupe based themselves in Robert Fraser's Mount Street flat, as Rufus Collins, one of their lead actors was friends with Fraser. Unfortunately Fraser had let his flat to J. Paul Getty, with the result that one time when Getty arrived back from Rome he found them living there. "They took things for granted – and when I say 'took', I mean *took*! Talitha had wonderful clothes and for weeks, months The Living Theatre rifled them, and we'd go to louche London nightclubs and see people wearing her clothes. Mostly men."

Seeing Chas squirm at the gangster image they have given him, "you've gone too far", Turner offers: "He means we haven't really got anywhere." Pherber spins it again: "He means we've got to go much further out." And Turner spins again: "We have to go much further, much further back, and faster."

These time and spatial shifts that recur continually, always seeming to have a logic, but in fact not always having their perceived logic, are more than Cammell's interest in Borges. Borges was a follower of J.W. Dunne, as revealed in his essay 'Time and J.W.Dunne' (1940). Roeg, too, had picked up on *An Experiment With Time* (1927), a work that was noticeably employed by T.S. Eliot (*Burnt Norton*) and J.B. Priestley. What was important to Roeg was the idea of precognition, discovering the following day that the dream from the night before foreshadows the reality to follow. Dunne's thesis was that dreams were merely a displacement in time, because all moments in time are perceived at the same time, but that our consciousness cannot handle that possibility in everyday life, and that only in sleep or trance states was it possible to pierce the mental barriers. Or the notion of infinite regression, where you need to step back to paint yourself into the picture of the world, then step back again to paint that picture in, and then . . . For Roeg, in exploring these ideas in a visual sense, it wasn't always about going back and forth with time, but sometimes sideways, proposing a state that is not before, during or after.

As much as Burroughs' films or the ideas of cut-ups can be seen as means to be random, Frank Mazzola points out that this is not how the editing was done. What the cut-ups did indicate was the idea that time could be dislocated and used. Roeg was already thinking along these lines; this is not only evident from his interest in Dunne's work, but also from films he had worked on, like *Petulia*.

When *Last Year at Marienbad* appeared, this just added to his interest in time movement. I write this as if seeing *Marienbad* happened after, but it was before . . . you see the reason I trust. Though Resnais and Alain Robbe-Grillet offer different viewpoints on an interpretation of the film, the only real meaning is that of the spectator, "the only 'character' who matters is the spectator. The whole story is happening *in his head*, and is precisely being *imagined* by him," said Robbe-Grillet. Whether the film is in the memory of one or other of the characters, an interior monologue, whether it is about persuading someone to remember something, or to invent that memory, or whether it is just a film, what you see is in the present alone, no more, as Robbe-Grillet reminds us. "The universe in which the film takes place is, characteristically, that of a perpetual present which makes any recourse to memory impossible." To go further on the spatial line, what is brought home is that within a shot, when the camera moves around and returns, something is not as before. As Resnais said, his interest is "non-chronological, a film where the vision would change each moment, where the décor, the situation would be completely modified in the course of the same scene". This kind of licence is noticeable in *Performance*, where our idea of the room in Turner's house shifts as things seem to move around. Likewise the office in Mount Street, with the nightclub seemingly not being downstairs. As Roy Armes says in connection with *Marienbad*: "The use of an imaginary geography is quite common in the cinema and Resnais uses the same technique with the three baroque castles (Nymphenburg, Schleissheim and Amalienburg) that served as locations for Marienbad, but edits the fragments of the film in such a way that the same doorway constantly gives access to a new room and the garden is constantly changing, sometimes with paths and hedges, at others with pools and fountains, the same statue being found in a variety of places and occasionally absent from where it was before. In this way a labyrinth is constructed and indeed a whole spatial reality that has little connection with the world as we know it."

Having suggested that Chas' act has "been on the road a million years", that people are as fascinated by the glamour of fear, the glamour of the criminal performance, Turner turns it to further erudition with the motto "a thousand years old", which was, according to Pherber, the last words of the Old Man of the Mountain: "Nothing is true. Everything is permitted."

"Imagine yourself being a thousand years younger." And they spin the mirror again and Pherber takes Chas to another time, another place, as she dresses him in Middle Eastern attire, down to the accessories of a dagger in his sash, a wig on his head and suitable eyeliner to fit the part. Chas admires his image in the mirror, takes on the stance of the assassin, not the Western gangster. In an earlier draft of the script, as she dresses him in a shirt, Pherber says: "This is Persian. The shirt of an Assassin." Chas: "An assassin? This shirt?" And she explains: "The followers of Hassan-i-Sabbah . . . The Old Man of the Mountains, were called the Hashishi. Near to his castle, Hassan had made a garden . . ." And Turner, who has gone through a curtain to find a book, returns to read from Marco Polo and inform us all about the Hashashin, the Order of the Assassins, who derive their name from hashish. And we enter another part of the labyrinth, chasing through the drug culture and its overlap in the history of assassination.

The name 'Old Man of the Mountain', whether rightly or wrongly, was applied to Hassan-i-Sabbah, a wealthy man who commanded a group of assassins who existed from around 1092 to 1275, though it's difficult to give dates and true information as the accounts generally used are based on Marco Polo's, which in turn are perhaps a concoction based on various second-hand accounts and hearsay. Polo wasn't in the area of Alamut (which means Eagle's Nest) until 1273. Hassan-i-Sabbah himself was killed in 1194. We like to associate the term 'assassin' with the idea that it is derived from the Arabic Hashishin, users of hashish, that the killers had at some point been drugged on hashish, but this is challenged these days, some saying that it is a mishearing of the word for his disciples, 'Asasiyun', meaning people who are faithful to the Asas, the foundation of the faith. Sabbah founded the Order of the Assassins. Whether the story as recounted by Marco Polo is true or not, this is what Turner reads out to illustrate mention of the Old Man of the Mountain. This leader was a prophet, a magic man, who had his followers in his grip, promising them a garden of paradise, where lovely young women and beautiful plants and flowers were their prize if they obeyed his orders. Gardens and paradise were a usual merging, the Garden of Eden, the terrain of Adam and Eve, was not far from here. If they failed in their mission, he would send his angels to retrieve their bodies and they would still enter the paradise. "Go thou and slay; and when thou returnest my Angels shall bear thee into Paradise. And shouldst thou die, natheless even so will I send my Angels to carry thee back into Paradise." Hassan-i-Sabbah was a learned person, as were his followers; for he did not expect them to carry out the assassinations in public, but to study and have knowledge about the culture they were to enter and thus discover the best way to execute their mission. It was stated that the murders were specific, not random, and that the targets were politicians or generals, not the ordinary people.

Sir John Mandeville names Hassan ben Sabbah as Catolonabes in his *Travels*, and recounts another variation of Marco Polo's account, with the delights of the garden being maidens "not older than fifteen". Mandeville used Odoric of Pordenone as his real key source, not Marco Polo. Sir John Mandeville, a name used for convenience, as he could also be one of a number of Belgians – Jehan de Bourgogne, Jean à la Barbe, Jan de Langhe, or Jean d'Outremeuse – all often cited or discredited, was notorious for using a variety of sources, most of them traced, and was regarded as a masterful fabulist in his weavings and elaborations, a commendable precursor of Borges and his labyrinthine ways. It should also be noticed in passing that Benjamin of Tudela, who travelled 100 years before Polo, mentions Al-Hashshashin and their leader as 'the Old Man,' and claims that another place, Kadmus, was their home.

In the Sixties it suited the legends to align 'assassin' as a derivative of 'hashishin', something not found in Muslim chronicles, and thus to carry forward the idea that the killers were users of hashish. George Andrews and Simon Vinkenoog's *The Book of Grass,* a popular counter-culture reference, carried around in backpacks, also gave details of the Hashish Club (Club des Hachichins) at the Hôtel Pimodan on the Ile Saint-Louis in Paris, which took place on the upper floor in the 1840s and 1850s, where at various times Théophile Gautier, Alexandre Dumas, Honoré de Balzac, Gérard de Nerval, Charles Baudelaire and others passed through the portals to partake of the drug, and to variously recount their experiences.

In his interview with David Del Valle in 1988, Donald Cammell says that the line "Nothing is true. Everything is permitted" is drawn from Nietzsche. "*Performance* is about the transvaluation of all values. Perhaps the film is Nietzschean in the sense that I believe in living one's life that way. The film brings the Neanderthal gangster and the effete yellow book world of the rock star into one demonic fusion." The line is found in the third essay of *On the Genealogy of Morals*, Section 24. It is drawn from Nietzsche, but he attributes it not to Hassan-i-Sabbah, but to the Order of Assassins, who were "free spirits *par excellence*". It seems that Dostoevsky's *Brothers Karamazov* is cited as Nietzsche's source, but the Nietzschean expert Walter Kaufmann assures that he had never read the book, and it wasn't in translation in French until after his book was published.

Perhaps Cammell has first read it in Nietzsche, or perhaps he had come to it from either Brion Gysin or William Burroughs. Donald Cammell and Deborah Dixon were good friends of Gysin, seeing him in Paris and Morocco. It is likely that Gysin had spoken of these ideas, even though it was Burroughs who was to popularise the slogan. The first time it appeared was in *The Ticket that Exploded*. Burroughs also features Hassan and his Garden of Delights in *The Soft Machine*, *The Ticket that Exploded* and *Nova Express*.

There are suggestions in studies on Burroughs that he had probably heard of Hassan-i-Sabbah either from Gysin, or from Betty Bouthoul's *Le vieux de la montagne* (1958), which was itself a revised edition of *Le grand maître des Assassins* (1936).

And as we emerge, we find Pherber asking if Chas can hold the image on the one of the Garden of Paradise, the garden where those who kill return to nirvana with the maidens. We suspect that she intends to lead him into a sexual relationship. The scene cuts to the bed. But the sex does not materialise, not as we see it. In a sequence from an earlier script they start to move towards sexual play. Chas kisses her "with passion, clumsily, rather aggressively – a reminder of his usual relations with Dana . . ." and Pherber has to stop him, saying she doesn't like violence. "No, no. You mustn't be violent, baby. I don't dig violence." Now, though, whilst she teases him sexually, there seems no intent on sexual conquest as an end point, or any point. What we see is the exploration of gender identity as Pherber leads him through the paths of what is male and what is female, how they merge, how one is in the other. And vice versa. This is the side that Chas refuses to accept, and though she playfully uses the vanity mirror to insert one part of one body on the other, it only makes him feel more aggressive. He feels that they are trying to steal his identity, rather than just have a look, to see what it is about him, if there's a demon at the core, because Turner has lost his demon . . . has become "stuck", unable to move, the Borgean tiger has vanished, the psychic energy that drove him before. We know that Chas' demon is, or was, or still is . . . Joey Maddocks. The mirror reveals it.

This idea of merging the male and female was a Cammell issue that seems to have been carried throughout his life into his other film projects, realised and not. It seems to be fundamental to his relationship with his wife, China, with whom he collaborated on all scripts, with "the possibility of merging his personality" with hers, as his brother David states. And it is interesting that the one person who leads the discourse on identity is Pherber, the one who looks the most like a female in her physical characteristics, with a female haircut, female face and understated make-up.

When a camera manipulates a mirror's reflection to deceive the film audience into believing the image seen is the same image as seen by the character, we abide by the rules and accept the deception, giving it little more than a fleeting thought. With *Performance* it is not the same. It is unacceptable, particularly with Pherber, who has quietly controlled key movements in the film. Since her earliest scene with Chas in the basement, where we were seduced into believing she wore no trousers, we have been aware of any further deception or manipulation on her part. Which is not to say that we can resolve anything or everything. The visual riddles, as with the language games, are part of the drug experience and also another reminder that Lewis Carroll's Alice is always present, always creating its own underworld. Nic Roeg has noted how this children's classic is part of his make-up, as it is for many of his audience.

Though the camera wants us to reflect on our own bisexuality, it is unable to trick or convince us this time. But was it ever so? Standing before Velázquez's *Rokeby Venus* (aka *Venus at Her Mirror*) in London's National Gallery, we can contemplate at length the logic and implications of that mirror's reflection to the degree that we come away with questions, not answers.

Though we've seen the bedcover before, brought from Hindu Kush, a mountain range in Pakistan, not Persia, after seeing a close-up of the *Amanita muscaria*, this spread appears in a different light, as a giant red mushroom cap. There is a precedent with the American-based Pop artist Claes Oldenburg, who was staying in London in the mid-Sixties and was exhibiting at Robert Fraser's gallery. He recalls Mick Jagger at the opening of his show. Paul McCartney, too. One of the features of Oldenburg's work was to make large sculptures using non-rigid materials, termed soft sculptures. Invariably they would be made from plastic and stuffed with kapok. They looked floppy, useless, like a punctured beach ball waiting to be discarded. For Oldenburg they had dreamtime qualities, reminded one of sleep, or relaxing before sleep or on waking. Examples would include a soft, crumpled typewriter with its keys ineffectual, hanging on threads, or musical instruments, telephones, a giant light switch. Food was another favourite, large hamburgers, ice creams, pastries. All were usually much larger than the objects they represented. Most related to manufactured objects, not natural ones. And though I cite the resonance with the mushroom bedspread, this object is a representation of nature, something that Oldenburg would not have been interested in at that time. Perversely, though, the real mushroom cap is rigid, and any attempt to bend it will make it snap.

These paths in the labyrinth can be stepped onto and stepped back from. Again a scene is cut short, Chas needing to explain about Joey, when Pherber says that he should go downstairs and talk with Turner, talk to him about demons perhaps.

"Juggling all those balls, millions of them." This film, like this book, works to keep balls in the air, the supreme act of juggling, keeping on the edge, keeping one's nerve, holding one's breath . . . And that's what was happening on set. Ideas were posited, but not resolved. Unnerving, but exciting. Roeg said in a 1972 interview with Gordon Gow: "This whole point about identity emerged as Donald and I talked together during the scripting phase. But it wasn't a finished screenplay when we went on the floor. Various things came to the surface – some things high in Donald's mind, and some things high in mine. Identity was certainly high in my mind."

By filming chronologically one can generate and evolve the narrative, watching and waiting for something to 'happen'. They had a rough mapping for an end, a possible end, but nothing was fixed, anything was possible.

A New York magazine, *Jazz and Pop*, must have gone to press without checking how the film had changed from the earlier outline they were given. Their version says that after Chas has contacted Tony to organise a passport, "The police make a lightning raid on the house. Chas at first thinks they have come for him. But he soon discovers they suspect Turner of using drugs. Rather than allow a search that will reveal Chas' gun and tell-tale belongings, Turner hands the drugs over to the police and leaves with them. Pherber is furious with Turner's sacrifice, but Lucy agrees to take Chas' passport pictures to a prearranged rendezvous. Rosebloom and Moody meanwhile have tracked down Farrell and forced information from him. Lucy is followed back to the house. Chas is now enjoying a tender relationship with Lucy, who wants him to stay. Going downstairs, he finds Rosebloom and Moody waiting. He leaves with them as Flowers arrives. Turner, out on bail, watches, incuriously, from the window as the car drives off. Left behind is Chas' expensive camel hair coat, which Turner carefully hangs up."

Holding one's nerve is easier when you are a writer at a desk, a painter at an easel, or a person with a camera making a home movie. It's not so easy when you have a cast before you and a full crew behind the camera, everyone wanting to know what happens next, all with different viewpoints and questions in mind. Mike Molloy recounted after a long day's stint behind the camera, "Nobody knows what's happening. Donald is rewriting the script every night, depending on what happens between Mick and Jimmy in front of the cameras during the day, and what he thinks Mick is about to do next. Donald's going off on all sorts of tangents and trying to relay the tangents to the actors, and it's hard to get his thoughts across. The actors are freaking out. Mick and Jimmy." From her position as continuity, Annabel could watch: "Jagger's picking up on Donald's ideas. He's throwing a lot of ideas back at Donald. But it's very hard on Jimmy, he's the one who's suffering at this incredible change of identity he's being forced through. Donald's making him so uptight."

Donald was working with these tensions, but perhaps it wasn't the best way for James Fox to work, despite the performance he was turning in. His father, who was his agent, didn't help matters. He had not wanted him to take the role in the first place, wearing a wig and exploring bisexuality. At one point "James' father sent a message by chauffeur while we were in the middle of a scene," Roeg said. "I never saw the letter, but James intimated that his father didn't want him to go on with it, had heard terrible things about it."

Fox agreed that it was hard. He was trying to follow the exploration, the "mindscrewing" as he put it. But it wasn't easy to take a character down that line. "The dressing up, the bisexuality, the actual drug experiences. Well, these things had to be discovered in Chas and that was a hard journey." The others were working with parts closer to their own selves.

"So that's what they did. They basically tried to reconstruct him. Now that is a difficult journey for me as an actor to go through because we were so intensely committed to the film."

When asked if he ever felt a film was getting away from him, Roeg said: "Yes, it should do. That's when it gets exciting. The screaming confusion of atoms and molecules holding that telephone together has to be acknowledged in our understanding of the nature of things. I like to feel like a jockey, in some way, to let it have its head."

Chas goes down a flight to see Turner in his room. He finds Lucy dancing to the music. Though we hear 'Poor White Hound Dog', it was 'Leaving Trunk' by Taj Mahal being played during the shoot. "That's the thing with films," said Jagger. "Nobody knew what music we were going to use or records. Someone said maybe we'll use 'Leaving Trunk' because it's good to dance to. Then we just did something in the same tempo. The whole thing of films is a cheat." Or a manipulation and illusion.

Lucy wears Chas' camel hair coat and a scarf belonging to Donald. She is wary initially at how Chas will react to her playing with his gangster image. Then she removes them, perhaps through fear, or perhaps she has changed her mind about Chas. She need not be afraid, for Chas is still feeling the effects of his trip. He has not been re-orientated as yet, perhaps never will.

Jagger as performer honed his style from various sources, but two who played a key role were black artists. The first was James Brown, whom he had watched from the wings at the Apollo some years before, and the second, and most notable, was Tina Turner. He had also studied her in performance from the wings when they toured together, "every nuance, every gesture, every strut and bump and grind", to the extent that he had said to a friend: "I *am* Tina Turner." That's the image he had of himself when performing.

Chas is assaulted by the music, he knows a thing or two about violence, but he can't stop this aural assault. He goes with the vibe. As his mind whirls inwards, echoes of the whorls of the large shell on the mosaic table, encouraged by Turner using a fluorescent light, a phallic menace, a spear of light, boring it into his head, still weakened by the invading blood of the mushroom, Chas moves through to the imaginary. This will turn into another of the memorable sections of the film.

'Memo From Turner' is almost a detachable promo film for the song, though taken out of context detracts from its pertinence. This is not entertainment, pure and simple. Here, as throughout the film, Roeg's camera is always moving, "even manic". Roeg doesn't want his camera to be unobtrusive. "To me, the zoom calls attention to the fact that the camera can go where the human eye can't." Shooting on location helps one to be inventive. Harry Flowers' office was not shot in Lowndes Square, but upstairs in a neglected boardroom, on the top floor above a Chinese restaurant, the Chuen Cheng Ku, at 17 Wardour Street. David Cammell had been involved in a nightclub on those premises some years earlier. It had quite a reputation, with celebrated visitors, including Princess Margaret. It was called Le Condor, though it is repeatedly mis-written as El Condor. Names have meanings, often mischievous ones. Le Condor is a play on 'Le Con d'or,' the golden cunt, and has a literary allusion, to a book by Louis Aragon, writing as Albert de Routisie. His infamous secret novel, *Le Con d'Irène*, first appeared in 1928 in Paris, hand in hand with, and bearing the same discreet publishing mark as, Georges Bataille's first edition of *Story of the Eye* (using the pseudonym Lord Auch), both supplied with relevant illustrations by André Masson.

'Memo From Turner' was written by Cammell and Jagger, playing on ideas that merged the two worlds. With Turner dressed as Harry Flowers, poised and posed in the office where the business operates, earlier events are paralleled and merged. Chas' new boss and father figure becomes the analyst, leading him through the tunnels, mocking their lifestyle and confronting his sexuality. Asked to strip off, all the associates are set in action, with Chas the only exception. He doesn't strip. This is Chas' viewpoint. But Chas never saw the Magritte painting propped against the mirror. Observer and observed. Bifurcating. This must be Turner too, the analyst entering the head, boring into the unconscious, penetrating with music to add to the lingering effects of the drug.

There is a reference to *The Soft Machine*, the novel by Burroughs, partly for its meaning, 'the human body', and partly to acknowledge a slight use of cut-ups to achieve the lyrics.

The final gesture, breaking glass, ends the session. The sound ricochets through a dying image to a Baconesque tableau, a way to contain the homosexual merger of the art and criminal worlds. The nude bodies are splayed on the floor, distorted and entangled, exhausted or dead, arranged as in a painting, one that doesn't exist, but constructed enough for us to imagine it could be real.

There were slight issues when Donald asked the actors to strip off for the scene. It was the first they knew about it and they were none too pleased. Stanley Meadows, playing Rosebloom, recalled: "Donald wanted me to take my clothes off – one of his last-minute inspirations!" When Meadows said no, Donald said: "What if Fellini asked you to do it?" Meadows reminded Donald that he was not Fellini. "Fortunately my contract stipulated I was not to display my genitals in front of the technicians." Johnny Shannon was having "none of that" either. "I didn't want the nude bit. Imagine, round Lambeth, people saying, 'Seen Johnny Shannon's fat arse up there?'" John Bindon was up for it. "Tony Mordon was adamant, I'm not going to do it, no way," Shannon recalled with regard to his associate. "Suddenly Donald took him to lunch, had a couple of bottles of wine, came back, and they were suggesting better ways to do it."

No matter their hesitation, the abiding image is one of a naked Bindon in the chair, with the roses in the vase bobbing up and down before him in time to the music.

This Bacon art reference is usually the only one that is pursued in any detail in terms of this film, emphasising the idea that Francis Bacon's interests overlapped into the world of the Krays and other East End criminals, because his preference for lovers was 'rough trade', boys who might be partial to giving him a beating or whipping.

Francis Bacon first met the Krays in Tangier in early 1962. Though the Krays were there on business, as guests of Billy Hill, Ronnie shared the same interest as Bacon – the local boys. Their introduction was made by a mutual friend, the actor Stanley Baker, there on holiday. The four of them went out to dinner, and Bacon witnessed Ronnie humiliate a local boy beckoned to the table. Bacon was shocked, but, though repelled, he was also fascinated. Bacon believed that East End criminals at that time "possessed some ruthlessly virile sense of amorality", and he liked the idea of "succumbing to a man like Ron who was beyond good and evil, totally immoral, and would stop at nothing".

What is important with regard to Bacon is that, like Artaud, he was searching for a way to make the paint "come across directly onto the nervous system". Not only to work on the painter, but on the spectator, too. The bodies are sprawled on the floor with all their theatricality, centred for us, as we peer down that tunnel, looking through the keyhole.

So that we understand we are still holding together references that perform on each other, Francis Bacon, in one of his interviews with David Sylvester, mentions a letter in which "Van Gogh speaks of the need to make changes in reality, which become lies that are truer than the literal truth. This is the only possible way the painter can bring back the intensity of the reality that he is trying to capture. I believe that reality in art is something profoundly artificial and that it has to be recreated."

Everything else has slipped Chas' mind. He has forgotten to have his passport photograph collected. When he goes down with Turner to make the call, on the payphone, it is as if Turner too has a death wish, suggesting the photo be collected from their home. As is only to be expected, at the other end of the line, Chas' friend Tony, propped up in bed, has company in the shape of Rosebloom and Moody, both seated comfortably, probably having waited for some while. Rosie has even brought his copy of Borges with him, although set it aside for the moment. Moody confirms his sexuality, looking at Tony's wife in such a way that she can expect him to come back knocking at her door.

For some reason the Vladimir Tretchikoff print of the pink-topped *Miss Wong* seen earlier on the wall has now been replaced by the more popular yellow-topped *Chinese Girl*, a bestseller of the period, displayed in many ordinary homes throughout the Sixties. Among the other adornments are flamenco dolls, brought back from trips to Spain, perhaps visiting friends who took to avoiding the long arm of the law, as well as a carved model of a camel. Private jokes abound.

Pherber has been joined in the bedroom by Lucy, who has taken a shine to Chas. She is pleased to discover that Pherber has not had sex with this man, a gangster, proof shown in the shape of his gun. She wonders whether he should flee to the mountains of Persia, a place where she's sure he can join the bandits.

Turner knows that Chas will be leaving soon. He still seems in two minds as to whether he has achieved anything with the intruder. He watches Chas sleep. He joins him in the bed, to rest. There follows a shot that is offered for viewers to read as they want, depending on the mosaic each has constructed. Whether you wish to keep your readings open, or move towards closure, questions still seem pending.

As Chas wakes he feels a body next to him, a body that we can see is Turner. Yet as this body turns over to embrace Chas it merges into Lucy, and the scene that flows is a tender love scene and its post-coital aftermath, with Chas transformed into a caring man, showing an interest in the feelings of another person, extending further as he offers to do something for her, a small gesture, but enough, an offer to go upstairs and bring down her shampoo.

As an earlier draft says: "He keeps smiling and kissing her face with a sort of incredulous delight. He is gentle . . . he seems conscious of his extreme good fortune in being entrusted with this rare person."

All is not lost, no one is bad forever. Chas kisses her gently on the head. This will be the first time, perhaps the last time, he will do something for another without expecting something in return.

For Lucy, a moment with Chas has been found. She has given him all she has to give. She has given herself. She has given a sparkling amethyst, a geode split open, revealing the wonder that resides within a seemingly hard case. She has given him another amethyst, a bit more polished, her own ring, a magic ring. And she would like to leave with him. She drops in odd phrases in her native tongue, French. The world is a bigger place. The planes are flying in the blue sky, beckoning departure. Take me away to America. Except he will be leaving by stealth in a freighter. We can dream. The original script bore the idea that Lucy suggested Marrakech as a suitable destiny, a North Africa that many of those involved in the film knew as a second home.

Persia is offered. There are bandits in Persia. He would be at home, she proposes. Though whether the mountains would be improved without the bandits is a question Turner has posed to Lucy. Je ne sais pas. I don't know.

It is now that Chas asks her name. Lucy. Just after we've seen the plane in the sky. There might not be diamonds, but there are amethysts. He has come through his trip and feels renewed; the amethyst has been split open to reveal its true inner core.

Is this the man that Turner had wanted to appear? He had gone in search of his demon and it appears that Chas has cast aside his demon, finally, and merged with the ambience of this house and its inhabitants.

Whether the question of Turner merging or changing into Lucy is intended as an issue for Chas, or just for the confusion of our perception, is for each to resolve. We have already seen those questions asked before in this house. Lucy likes to wear the clothes of others. It is not difficult to be deceived momentarily by a sleight of hand, a switch of clothes, camera cuts, shifts of time. I am a film. And yet the idea that Lucy is almost a boy, with an androgynous look, flat-chested and shortish hair, is there to be explored. There is a floating that shifts the ground between homosexuality and bisexuality. Donald Cammell had not resolved the issues either. In *The Performers*, he was still feeling his way towards the ending. "Something in Chas has changed. Perhaps, though, his screwed-up ego would refuse to face the fact that, for a little while anyway, he is not trying to demonstrate that he is 'nothing but a man'. Perhaps he has realised that these three people are not concerned with the demonic and pathetic problems of gender that rot the human race . . . that they don't waste their lives and loves trying to define their sexes."

That it should come so late is unfortunate, for this moment is to be fleeting, dispelled by the arrival of Rosie and the boys, come to collect their belongings and take him away.

Turner too has been contemplating Chas' fate. Has he found the demon in Chas, or did he negate Chas' demon with the use of the hallucinogenic? He needs to speak to him some more. Probably.

That we have seen Turner and Lucy momentarily confused, masked for a moment by wearing the same gown, is one thing. That Turner and Chas have been merged and separated, and merged again, is not in question.

In *Fahrenheit 451*, Julie Christie resolved the problem of identity by playing both parts, in fact acting the same way, just changing a few superficial points, a way to show that there was not much difference between the conformist and the radical.

When Chas goes to visit Turner in the bedroom, he knows what he will do. "I've got to shoot off." But will he shoot Turner? He is in two minds. Turner seems to decide it for him. He knows Chas has been sent to assassinate him. He can't find his demon anyway, it is dead, so he'll go with Chas, who he knows is not leaving the country, but leaving his body. He is bound for the garden of delights. And that's where Turner also wants to go. "I was fascinated by the idea of murder which might also be suicide."

These were notions that Cammell initially found inspiration in through Borges and Nabokov's *Despair*. For Roeg, too, this will recur as a way to draw films to an end. Tracy in *Eureka* says that her father, McCann, "needed someone to finish him off". In *Don't Look Now*, Baxter is willing his death. Likewise the Aborigine in *Walkabout*.

It is all seen in Artaud's *Van Gogh* text. "One does not commit suicide alone. No one was ever born alone. Nor has anyone died alone. But, in the case of suicide, a whole army of evil beings is needed to force the body to perform the unnatural act of depriving itself of its own life. And I believe that there is always someone else, at the extreme moment of death, to strip us of our own life.

"Van Gogh wanted to join that infinite for which, said he, one embarks as on a train to a star, and one embarks the day one has finally decided to finish with life."

Chas shoots him. Dead. And death becomes a transforming moment, a transcendental one. "Death is regarded as a transcendent moment there, and not as an end," Donald has said on various occasions. Though he says it "was something that I thought of at the last moment, a week before shooting the last sequence and when I suggested it to Nic he was tremendously excited and said now finally it's all going to make sense and that's what's missing. I was always worried about the end."

Chas walks out of the house, noticeably tieless, accompanied by 'the chaps', with overtones of being led away at the end of Cocteau's *Orphée*, and steps into the white chariot awaiting him, the white Rolls-Royce, lent by John Lennon, himself to be assassinated not too far into the future, the Rolls with its Spirit of Ecstasy mascot flying proudly on its bonnet. Whisking him away to another land, whether this one is in Richmond Park, or to a reshoot possibility.

It seems that some time after filming, Nico suggested to Donald another ending, something that would be "purely allegorical", as Donald wrote to Sandy Lieberson, which could be achieved if they shot a bit more footage.

After seeing Turner's face in the Rolls window:

"Cut to a close high-angle shot, looking down on a street from the building. The white Rolls-Royce comes into close shot (angle down on its roof). As it rolls up the street, we zoom out to show Central Park West. We continue to pull up and back as the Rolls turns into Central Park. It recedes across the park – a grayish, misty shot. As the camera angles up to follow the car, the New York skyline (of Fifth Avenue in the distance) comes into frame.

The white Rolls recedes across the Park."

Though this request was not taken up, over time the readings of the film have allowed for anything but a realistic interpretation. The fact that Jagger, who took so long to appear in the film, has placed the dying image, the train gone to a star, in a confusing light, has been enough.

Rosie goes around the house switching off the electrics, in the same way as Chas did earlier when he left his flat. Besides a mark of the end, it is also a connection to the post-war generation who still switch off lights when they leave a room, a way to conserve energy.

And for Lucy, left in the bath, there's a note placed on the side: "Gone to Persia X Chas".

Chas has wanted her to know that he has gone to the Garden of Paradise, even if she is not to know it as expressed by Turner in his reading from Marco Polo. Omar Pound, the son of Ezra, points out that the construction of Persian makes it "a superb language for puns" and "double entendre". The intricacy in all its arts has a subtlety and delicacy that hides symbols which create clusters of meanings for the Persian eye that are lost on those from the West.

Left behind in the basement cupboard, amongst the empty frames, is the empty shell of Jagger's body. There is no Turner on the premises. There must have been a hollow laugh when the filmmakers discovered that the so-called Rembrandt, Velázquez, Rubens and whatever other art that had hung in the house and that they had been forced to insure was nothing but cheap copies.

There's a thought as Chas walks towards the Rolls, ahead of him is a little boy . . . walking backwards. Is time regressing? Is Chas' life flashing before him? Who were those boys fighting on the steps earlier, at Joey's death? Has it all been in vain?

It is not the same thing as when Frank Mitchell was taken from the hidey-hole provided by the Krays, ushered into a van to be executed, dumped at sea. Or Ginger Marks' body taken for burial beneath a motorway under construction, as believed at the time. Given that Jimmy Evans and the Krays are references in the research, these are ideas that are permissible.

That we see Turner's head look at us, the viewer, through the car window, gives us the idea that Chas and Turner have merged. Even if Harry Flowers sees only Chas climb into his car.

There is a more prosaic reading, rather than a mosaic reading, in that, in the late Sixties, whenever luxury cars, particularly Rolls-Royces, and particularly a white one, should appear, one peered across to see which star was inside, for who else would be in such a car? Who did you see? You saw whom you wanted. "Do you know who I saw today, I saw John Lennon, I saw Mick Jagger, I saw . . ." "You couldn't have done. He was on the news. He was in New York." "Well, I thought I saw Mick Jagger . . . It was someone just like him. You sure he was in New York?"

The bullet that travels into Turner's head, before it strikes the mirror and Borges, is a camera venturing inside the tubes of a body. Given the myths that have proliferated around this film, it is no surprise that rumours circulated that it was a camera travelling up Anita's vagina to capture the sequence. The reality was that it was shot at the Cancer Research Centre in London: "There was a guy there who was into microscopic photography and I got him to shoot it through a cadaver's tubing," says David Cammell.

Because the image of Borges is shattered in the process of the killing, readings have always started there. Donald said in his interview with David Del Valle, when asked if Chas had absorbed Turner's persona: "In a sense, yes. I was thinking of Jorge Luis Borges and the Spanish bullfighter El Cordobés, who kisses the bull between the eyes before placing his sword therein. Jagger is very much that bullfighter. In terms of painting, if you look at the 'Memo From Turner' number, Jagger's character has already assumed the Harry Flowers persona (in terms of Chas' perception), so this further absorption seems natural."

It would be feasible to extract ideas from any number of Borges stories, as has been done already. That 'The South' was clearly employed and prefigures the ending should not be ignored, Turner like Dahlmann offering himself to the professional killer as a preferable way to die. Likewise, there is the echo with the sacrificial ending of *Odd Man Out*, Donald's secret film within the film.

Donald is clear that Borges is at the core, that "one man is all men", as he phrases it. At different times he records it. In his contribution to the film that Paul Joyce made on Nic Roeg, Donald talked through the *Performance* section, saying: "At the moment of truth, when two men seek each other out, at the moment of destiny, the pattern of their lives may have become so similar that to all intents and purposes they become one man. This is a thing that primitive musicians and aborigines and so on work towards with pointed sticks and spells, stealing of another man's soul."

And there is always an angle to be extracted from the idea that the author of *The Revenger's Tragedy*, Cyril Tourneur, is adding another piece to the mosaic, whether truly an assassin or not. What better way than that an error should contribute to the turns of a labyrinthine course. Though we've barely touched on it, Cammell has regularly insisted on the humour involved in the film. Cammell, Jagger and Pallenberg had sharp wits, knew how to handle the knife, on screen and off. It's for you to decide who came up trumps and what didn't.

And what was the role of Harry Flowers when Chas lined up his sights on Turner's head? We were never party to that. Turner had become Flowers, at least in Chas' mind. What role did Flowers have in Chas' life? Did he feel betrayed by Flowers, his father figure, for his part in adding fuel to the conflict with Joey? We shall never know.

But then nothing is closed. That was never the intention.

Start again.

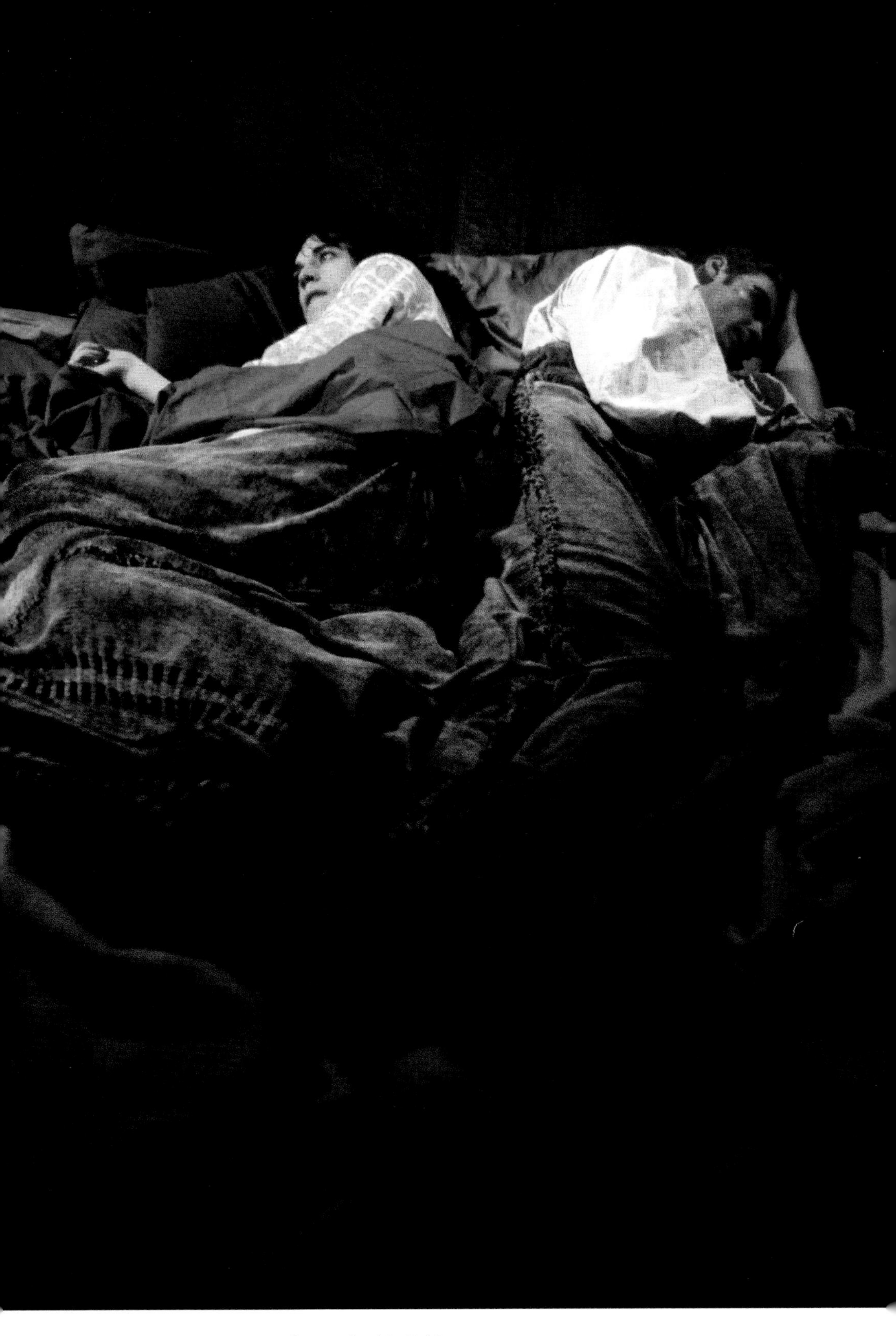

Turner contemplates his fate. RICHARD POLAK/REX FEATURES

Lucy marks the change in Chas. WARNER BROS/PHOTOFEST

Lucy reviews the situation. WARNER BROS/PHOTOFEST

Pherber plays her final card. WARNER BROS/PHOTOFEST

The question of identities takes another turn. WARNER BROS/PHOTOFEST

James Fox during filming. ANDREW MACLEAR/HULTON ARCHIVE/GETTY IMAGES

Turner imagined as Flowers, with Magritte's *Portrait of Alex Salkin* echoing uncanny resemblances. DICK POLAK

Turner performs for the chaps. WARNER BROS

Chas and Turner get into the pulse. WARNER BROS/PHOTOFEST

Turner's bedroom with the travelling polar bear rug. WARNER BROS

Jagger in Powis Square preparing for his departure in the white Rolls-Royce loaned by John Lennon.
JOE BANGAY/DAILY EXPRESS/HULTON ARCHIVE/GETTY IMAGES

Jack Nitzsche. MICHAEL OCHS ARCHIVES/GETTY IMAGES

Vice. And Versa.

Mick Jagger. **And Mick Jagger.**

James Fox. **And James Fox.**

See them all in a film about fantasy. And reality. Vice. And versa.

James Fox / Mick Jagger / Anita Pallenberg / Michele Breton

Written by Donald Cammell / Directed by Donald Cammell & Nicolas Roeg / Produced by Sanford Lieberson in Technicolor
A Goodtimes Enterprises Production from Warner Bros.

The focal idea of the Warner Bros publicity machine.

Chas is led away. RONALD GRANT ARCHIVE

Heurtebise and the Princess are led away at the end of Jean Cocteau's *Orphée* (1950).

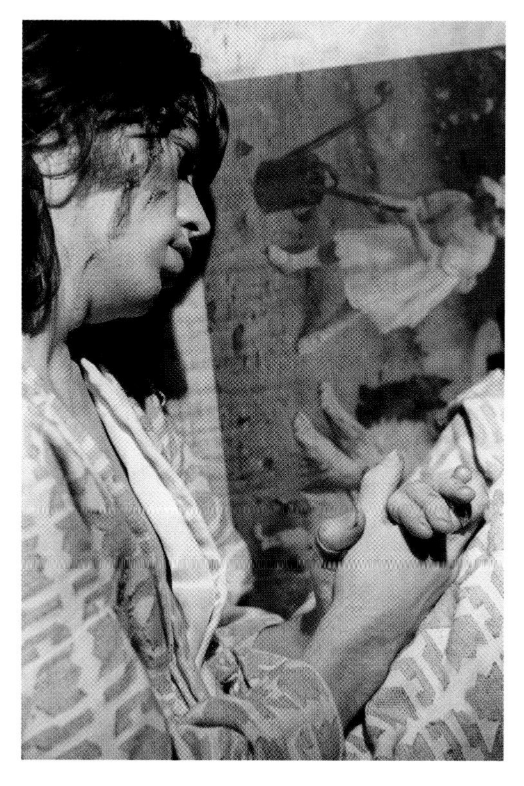

Turner's empty shell is deposited in the basement cupboard with the discards. WARNER BROS

On set photo of Jagger used as the cover for the *Time Out* fold-out poster supplement to launch the UK release of *Performance* in January 1971.

11) I see a red door

THE problems that were to beset the editing were already set in motion during filming. Having given the production carte blanche, allowing the directors to film on location away from the usual prying eyes (no wonder Roeg likes the motif of 'we are always being watched'), when a suit did arrive on set, mackintosh folded over his arm, as Annabel Davis-Goff noted, he was frankly not pleased at what he saw. When another executive arrived from Hollywood and pointed out that they were not keeping to the script, only to be asked where precisely they had strayed, the directors knowing full well there was no script to keep to at this point, it was only a matter of time. And when someone comments that even the bath water is dirty . . . you know that trouble will happen.

As Donald Cammell told Derek Malcolm in *The Guardian* when the film was released in 1971: "It has been a history of opposition all along, right from the rough cut, which Ken Hyman, then head of production, hated. Surprisingly, he backed it in the first place and left us alone until the eleventh week of shooting, then he came on the set and was horrified. He looked at Mick Jagger and shouted to a henchman: 'Hey, Dave, this guy is bi.' He said it was the dirtiest movie he'd ever seen and wanted to stop the shooting there and then. Fortunately, there were only twelve days to go, so his financial advisers persuaded him to let us finish it."

In the end it had come in more or less on schedule, taking nine days more than anticipated, and only $150,000 over budget, which was regarded as negligible. Nevertheless, Ken Hyman had not liked it. He felt that Sandy Lieberson had betrayed him. "How could I have possibly done this to him, a friend, somebody who he considered a colleague. He was disgusted he said. It was dirty. He described it as dirty."

A fundamental mistake, Lieberson thought, was that instead of being somewhat economical with what they showed by way of rushes, selecting 20 minutes "of takes and rough sequences", a sample of a day's shoot, they were projecting everything, putting to sleep the executives who came for viewings after their lunch. The moment came, though, when the bathroom scenes were projected and sleep became a thing of the past, and trouble could be foreseen.

Donald Cammell went away for a short break to Morocco before they started on the edit. A rough version was produced by February, and then Antony Gibbs was brought in to finish the first edit. Gibbs' credentials marked him as a key component in British films of that period, with *A Taste of Honey*, *The Loneliness of the Long Distance Runner*, *Tom Jones*, *The Knack* . . . and, just prior to *Performance*, Dick Lester's *Petulia* and the film version of Pinter's *The Birthday Party* set alongside his name. The American editor, Dede Allen, acknowledged Gibbs as a direct influence on her work on *Bonnie and Clyde*. Nic Roeg had shot *Petulia* and would have Gibbs edit his next film, *Walkabout*.

Once filming for *Performance* was finished, the Stones went back to business, launching the *Beggars Banquet* album, in slapstick custard pie fashion at the Kensington Gore Hotel, and then jumped straight into shooting a light pastiche of family entertainment with their *Rolling Stones Rock and Roll Circus*, even if they delayed its completion and release for almost 30 years. A change of air was needed, so Mick and Marianne, with Keith and Anita, left for Brazil, setting sail from Lisbon on a boat that took 10 days. That slow trip is where the sobriquet 'The Glimmer Twins' originated, suggested by a passenger who was nagging at them to reveal their identity, "just give us a glimmer".

Marianne thought the trip was "a chance to heal the wounds (and cool out our accelerating drug habits). Keith and I were still feeling very jangled from Mick and Anita's affair on the set. There was no residual emotional link for Anita. Like all her affairs it was a fling, and when it was over that was it. But Mick obviously did not feel the same way, and the shadow of *Performance* cast a pall over the whole trip. Mick was continually whispering come-ons in Anita's ear, but for Anita it was over."

Warner Brothers was in a transitional stage. The company owned by Seven Arts changed hands to Kinney National Services in 1969. That takeover was to save *Performance*. Warners had been threatening never to release the film. But Lieberson found an ally in Fred Weintraub, a new executive who had been responsible for Warners financing *Woodstock*.

He liked what Lieberson had told him about *Performance* and persuaded Warners, in the shape of Ted Ashley, the new chairman, and John Calley, the head of production, to go ahead with it.

Thus, the edit by Antony Gibbs was test-screened in July 1969, although in a second-rate suburban cinema in Santa Monica, where the audience had already sat through *Midnight Cowboy*, a re-run film released six months previously, as Lieberson recalls. *Performance* was to be added after the main bill, to test out audience reaction. Also in attendance were Warners executives, including Ashley, Calley and many of the publicity personnel. Although antagonism was felt during the early scenes, the crunch came with the fight scene in Chas' flat. "The beating was much more explicit in that edit, and longer." People shouted for the film to be stopped. Twenty minutes later, after many had left, the projection recommenced. The Warner executives left in a hurry directly it ended. Legend recounts that one of the executives' wives discovered her earlier meal hadn't been digested properly and redecorated the floor, starting with her neighbour's shoes. The next day Cammell, Roeg and Lieberson were informed that Warners didn't want to release the film. Dr Aaron Stern, who was a psychiatrist and head of the ratings board of the Motion Picture Producers' Association, told Ashley, who had invited him along, that it was too disturbing. Stern said that it would be "terrible for Warner Bros to release this kind of movie, and there was no way in the world he would give it anything other than an X-rating". It seems Warners and the other major studios had an agreement with the board that they wouldn't produce X-rated films.

Nic Roeg said that they went to a party that evening "and people walked away from us. We found ourselves in a room on our own." Paul Mayersberg, who had travelled across the Atlantic with them for meetings to discuss future projects, said they were taken aback by the response. "They didn't expect this absolute vituperative 'we're going to bury it' response. That was quite shocking. They could see careers going down the tubes as they spoke." Roeg took it further: "They were going to sue me, Warner Bros, because directors have to sign up to a professional standard."

The other concern was that the main draw, Mick Jagger, didn't appear soon enough. Though there was violence and sex in the film, and stories are told that these were what they objected to vehemently, this was not the complete case. Sex sold movies. Violence too. Hollywood likes to have a hypocritical view on such matters. But there was also the matter of its ending. The earlier idea had been to include a drugs bust, but instead there was an incomprehensible mindfuck, which was not what they had bargained for.

It is usually recalled that the first part of the film played slow, like the second part. And although changes were to be made to the second, they were not as major as the edit to the first. To call the second section slow is relative. To this writer it moves along at a fair pace, but what people understand as slow refers to a surface pace, where little appears to be happening, except hippy types taking drugs, having sex, bathing, cooking, reading, talking . . . that's not 'action', whereas on an intellectual level, it pours one thought and idea after another, overlapping and making the viewer's head spin at times. I say that to help imagine how the first half ran, as a copy of the original cut is not available, though reportedly one does exist.

There's a fundamental difference in the way people perceive things. For Clive Donner, talking about his 1963 film about the relationship of three men in a house, *The Caretaker*: "It seemed to me that within the situation, and within the relationships that developed between the characters, there was enough action, enough excitement seen through the eye of a film camera, without imposing conventional film action treatment." Pinter concurred and called it "exciting cinema".

Nic had found that *Walkabout,* the film he had been preparing prior to shooting *Performance,* was ready, so he left for Australia, unable to delay any longer. He had to forsake any involvement in the next stage of editing or any of the business to get the film released. Sandy Lieberson, too, had another production, *Mary, Queen of Scots*, to oversee. Though they all discussed what should be done, Donald was left to handle the re-edit and make decisions on a daily basis, reporting back to Nic periodically.

The first editor who Warners assigned for the re-edit was totally unacceptable and not sympathetic to the film. Donald then met Frank Mazzola, who not only was to work on the edit of *Performance*, but also was to work with Donald on all his subsequent films. In other words, they hit it off from the start. "I could sense the soul and the spirit in the guy." And though Mazzola was warned at Warners that if he did the film "I'd be black-balled", he pressed ahead. As a result he was uncredited officially, but not subsequently. He received instructions that he couldn't cut the film on the Warners lot, so he took it over to the Sam Goldwyn Studios and worked there.

Mazzola was born and bred in Los Angeles, his parents being vaudeville actors. Frank started acting young, had a minor role in *Rebel Without a Cause*, with additional credit for authenticity as "rebel consultant" on the set because of his gang culture background. As an editor he had worked for 13 years prior to meeting Cammell, and was steeped in European cinema, particularly the *nouvelle vague*.

Frank loved the film. "I said I have got to work on this film." Donald had told him: "I want to inter-cut; I want to flash forward. I want to throw away time." He told the critic Kieron Corless: "We were working from seven o'clock in the evening to five in the morning. Every time we had an idea we were just trying it." Frank obtained separate dialogue, effects and music tracks, "because I wanted to cut everything against the picture." Donald "liked to talk a lot in the editing room. He'd pick up a book and start reading – Borges or something like that – and then he'd come over and look at what was going on and start talking and the energy would rise. I would be cutting and all of a sudden the film would just take over. It was like stepping into a world of magic. Things would start flying through my hands. I could feel the electricity in the film going through my teeth. The film took on its own life and I was trying to chase it."

They started at the end of February and took about eight weeks, doing three edits. Mazzola recalls that the third edit, the one they showed to John Calley, is not the cut as seen today. "The cut he approved isn't the cut that most people have seen. There are pieces missing. I don't know when those cuts were made, but the longest cut I've seen of the film as it currently exists isn't Donald's and my cut."

In order to reduce the first section, Mazzola pared down many shots to the essential action. As they were shot stylistically it worked. Pull pants up, sit down, stand up. This speeded up the action and set a rhythm. It was all the early scenes, though he recalls: "I added the close-up of the gun smashing the mirror at the end of 'Memo From T'. I thought the end of the sequence needed to be punctuated in some way." But the re-editing was mainly on the first part, as they were told to reduce that and insert Jagger sooner. Looking through the footage they found some of Jagger spraying the walls, so they added that as a response to the latter request. All of the chance and cut-up techniques that are often suggested were not part of this strategy. The edits were carefully cut, the pace and rhythm being instrumental to the whole process. It was the concept behind the Burroughs/Gysin cut-up technique, the movement of time back and forth, as already encountered in Dunne and Borges, that appealed to both Cammell and Roeg.

The film was edited until Donald felt it to be satisfactory. The main work had been to reduce the early scenes, and yet retain the sense of the story. Although some of the violence in the fight was removed, the razor slicing across the shoe was not removed until much later. Compression was further achieved by sliding footage back and forth, running dialogue from one scene into another, making the whole section run differently. If one had seen the first version I can guess it was a surprise. Now it had taken a radical departure, a blessing in disguise for the film, as the decision to re-edit had chanced upon a fresh approach to editing, at least in mainstream cinema. "The whole edit was about throwing time away; cutting forwards and backwards," Mazzola said.

Whether the film is more violent after the edit, only a few people are able to judge. It is a violent film, but it is a film about violence. It has gained a further violent layer in the actual editing process, by the very nature of the editing. Whether one sees less overt violence is another matter; the inference of violence is certainly strong. As often happens by removing shots, whether of violent or sexual material, the contentious aspect increases rather than decreases, because the viewer's imagination fills in the missing parts. Ken Russell, who had jousts with the censor at this time with *The Devils*, could attest to that. Even the censor was to agree with Russell that *The Devils* was more sexual without the shots he removed than with them.

It should be borne in mind that Cammell had praised John Boorman's *Point Blank*, and had encouraged James Fox, in particular, to understand that the violence he wanted was not only overt behaviour, but had to be in his very being, in the way he moved, talked, held himself. Cammell wanted a kind of sensuous violence, or as critic Stephen Farber expresses it: "What's persistently brutal about the film is the fierceness of Lee Marvin's every twitch." He points out that the editing bears this violence too: "The establishing shots that we've come to expect in Hollywood movies are almost all omitted, and we're constantly being thrust into a scene before we have our bearings, forced to catch up with what's going on. The very rhythm of the film is that of an assault."

Though Cammell and Mazzola were pleased with what they had achieved, Donald found that "Nic Roeg hated it like that, and there's an argument that in its original form it may or may not have been better. Certainly Mick preferred it as a straightforward story at the beginning." It became "a really interesting montage of images" as a result. Donald felt his painting background was brought to the fore at this point. China Cammell, his future wife, said that Donald "thought everything existed all at one time. And how it mastered itself was just a function of the brain. The brain couldn't process everything happening at the same time. And that's how he got that editing technique, by that way of thinking, that everything happens like a painting, all at once, bam, and the processes in little flashes."

The second edit was not well received: "they still said it was too sexy, too violent." Donald recalled that Nic wasn't pleased either. "Nic said I don't like it, you've gone over the top with it. Then we re-edited again, same thing happened. Nic said I'm going to take my name off it. He said he would take his name off the picture, which upset me and so on." Sandy isn't so sure it was as straightforward as that, or put so bluntly, or "formally". The opinion was that all the care they had taken to capture the violence of the underworld, and to implicate its homosexual aspects, had been reduced, if not lost. "That was something that all of us thought was terribly important and hadn't ever been revealed before in a British film," Lieberson said.

Not only had there been two directors, but there had been four editors, indeed more, at work on *Performance*, each striving differently with the material at hand. Whilst Mazzola is now credited, even if uncredited on the film itself, with editing, he himself states that basically he worked on the first half. And that Antony Gibbs had prepared the version taken for test-showing. It also has to be reiterated that Antony Gibbs had edited Dick Lester's *Petulia* just prior to *Performance*, a film that Nic Roeg had photographed. *Petulia* was a jolt to the system, noticeably constructed using time disorientation, beginning with the middle of the narrative and then zigzagging through flashbacks and flash-forwards, Lester displaying his Godardian interest, Godard having famously responded to a question of whether a film should have a beginning, a middle and an end, with "Yes, but not necessarily in that order."

Besides the ideas to do with time as mentioned in terms of Burroughs, Borges, Dunne and *Petulia*, Nic has always pointed out the early effect of Alain Resnais' *Last Year at Marienbad*. "When *Last Year at Marienbad* came out, all of these hard-nosed, rock-faced people would storm out saying Resnais didn't know anything about putting together a narrative. They couldn't accept an actor going upstairs in a blazer and coming downstairs in a dinner jacket. But in every commercial today, you see mommy putting a pie in the oven, then you cut to the kids eating it. No questions asked. People accept ellipticism more in other forms, but the cinema is so far behind." Resnais himself, looking back, tries to explain it simply. "One thing that interested me at the time was to see if you could construct a narrative without respecting chronology. Robbe-Grillet pointed out to me that when you use your imagination, you don't think chronologically. If I think about what I'm going to do when I get back to Paris, I don't think, tonight I'll have dinner in Cannes, tomorrow morning I'll take the train, then get a taxi home, punch in the code to get into my house, take the lift upstairs, go in and read the post. I think, there's a stack of letters waiting for me, I must get home and open them. The editing happens instantaneously."

"*Performance* was edited but no release date was promised. Warner Brothers apparently had doubts about the violence and whether the film was really commercial," Fox wrote in his autobiography. "I was disappointed." Fox had already been there to some extent with the other film that he thought portrayed him at his best. As Fox's co-star Dirk Bogarde explained with regard to *The Servant*: "It was quite another thing to get it shown when we finally finished. No one wanted this effort, no one was even prepared to give it a single showing. Obscure, obscene, too complicated, too dark, too slow, and naturally too uncommercial. Even the slight of obscenity didn't help it; it was removed from our hands and placed on the Distributors' shelves to gather dust like a poor wine. It seemed that the whole endeavour had not paid off, the courage had been in vain, the money, such as there had been, was lost, written off as a company loss."

Similarly, if it had been left to Ken Hyman, *Performance* would have been shelved . . . forever. It is even suggested that he tried to bury the negative on the backlot. When John Calley moved to get the film released, Ted Ashley said it needed further cuts from the version that Calley had approved. Donald was not pleased. He talked with Mick Jagger and they sent a telegram to Ted Ashley, the president of Warner Bros, on June 18, 1969.

> Re *Performance*
> This film is about the perverted love affair between Homo Sapiens and Lady Violence. In common with its subject, it is necessarily horrifying, paradoxical, and absurd. To make such a film means accepting that the subject is loaded with every taboo in the book.
>
> You seem to want to emasculate (1) the most savage and (2) the most affectionate scenes in our movie. If *Performance* does not upset audiences it is nothing. If this fact upsets you, the alternative is to sell it fast and no more bullshit. Your misguided censorship will ultimately diminish said audiences in quality and quantity.
>
> Cordially, Mick Jagger, Donald Cammell.

What sounds extraordinary is that Cammell, for surely he was the author, should write in this tone to the head of the company, even if it sounds justified. What perhaps is not noticed is that Donald Cammell had become an ardent reader of Artaud. It had affected him enormously as we have noted. One has the impression that Cammell is writing in the 'idiom' of Artaud as found in the *Artaud Anthology*, by which I mean the Jacques Rivière letters (with which the book opens) and indeed others in that volume. I also mean the general tone, and also the 'you' form of address. There is no one specific text that this telegram alludes to. Jagger would also have been on board for such a tone, as he too was an Artaud reader and later contemplated playing Artaud in a film by Marcus Reichert, even shooting several test scenes for it.

Following the letter to Ted Ashley, Donald wrote to Stanley Kubrick and other directors he admired on June 23, asking for help, explaining that Ted Ashley had insisted that cuts be made before release. The scenes involved were:

"i) the flogging of Chas (James Fox) by his *ex-boyfriend, Joey*. (My italics.)
ii) the subsequent shooting of Joey by Chas.
iii) the amorous episode which shows the cheerful mutual fucking of

> Turner (Mick Jagger) and his two girl friends on the morning that the doomed Chas installs himself in their basement."

He then went on to summarise:

> "the cuts comprise about 70 per cent of the flogging scene, the entire scene of Joey's dialogue with Chas after the latter has shot him (Joey now dies neatly, invisibly and inarticulately off screen); and 90 per cent of the love making scene shot in 16mm where real live and laughing human bodies were exposed on the screen for just over a minute."

In Britain, before it could be released, it was to be subjected to further cuts at the hands of John Trevelyan and the British Board of Film Censors. "The head-shaving scene is cut to ribbons," Cammell noted, "you just see the start and the finish. Nic got some beautiful close-ups. The guy began to bleed from a real nick and we got a shot of that but Trevelyan cut it. He said that delinquents would be going out and shaving everybody." With regard to that sequence, Trevelyan said: "I again don't know whether a scene will make people copy it, though it did occur to me that with all this juvenile violence, there's much more than you think. This head-shaving is a very nasty thing to do to anybody." But he did want the sado-masochism to be played down. Cammell said Trevelyan asked "for the removal of intercut shots of Chas' girlfriend clawing his back inserted into the flogging sequence. He said he could not countenance an explicit statement of Chas' sado-masochism." When Cammell pointed out that the deletion of this piece of character development would make the scene gratuitously violent, Trevelyan agreed.

"I must say that I think, and still accept, that the scenes of violence in *Performance* were justified," Trevelyan said. "They were not put in for commercial effect. That does not solve my problem because we've declared for years a policy against excessive violence and the beat-up scene in *Performance* was about the most savage I have seen on the screen. It's brilliantly done but we had to do it."

And then after that hurdle, Derek Malcolm noted: "Warner Brothers Distributors exercised their own censorship and removed the intercutting anyhow." Malcolm attests that between the first press show and the second, which he also attended, shots had been removed.

I saw the film on December 4, 1969 in a viewing theatre in St Anne's Court in Soho. Donald and I watched it with a friend I had brought along. I suspect that the version with the razor-cutting of the shoe that I saw at that private screening was the version Malcolm first saw. It seems strange to cut further after the battles with the censor had been completed. But as Donald said: "There are a number of people at Warners who hate the film and all it represents."

A sampling of films that had altercations around that period with the British Board of Film Censors helps to give a perspective. In 1966, *Blowup* had retained its bared breasts and a flash of pubic hair. Ken Russell's *Women in Love* (1969) survived the male nudity, provided the fighting was kept in motion, so that there was no focus on the penes. Russell's *The Devils* (1971) was to be his next confrontation, this time with a degree of torture and the naked orgy of the nuns. Joseph Strick's film of Genet's *The Balcony* (1962) had allowed the first lesbian kiss, but Robert Aldrich's *The Killing of Sister George* (1968) went further and the lesbian kissing and breast fondling had to be pulled back. Buñuel's *Belle de Jour* (1967) had allowed whipping, but Robbe-Grillet's *Trans-Europ-Express* (1967) was rejected for its sadism. Sam Peckinpah's *The Wild Bunch* (1969) had gone to the limits with its violent bloodbaths, and his *Straw Dogs* (1971) took violence further than *Performance*.

Theatre censorship was abolished in 1968, and Nic Roeg recalls sitting on a censorship working party committee and asking if the theatre was free of censorship, why not film, gaining the response: "Anybody can just walk into cinema, but in theatre, you make a conscious effort and it's part of the culture."

After filming is the only time Jagger has gone on record at length to reveal his thoughts and dissatisfaction with the work. "As a film, *Performance* really wasn't successful, so therefore I wasn't very successful in it. To a certain extent it is successful, but to film people, i.e. the industry, it had a very strange effect which no one could really work out, least of all me. I mean, it seemed a pretty ordinary film to me. I thought it was all right considering it was my first attempt. None of it was me. It was a team effort between the director and me. He suggests what you should do and you either do it or you don't. I wasn't portraying myself (*laughs*), and that's precisely what people thought I was – but then that's what acting is.

Making people believe that's what you are. (…) People in the film industry really thought that I was like that and they'd seen hundreds of films featuring hundreds of actors that weren't anything like the parts they portrayed. People acting as soldiers or officers but who've never been in the army. People acting as though they were upper class when in fact they were from the gutter.

"When I came along and did that film they thought Jesus, we can never have a guy like that in a film, he's a junkie Satanist. They believed every fucking piece of it, which makes me laugh! Bloody incredible! I'll tell you, it's very difficult to do that sort of role at fucking six o'clock in the morning."

12) and I want it painted black

THE other performance, the one that really makes it, was the soundtrack. If anything was to take on the tags 'groundbreaking', 'influential', 'revolutionary' or 'experimental', it was the work of Jack Nitzsche on *Performance*. Brought in without his hands tied, in the same way as the two directors had started off shooting the film, he contributed a mix of styles, tastes and influences to the final work that was fresh to mainstream cinema.

The initial idea had been for Mick Jagger to write the music, hopefully with his writing partner, Keith Richards, and then for the Stones to record it. However, that idea seemed to go out the window as Richards became more and more irritated by the rumours, or indeed the shenanigans, that went on inside the house in Lowndes Square. The upshot was that he refused to write any music for the film, instead working on songs for a future Stones album, *Let It Bleed*.

A version of 'Memo From Turner' was recorded with Keith playing guitar. Donald Cammell thought Keith had contributed 'negative energy' to the session and that it lacked punch. But it seems that Richards never played on the session, or any other, and the version as heard in the film is more than just the London recording with Ry Cooder re-recorded in LA.

Jack Nitzsche, who had already worked with the Stones, played Keith the film score he had written for Christian Marquand's *Candy*, which had been rejected. Keith was impressed and told Jagger that Nitzsche could do the music for *Performance*. "He's just this *obsessive* . . . beautiful . . . freak. . . . an American Brian Jones if you like These great spates of rampant irrationality. (. . .) Personally I've always felt he was never given enough credit for his work with Spector. I mean, when you consider how vital the arranger was to those productions. The need to understand spacings for instruments and the weight of the sound itself."

Nitzsche had entered The Rolling Stones' world some years earlier in

1965. He was known as Phil Spector's arranger, many seeing him as the main cog in the famed 'wall of sound'. He was only paid $50 per chart to arrange what became The Crystals' hits – 'He's a Rebel', 'Da Doo Ron Ron', 'Then He Kissed Me' – The Ronettes' 'Be My Baby' and later The Righteous Brothers' 'Unchained Melody' and Ike & Tina Turner's 'River Deep-Mountain High', but he wasn't overly concerned.

His first meeting with the Stones had come about in London when he accompanied Spector to a Regent Sound Studios' recording. The following year in America he was involved in organising their appearance on The T.A.M.I. Show, a television event "packed to the rafters with possessed teeny-boppers" and suggested they try the RCA Studios for recording when they enquired about a studio where they could work while in town.

It was at the end of a 20-hour session at RCA in Hollywood, with only Mick and Keith still awake and standing, that Phil Spector picked up Bill's bass and Jack Nitzsche sat at the harpsichord. The song the four of them recorded was 'Paint It Black'.

Nitzsche was to play piano at a number of recordings. The first time he was asked to contribute he deferred, saying he wasn't an experienced studio musician. "That's all right, neither are we," Jagger replied. Nitzsche always said his biggest palpable influence was on 'Paint It Black'. "They didn't know what to play on the back-up and I started playing the piano gypsy style and they just picked it up. I thought it was just a joke."

He was impressed by the Stones at the various sessions. "There was no guidance at all on those records. And very little need for it. What the fuck, this was the first time a band got together and just played. They changed my whole idea of recording. Before I'd just been doing sessions, three hours to get the tunes down. Working with the Stones made sense right away. Booked studio time for 24 hours a day for two weeks and if ya' didn't get it, fuck it. The great new thing about them was they'd record a song the way they had written it. If it didn't work nobody thought twice about making it a tango! They tried every way possible. Nobody had that big ego thing about keeping a song a certain way. That changed me. That was the first really free feeling I had in the studio."

Rolling Stones discographies seem to abound with irregularities, and 'Memo From Turner' might well be part of that unintentional confusion. It is suggested that the song was recorded as part of the March to June

Olympic Studios sessions, probably during the period May 13 to 21, for *Beggars Banquet*. Ry Cooder was there, brought along by Nitzsche, and he contributed to a couple of tracks, 'No Expectations' and 'Prodigal Son', though he is not credited on the album. It was later, on another album, *Let It Bleed*, that a friction developed between Cooder and Richards that ended his involvement with the Stones, the dispute being over the origin of the riff for 'Honky Tonk Women'.

Time shifting or not, it would seem that it might have been difficult to record a song for *Performance* that had probably not been written at that point.

Donald Cammell was getting worried that Mick had said he would supply a song and more for the film, but nothing had materialised, despite repeated enquiries. Finally, with the shoot under way, Donald took Mick into a pub in Brewer Street and asked what had happened, where was the song. Mick broke down, almost in tears, and said he'd blown it. Keith was having no part in this project. It seems that Cammell wrote the lyrics, with Jagger, and that it was demoed early in September, with Steve Winwood playing guitar, bass, piano and organ, and Jim Capaldi on drums. This was enough to be able to lip-synch when filming, for it wasn't recorded again until after the shoot was over, on November 17, this time at Olympic Studios, using the earlier version, but with new vocals and Al Kooper added on guitar. Three takes were made. Keith was not at either session.

Though Ry Cooder had started working as a blues act, initially with singer Jackie DeShannon, in 1965 he formed the Rising Sons with Taj Mahal, and when it collapsed undertook session work, notably giving a distinct sound to Captain Beefheart's first album, *Safe as Milk*. He declined an invite to join the group, since working as a session musician was preferable at that time. Later he composed for films, 1984's *Paris, Texas* for Wim Wenders being an early highlight. As far as Cooder was concerned, people didn't seem to understand that music on film is "sub-textual" and "an interior sound". This is what Cooder thought came through with Nitzsche. "When Jack Nitzsche started doing that on films in the Sixties, the engineers didn't like it, the producers didn't like it, everybody said, 'This guy's nuts. He's crackers, what do you want him for? He's gonna ruin your film.' But quickly that changed and the people who made the films got younger all of a sudden and they expected to hear something from their own experience in there." Part of the mistake, as Cooder saw it, was to use rock'n'roll in films. The idea of using rock'n'roll like a knife in films (as Steve Woolley suggested, "You twist it and nostalgia comes pouring out") would be anathema to Cooder and Nitzsche. "Personally I don't have much use for it. Only because it's so one-way all the time. I like rock'n'roll all right once in a while, but to me it's a narrow path that you're going on because it has more to do with performance than some kind of style and some progression. Jack Nitzsche had a lot of trouble because every time somebody played an electric guitar on one of those scores it'd stop the show like that. I could never understand that. We'd look at these things, and I was pretty young, and I didn't know anything at all. I had no idea what was going on except that I could see these goddam electric guitars fucking up this imagery."

Mick Jagger called Jack Nitzsche and asked him to come to London to see *Performance*. "It blew my mind. But it's tamer without music – didn't take you to that crazy place. (…) At the beginning he said we could score it together, so I said, 'What do I need you for?' and he said, 'You're right.' So I just brought in all my friends and we did whatever we felt like doing. That was fun."

Nitzsche took the film back to his place off Laurel Canyon, to what is often referred to as a 'witch's cottage', and worked with the aid of cocaine, brought in regularly by Donald Cammell.

As Nitzsche recalled, it was the only film he had done "where nobody interfered". Though Jackie DeShannon didn't work on this soundtrack, she gives a clue to the breadth of Nitzsche's interests by talking about the 'Needles and Pins' recording she made a few years earlier at LA's Western Studios. Written for her by Sonny Bono and Nitzsche, and recorded in a couple of takes, it mixed folk with pop and had an attachment to Nitzsche's dense wall of sound. "I knew it was something special, that we were doing something new here by melding all our diverse influences," said DeShannon. "Jack and I were musical soul mates. We could go from Stockhausen to Aaron Copland to Lightnin' Hopkins in a flash, then move on to Mexican street music and Bartok. That's how we spent our time together."

Nitzsche called up Cooder. "I'm gonna do this movie music now: this guy's made this film, Jagger's in it, and there's a song and it's a pretty weird movie." Cooder thought it sounded interesting. "Come on down and we'll get started."

Cooder went down to Western Studios with his guitars. "We were still using screen projection (...) they would roll the film," he explained to Jonathan Romney for a *Wire* interview. "It was a pretty good sized screen, in this big old studio, and Nitzsche'd be shuffling his score paper and making notes; and I'm sitting there and this scene comes up and he says, 'Well, do it.' Shuffling . . . And I say, 'Well, I don't know, whaddya think I oughta do, Jack?' Nic Roeg came over and said, 'This scene is incredibly sad, it's so tragic because this man and this woman . . . and what they're feeling and what they're thinking . . .' He went on, this long thing. I went, 'Oh God, no. I don't understand.' Jack says, 'Just play bottleneck, all right? You don't have a lot of time.' OK, here I go. But I found this is kind of cool: watch and see and play. And then wait. And then watch and see and play. Somebody gets up and moves, then some little look in the face and go for that. [*Laugh*] Roeg goes, 'Fantastic! What you've done for this scene is incredible! How you've made these actors portray and work, what I've never believed and I didn't think . . .' I thought, 'OK. I can do this.'"

Nitzsche had no intention of resorting to film libraries, or taking tracks already written. They had the 'Memo From Turner' track, but Nitzsche didn't like the result, nor did Jagger it seems. They decided to scrap it and start from scratch, taking only Jagger's vocal and working with a click track. Russ Titelman "played the Keith Richards-sounding 'jing-a-jing' on rhythm guitar", as he phrased it, and Ry Cooder played slide. Who else appears is not known, although Gene Parsons is probably on drums. "It's all an illusion and an illusion on top of other illusions," was how Jagger spoke of the song at the time. "There's so many illusions that I've forgotten after a while." Two other versions from the London takes are in circulation, one available on the album *Metamorphosis* and the other online at YouTube.

The Last Poets' 'Wake Up, Niggers' was already chosen, a 'ready made', suggested by Anita. And Jagger had been filmed doing the extracts of Robert Johnson songs. For the rest, Nitzsche would build a sound texture of musics and effects, whatever he felt was necessary.

What was fortuitous was the group of friends Nitzsche assembled to work with him. Randy Newman, who would later make his own contribution to film music, opens the soundtrack with 'Gone Dead Train', written by Nitzsche with Russ Titelman. Newman is not known for his blues singing, but this up-tempo rock song benefits from his gravel-tired voice. Randy was the core of the band, along with Cooder and Titelman. Though the song was based on King Solomon Hill's 'Gone Dead Train', it was so loose that it bears little resemblance. The original lyrics were to do with an actual train, a Death Train, which was probably part of the reason for its inclusion at the head, and its reprise at the end of the film. Titelman said, "Jack wanted to lyrically use all this voodoo and blues terminology for this story of this faded rock star, a burnt-out character who can't get it up anymore. I saw the track part as Chuck Berry-like in feel but more raucous."

The music credits on *Performance* have been pieced together over the years, added to each time it is written about. At the time of recording, Russ Titelman and Lowell George were learning sitar at the Kinara School of Music, a place that Ravi Shankar had opened. As Nitzsche was moving away from using the regular instrumentation, finding his course would later fit the term 'world music' more appropriately, Titelman offered to borrow some instruments from the school; a "tamboura and veena" were two that were mentioned.

This ethnic angle can be heard, whether blues, or the influence of Native Americans with Buffy Sainte-Marie playing Indian mouth bow, an instrument rarely recorded at that time, or the influence of North African and Middle Eastern music, with instruments such as the santur, tamboura, veena, sitar and tabla. None were used for colouring, all were part of the essential weave.

It should be observed that two women, Sainte-Marie and Merry Clayton, are fundamental to this soundtrack, both working with their mouths, whether a calming or wailing gospel voice, or as an echo chamber with the mouth bow. Both women are what make this soundtrack quite distinctive and original. Given that the Stones' sound is very much a male music, it shows Nitzsche's working plane included women.

It's true to say that Ry Cooder's guitar and bottleneck playing is what is usually picked up on because he was a fresh, young voice. Or perhaps it was that 'Get Away' has inroads into 'Rollin' & Tumblin', leaning more towards Robert Johnson's 'Travelin' Riverside Blues' and then John Lee

Hooker's 'Boom Boom' in the second part, which is not surprising if he'd just watched part of the film and seen Jagger's take on Johnson and Hooker in his guitar-plucking scene. 'Powis Square', too, was a decided tribute to Blind Willie Johnson's 'Dark Was the Night', a song that was a particular Cooder favourite and which was worked on again in *Paris, Texas*. The dulcimer on 'The Hashishin' though was new.

To counter this instrumentation, Nitzsche brought in an early Moog synthesiser soundscape artist, Bernard Krause. It was not the same one as seen in Turner's room in the film, which was a Moog Series III modular synthesiser that Jagger had bought and later sold to a Berlin studio. It eventually found its way into the hands of Christophe Franke of Tangerine Dream.

The crowning glory was the inspired way of riding the wail of the gospel singer, Merry Clayton, across the sound layers. Her contribution was so memorable that she was later called in to give an extra dimension, a featured role, with Jagger on the vocals to 'Gimme Shelter'. Here, for *Performance*, she multiplies to become the Merry Clayton Singers for the final choral work, a fitting end as it nods towards the vocal compositions of the Hungarian György Ligeti.

13) let's have a look

PERFORMANCE was released in America on July 30, 1970, the summer vacation being the best time to release a film that you expect to slip through the net and sink. It is an ideal way for commitments to be fulfilled, contracts to be complied with. This applies equally to big companies and artists. The music business is filled with these manoeuvres. What looked a great idea at one time is put onto the killing floor instead of going through the arduous and expensive procedures of courtrooms and litigations. *Performance* even carried the mark of an X-rating, the kiss of death.

Before the American version could be released, some dubbing had to be made. The main casualty was Harry Flowers. Hardly anyone could understand a word Johnny Shannon said. Nor John Bindon. Nor Laraine Wickens. Blimey! Once the deed was done, a body blow had been made to another vital ingredient. As Donald noted, what "we hadn't anticipated was the language problem. (...) The studio people would sit at the screenings with strained expressions as though this was a Japanese movie with Czech subtitles."

The press reaction was not particularly enthusiastic. Much play has been made of the vituperative reviews. Yet *The New York Times* ran the first review in praise of the film on August 16 by Peter Schjeldahl, a poet often associated with the New York School and a leading art critic. His praise was measured, like his poems. "There are movies about violence and then there are violent movies. *Performance*, that perfect, poisonous cinematic flower, is a violent movie. (...) It is not a movie for everybody, but it is a very exciting movie and for those who do not necessarily include sweetness and light in their definitions of beauty, even a very beautiful one as well. The principal pleasures of *Performance* are those of its flesh. The inspired acting of all hands, especially Jagger and Fox; Mr Roeg's ravishing camera-work and an overall attention to nuances of speech and gesture and décor, both 'significant' and purely ornamental, gives the movie a texture as hypnotic in its density and intricacy as a tantric mandala." By the end Schjeldahl was sure of his experience. "And though one emerges from the theater unedified and feeling a little scorched, it is at least with the accompanying conviction that one has just spent two hours in the presence of something extraordinary."

This seems to have stirred the paper's film critic, John Simon, to launch an attack the following week, on August 23, which is memorable for its opening line: "You do not have to be a drug addict, pederast, sadomasochist or nitwit to enjoy *Performance*, but being one or more of those things would help." The review worked, because it is often quoted, while Schjeldahl's has been virtually buried. Likewise, another blast from Richard Schickel in *Life* magazine runs around loose, clutching its sick bag: "the most disgusting, the most completely worthless film I have seen since I began reviewing". (Nic Roeg used to carry the review in his pocket as a memento mori, and for comic relief.)

There are others that need some airing too, such as Arthur Knight in the *Saturday Review*, who offers his brief appraisal. "Even perversion can have dramatic validity; but perversion exploited for its own sake, as in *Performance*, represents perhaps the nadir of tastelessness." After a suitable attack, it ends: "*Performance* is a picture without a single visible excuse for its existence." They were coming together like a veritable gang of droogs, out for a good kicking in the underpass. The respected Andrew Sarris in the *Village Voice* phrased it another way: "We are going through a period when movies seem to be stranger than ever, but *Performance* is almost in a class by itself in its strangeness. Indeed, in some ways *Performance* is the most deliberately decadent movie I have ever seen. If movies had odors, *Performance* would stink but in an original way."

Rolling Stone came to the defence, liking all aspects of the film. "*Performance* is a stunning film, stunning in the sense of a body blow, and if *Woodstock* presented one sort of reality, *Performance* presents another sort, a dark yin to *Woodstocks'* yang. The Maysles brothers aside, *this* is the Altamont movie. We have to deal with Altamont – and of course Jagger knew about Altamont even before it happened. *Performance* was shot nearly two years ago, long before the apocalypse at the Speedway, but it's all here in final form – future tidings neatly catalogued and even pre-analysed. A line from Jagger's song: 'We were eating eggs in Sammy's when the black man drew his knife.' This is a weird movie, friends."

The support, as indeed the seed for its future growth, would have to come from the alternative press and specialist magazines. Stephen Farber in *Cinema* is one example. "*Performance* is the first film to render the drug experience imaginatively and compellingly; more than that, it is the definitive statement of the drug experience as mystical conversion, a radical assault on conventional values, and the key to the transformation of life."

It was only in general release for eight weeks, and usually only played in one venue in the major cities. After its more or less guaranteed disposal in America, despite good attendance records, the film was withdrawn and requests for it not fulfilled, according to Cammell. But where it could, it continued to play pockets here and there, late-night showings. It never went away. Its reputation just grew. When an older generation tries to forbid their siblings from doing or seeing something, there must be a reason, and there will always be those who say, "Let's have a look."

Whatever the views of the high-ranking executives at Warners, those working the publicity machine were enthusiastic, many undoubtedly relating to the film's subject matter. The main idea was to juxtapose images of Jagger as the long-haired, feminine rock star against the gangster with slicked-back hair. When the full sheet of images was used, they added Fox as gangster against Fox in hippyish mode, and the threesome of Jagger with the two women against another of Jagger reclining with Fox. Both sides are shown with the heading, one that has stuck: "Vice. And Versa." The full caption beneath reads: "This film is about madness. And sanity. Fantasy. And reality. Death. And life. Vice. And versa." The publicity department never wavered from this marketing success. They were not caught lacking. They enjoyed their work, as Harry Flowers would say.

The British launch of the film was organised as a benefit for the drugs advice charity Release, and was held at the Odeon Leicester Square in January 1971. Caroline Coon, who ran the organisation, sought to maximise the publicity by approaching *Time Out*'s owner, Tony Elliott. He rose to the occasion by giving major coverage in the magazine, including on its cover, and also produced a 'poster magazine' that has to be one of the best celebrations a British film has ever received. With interviews, photographs and comments, this supplement today has become a much sought-after collector's item.

Though Jagger had promised to attend the opening, he didn't show. Because of the delays, more than two years had elapsed since filming had ended. He had shot another film, *Ned Kelly*, which had drawn a negative response, and he thought the same might happen to *Performance*, particularly after its reception in the States. Stanley Meadows (Rosebloom) recalled that the Odeon was packed. He attended with John Bindon. "When the film ended we walked out together and people were literally cringing, as if we were real villains."

As was to be expected, in general the reviews were better in the UK. Where the Americans were unable to understand the British accent, or the nuances of British life, on native soil they homed in on that aspect.

Tom Milne in *The Observer* opened with: "Every once in a while a film turns up which hits the contemporary nail so squarely on the head that it really defies criticism or interpretation. Such a film is *Performance*, an extraordinary kaleidoscope of sex, violence and mystic yearning that finally resolves itself into a sort of heraldic shield emblazoned with the device 'This Is Now'." Unlike many of the American reviews, Milne also recognised that the film was not solely about maleness, that there was a female side to the film. "But the point of this merging of causes and effects, of roles and characters, is only completed when one realises that nothing is true in the film, everything is permitted in the way of deception. Not only does the pop star enjoy a *ménage à trois* with two girls, one lushly feminine and the other ambivalently boyish, but the film uses all three actors interchangeably, delightedly deceiving the eye and ultimately incorporating even Chas into a unisex quartet which seems to act with one mind."

Others in the Fleet Street press, as it was still known at the time, picked up on the film, particularly the broadsheets. "Richly original, resourceful and imaginative, a real live movie, in fact, just when we were beginning to think that maybe it wasn't possible any more from home-grown talent," wrote Derek Malcolm in *The Guardian*.

Philip French wrote an analysis in *Sight & Sound*, probably the first serious lengthy appraisal of the film, and Jan Dawson complemented it with further support in the *Monthly Film Bulletin*. Both indicated the film's complexity. "But what is adorable about *Performance*," Dawson wrote, "is not the fact that Donald Cammell should have written a script under the influence of such dauntingly heavyweight writers but that he and his co-director Nicolas Roeg should have succeeded in creating a purely cinematic language for expressing their ideas."

The British had a film to be proud of. The serious critics did not offer pithy comments for the billboards, but considered responses for the reader and encouragements to see the film.

The filmmakers themselves had been shocked by the American response. And by the treatment they had received from Warner Bros. Roeg wondered: "Can people really imagine that someone who's spent so much time in film doesn't know what foot he's putting forward?" In a rare interview at the time, Donald tried to summarise the film and his feelings in *The Guardian*: "The film is simply about an idea. It's a movie that gets into an allegorical area and it moves from a definition of what violence is to an explanation of a way of being. It is an attempt, maybe successful and maybe not, to use a film for exploring the nature of violence as seen from the point of view of an artist. It says that this crook leads this fading pop star to realise that violence is a facet of creative art, that his energy is derived from the same sources as those of the crook. And that that energy is always dangerous, sometimes fatal. How can saying this honestly and openly be considered dirty, or even retrograde?"

To complement the film, a single, 'Memo From Turner', was released in November 1970, with the soundtrack album appearing with the film, "the strongest soundtrack since *Woodstock*" the promotion proclaimed. A novelisation was also published, both here and in America. Though the film could have stayed on the circuit longer, it was pulled after only two weeks.

Ultimately, Fox was pleased with what they had achieved. "I don't think any other English movie has dealt with that subculture like that, where we're so obsessed with class in this country but not with sub-culture. And sub-culture is much more interesting."

Mick Jagger has rarely spoken about the film since its release. His life is so full that there is no reason why he should keep returning to past works, or even be able to recall details. When he has done, it has been hard to say anything new, because he had given such an extensive interview with *Time Out*. Whilst everyone else was starting to read into the finished work, and close it down, Jagger was still seeing how to take it further. "The thing is that it's very easy for people to believe that's what I'm like. It was easy to do in a way because it's just another facet of me if I felt inclined to go that way. But now when I look at it there's so many things I could have done to make it stranger or to make it more real, to my mind, of how Turner would be and how he would live."

Marianne Faithfull felt that *Performance* changed everything, marked the end of an era. "For one instant we looked back and, although we didn't become pillars of salt, I found that when I turned round again there was no ground beneath my feet." Donald saw it as the end of a period too. "*Performance* is a landmark and a swansong for the era of Swinging London, not a success when it came out. Warner Bros wanted none of it." The industry might not have done, but Alexander Walker was certain in thinking of its place when he wrote his book *Hollywood, England* in 1974, summarising the British film industry of the Sixties: "It is hard to think of half-a-dozen films which were created *as films* during the era, and not simply re-created as the screen versions of other tried and proven works: *A Hard Day's Night*, *If*. . . certainly, and shall we admit *Blowup* and stretch the limits of the 1960s to include *Performance*? At least there are four films that seize the essence of the 1960s and express it in concepts that have an authentic aesthetic freshness that hasn't been drained off from the theatrical production or the printed word. They are also four of the most sheerly 'visual' films the decade produced."

By releasing the film with a delay, anything levelled against the violence was more or less irrelevant. The massacre and bloodbath at both the top and tail of *The Wild Bunch* in 1969 was far in excess of anything achieved to date. Sam Peckinpah and his editors, Lou Lombardo and Robert Wolfe, worked through 333,000 feet of film, taken from 1,288 camera set-ups, for over a year to make the art of violence into something unforgettable and another core effort that would further define montage. *Bonnie and Clyde* (1967) had already offered us the 'dance of death' violence, along with the idea of a stronger female persona at that mid-Sixties social turning point.

James Fox found it hard to get the film out of his system. "I stayed friends with John, and Beryl and Tommy and I was around them for quite a few months trying to come off the picture. (. . .) I really split from Donald and Mick and Deborah and Chris and people like that. I didn't really have any friends. I think I kinda just disappeared for a while after three or four months." Johnny Shannon thought that Fox had been "brainwashed or kidnapped by some religious cult for my money. He told (Fox): 'If you want me to thump them for you, Jim, I will.'"

In the period between filming and release, the Stones returned to business. As with any major band, the job absorbed enormous amounts of time and concentration. For the Stones and Jagger, though, there were a number of additional momentous events between late 1968 and late 1970, both personal and professional, which were to dramatically take forward the myths around the band.

The trauma and tragedy surrounding Brian Jones' demise and death were one thing. Whilst there must have been some relief at having him out of the band, no one foresaw his death or paid attention enough to prevent it. The idea of the free concert in Hyde Park, with half a million in attendance, being turned into a tribute for their former bandmate stood little chance of working out positively. A show was conjured up, one that is best remembered for Jagger's white dress, designed by Mr Fish, the reading from Shelley's *Adonais*, and the release of hundreds of white butterflies, a good percentage of which had expired in the boxes or quickly collapsed on the audience once set free.

No sooner had Mick and Marianne departed for Australia, where they were to film *Ned Kelly*, than the distressed Marianne overdosed and was hospitalised in a coma. The utter despair of losing their baby after seven months, added to the guilt over Brian's death, had been too much for her.

The next disaster was not having the right judgement in duplicating a free concert on the *Let It Bleed* tour. After the fact, the band admitted that they had not understood the nature of violence in American society. It wasn't until they were standing on the stage at Altamont and saw the behaviour of the Hells Angels and the way Meredith Hunter had his life ripped from him that the full horror was brought home. It was all very well for Donald Cammell and others to point out that *Performance* had in its turn been prescient, but words were not the same as the horror and vulnerability of being on the spot. Many have commented that the consequence of that day in December 1969 was that Jagger pulled back from the edge. The Stones realised how much they were part of society's fabric, and that they had responsibilities too. If they generated audience energy, violence, or good times, they had to basically accept the consequences of what might happen.

Part of the weave that contributes to the horror of Altamont lies in the songs the Stones were composing in that era. Like any repertoire from any set of musicians, there are always going to be readings that connect the lyrics to their lives, particularly as many do bear some relationship to personal events. For the Stones there was the unfortunate collision of one song, 'Sympathy for the Devil', with that period. The song came about when Marianne gave Mick a copy of Mikhail Bulgakov's *The Master and Margarita* to read. He took his idea from it, condensing elements to make a song that had nothing to do with black magic. That he had been reading about magic, that he was loosely connected with Kenneth Anger, in London for some years, trying to get Mick to be in his films in one way or another, and that *Performance* was made by Donald Cammell, who had a connection of some type to Aleister Crowley, plus a number of other threads that waved around like a Medusa headpiece, only strengthened the idea that contributed to the Altamont legend. And, ultimately, in one way, it helped *Performance* be seen as a document of those times. But you can't stop people believing what they want. "The most indelible misconception to come out of *Let It Bleed* was the silly notion of Mick as the disciple of Satan," Marianne wrote. That song was "pure papier mâché Satanism".

Whether Warners were encouraged to let *Performance* appear to feed off Altamont or the subsequent film by the Maysles Brothers, *Gimme Shelter*, is only speculation. But myths feed other myths. Legends grow.

14) not fade away

WHAT makes one film become a cult rather than another? Are there factors that we can put our finger on in terms of this film, *Performance*? But if the answers were that easy, then cult works could be fabricated. The truth is that it happens in spite of any attempts to 'cultivate' that position.

"Ahead of its time" repeats like a mantra as one reads through reviews, essays or references to the film. Warners used that term as a marketing ploy in 1977 when the film was reissued. "Ten years ahead of its time . . . are you now ready for *Performance*?" was the advertising slogan. In 1967 in his 'pop' column in the *Sunday Times*, Tony Palmer chided *Melody Maker* for writing that Zappa and the Mothers of Invention were "ahead of their time" by saying they are not, "they are of now". Zappa was sharper and able to perceive what others did not see. By now I think it is quite apparent that *Performance* was of its time, "preserves a whole era under glass" as Marianne Faithfull reflected. I've tried to pull out some of the threads. There are others. How many films can be pursued in this fashion to show a mapping of its history? Despite all the viewings over the years, from the private theatre to the big cinema screening, from television to video, where control of the projection became possible, and today on DVD where everything is possible, and permitted, I still see further aspects that enhance or indeed contradict previous thoughts.

It wasn't until last year, watching the DVD, that I noticed the little boy going backwards at the end. How it was achieved is obvious, but why is another matter. Does it have some deep meaning? With a film so weighted one would like to think so. It is for you to unravel. Or treat as a mystery. Like all readings, it will depend on your personal levels of knowledge to give depth to the contexts, as well as the pure pleasure of reading the text. A viewer coming from the Sixties is presented with one form of resonance. But a film transcending its time and gaining cult status is dependent on its relevance for others in the eras that follow. Each generation looks to the film and extracts what it requires. Just by being of its time doesn't make it a cult work.

Though this is fundamentally Donald Cammell's film, it is also a team work. Donald was keen to emphasise that he enjoyed working with others, with merging ideas and talents, and that he stood against the concept of the *auteur* approach to filmmaking. But, as became evident, life is not always black and white, or runs fairly . . . and the film that Donald felt was basically his film seemed to slip away and was regularly credited to his co-director, Nic Roeg.

This was not helped by the fact that Donald Cammell, for all his efforts, succeeded in bringing only three other films to the screen: *Demon Seed* (1977), *White of the Eye* (1987), *Wild Side* (1995). Each has its own surrounding saga. And besides them there was the recurrent presence, indeed one could say nightmare, of Marlon Brando, who seemed to blight that elusive dream of achieving some form of cinematic paradise. And yet *Performance* was in some respects that paradise, that garden of delights. Cammell would not be the first, or the last, to have an early success (whether or not perceived as that at the time), only to have countless other projects slip through his fingers. And yet, there can be a madness that drives the artist forward, refusing attempts to lift that foot from the pedal. For such an artist there is nothing unless one is placing everything on the line at each attempt. The only performance that makes it, that really makes it, is the one that leads to madness. How right you are.

Donald died in April 1996 by placing a gun against his forehead and firing it downwards, so that the bullet lodged in the back of his throat. It was not exactly the same as Turner's shooting in *Performance*, just similar. Reportedly it took him 30 minutes to die, during which time he remained conscious and asked his wife, China: "Can you see the picture of Borges now?" Whether it is true or not, today it is part of the legend.

Nic Roeg has since achieved fame in his own right as a director, and has the *auteur* label attached to him, whether he wants it or not. His whole life has been in films. He was about to direct *Walkabout* when *Performance* came along. Claims are made that various cinematic techniques that appeared in *Performance*, such as non-linear narrative, or a mosaic form of montage, were later repeated in his other films, suggesting that he capitalised on them, and allowed his fame to be built on someone else's ideas. A trace of Nic's earlier work, which is all I've had space to accommodate here, shows that it is not as black and white as that. We all learn from each work as we progress, taking on board and adapting interests that we already have. Part of the reason Donald and Nic worked together was the similarity of their interests, a feeling that they could merge what each had to contribute and make it stronger.

Far from Roeg seeming to gain credit for *Performance*, at times it has sounded as if he's been embarrassed to be given any recognition, to the degree that for many years he ignored his part in the film. But there is no getting away from it, the friction between the directors, whether personal or stirred by the media, or others, has added to the saga surrounding the film. It has not been the reason for its cult status, but it has been one of the factors kept in the air, one of the balls in the 'cult juggled arena'.

Once Cammell had other films to his name, the credit for *Performance* started to shift back towards him, often removing any directing credentials for Roeg. It has been a lifetime of a swinging pendulum. Sometimes, they probably rued the day the idea of co-directing was suggested, and yet that approach was instrumental in making the film what it is today.

Performance has benefited from the subsequent films made by Roeg, the remarkable flow of *Walkabout* (1971), *Don't Look Now* (1973), *The Man Who Fell to Earth* (1976), *Bad Timing* (1980) and *Eureka* (1983), all of which have ideas, motifs and visuals that repeat or are developed, so that we take them on board as a vocabulary that enables us to appreciate and rediscover them in any subsequent viewings of *Performance*. Because of this rich vein of gold struck by Roeg, *Performance* has gained further credence.

Two factors seem to come into play when it comes to the impact that Mick Jagger and The Rolling Stones have had on the cult credentials of *Performance*. There's the obvious fact that the Stones have had a lifetime in the music business, and have remained before the public eye not only for their musical achievements but also for the succession of scandals that various members have attracted over the decades, encompassing dramas around drugs, killings and debauched lifestyles, seemingly at least.

The other connects to that word 'seemingly' in relation to Mick Jagger, for we all think we know this person called Mick Jagger. At some stage he must have realised that his shifting image and identity had struck a chord, a very convenient chord, one that he could use to retain his sanity and his private life. That he has been derided as a result is a mark of its success. In fact, it reflects our irritation at not being able to knock him off his perch, a typically British way of responding to the success of others.

That Oldham instigated the 'bad boy' idea to counter The Beatles' 'good boy' image in the early days was the seed. There is nothing better than the notion of 'bad' to work with. It is the pithy and insulting reviews that are recalled in the history of *Performance,* not the praise or the considered commentaries.

It has made Jagger's job easier that the stories surrounding the shoot have been so salacious. His response is his get-out card: "Those stories are so good I couldn't possibly deny them." That answer in various forms has been his lifelong way to proceed. By writing no autobiography, and not sanctioning any official biography, everything can be denied, or accepted with a laugh. Carey Schofield remarked many years back, in 1983: "As with a holy man or a mass killer, it hardly matters whether or not they are true."

One of the other intriguing factors is the way in which Mick Jagger and Keith Richards have pushed around some of their personal spats in public. Other bands have ruptured as a result. All of us have friends that we have kept for years, or lost over the years. All of us can relate to friendship. Whilst retaining a private life on the one hand, they have conducted a strand of it in public. And it has worked. And still works. Richards' recent autobiography became a bestseller and gossip once again rode the waves. The myths keep rolling.

And what about Anita Pallenberg? At one point she was part of that Rolling Stones circus, her involvement taking in three of the band, an influence that seems unparalleled among any of the other women associated with the group over the years. And then Anita became detached, freed from the whole apparatus, and for years she was game for the media hounds, attracting attention for the worst aspects: an accidental killing and drug abuse. Today, when photos appear in the media, usually in an unflattering light, their intent is to say that we, the public, have won, that she has been put in her place. Her story is something that people would read because of her fall. Whilst it has been rumoured that she was writing her autobiography, nothing has materialised. Further rumours abound that she has been paid *not* to write her side of events. But what could she possibly say that we don't already know or have speculated upon, given the numerous interviews she has given over the years? Her aura of decadence and destruction could only be enhanced, her bad girl image could never be cleaned up. The only ones who would be unhappy, despite any pretence otherwise, are those who might suffer from the fallout, not knowing what damage a loose cannon might cause.

To take the story of *Performance* back to speculation: did she or didn't she have sex with Mick Jagger on the film, whether in filming itself or downstairs in the dressing room? For years Donald toyed with the question, manipulating it. Keith Richards has said recently that he didn't actually know for some time, though finally he knew just from Mick's behaviour. Jagger said nothing himself, of course. And Anita has variously said she did, and then in later years that she didn't, and that it was all a fabrication by Donald, playing games, being mischievous, stirring up the publicity machine . . . effectively.

And yet at times one gets the impression, or perhaps she said it in the scores of interviews, that she didn't have any relationship with Donald, which is a quite bizarre thing to say . . . though perhaps she means no relationship with him during the film shoot, because that question has arisen too. The sexual story has a sense of betrayal, and that is the real issue. The myths are their own labyrinth.

Marianne, who has had her own problems, is another part of the giant labyrinth surrounding the Stones. She thinks: "Anita really went off her rocker. For years. Into an abyss. And I don't think it was really her fault at all, I've never thought Anita was an evil person. I never blamed her, even at the time, for that affair with Mick. God, she was so gorgeous and someone that beautiful can do what they want, really. But the price is high, it always is."

Another legend, Louise Brooks, once wrote a text about 'Why I Will Never Write My Memoirs' in which she acknowledged the importance of the sexual angle. "In writing the history of a life I believe absolutely that the reader cannot understand the character and deeds of the subject unless he is given a basic understanding of that person's sexual loves and hates and conflicts. It is the only way the reader can make sense out of innumerable apparently senseless actions."

James Fox's contribution to the film's cult status has always been about the idea that he walked away, quit acting and turned to religion for his salvation, becoming an evangelical Christian, working with The Navigators. For years misreporting had attributed this to the shock of the drugs and decadence on the set. When he returned to acting years later in a more balanced way, with a family and his religious beliefs in order, the record could be set straight. As I've intimated, his lifestyle and the tracks of his demise were already on the slippery slope before his involvement with the film. "People think *Performance* blew my mind . . . my mind was blown long before that."

His world today is very different, though he acknowledges *The Servant* and *Performance* as his two films of distinction. With that in mind, when he has spoken about the film, he prefers not to make too many comments, quoting the line from John Ford's *The Man Who Shot Liberty Valance*: "When the legend becomes fact, print the legend."

For some years John Bindon made the headlines, on two levels: first with the murder he was tried for, which showed the public his dark side as a villain; and secondly, through the stories about his relationship with Princess Margaret, some aspects of which are still a mystery, or cloaked enough for us to fill in what we want to believe. Anything to do with the Royal family and a commoner, or even worse, a villain, is assured of attracting the interest of the British populace.

Hand in hand is the glamorisation of the British criminal, going back to the Great Train Robbers, and their 'cheeky' robbery, which was corrected by dishing out hefty sentences. This simply set in motion further attention on the criminal fraternity, including the glamour around the Krays, which in the decades since has enabled perpetrators of criminal activities to write their life stories on emergence from prison, their slates wiped clean, economical truth and a sprinkling of tales keeping the public amused.

It has always been stated that the editing by Frank Mazzola struck the right nail, and likewise the soundtrack by Jack Nitzsche found the right note, both being instrumental in the success stories of those men. It is not so much a matter of one factor or another that lifts a film onto another plane, but a whole range of ideas and activities, perhaps a steady stream of them flowing, even overlapping, and continue to build. We also have to take on board the recurrent interest that Aleister Crowley brings to the palette, even perhaps traces of Kenneth Anger's star, although it has probably faded a bit today. And the ever-present respect given to Christopher Gibbs for his contribution to the style of the period. And the stories of David Litvinoff's influence, enigmatic traces of his life regularly leaking out, a thorough biography needed before it's too late.

The role of the Mars bar incident, in Marianne's life and mythology, will never be shaken off. That it is included in this film, in any way, adds a juggling ball to that 'cult event'.

Whilst few of us will have seen the 'out-takes' of the sex scene in *Performance,* or the subsequent short film entitled *Performance Trims*, there is another story, which now seems whimsical. Indeed, evidence in the form of stills reproduced in various books only adds to the legend.

In late November 1970, Sandy Lieberson took a 10-minute film, entitled *Performance Trims*, to the first Wet Dream Film Festival in Amsterdam. It was taken from the 16 mm footage of the sex scenes in *Performance* and had no soundtrack. The book documenting the first and second festival that appeared in 1973 states that it is the "Possession of Sandy Lieberson, England." The notes go on to state: "SUCK would like to thank Sandy Lieberson for flying over to Amsterdam with the cock-bits from Mick Jagger's *Performance*. Sandy produced the film. But we understand that Warner Brothers, who distribute the film, have threatened Sandy with a lawsuit over this. So thank you again, Sandy me darling. (Get stuffed, Warner Bros.) The revealed apparatus of the King of The Rolling Stones in the cuts from *Performance* got much applause, but also disappointed people because Jagger's cock of course isn't any different from other cocks."

Lieberson was a friend of Jim Haynes, one of the organisers of the Wet Dream Film Festival, and had responded to a request when "asked if he had any interesting movies, or interesting bits from *Performance* or other films which we might screen" by offering some censored footage from the film. He brought the reel, and took it away afterwards, "to make sure that nothing happened to the print". It transpires that Richard Neville thought some of the footage would look good in *Oz*, so he went into the projection room in the Kosmos and clipped frames of Jagger in bed with Michèle Breton. Neville apologised one month later to Jim Haynes in a letter dated December 28, 1970: "I am sorry to hear that my purloining of 3 frames from PERFORMANCE off-cuts has created such anxiety amongst

SUCK people. It did not occur to me that you or Bill would be particularly interested so I didn't bother to even mention my intention to you. For this I am sorry and I realise now that I should have. When I saw Mick Jagger's naked front I thought this could make an exciting OZ graphic so, along with Jay Landesman, Albie went to the BBK, snipped out 3 frames and re-spliced the film. When Sandy Lieberson came back to London I began to realise how seriously everyone regarded my action and I promised we would not publish the picture until we contacted Mick Jagger and that further I would return the negatives directly to him." It was published in *OZ* #32, despite the suggestion it would not be. Jagger laughed about the whole incident over lunch with Jim Haynes in Paris much later.

Performance has had its influence and admiration acknowledged by a variety of filmmakers, including Bernardo Bertolucci, Stanley Kubrick, Paul Schrader, Quentin Tarantino, Martin Scorsese, who referenced 'Memo From Turner' in *Good Fellas* (1990), and others. The ending of *Sexy Beast* (2000) is a direct reference to *Performance*, as the camera zooms through the swimming pool, burrowing its way into the underground connection.

And it hasn't gone unnoticed that musicians have worked with ideas from the film, the first being Big Audio Dynamite with 'E=MC2', then Happy Mondays with 'Mad Cyril' and William Orbit's recording of 'Harry Flowers'.

It is perhaps fortunate that lines seen in the earlier scripts, where words like "groovy" were included, never made it to the screen, because if there's anything that dates a film or makes people cringe today it is such language.

What does seem to be in its favour, and which is reflected in its citing as "the world's most expensive home movie", is the idea that it has that element of documentary. There is relatively little perceptive documentary footage of the time, specifically of fringe activities. Most of what is shown comes from places such as the BBC archives. In other words, mainly official sources. Peter Whitehead is a notable exception for shooting *Tonite Let's All Make Love in London* (1967). Of course there is more, and it is in black and white predominantly, but for those around at the time it was unusual to find a stills camera, let alone a film camera, in action at any event. *Performance*, with the naturalness of its behaviour in the bath and bed, in particular, seems perversely to convey that documentary aspect.

And there are still repercussions. When the most complete cut of the film was submitted to the British Board of Film Classification (formerly the British Board of Film Censors) in January 2004, the question arose as to the age of Michèle Breton at the time of filming, and whether she qualified for protection under the Protection of Children Act, in the light of the new definition of the Sex Offences Act (2003), that redefined a child as being a person under 18, where before it was 16. Despite all the information on Breton's age that had been given out in interviews by Donald, it was the sight of her underdeveloped physique that made the examiners think twice. As it was apparently impossible to obtain proof of the actress' age, and there was no actual shot on screen of the actress participating in any sexual activity, being almost a bystander to the action, the film was passed uncut with an 18 certificate.

15) also part of the trip

A PREFACE is often written after the book is written and then included at the front to say what is about to be read, or even what the writer intends to write, even though as he writes he knows that it has already been written.

This is written after the fact. I knew what I hoped to write, what I hoped to explore. I know that I took other paths in the process, that I created a different mosaic from what I had imagined prior to starting. But I would have it no other way.

Performance is a film that moves quickly, takes us through an enormous number of possibilities, with references that we can either ignore or connect with. There is no intention to supply a meaning or meanings, it lives in the world of open texts. If you dislike that form of art then you can move on. If you like your time to be absorbed that way, then you can stay, yesterday till tomorrow. You have all the time in the world. Especially today, when technology allows the film to be pleasured at our own pace, again, and again, and then some more. Everything is possible. Everything is permitted.

I have tried to show certain pieces of a mosaic in the limited space and time of this book. There was more I didn't pursue, or didn't see, or that didn't come within the compass of my interests. Once you take the plunge, you can feel the swell of the immersion, the desire to go forward while at the same time experiencing the lures which distract one. As one critic suggested, we try to come to terms with all these ideas and possible meanings and weave our own text, but don't always feel we've achieved it. Ultimately, we still have an open text and the film is waiting to be read again. Or, as Raymond Durgnat said, it is an interpretation "not in the sense one interprets an obscure passage into a clearer one, but in the sense that a player interprets a composer's score".

Where some would use the idea of the jigsaw coming together, I was thinking of the mosaic starting to build, for there is no slotting together, only a mosaic captured and held in place by a fixing agent.

While some have attached praise of the order of 'best British film' and similar accolades, others have attacked *Performance* in the vilest manner possible. No one can deny, though, that its history has granted it an attention not given to many. For various reasons it is an extraordinary film, one that has given endless hours of pleasure, whether through the acting, the script or cinematic ideas. That a film that actually had so much loaded against its chance to succeed has defied all the odds and lives on has to give hope to those who want to strive to make their own project.

In one sense this book was begun in December 1969, a few weeks before *Performance* had its first public showing in Britain. Today it appears, more than 40 years later, with the same title, but in a different form. According to my archives, it was on December 6 that I met Donald Cammell at a Soho viewing theatre in St Anne's Court, off Wardour Street, and watched the film in a slightly longer version than the one released. Donald rushed off afterwards to see Blood, Sweat & Tears at the Royal Albert Hall, if I recall. I went home to start work on the novelisation, clutching a continuity script, only to be pulled up short because of contractual difficulties between the publisher, Sphere, and Warner Bros.

In the early Eighties, with the arrival of video, it was possible to catch a television broadcast of the film and use it in my classes at the art school in Rochester, in what was later to be given the illustrious title Film and Media Studies. Over the years I showed extracts or full screenings to my students, accumulating notes in the process. Those are the early days of my relationship with the film.

I have always thought that it was better to work with the documents of the period, rather than to view with hindsight, particularly as that possibility was open to me. In other words, to take on board the resources that those involved had access to. It is all very well to discuss Artaud, for example, but if the only books available in English at the time numbered three, then the ideas were probably derived from those available works.

My own bookshelves, archives and scrapbooks have been my resource. My own involvements in the late Sixties overlapped with the world mapped out by Barry Miles in his books. I was also involved at the Royal Court where Marianne Faithfull acted in Chekhov and Edward Bond's play. People know about these events, but I was there, saw many of them, and participated in some. My involvements in film, music, art, literature and crime writing have taken me across many of the aspects included in *Performance*. I determined to use an archival basis because comments at the time, whilst certainly hiding some things, are more interesting than many made today, which might be twisted by faulty memories or other preoccupations. It is a kaleidoscopic approach, a sense of a mosaic in the making. My approach has always been in the spirit of the film itself, an interdisciplinary and intertextual one.

I have not necessarily sought to do new interviews with those concerned, as an enormous number have been produced already, many dating from nearer the time of the film. My fear was that, by doing new interviews, how much more could be obtained and how much more might just cloud the issues, either opening up the stories or bending them further to improve reputations?

The question is always whether the information is correct. Many of those involved lead such busy and concentrated lives that they can't recall everything, let alone rummage through the ravages of tiredness, drugs, drink or whatever. It's bad enough for the rest of us to remember our lives. Criminals recall, sometimes with selective memories, for good reason. The books written can only be as good as the resources. Even when one is involved in certain events one sometimes cannot verify the documented evidence.

I've thought to write this book before, then left it aside. There were questions that one could ask those involved, but now it is too late, or more difficult to seek answers, or trust the answers. Many have painted the key areas, repeatedly, with different brushes, over time, but some views have been omitted or not worked on at all. So I've tried bringing some more things into the picture. I have intercut thoughts and dialogues with numerous people directly on the film, or on ideas that are central to this film. As this goes back many years, to the Seventies basically, many of those spoken to, directly or in letters, have been forgotten, in the sense of putting a name to a thought or idea. Only in the last two decades, when I've wondered about writing at length, did I have a clearer picture in my head of those I had spoken to. That said, I've still forgotten names.

Nevertheless, I wish to thank all these people who in their various ways have contributed, either recently or over some years, to filling in details of the mapping I have given to this remarkable film.

The main participants have spoken many times in interviews for books and documentary programmes right from the start. Many repeat the same points, with slight variations. In more recent times the variations have been greater, whether through a lack or confusion of memory, or for other reasons. It is the earlier documentation that has been favoured. Only one person acknowledged that they had "got stoned" before recording the conversation, and that was Jon Savage, interviewing Donald Cammell, the reprinted version where this is stated being an extract from a longer interview published earlier.

The intent has been to be more informational than interpretative, to offer lines for others to pursue if they wish to take a path into other areas of the labyrinth. I wanted to present a context for the film, so that it didn't only suit the person already informed on some of the areas, but it enabled a newcomer to read between the covers of one book a sense of the biography of the film. I have not included extensive biographies of Donald Cammell or any of those involved because I was intent on a biography of the film itself.

My own library includes a large number of cultural scrapbooks, started in 1964, where I've stored clippings from newspapers and other publications that I would not otherwise have kept. Sources like *The Guardian, Independent, Observer, Sunday Times, Melody Maker, NME, TLS, City Limits, Libération, Le Monde* and many more found their way in there, whereas many specialist magazines in art, cinema, theatre, music and literature are not clipped, but have been retained in their entirety, the rise and fall of some of these collections following my fluctuating interests. As for the rest, the books, records, videos, DVDs . . . these are from my library, my house basically. I had thought I would resort to other libraries, but when I did seek things, I found the libraries wanting, which reinforced my reasons for starting my own working collection all those years ago in the mid-Sixties, indeed the germ of the idea coming from something William Burroughs wrote about building up one's own resources, not leaving it for other official agencies to control what should be our reference bank. Out of the blue, arriving on the last train, was an archive from Peter Playdon. He had researched extensively for many years to write an in-depth dissertation on the film. Amongst his papers were many interesting documents that either added to my approach or countered some of my impressions. I thank him for his work, his archive and the areas he has explored diligently.

The point of intertextual work is that it can go on forever. One has to determine for oneself where you go and where you stop. At times it was like juggling, holding 14 balls in the air, or more. At times, to mix images, it was like making a mosaic and wondering whether I was standing on the cradle, like Donald Sutherland in *Don't Look Now*, waiting for all to crash to the floor. But fear is the game. Fear is the risk. There's no point otherwise. As Borges says, if you know what you're doing it's not interesting. And yet, of course, one has a sense of the book one wants to write and one edits and selects accordingly.

And so the use of other libraries never materialised. But I do have other people to thank for their contributions. Many go back over the years. Some are good friends. Paul Mayersberg has been one person who has talked through ideas on film, in general, as well as ideas to do with his work with Nic Roeg, *Performance* and our other common interests. I thank him for his repeated clarity in exploring ideas in conversations and interviews that have been published.

Though I had chatted to some of those involved on either side of the camera over the years, it has always been informally. I have spoken to a few people in recent times who have not often been asked to reflect, often about specific issues that I wanted addressing. David Cammell has been helpful in many ways, not only in his recall, but also in filling in points not covered before. As indeed was Deborah (Dixon) Roberts, who went through the vital years with me to pick up on some of my suppositions and shape the gaps in my thoughts. I was particularly pleased that Deborah found a photo that confirms one of the myths surrounding the film, which she thought would amuse me, but which has done more than that. Special mention and gratitude also to Annabel Davis-Goff, who engaged in a good dialogue and painted in points constructively. I thank the three of them wholeheartedly.

David Barraclough is more than an editor. He had wanted me to write the book many years ago when he was working for another publisher. His renewed contact was a surprise and welcomed, and has led to fruitful meetings, meals and other dialogues. His sharpness in refining or making me clarify certain flights of ideas has been much appreciated. Likewise, many thanks also to the picture editor, Jacqui Black, who located fresh photos from others who had visited the set, enabling us to present a mosaic of a visual narrative.

And there are others, some of whom have helped me at great length over a period, others who have just helped on specific lines of thinking or enquiry. I thank Stephen Barber, Daniel Bird, Kieron Corless, John Cussans, Hanna de Heus, Ken Hughes, David Hyman, Cameron Lindo, Sophie Marceau, Mike Molloy, Lynda Morris, Kim Newman, Bernard Noël, Mike O'Pray, Kieron Pim, Will Rowe, Tony Rudolf, Raúl Ruiz, Andrew Sclanders, Iain Sinclair, Terry Smith, Brad Stevens, Lynne Tillman, Sam Umland, Paul Woods, Susannah York, Andrzej Zulawski, and the irresistible few who shall remain anonymous.

This book is dedicated to the memory of Donald Cammell, who first opened the door to this film, and to my wife, Catherine, who has followed the writing of this book at every step, reading, commenting, notating in the margins, painting colours in the air . . .

The idea that James Fox should use the remark from John Ford's *The Man Who Shot Liberty Valance*, saying: "When the legend becomes fact, print the legend," or that Mick Jagger should respond to the salacious rumours with: "those stories are so good I couldn't possibly deny them", leads me to quote Jean Cocteau: "History is a truth that in the long run becomes a lie, whereas myth is a lie that in the long run becomes a truth."

Nico used to enjoy telling lies, according to her friends. "People like us are in the eye of the press, and it's fun to play games with them." She lied to deceive, as she said, not to play games like the others. She had her own personal and sad agenda, far removed from most of those involved here. The cast of those in this book might or might not have been economical with the truth, to varying degrees at various times. It is not important if some facts are not precise, such as when Anita met Jones, or Cammell, or whether Nico and Anita were confused. It adds to the allure of the whole episode, the whole adventure. Rather than offer a pedantic record of facts and dates, with variables, the idea has been to give a sense of period, events, things that happened, perspectives that those involved might have brought, or seem to have brought, to the occasion. There are plenty of biographies of those involved, more on some than others. All were helpful, but none were bibles.

I like to recall Robbe-Grillet's remark: "I reject the two basic characteristics of autobiography. First, that you can't start an autobiography if you haven't got an overall view of your life. (...) And secondly, the idea that you have to tell the truth. Surely that's never been the case." Jonathan Romney, drawing the interview to a close, pushed on the point that if Robbe-Grillet lied in his books, does the same apply to interviews: "Oh yes. If something seems to me more interesting than the truth . . ."

Nic Roeg has a healthy disregard too: "The past changes all the time for me. Finally, I come to the conclusion of never talking about it. Even if I described it exactly, I'd finally have to say it was not exactly that way. I think biography is probably more accurate than autobiography because a biographer is likely to think up fresher lies."

What I like about *Performance* is that it is one of the few films that never seems to satiate one's thirst at each viewing. There are no doors to close, just doors to swing on. If it were a painting by Hieronymus Bosch, we would not complain at the excess of imagery. If it were James Joyce's *Ulysses*, we would choose to either read it or never open it. It is a film that takes less than two hours to watch. If you do not want that experience, turn away. If you do, proceed. Nothing else matters.

Raúl Ruiz, in his *Poetics of Cinema*, makes a point before setting off on his journey with the reader: "One last remark: I am not a scholar and the majority of my references have been culled from my personal library, allowing me to check them without difficulty. But I read in zigzags, I travel from one book to the next, and this is not without risks. It is quite possible that here and there, certain interpretations or comparisons are stretched or simply gratuitous. However, this book is a journey – and travellers should be aware that paths leading nowhere are also part of the trip."

16) credits

Performance (UK)

(Filmed July to November 1968)
(Released August 1970 (USA), January 1971 (UK))

Written by Donald Cammell
Directed by Donald Cammell & Nicolas Roeg

Chas Devlin	James Fox
Turner	Mick Jagger
Pherber	Anita Pallenberg
Lucy	Michèle Breton
Harry Flowers	Johnny Shannon
Rosebloom	Stanley Meadows
Moody	John Bindon
Joey Maddocks	Anthony Valentine
Dennis	Anthony Morton
Tony Farrell	Kenneth Colley
Harley-Brown	Allan Cuthbertson
Lorraine	Laraine Wickens
Chauffeur	John Sterland
Dana	Ann Sidney
Noel	Noel Swabey
Noel (voice)	Ian McShane (uncredited)
Workman	Reg Lye (uncredited)
Steve	Billy Murray (uncredited)
Fraser	Anthony Roye (uncredited)
Jack Harrison	Leon Eagles (uncredited)
O'Brien	John Poole (uncredited)
Mrs Farrell	Jane Lapotaire (uncredited)
Mrs Devlin	Mary Quinn (uncredited)

Noel's mother	Helen Booth (uncredited)
Gordon	Ralph Nossek (uncredited)
Herbert	Reg Lye (uncredited)
Pooley	Terry Duggan (uncredited)
Mr Goulandris	Andreas Lysandrou (uncredited)
Detective Sergeant	Edmond Bennett (uncredited)
Constable	Jay Denyer (uncredited)
Ticket Clerk	John Caesar (uncredited)
Myers Twins	Dennis & John Myers (uncredited)
Producer	Sanford Lieberson
Associate Producer	David Cammell
Director of Photography	Nicolas Roeg
Editors	Antony Gibbs
	Brian Smedley-Aston
	Frank Mazzola (uncredited)
	Tony Palmer (uncredited)
Art Director	John Clark
Assistant Director	Richard Burge
Second Assistant Director	Peter Jacques (uncredited)
Unit Manager	Kevin Kavanagh
Production Manager	Robert Lynn
Design Consultant	Christopher Gibbs
Technical Advisor	Deborah Dixon
Technical Advisor & Dialogue Coach	David Litvinoff
Set Dresser	Peter Young
Continuity	Annabel Davis-Goff
Casting Director	Miriam Brickman (uncredited)
Camera Operator	Mike Molloy
Electrician	Paul Borg (uncredited)

Focus Puller	Peter Hannan (uncredited)
Sound Recordist	Ron Barron
Sound Editor	Alan Pattillo
Dubbing Mixer	Gerry Humphreys (uncredited)
Sound Re-recording Mixer	Gerry Humphreys (uncredited)
Wardrobe	Billy Jay
	Emma Porteus
Make-up	Paul Rabiger
	Linda DeVetta
Hairdresser	Helen Lennox
Production Companies	Warner Bros Inc / A Goodtimes Enterprises production
Original Music	Jack Nitzsche
Conductor	Randy Newman
Singers	Mick Jagger
	Merry Clayton/The Merry Clayton Singers
	Buffy Sainte-Marie
	Randy Newman
Musicians	Ry Cooder (guitars, dulcimer)
	Randy Newman (piano)
	Russ Titelman (percussion, guitar)
	Lowell George (guitar)
	Buffy Sainte-Marie (mouth bow)
	Bernard Krause (Moog synthesiser)
	Nasser Rastegar-Nejad (santur)
	Amiya Dasgupta (sitar)
	Milt Holland (drums, percussion)
	Gene Parsons (drums, guitars)
	Bobby West (bass)

'Gone Dead Train', vocal by Randy Newman
'Performance', vocal by Merry Clayton
'Get Away', bottleneck guitar solo by Ry Cooder
'Powis Square', bottleneck guitar solo by Ry Cooder
'Rolls Royce And Acid'
'Dyed, Dead, Red', mouth bow solo & vocal by Buffy Sainte-Marie
'Harry Flowers'
'Memo From Turner', vocal by Mick Jagger
'The Hashishin', mouth bow solo by Buffy Sainte-Marie, dulcimer solo by Ry Cooder
'Wake Up, Niggers', vocal & congas by The Last Poets
'Poor White Hound Dog', vocal by Merry Clayton
'Natural Magic'
'Turner's Murder', vocal by The Merry Clayton Singers

All music written and arranged by Jack Nitzsche, except 'Gone Dead Train', which is by Nitzsche & Russ Titelman, 'Memo From Turner' written by Mick Jagger & Keith Richards (& Donald Cammell), and 'Wake Up, Niggers', which is written by The Last Poets (Jalaluddin Mansur Nuriddin, Omar Ben Hassan & Abiodun Oyewole).

selected resources

Books, magazines, newspapers . . .

Abadie, Daniel (ed), *Jackson Pollock* (Centre Georges Pompidou, 1982)
Abadie, Daniel (ed), *Tàpies* (Jeu de Paume, 1994)
Ableman, Paul, *Test:* (Methuen, 1966)
Adams Sitney, P. (ed), *The Avant-Garde Film* (New York University Press, 1978)
Adams Sitney, P., *Visionary Film* (Oxford, 1974)
Aftel, Mandy, *Death of a Rolling Stone* (Sidgwick & Jackson, 1982)
Aldridge, John, *Satisfaction* (Proteus Books, 1984)
Almendros, Nestor, *A Man with a Camera* (Faber & Faber, 1980)
Alvarez, Al, 'Roeg Time' (*Inter/view,* July 1988)
Anderson, Christopher, *Jagger Unauthorised* (Simon & Schuster, 1993)
Andrew, George & Vinkenoog, Simon, *The Book of Grass* (Peter Owen, 1967)
Antonioni, Michelangelo, *Screenplays* (Souvenir Press, 1963)
Armes, Roy, *The Cinema of Alain Resnais* (Zwemmer, 1968)
Artaud, Antonin, *Artaud Anthology* (City Lights, 1965)
Artaud, Antonin, *Obliques / Artaud*, 1976
Artaud, Antonin, *Oeuvres Complètes XIII* (Gallimard, 1974)
Artaud, Antonin, *Selected Writings* (Farrar, Straus & Giroux, 1976)
Artaud, Antonin, *The Theater & Its Double* (Grove Press, 1958)
Ashton, Dore, *The Life and Times of the New York School* (Adams & Dart, 1972)
Baddeley, Gavin & Woods, Paul, *God's Assassins* (Ian Allan, 2009)
Baker, Phil, *Burroughs* (Reaktion, 2010)
Balch, Anthony, 'Interview: Breakthrough in Grey Room . . .' (*Cinema Rising* 1, April 1972)
Baldick, Robert, *The Life of J.-K.Huysmans* (Oxford, 1955)
Balthus, *Balthus* (Centre Georges Pompidou, 1984)
Barber, Chris, 'Performance' (*Eyeball* 4, 1996)
Barber, Lynn, 'Lady Rolling Stone' (*The Observer*, February 2008)
Barber, Stephen, *Antonin Artaud: Blows and Bombs* (Faber & Faber, 1993)
Barber, Stephen, *Terminal Curses* (Solar, 2008)

Barlow, Sarah & White, John (eds), *Fifty Key British Films* (Routledge, 2008)
Barthes, Roland, *Image-Music-Text* (Fontana, 1977)
Barthes, Roland, *The Pleasure of the Text* (Farrar, Straus & Giroux, 1975)
Bataille, Georges, *Les Larmes d'Eros* (Pauvert, 1961)
Battcock, Gregory (ed), *Minimal Art* (Dutton, 1968)
Battcock, Gregory (ed), *The New American Cinema* (Dutton, 1967)
Baudelaire, Charles, *Intimate Journals* (Panther, 1969)
Beard, Paul & Hill, Lee, 'The Man That Time Forgot' (*Neon*, August 1997)
Beaton, Cecil, *Beaton in the Sixties* (Phoenix, 2004)
Beaton, Cecil, *Cecil Beaton's Diaries 1963–74* (Weidenfeld & Nicolson, 1978)
Beckett, Samuel, *Waiting for Godot* (Faber & Faber, 1959)
Berger, John, *About Looking* (Writers & Readers, 1980)
Berne, Eric, *Games People Play* (Penguin, 1967)
Biguenet, John & Whalen, Tom, 'An Interview with Jorge Luis Borges' (*New Orleans Review*, Fall 1982)
Biskind, Peter, *Easy Riders, Raging Bulls* (Bloomsbury, 1998)
Bockris, Victor, *Keith Richards* (Omnibus, 2006)
Bogarde, Dirk, *Snakes and Ladders* (Penguin, 1988)
Bond, Edward, *Early Morning* (Calder & Boyars, 1968)
Bond, Edward, *Lear* (Eyre Methuen, 1972)
Bond, Edward, *Saved* (Methuen, 1965)
Booth, Stanley, *Keith: Till I Roll Over Dead* (Headline, 1994)
Booth, Stanley, *The True Adventures of The Rolling Stones* (Sphere, 1986)
Borges, Jorge Luis, *Collected Fictions* (Viking, 1998)
Borges, Jorge Luis, *Fictions* (Calder, 1965)
Borges, Jorge Luis, *Labyrinths* (New Directions, 1964)
Borges, Jorge Luis, *A Personal Anthology* (Cape, 1968)
Borges, Jorge Luis, *Selected Non-Fictions* (Viking, 1999)
Boyle Family, *Beyond Image: Boyle Family* (Arts Council, 1986)
Brett, Guy, *Kinetic Art* (Studio Vista, 1968)
Brook, Peter, *The Empty Space* (McGibbon & Kee, 1968)
Brooks, Louise, 'Why I Will Never Write My Memoirs' (*Film Culture* 67–69, 1979)
Brown, Mick, *Performance* (Bloomsbury, 1999)
Brown, Norman O., *Love's Body* (Vintage, 1966)
Buck, Paul, *A Public Intimacy* (Book Works, 2011)
Buck, Paul, 'Caught in the Act: An Interview with Paul Mayersberg' (*Rapid Eye* 2, 1992)

Buck, Paul, 'Violent Silence: An Interview with Paul Mayersberg' (*Divinity* 4, Winter 1993)
Buck, Paul, 'Who Fucked Madonna?' (*Frozen Tears* III, 2007)
Burgin, Richard, *Conversations with Borges* (Avon, 1970)
Burroughs, William, *The Naked Lunch* (Calder, 1964)
Burroughs, William, *Nova Express* (Cape, 1966)
Burroughs, William, *The Soft Machine* (Calder & Boyars, 1968)
Burroughs, William, *The Ticket that Exploded* (Calder & Boyars, 1968)
Burroughs, William, 'the beginning is also the end' (*Transatlantic Review* 14, Autumn 1963)
Cadwallader, Graham, 'Inside Performance' (*Sight & Sound*, Spring 1971)
Calendo, John, 'Dietrich and the Devil' (*Inter/View* 26, October 1972)
Calendo, John, 'Dietrich and the Devil (part two)' (*Inter/View* 27, November 1972)
Cameron, Ian (ed), *The Films of Jean-Luc Godard* (Studio Vista, 1967)
Cammell, C.R., *Aleister Crowley* (NEL, 1969)
Cammell, Donald, *Performance* (Faber & Faber, 2001)
Campbell, Duncan, *That Was Business, This is Personal* (Mandarin, 1991)
Campbell, James, *Paris Interzone* (Secker & Warburg, 1994)
Campion, Chris, 'The Uncensored Don' (*Dazed & Confused* 62, February 2000)
Carey, Gary, *Marlon Brando: The Only Contender* (Robson, 1976)
Carroll, Lewis, *The Annotated Alice* (Penguin, 1965)
Catoir, Barbara, *Conversations avec Antoni Tàpies* (Cercle d'Art, 1988)
Catterall, Ali & Wells, Simon, *Your Face Here* (Fourth Estate, 2001)
Caute, David, *Joseph Losey* (Faber, 1994)
Chandler, Raymond, *Pearls are a Nuisance* (Penguin, 1964)
Chang, Chris, 'Cinema Sex Magick: the Films of Donald Cammell' (*Film Comment*, July/August 1996)
Charone, Barbara, *Keith Richards* (Futura, 1979)
Chibnall, Steve & Murphy, Robert (eds), *British Crime Cinema* (Routledge, 1999)
Christ, Ronald, 'An Interview with Jorge Luis Borges' (*Paris Review* 40, Winter-Spring 1967)
Cioran, E.M., *Anathemas and Admirations* (Quartet, 1992)
City Lights Journal 1, 2 & 3 (1963, 1964 & 1966)
Clair, Jean, *Art en France* (Chêne, 1972)
Clarkson, Wensley, *Bindon* (Blake, 2007)
Clerk, Carol, 'Crimes and Misdemeanours' (*Uncut* 40, September 2000)

Cocteau, Jean, *Five Plays* (Hill & Wang, 1961)
Cocteau, Jean, *Two Screenplays* (Calder & Boyars, 1970)
Cohn, Nik, *Today There are No Gentlemen* (Weidenfeld & Nicolson, 1971)
Combs, Richard, 'Looking at the Rubber Duck: Nicolas Roeg on François Truffaut' (*Sight & Sound*, Winter 1984/85)
Combs, Richard, 'Relatively Speaking' (*Monthly Film Bulletin*, August 1985)
Comolli, Jean-Louis, 'The Phantom of Personality' (*Cahiers du Cinéma in English* 11, September 1967)
Cook, Richard, 'Roegery' (*New Musical Express*, May 1983)
Cooper, David, *Psychiatry & Anti-psychiatry* (Tavistock, 1967)
Cozarinsky, Edgardo, *Borges In/And/On Film* (Lumen, 1988)
Cros, Jean-Louis & Lefévre, Raymond, 'Pour rehabiliter Nicholas Roeg' (*Image et Son* 362, June 1981)
Dalle Vacche, Angela, *Cinema and Painting* (Athlone, 1996)
Dalton, David, *The Rolling Stones* (W.H. Allen, 1975)
Dalton, David, *The Rolling Stones: The First Twenty Five Years* (Thames & Hudson, 1981)
Dalton, David & Farren, Mick, *Rolling Stones in Their Own Words* (Omnibus, 1980)
Danks, Adrian, 'What's Been Puzzling You is the Nature of My Game' (*Senses of Cinema*, 2001, online journal)
Dawson, Jan, 'Performance' (*Monthly Film Bulletin*, February 1971)
De Rham, Edith, *Joseph Losey* (Deutsch, 1991)
Del Valle, David, 'Memo from Cammell' (*Video Watchdog* 35, 1996)
Di Lauro, Al & Rabkin, Gerald, *Dirty Movies* (Chelsea House, 1976)
Donoghue, Albert & Short, Martin, *With a Gun in My Hand* (Blake, 2008)
DuCane, John, 'Donald Cammell: Performance to Ishtar' (*Cinema Rising* 1, April 1972)
Dunne, J.W., *An Experiment with Time* (Faber & Faber, 1958)
Dwoskin, Stephen, *Film Is* (Owen, 1975)
Ehrmann, Jacques (ed), *Game, Play, Literature* (Beacon, 1971)
Eliade, Mircea, *Myths, Dreams & Mysteries* (Fontana, 1968)
Elliott, Tony, 'Jagger on Performance' (*Time Out*, January 1971)
Esslin, Martin, *The Theatre of the Absurd* (Penguin, 1961)
Evans, Jimmy & Short, Martin, *The Survivor* (Mainstream, 2001 & 2002)
Faithfull, Marianne, with Dalton, David, *Faithfull* (Penguin, 1994)
Faithfull, Marianne, with Dalton, David, *Marianne Faithfull: Memories, Dreams and Reflections* (HarperCollins, 2008)

Farber, Stephen, 'Performance: The Nightmare Journey' (*Cinema*, Fall 1970)
Farson, Daniel, *The Gilded Gutter Life of Francis Bacon* (Vintage, 1993)
Feineman, Neil, *Nicolas Roeg* (Twayne, 1978)
Finnegan, Ruth, *Oral Poetry* (Cambridge, 1977)
Ford, Christopher, 'Nothing Queer About Johnny Shannon' (*The Guardian*, January 1971)
Fordham, Peta, *Inside the Underworld* (Panther, 1974)
Foreman, Freddie, *The Godfather of British Crime* (Blake, 2007)
Foreman, Freddie & Lambrianou, Tony, with Clerk, Carol, *Getting it Straight* (Pan, 2007)
Foster, Hal, 'On Richard Hamilton' (*London Review of Books*, October 2011)
Foucault, Michel, *Madness & Civilisation* (Vintage, 1973)
Fox, James, *Comeback* (Hodder & Stoughton, 1983)
French, Philip, 'Performance' (*Sight & Sound*, Spring 1971)
Freud, Sigmund, *Art and Literature* (Penguin, 1985)
Friedman, B.H., *Jackson Pollock* (Weidenfeld & Nicolson, 1972)
Fromm, Erich, *The Anatomy of Human Destructiveness* (Penguin, 1977)
Gaskill, William, *A Sense of Direction* (Faber & Faber, 1988)
Gaskill, William, 'On Saved' (Royal Court programme, 1965/66)
Gavronsky, Serge, *Towards a New Poetics* (University of California Press, 1994)
Geley, Gustave, *From the Unconscious to the Conscious* (Collins, 1920)
Genet, Jean, *Miracle of the Rose* (Blond, 1965)
Genet, Jean, *Our Lady of the Flowers* (Panther, 1966)
Genet, Jean, *The Thief's Journal* (Blond, 1965)
Gilbey, Ryan, 'Nicolas Roeg: I Don't Want to be Ahead of My Time' (*The Guardian*, March 2011)
Giles, Jane, *The Cinema of Jean Genet* (BFI, 1991)
Girodias, Maurice (ed), *The Olympia Reader* (Ballantine, 1967)
Giuliano, Geoffrey, *Paint It Black* (Virgin, 1994)
Godard, Jean-Luc, *Godard par Godard* (Cahiers du Cinéma/Editions de l'Etoile, 1985)
Godard, Jean-Luc, *Pierrot le Fou* (Lorrimer, 1969)
Goffman, Erving, *The Presentation of Self in Everyday Life* (Penguin, 1969)
Gomez, Joseph A., 'Performance and Jorge Luis Borges' (*Literature/Film Quarterly*, Spring 1977)
Goodwin, Michael, 'Performance' (*Rolling Stone* 65, September 1970)
Gow, Gordon, 'Identity: An Interview with Nicholas Roeg' (*Films & Filming*, January 1972)

Gow, Gordon, 'Performance' (*Films & Filming*, April 1971)
Green, Jonathan, *Days in the Life* (Pimlico, 1998)
Gross, Larry, 'Film Après Noir' (*Film Comment*, July–August 1976)
Grotowski, Jerzy, *Towards a Poor Theatre* (Eyre Methuen, 1968)
Guibert, Rita, *Seven Voices* (Vintage, 1973)
Gysin, Brion, 'Statement on the *Cutup* Method and Permutated Poems' (*Fluxus* 1, 1965)
Hacker, Jonathan & Price, David, *Take Ten Contemporary British Film Directors* (Oxford, 1991)
Hall, Peter, 'On Directing Pinter' in *New Theatre Voices of the Seventies* (Eyre Methuen, 1981)
Richard Hamilton (Tate, 1992)
Handke, Peter, *Offending the Audience and Self-Accusation* (Methuen, 1971)
Hay, David & Davis, Elliott, 'Nicolas Roeg' (*Cinema Papers* 2, April 1974)
Hayden-Guest, Anthony, 'She-Devil: The Lives and Loves of Anita Pallenberg' (*Sunday Correspondent*, February 1990)
Haynes, Jim, *Thanks for Coming* (Faber & Faber, 1984)
Heckman, Don, 'Performance' (*Jazz & Pop*, April/May 1969)
Heinrich, Clark, *Strange Fruit* (Bloomsbury, 1995)
Hern, Nicholas, *Peter Handke, Theatre and Anti-theatre* (Wolff, 1971)
Hirsch, Foster, 'Underground Chic: Performance' (*Film Heritage*, Spring 1971)
Hodge, Vicki, 'Princess Margaret, the East End Killer and Me' (*The Mail on Sunday*, June 2002)
Hodkinson, Mark, *Marianne Faithfull* (Omnibus, 1991)
Hoffenberg, Mason, *Sin for Breakfast* (Traveller's Companion, 1967)
Hohl, Reinhold, *Giacometti* (Thames & Hudson, 1972)
Hotchner, A.E., *Blown Away: The Rolling Stones and the Death of the Sixties* (Simon & Schuster, 1990)
Huges, Bart, 'The Hole to Luck' (*Transatlantic Review* 23, Winter 1966/1967)
Huges, Bart, 'Letter' (*Residu* 2 / *The Mongol Review*, Spring 1966)
Hughes, William, *Performance* (Tandem, 1970)
Huxley, Aldous, *The Doors of Perception & Heaven and Hell* (Penguin, 1959)
Huysmans, J.-K., *Against Nature* (Penguin, 1959)
Huysmans, J.-K., *Certains* (Librarie Plon, 1908)
Iampolski, Mikhail, *The Memory of Tiresias* (University of California Press, 1998)
Izod, John, *The Films of Nicolas Roeg* (Macmillan, 1992)
Jackson, Kevin, 'The Performance of a Lifetime' (*The Independent*, March 2000)

Jackson, Kevin, 'Sympathy for the Devil' (*The Guardian*, May 1996)
Jackson, Laura, *Golden Stone* (Smith Gryphon, 1992)
Jackson, Laura, *Heart of Stone: The Unauthorized Life of Mick Jagger* (Smith Gryphon, 1997)
Jean, Raymond, *La Lectrice* (Actes Sud, 1986)
Kaufmann, Walter, *Nietzsche* (Princeton, 1974)
Kearney, Patrick, *The Olympia Press: A Handlist* (private, 1975)
Kennedy, Harlan, 'The Illusions of Nicolas Roeg' (*American Film*, Jan–Feb 1980)
Kennedy, Harlan, 'Interview with Nicolas Roeg' (*Film Comment*, March/April 1983)
Kinder, Marsha & Houston, Beverle, *Close-Up: A Critical Perspective on Film* (Harcourt Brace Jovanovich, 1972)
Kinder, Marsha & Houston, Beverle, 'Insiders and Outsiders in the Films of Nicolas Roeg' (*Quarterly Review of Film Studies*, Summer 1978)
Knickerbocker, Conrad, 'William Burroughs: An Interview' (*Paris Review* 35, Fall 1965)
Knight, Arthur, 'A Matter of Taste' (*Saturday Review*, August 1970)
Kolker, Robert Phillip, 'The Open Texts of Nicolas Roeg' (*Sight & Sound*, Spring 1977)
Kroll, Jack, 'A Last Word on Performance' (*Art in America*, March 1971)
Kultermann, Udo, *Art-Events and Happenings* (Mathews Miller Dunbar, 1971)
Lambrianou, Tony, with Clerk, Carol, *Inside the Firm* (Blake, 2009)
Lanza, Joseph, *Fragile Geometry* (Paj Publications, 1989)
Lawrenson, Helen, 'Mick Jagger, I Love You' (*Esquire*, June 1969)
Leeman, Richard, *Cy Twombly* (Thames & Hudson, 2005)
Leiris, Michel, *Francis Bacon* (Thames & Hudson, 1987)
Levy, William (ed), *Wet Dreams: Films and Adventures* (Joy Publications, 1973)
Libin, R. Joseph, 'Donald Cammel: Performance Pluperfect' (*Inter/View*, July 1972)
Lichtenstein, Rachel & Sinclair, Iain, *Rodinsky's Room* (Granta, 1999)
Lippard, Lucy, *Pop Art* (Thames & Hudson, 1966)
Lippard, Lucy (ed), *Surrealists on Art* (Prentice-Hall, 1970)
Lorenz, Konrad, *On Aggression* (Methuen, 1967)
MacCabe, Colin, *Performance* (BFI, 1998)
Magritte, René, *Ecrits complets* (Flammarion, 1979)
Malcolm, Derek, 'What a Performance' (*The Guardian*, January 1971)

Mandeville, Sir John, *The Travels of Sir John Mandeville* (Penguin, 1983)
Manguel, Alberto, *A History of Reading* (Flamingo, 1997)
Manso, Peter, *Brando* (Weidenfeld & Nicolson, 1994)
Matthews, Tom Dewe, *Censored* (Chatto & Windus, 1994)
Mayersberg, Paul, 'The Story So Far . . . The Man Who Fell to Earth' (*Sight & Sound*, Autumn 1975)
Mayersberg, Paul & Shivas, Mark, 'Nouvel Entretien avec Joseph Losey' (*Cahiers du Cinéma*, March 1964)
McClure, Michael, *The Beard* (Grove, 1967)
McClure, Michael, *Meat Science Essays* (City Lights, 1966)
Macdonald, Kevin, 'Donald Cammell: When He Shot Himself, Did He Set the Scenes for His Finest Show?' (*The Observer*, May 1998)
McMahon, Joseph H., *The Imagination of Jean Genet* (Yale, 1963)
McVicar, John, *McVicar by Himself* (Arrow, 1979)
McVicar, John, 'Violence is Golden' (*20/20* 9, December 1989)
Meades, Jonathan, *Peter Knows What Dick Likes* (Paladin, 1989)
Melly, George, *Revolt into Style* (Penguin, 1970)
Michaux, Henri, *Infinite Turbulence* (Calder & Boyars, 1975)
Michaux, Henri, *The Major Ordeals of the Mind* (Secker & Warburg, 1974)
Michaux, Henri, *Miserable Miracle* (City Lights, 1963)
Miles, Barry, *In the Sixties* (Pimlico, 2003)
Miles, Barry, *London Calling* (Atlantic, 2011)
Miles, Barry, *Mick Jagger in His Own Words* (Omnibus, 1982)
Miles, Barry, *William Burroughs: El Hombre Invisible* (Virgin, 1992)
Miles, Barry, 'Jagger: Interview' (*International Times* 31, May 1968)
Miles, Sarah, *Serves Me Right* (Macmillan, 1994)
Millar, Gavin, 'Writes in Praise of Performance' (*The Listener*, January 1971)
Milne, Tom, *Losey on Losey* (Secker & Warburg, 1967)
Milne, Tom, 'Making It All the Way' (*The Observer*, January 1971)
Milne, Tom, 'The Man Who Fell to Earth' (*Sight & Sound*, Summer 1976)
Milne, Tom & Houston, Penelope, 'Don't Look Now' (*Sight & Sound*, Winter 1973–1974)
Monaco, James, *The New Wave* (Oxford, 1976)
Monegal, Emir Rodríguez, *Jorge Luis Borges: A Literary Biography* (Paragon, 1988)
Morgan, Ted, *Literary Outlaw: The Life and Times of William S. Burroughs* (Holt, 1988)
Morphet, Richard, 'Introduction' in *Richard Hamilton* (Tate, 1970)

Morphet, Richard, 'Richard Hamilton: The Longer View' in *Richard Hamilton* (Tate, 1992)
Morton, James, *Gangland* (Little, Brown, 1992)
Mottram, Eric, *William Burroughs: The Algebra of Need* (Boyars, 1977)
Müller, Grégoire, *The New Avant-Garde* (Pall Mall, 1972)
Nabokov, Vladimir, *Despair* (Penguin, 1981)
Narboni, Jean & Milne, Tom (eds), *Godard on Godard* (Secker & Warburg, 1972)
Nichols, Bill, 'Redemption & Performance' (*Take One*, January 1974)
Nietzsche, Walter, *On the Genealogy of Morals* (Vintage, 1969)
Noël, Bernard, *L'enfer Dit-on . . .* (Herscher, 1983)
Noël, Bernard, *Magritte* (Bonfini, 1977)
Norman, Philip, *The Stones* (Elm Tree Books, 1984)
Norse, Harold, *Memoirs of a Bastard Angel* (Bloomsbury, 1990)
Nuttall, Jeff, *Bomb Culture* (MacGibbon & Kee, 1968)
Nuttall, Jeff, *Performance Art 1: Memoirs; 2: Scripts* (Calder, 1979)
Nuttall, Jeff, 'Thoughts of Chairman Me' (*Unit* 10, February 1968)
Odier, Daniel, *The Job: Interview with William Burroughs* (Cape, 1970)
Oldenburg, Claes, *Notes in Hand* (Petersburg, 1971)
Palmer, James & Riley, Michael, *The Films of Joseph Losey* (Cambridge, 1993)
Paytress, Mark, *The Rolling Stones: Off the Record* (Omnibus, 2003)
Pearsall, Ronald, *The Worm in the Bud* (Penguin, 1971)
Pearson, John, *Notorious* (Century, 2010)
Pearson, John, *The Profession of Violence* (Weidenfeld & Nicolson, 1972)
Peary, Danny, *Cult Movies* (Vermilion, 1982)
Penman, Ian, 'A Lizard: A True Star' (*Uncut* 52, September 2001)
Penrose, Roland, *Tàpies* (Rizzoli, 1978)
Performance Poster Magazine (*Time Out*, January 1971)
Perkins, Michael, *The Secret Record* (Morrow, 1976)
Peschel, Enid Rhodes, *Intoxication and Literature* (Yale French Studies 50, 1974)
Phelps, Guy, *Film Censorship* (Gollancz, 1975)
Pinter, Harold, *The Birthday Party* (Methuen, 1960)
Pinter, Harold, *The Caretaker* (Methuen, 1960)
Pinter, Harold & Donner, Clive, 'Interview on The Caretaker' (*Transatlantic Review* 13, Summer 1963)
Playdon, Peter, *Performance* (unpublished thesis)
Poe, Edgar Allan, *Selected Writings* (Penguin, 1967)

Polo, Marco, *The Travels* (Penguin, 1967)
Pound, Omar, *Arabic & Persian Poems* (Fulcrum, 1970)
Prince, Richard, *American Prayer* (Gagosian Gallery/Bibliothèque Nationale de France, 2011)
Rawlings, Terry, *Who Killed Christopher Robin?* (Boxtree, 1994)
Raymond, Derek, *The Hidden Files* (Little, Brown, 1992)
Ribowski, Mark, *He's a Rebel* (Dutton, 1989)
Richards, Keith, with Fox, James, *Life* (Weidenfeld & Nicolson, 2010)
Richardson, Charlie, *My Manor* (Pan, 1992)
Robbe-Grillet, Alain, *Last Year at Marienbad* (Calder, 1962)
Robbe-Grillet, Alain, *Obliques / Robbe-Grillet*, 1978
Robbe-Grillet, Alain, *Snapshots & Towards a New Novel* (Calder, 1965)
Rodley, Chris, 'Marlon, Madness and Me' (*20/20* 1, April 1989)
Rolling Stone: The Groupies and Other Girls, February 1969
Rolling Stone Interviews 1967–1980 (Arthur Barker, 1981)
The Rolling Stones / Ultimate Music Guide (Uncut, 2011)
Romney, Jonathan, 'Tracking Across the Widescreen: An Interview with Ry Cooder' (*Wire* 138, August 1995)
Romney, Jonathan & Wootton, Adrian, *Celluloid Jukebox* (BFI, 1995)
Roskill, Mark (ed), *The Letters of Van Gogh* (Fontana, 1963)
Roszak, Theodore, *The Making of a Counter-Culture* (Faber & Faber, 1970)
Roud, Richard, *Godard* (Secker & Warburg, 1967)
Ruiz, Raúl, *Poetics of Cinema* (Dis Voir, 1995)
Russell, Ethan A., *Let It Bleed* (Springboard, 2009)
Russell, John, *Francis Bacon* (Thames & Hudson, 1993)
Salwolke, Scott, *Nicolas Roeg Film by Film* (McFarland & Co, 1993)
Sanchez, Tony, *Up and Down with The Rolling Stones* (Blake, 1991)
Sandford, Christopher, *Mick Jagger: Primitive Cool* (Gollancz, 1993)
Sarris, Andrew, 'Film in Focus' (*Village Voice*, July 1970)
Sartre, Jean-Paul, *Situations* (Fawcett, 1965)
Sartre, Jean-Paul, 'In Camera' in *Three European Plays* (Penguin, 1958)
Savage, Jon, 'Hassan Told Me to Do It' (*VAGUE* 23, 1990)
Savage, Jon, 'Snapshots of the Sixties' (*Sight & Sound*, May 1993)
Savage, Jon, 'Tuning into Wonders' (*Sight & Sound*, September 1995)
Scaduto, Anthony, *Mick Jagger* (W.H. Allen, 1974)
Schechner, Richard, 'Puzzling Pinter' (*Tulane Drama Review* 34, Winter 1966)
Schickel, Richard, 'A Completely Worthless Film' (*Life*, October 1970)

Schjeldahl, Peter, 'One Emerges a Little Scorched, But . . .' (*New York Times*, August 1970)
Schofield, Carey, *Jagger* (Methuen, 1983)
Severin, Steven, 'Total Recall, Nearly' (*The Guardian*, October 1997)
Shafto, Sally, *The Zanzibar Films and the Dandies of May 1968* (Zanzibar USA Publication, 2000)
Simon, John, 'The Most Loathsome Film of All?' (*New York Times*, August 1970)
Sinclair, Iain, *The Kodak Mantra Diaries* (Albion Village Press, 1971)
Sinclair, Iain, *Lights Out for the Territory* (Granta, 1997)
Sinclair, Iain (ed), *London: City of Disappearances* (Hamish Hamilton, 2006)
Sinclair, Iain, 'London, Necropolis of Fretful Ghosts' (*Sight & Sound*, June 1994)
Sinclair, Iain, 'Smart Guys' (*Sight & Sound*, August 1996)
Sinyard, Neil, *The Films of Nicolas Roeg* (Letts, 1991)
Sontag, Susan, *Against Interpretation* (Eyre & Spottiswoode, 1967)
Sontag, Susan, *Styles of Radical Will* (Secker & Warburg, 1969)
Spencer, Neil, 'Sympathy for the Devil' (*Uncut*, February 1998)
Spitz, Marc, *Jagger: Rebel, Rock Star, Rambler, Rogue* (Gotham, 2011)
Stark, Richard, *Point Blank* (Hodder Fawcett, 1962)
Steiner, George, *Extraterritorial* (Penguin, 1975)
Storr, Anthony, *Human Aggression* (Penguin, 1970)
Stratton, David, '*Performance*: A Review' and 'Dreams of Marrakesh: Extracts from the Original Screenplay of *Performance* by Donald Cammell' (*Cinema Papers*, January 1974)
Sturrock, John, *Paper Tigers* (Oxford, 1977)
Sullivan, Chris, 'Performance: Anita Pallenberg Talks About the Notorious Sixties Film' (*The Independent*, March 2007)
Sylvester, David, *Interviews with Francis Bacon* (Thames & Hudson, 1975 & 1987)
Sylvester, David, *Richard Hamilton* (Anthony d'Offay, 1991)
Talbot, David & Zheutlin, Barbara, 'Expecting to Fly: Jack Nitzsche' (*Crawdaddy*, November 1974)
Tessier, Max & Guérif, François, 'Nicolas Roeg' (*Revue du Cinéma*, October 1985)
Théorie d'ensemble (Editions du Seuil, 1968)
Toch, Hans, *Violent Men* (Penguin, 1972)
Trevelyan, John, *What the Censor Saw* (Michael Joseph, 1973)

Tuchman, Maurice, *The New York School* (Thames & Hudson, 1971)
Tulane Drama Review: Genet & Ionesco (1963)
Tulane Drama Review: Happenings (1965
Umland, Rebecca & Umland, Sam, *Donald Cammell* (FAB Press, 2006)
Vogel, Amos, *Film as a Subversive Art* (Weidenfeld & Nicolson, 1974)
Vyner, Harriet, *Groovy Bob* (Faber & Faber, 1999)
Wagner, Richard, 'The Search for the Self in the Films of Nicolas Roeg' (*Velvet Light Trap*, Autumn 1974)
Waldman, Diane, *Mark Rothko* (Thames & Hudson, 1978)
Walker, Alexander, *Hollywood, England* (Michael Joseph, 1974)
Walker, Alexander, *Sex in the Movies* (Penguin, 1968)
Waller, Nick, 'Persistence of Vision' (*Nuit Isis*, 1989)
Ward, John, *Alain Resnais, or the Theme of Time* (Secker & Warburg, 1968)
Webb, Peter, *The Erotic Arts* (Secker & Warburg, 1975)
Weiss, Peter, *Marat* (Calder & Boyars, 1965)
Wells, Simon, *The Great Rolling Stones Drugs Bust* (Omnibus, 2011)
Will, David & Willemen, Paul, *Roger Corman* (Edinburgh Film Festival with *Cinema* magazine, 1970)
Wilson, Colin, *Order of Assassins* (Panther, 1975)
Witts, Richard, *Nico: The Life and Lies of an Icon* (Virgin, 1993)
Wollen, Peter, 'Possession' (*Sight & Sound*, September 1995)
Wood, Jason, 'His Brilliant Career' (*The Guardian*, June 2005)
Wood, Rebekah, 'The Acid House' (*Neon*, March 1998)
Woods, Gerald, Thompson, Philip & Williams, John, *Art without Boundaries* (Thames & Hudson, 1972)
Wyman, Bill, with Coleman, Ray, *Stone Alone* (Viking, 1990)
Young, J.Z., *Programs of the Brain* (Oxford, 1978)

Relevant magazines since the late Sixties include: *Afterimage*, *Artforum*, *Artitudes*, *Art Monthly*, *Art Press*, *Artscribe*, *L'Art Vivant*, *Cahiers du Cinéma*, *Diacritics*, *Flash Art*, *International Times*, *Mojo*, *Monthly Film Bulletin*, *Opus*, *La Quinzaine Littéraire*, *Sight & Sound*, *Studio International*, *Substance*, *Uncut*, *The Wire* and *The Word*. Also, as noted earlier, an extensive scrapbook collection dating back to 1964.

Records, tapes . . .

Artaud, Antonin, *Pour en finir . . .* (including Van Gogh texts) (Dimanche, 1995)

Burroughs, William, *Call Me Burroughs* (The English Bookshop, 1965)

Captain Beefheart, *Safe as Milk* (Buddah, 1967)

Hooker, John Lee, various collections

Jagger, Mick, *Memo From Turner b/w Natural Magic* (Decca, 1970)

Johnson, Robert, *The Complete Recordings* (CBS, 1990)

Performance soundtrack (Warner Bros, 1970)

Rolling Stones, The, particularly pre-1970

Who, The, *Ready Steady Who* (Reaction, 1966) and memories of the live *Ready Steady Go* show itself, and 'Smokestack Lightning' at the Marquee c.1964–1965 (YouTube, extract)

Also various blues collections, and musics from North Africa and the Middle East.

Documentaries . . .

Abstract Expressionism I & II (Open University, 1983)

Art & the 60s: Politics and Performance (dir. Vanessa Engle, 2004)

Art as Performance (Open University, 1976)

Art on Film (Open University, 1976)

Being Mick (dir. Kevin Macdonald, 2001)

Borges & I (dir. David Wheatley, 1983)

Burroughs (dir. Howard Brookner, 1983)

The Cardinal and the Corpse (dir. Christopher Petit, 1992)

Donald Cammell: The Ultimate Performance (dir. Kevin Macdonald & Chris Rodley, 1998)

Empire of the Censors (dir. Saskia Baron, 1995)

Francis Bacon: The Brutality of Fact (dir. Michael Blackwood, 1984)

Go Go Go Said the Bird (dir. John Irvin, 1966)

Hollywood UK (BBC, 1993)

Influence and Controversy: Making 'Performance' (dir. Greg Carson, 2007)

Jackson Pollock: What Kind of Risk? (Open University, 1979)

Nothing As It Seems: The Films of Nicolas Roeg (dir. Paul Joyce, 1983)

The Other Francis Bacon (1998)

The Princess and the Gangster (dir. Craig Collinson, 2009)

Real Crime: Starring John Bindon (dir. Keith Wootton, 2002)

The Rolling Stones Rock and Roll Circus (dir. Michael Lindsay-Hogg, 1996)
The Rolling Stones: Stripped (dir. Jim Gable, 1995)
The Rolling Stones: We Love You (dir. Peter Whitehead, 1967)
The Secret Life of Princess Margaret (Carlton, 2005)
Signals Through the Flames: The Living Theatre (dir. Sheldon Rochlin, 1983)
The South Bank Show: Francis Bacon (dir. David Hinton, 1985)
A Technicolor Dream (dir. Stephen Gammond, 2008)
Tonite Let's All Make Love in London (dir. Peter Whitehead, 1967)
Visions: Profile on Godard (Channel 4, 1984)
Wholly Communion (dir. Peter Whitehead, 1965)

Films

Antonioni, Michelangelo: *L'Avventura* (1960), *Blowup* (1966)
Balch, Antony & Burroughs, William: *Towers Open Fire* (1963), *The Cut Ups* (1966)
Bergman, Ingmar: *Persona* (1966)
Boorman, John: *Point Blank* (1967)
Buñuel, Luis: *Un Chien Andalou* (1929)
Cammell, Donald: *Demon Seed* (1977), *White of the Eye* (1987), *Wild Side* (1995)
Cammell, Donald & Roeg, Nic: *Performance* (1970)
Cocteau, Jean: *The Blood of a Poet* (1930), *Orphée* (1950), *Testament of Orpheus* (1960)
Corman, Roger: *The Masque of the Red Death* (1964)
Deville, Michel: *La Lectrice* (1988)
Donner, Clive: *The Caretaker* (1963)
Fassbinder, Rainer Werner: *Despair* (1978)
Frears, Stephen: *The Hit* (1984)
Freeman, Robert: *The Touchables* (1968)
Friedkin, William: *The Birthday Party* (1968)
Genet, Jean: *Un Chant d'amour* (1950)
Glazer, Jonathan: *Sexy Beast* (2000)
Godard, Jean-Luc: (particularly) *Breathless* (1960), *Vivre Sa Vie* (1962), *Pierrot le Fou* (1965), *Alphaville* (1965), *Two or Three Things I Know About Her* (1967), *One Plus One* (1968)
Hitchcock, Alfred: *Notorious* (1946)
Hooper, Tobe: *The Texas Chain Saw Massacre* (1974)
Lester, Richard: *Petulia* (1968)